CONSCIOUSNESS, ENERGY AND FUTURE SCIENCE

Collected Articles from the
Journal of Future History on
the Evolution of Consciousness

Editor
J.J. Hurtak, Ph.D., Ph.D.

Academy For Future Science
Los Gatos, CA U.S.A.

Published by
The Academy For Future Science
P.O. Box FE
Los Gatos, CA 95031 USA
or
P.O. Box 3080
Sedona, AZ 86340 USA

www.affs.org
futurescience.org

Copyright © 2002 Academy For Future Science
Second printing, 2004
Third printing, 2023
All rights reserved.

This book is fully protected by copyright and no part of it may be reproduced in any form or by any means, including photocopying, utilized by an information storage and retrieval system, the internet or the world wide web, without permission from the copyright owners.

All pictures remain the copyright of the respective artists and are protected by this publication.

ISBN
1-892139-18-9

Edited by
J. J. Hurtak, Ph.D., Ph.D.

Book Design by
Lesley A. Photiadis

Cover Design
"Space & Time"
by Desiree Hurtak

Printed in the USA

CONTENTS

INTRODUCTION   ix
by J.J. Hurtak, Ph.D., Ph.D.

PART ONE

ARCHAEOLOGY

1 The Ryukyuan Submerged Landforms of the Late Quaternary   25
by Robert M. Schoch, Ph.D. & J.J. Hurtak, Ph.D, Ph.D.

2 Rock Circles of the Kofa Mountains in Southwestern Arizona: A Reconnaissance Study   47
by Steve Skotnicki, Ph.D.

3 From World Catastrophe to Global Migration   57
by J.J. Hurtak, Ph.D., Ph.D.

4 Rujum al-Hiri of Galilee: Stone Computer & Cosmic Timepiece   67
by Bruce D. Curtis, M.A., M.Div.

5 Stone Circles, Sky Circles, Sound Circles: New Evidence on Global "Round Numbers"   81
by Ulrike Granögger, M.Phil

6 The Sphinx as a Symbol of Evolution   89
by J.J. Hurtak, Ph.D., Ph.D.

7 How Old is the Sphinx? New Findings in Egypt   97
by Robert M. Schoch, Ph.D.

PART TWO

BIOLOGY

8 Genetics, Cloning & the Ethics of Survival   117
   by J.J. Hurtak, Ph.D., Ph.D.

9 DNA-RNA: The Genetic Blueprint of Life   127
   by Heleen L. Coetzee, Ph.D.

10 The Search for the DNA Code of Life
   & Its Applications   135
   by J.J. Hurtak, Ph.D., Ph.D.

11 A New Perspective of Life on Earth   143
   by Steve Skotnicki, Ph.D.

12 Biomagnetism & Bio-Electromagnetism:
   The Foundation of Life   151
   by Heleen Coetzee, Ph.D.

13 Microcosmic Music—A New Level
   of Intensity   159
   by Susan Alexjander, M.A.

14 Memory & the Synaptic Gap   165
   by Heleen L. Coetzee, Ph.D.

15 Who Are We, Anyway?   172
   by Gerald H. Vind, M.A.

PART THREE

ENVIRONMENT

16 Remote Sensing & the Rediscovery
   of Lost Worlds   185
   by J.J. Hurtak, Ph.D., Ph.D.

17 Environmentalism: In the Spirit of
    Sustainability   195
    by David Skinner, M.A.

18 Crisis of the Amazon: An Overview by a
    Visiting Scientist   207
    by J.J. Hurtak, Ph.D., Ph.D.

19 Understanding Living Energy & Our
    Living Environment   217
    by J.J. Hurtak, Ph.D., Ph.D.

20 Agriculture in Emerging Countries &
    Remote Sensing   227
    by Richard N. Quast, B.S., C.P.S.Sc.

21 Laser Remote Sensing of Forest &
    Crops in Genetic-Rich Tropical Areas   237
    by J.J. Hurtak, Ph.D., Ph.D.

22 The Quest to Terraform Mars   247
    by Desiree Hurtak, M.S.Sc.

23 Existing Space Law Concepts &
    Legislation Proposals   255
    by J.J. Hurtak, Ph.D., Ph.D.

24 Pyramidal Modeling of A Self-Sufficient
    Community   267
    by Alberto Rios Salinas, Architect &
    Alberto Rios Fernandez Jr., Architect

PART FOUR

Future Science

25 Beyond Newtonian Physics: The New
    Cosmology, & the Dialogue of an Open-

Ended Universe 279
by J.J. Hurtak, Ph.D., Ph.D.

26 A Critical Review of the Available Information Regarding Claims of Zero-Point Energy, Free Energy, & Over-Unity Experiments & Devices 286
by Patrick G. Bailey, Ph.D., Toby Grotz, & J.J. Hurtak, Ph.D, Ph.D.

27 Cold Fusion Research: Models & Potential Benefits 298
by J.J. Hurtak, Ph.D., Ph.D. & Patrick G. Bailey, Ph.D.

28 Sacred Geometry: Insights 313
by Patrick G. Bailey, Ph.D.

29 Liberating Universal Constants: The Physics of Immortality 321
by J.J. Hurtak, Ph.D., Ph.D.

30 Hydrogen: The Fuel For Future Transportation 331
by J.J. Hurtak, Ph.D., Ph.D.

PART FIVE

CONSCIOUSNESS

31 Paradoxes, Paradigms, & the Para-Rational 349
by Jeffrey Seth DeRuvo, M.A.

32 The Holographic Paradigm: Mind & the Awareness of Multiple Realities 361
by Marcus Weber, M.D. (Cand)

33 New Perspectives for Consciousness
 Evolution: At the Intersection of Science
 & Mysticism 369
 by Michelle D. Godfrey, M.A. (Cand)

34 The World of Archetypes 378
 by Mario Schiess

35 Threads in the Holographic Tapestry of
 Consciousness 387
 by Ben Taylor, Ph.D.

36 Seeking Higher Consciousness 395
 by Gerald H. Vind, M.A.

37 The Greater Unity of Sacred Geometries 403
 by J.J. Hurtak, Ph.D., Ph.D.

38 Age Eleven Speculations 413
 by Gerald H. Vind, M.A.

39 Awareness & Self-Determination versus the
 Technification of Knowledge on the Net 423
 by J.J. Hurtak, Ph.D., Ph.D.

40 The Organized Consciousness Universe 431
 by Gerald H. Vind, M.A.

Future Science is science guided by Consciousness.
— *J.J. Hurtak, Ph.D., Ph.D.*

Introduction

J.J. Hurtak, Ph.D., Ph.D.

The emerging frontiers of future science are those that assimilate global consciousness, ethical values and understanding by reaching beyond nonpersonal sciences with a greater humanistic understanding of life. Future Science recognizes that human consciousness has awesome powers of creative insight, that science can be engineered to make our planet a safe and healthy place for all creatures and plants, that zero-point energy may be harnessed for future flights into space. Clearly, humanity is beginning to take a quantum leap to gain the extraordinary ability to actually work beyond the confines of planet earth.

In today's world, we are being made aware of new options with changing scientific disciplines. In this light, we increasingly need some sort of conceptual framework within which to understand the meaning of a broad range of phenomena and experiences, from recorded music of human DNA to higher conscious awareness states, intentionality, unconscious processes, perception, latent energy powers of the mind, that are also redefining the direction and meaning of Life.

For example: The method of recombinant DNA demonstrated an unparalleled potential for the industry of medically important substances, such as

Introduction

human insulin, human growth hormone, a vaccine against the virus hepatitis, human interferon, and other breakthroughs, but has left us wondering about the effects of cloning. New stages of development, even more ingenious and promising, are taking shape now. The widespread opinion that genetic engineering is a threat to society raises concerns about the ethical and biological admissibility of a crude intrusion by man into the order of nature. Science has been forced to look for a redefinition of humanity as a vehicle for the Divine, containing more than the simple software of living matter.

We might even think of extending the range of critical thought to what some would term "the beginnings of *future science*"—a science expanded to redefine the direction of evolution itself by looking at the powers of consciousness and conscience as something greater than the sum of the activity of organic body parts. Traditional empirical science seeks only the reducible, whereas future science or broad-range sciences do not automatically bar all mental and consciousness experience from the status of genuine knowledge. Science itself must be a code of ethics since, if one grants the intrinsic worth of truth, then all sorts of consequences are generated by placing ourselves in the service of this one intrinsic value. As everything evolves, science too must evolve to seek values which can be uncovered within human nature itself. Techniques are now available for determining what is truly "good" for the human species, that is, what the intrinsic values of human beings are.

The New Directions of Investigation

The following articles from the *Journal of Future History* take into account the interconnection between consciousness and the new paradigms of science, including the new physics and biology. In the background of each writer, new connections in education, science, exploration and music have emerged from unique mental processes. Each article presented is a challenge to redefine the boundaries and positions of older scientific, cultural and theological positions through the discoveries and findings of researchers and writers who have been opened to the experiential side of an event or higher truth that transcends left-brain knowledge systems. In practice, an application of this greater synergism will allow us to gain insights from the new disciplines of the "cosmic Tree" so that we achieve a real advantage, a creative ladder of preparing for crises and preparing for oncoming generations, without stumbling on cynical skepticism and rudimentary "reductionism," and without having to commit to dualistic positions of philosophy that insist upon ultimate reality as unattainable or cosmic intelligence as beyond the human potential to reclaim a cosmic birthright.

Thus, the papers collected in this volume present a scientific-consciousness dialogue, outlining the emergence of a global mind that is connected with what some writers call the "Supermind." Aspects of biology and genetics are addressed, from viewpoints of how the human biocomputer works to descriptions of the multiple functions that constitute living matter and the workings of DNA. The writers also examine the problems relating to evidence of earlier human civilizations, the silent witness of ruins, buildings and places of worship.

Finally, the quest to overcome planetary limitations and extend a more meaningful human life into outer space through space law and terraforming planets for human habitation is discussed as part of a great extraterrestrial imperative. In all of this, we recognize the existence of a Divine Spirit that exists throughout the universe.

BACKGROUND OF WESTERN SCIENCE

With the rise of scientific civilization has come the rise of physical sciences that are interested in the things that are touched and tasted in the three-dimensional physical world, including living subatomic matter, almost to the exclusion of the higher evolution. As Western science developed it became restricted to a limited focus on the "matter" of evolution. From that restriction came both modern science's power to create manipulative technologies and the limitation of its epistemology. This is the ideological seedbed of all sorts of classical problems—the mind-body problem, action at a distance, free will versus determinism, science versus spirit, and so on. And while this restriction of science, to only a portion of the greater evolutionary process, was useful and justifiable for a particular period of history, its mistake was to become so enamored with the powers of prediction-and-control science that the "object" of science became misunderstood. In effect, we created a science that has become valueless.

Planning for the future must insist on human-orientated values rather than the present object-orientated "value-free" conception of science. Science, if it is allowed to awaken to the "new paradigms," will encourage people to seek and authenticate their inner truth by reference to the new physics, quantum being, holographic imaging, and chaos theory. But our current, incipient culture relies more heavily on material assumptions than do these revolutions within science. The emerging view of the 21st Century implies a revolution not only in the meaning of science, but also in the meaning of truth and the way we rethink truth in the universe. It in no way denies the power of empiricism for the purposes for which it was devised: prediction, control, and manipulation of the physical environment. Yet it does question the modern tendency to yield authority to the reductionist scientific worldview as the ultimate reality by which we should limit our perceptions.

Such indications of a shift in the metaphysical premises of the public at large, or the younger part of it, might be explained away as a mere fad, without the foundations of real exploration and field investigation. But more significant in a way are indications that increasing numbers of educators and scientists, persons with recognized scientific training who are on the staffs of research organizations and universities with high standards and who hold membership in recognized scientific associations in the USA, Germany, Russia and Japan, are manifesting more and more interest in developing scientific means to explain the increase in an extraordinarily widening range of experiences. More graduate students are beginning to experience nuances of the new "paradigms" of life with a profound intellectual sophistication.

THE "NEW PARADIGM"

Looking beyond the schism between science and religion, we recognize important overlapping areas between biology, psychology, physics and mysticism in the great nest of being. To begin with, we reach across disciplines and synthesize the teachings of anthropology, psychology, physics, sociology, religion and mysticism on a global level in the experience of Spirit beyond the formal concepts of God and soul. Next, we look at issues and answers in the biological-medical sciences that hold to the reality of brain reliability, mathematical methods in psychology, experimental ways of making life longer. This is followed by a next level that integrates the history of evolution through the disciplines of archaeology, geology and environmental science so that we can see the interlocking pathways of earlier evolutionary directions. Finally come the meta-sciences that are interested in the production of events and realities out of the latent powers of the mind, phantasmagoria triggered by the mind, cybernetics and allied fields, and new areas of research on the meaning of life from a cosmic perspective.

But as we contemplate the integration of science and religion, it becomes clear that the question of improving the human condition through technology without conscience—without attention to the educational process necessary to provide an awakened and extended consciousness—is very much a question of the improvement of means without regard to ends. *Science* without *con-science*, the consciousness of technology's implications, does not afford us a very pleasant prospect for our future.

What constitutes being a well-educated man or woman? What abilities will assure our personal freedoms of the decades ahead? The following elements are crucial:

>An informed acquaintance with the experimental and mathematical methods of biological and physical science

>An informed acquaintance with the historical and quantitative techniques and the main forms of analysis needed for investigating development and workings of modern society

>An informed acquaintance with the major philosophical and religious conceptions of humankind; an awareness of other times and other cultures

>Some understanding of and experience in thinking about ethical and moral problems, standards, manners and spiritual awareness of the changes that are occurring within the dimensions of universal intelligence

>The ability to think beyond what we read, heard, or saw, and to reach into ourselves and the Mind-2 universe for deeper answers

In envisioning a more productive education for the future, we must also weave self-esteem and responsibility into the total educational program. This means setting realistic expectations, providing a sensible structure, forgiving others, taking a risk, appreciating the benefits of a multi-cultural society, accepting emotional expressions and negotiating rather than being abusive. Affirming accountability for ourselves requires taking responsibility for our decisions and actions, being a person of integrity, understanding and affirming our values, attending to our physical health and taking responsibility for actions as leaders and teachers.

More importantly, as we formulate a real-life curriculum for the future, we must understand the inner relationship between mind and consciousness. Research on perception has altered science's view of "consciousness" and "reality." No longer is "reality" viewed only on the basis of scientists' mutually negotiated experiences as to what is logically acceptable, so that the difference between so-called "objective data" (for example, the read-out of a measuring instrument) and "subjective data" (an inner image) is one of degree only. Consciousness is being seen now not as a "thing" but as the scientific variable that connects with unlimited data constructs and actually causes "paradigm shifts" in each of the sciences.

Research done at Stanford University in 1994 and 1995 found that the mind has very sophisticated biomagnetic fields. There exist ion currents resulting from the electric activity of cellular membranes. Another kind of energy within the mind stems from ferromagnetic particles that are inherent or deliberately introduced into the organism of our body. The modulations of these internal magnetic fields many believe set in motion what could be called a semi-conducting quantum interference process, allowing cells, especially pyramidal cells, to work as a computer network to send and receive information.

The mind matrix can exhibit a remarkable list of potential energy transmitters and waveform patterns, but the triggering mechanism still remains in the human will. With the heightening of consciousness through the human will, creativity can be positively directed. Mind energy can even produce biological changes in molecules and atoms capable of changing protein and minerals into other forms.

In the early 1970s at Stanford Research Institute, experiments in remote viewing demonstrated the mind's ability to "reach" global targets, in violation of traditional rules of science. More work is needed in this area to understand how consciousness evolution arises in some sense out of mind, while it is also clearly beyond the physical mind. Much of the revolutionary work in this field was done by Russell Targ and Dr. Harold Puthoff of Stanford Research Institute-International, and by my late colleague, Dr. Andrija Puharich.

Their research demonstrated that mind energy is not affected by distance; apparently it has the same intensity anywhere on earth. This might indicate that we can receive thoughts that can lead us to a greater understanding of science, even to the point where mind energy can be conditioned by the higher patterns of pure energy; that is to say, the mind can experience higher states of universal experience in the endowments of universal intelligence.

THE NEW SCIENCE OF CONSCIOUSNESS AND THE FUTURE

Ultimately, the reality behind the phenomenal world is contacted not only through the physical senses but through deep intuition, or what was historically called "the consciousness qualities" of the mind.

While consciousness is too often seen as the end-product or by-product of material evolution, it can be argued that a greater consciousness first preceded physical evolution and continues to direct mental unfoldment. The mind constructs its unity out of interference patterns of energy and at the same time is everywhere and continuous as an external reality.

As the human mind is confirmed more and more to be like a holographic process of information storage and retrieval, we will ask ourselves:

> What sort of conceptual frameworks and organizing metaphors of a new language can be used to help us understand the many facets and dimensions of global consciousness operating in multiple dimensions of reality all considered together?

> What is the pragmatic difference between science and future science?

Introduction

—In discovering future histories of life "future science" crosses frontiers that have not been crossed by traditional science, connecting past, present, and future in a genuine participation with multi-worlds.

What is the difference between traditional "narrow-range" Western science and future science?

—In the future sciences, we recognize that "broad" science deals with models and metaphors representing certain aspects of experienced reality, and that any model or metaphor may be permissible if it is useful in helping to order knowledge, even though it may seem to conflict with another model which is also useful. Every metaphor and metaphysical sign and word is a holon, a library of meaning between the human and universal mind.

What is future science?

—It is the recognition that "understanding" comes, not alone from being detached, objective, analytical, coldly clinical, but also from cooperating with or identifying with the observed and experiencing it subjectively and then investigating it, using scientific methodologies. This implies a real partnership between the researcher and the phenomenon, individual, or culture being researched and an attitude of "exploring together" and sharing understanding.

In future science, *reality* must appear no longer to exist exclusively in the mind, for that (mis)perception breeds individualism. This suggests the necessity for strategies of reconciling the "many realities" of creative mental wave-patterns into a collective reality needed for the meeting between the familiar sensory images of the human evolution with the stimulating sources of greater vision and expansion of the collective consciousness. Reality should be understood as being composed of different grades or levels, reaching from the lowest and most dense and least conscious to the highest and most subtle and most conscious. At the one end of this continuum of being or spectrum of consciousness is what we in the West would call "matter" or the insentient and the nonconscious, and at the other end is "spirit" or "Godhead" or the "superconscious," which in Eastern thought is said to be the all-pervading ground of the entire sequence.

The central claim is that men and women can grow and develop (or evolve) all the way up the hierarchy to Spirit itself, therein to realize a supreme identity with the Godhead in this realm. The *Homo noeticus* can equally be called the self-evolving person, the responsible-for-himself person, but understanding the collective, the self-actualizing person, etc. In any case, it is quite clear that no social reforms, no beautiful constitutions or finely worded programs or laws will be of any consequence unless people are healthy enough, evolved enough, strong enough, good enough to understand and to want to put science into practice in the right way.

Prospects For The Future

At this time, everything in our personal experience affirms the importance of our ability to choose, and our deep inner guidance is bringing us toward the better choice. This poses a fundamental dilemma: Either we must deny our own innate wisdom because science knows better, or we have to face the intrinsic inability of science in its present form to give us an adequate cosmology and conscious philosophy to live by and to guide our society. Amidst the quantum urgency of the first part of the 21st Century, it is essential for science as a body of knowledge, including knowledge of genetics (related to cloning) and psychophysiology, and for research on the structure and understanding capabilities of the brain, to produce a language system that is in support of consciousness development.

Introduction

In the following pages we submit observations on how past and future evolutionary experiences are linked in the cosmos of the mind, in the holistic fields-within-fields relationship of the realm of consciousness. Consciousness, in its most developed form, is here used to explain the mysteries of creation, the nature of the universe, and the extraordinary potential of the human spirit. These findings, when verified, may serve to heal the "flaw" in the contemporary world view of science and unfold the continual nature of future science.

We must further realize that the teaching is not in books divorced from life experience, for the books are secondary. In essence, our future survival in the West requires us to recognize that education needs a detoxification—that is, a withdrawal from left-brain processes that are "fixed on linear scripting." Our education must begin with the fuller script of life which is in the mothering, nurturing aspect of rejuvenation. Thus, education should seek in a quiet way to recreate a total integration of the life experience while allowing for the creation of a sacred space whereby the mind, body and spirit can come together in a creative learning process of sustainable health, the raising of consciousness and the rejuvenation not only of our singular mind, body and spirit but collectively of the planetary mind, body and spirit. This is what the ancients, what the shamans of Africa, as well as the Indian cultures of North and South America, called the subearthly angelic spirits, the earthly Mother-Father which seeds the topsoil for rejuvenation. This is what we see in the psychoanalytical understanding of the life forces of joy influenced by sun, water and air that we see as the new birth or Beauty of the new embryological self, brought about by the balancing of power with peace and work with joy. And finally, there is the integration of the uppermost part of the psyche, which is divine unfoldment, love and wisdom interconnected with the divine host or mastery over our hectic, chaotic world which has lost contact and thus interest in the basic forces of the universe.

With a sense now of urgency, knowing how earlier

great civilizations were lost due to environmental destruction and limited philosophies, we need to recover the larger sense of the global mind. In waking up to future science, we recover something long lost, something very old and renewed, in ourselves individually and in the collective consciousness of humankind.

A new cosmology of consciousness must be born at this time. On this basis, a serious and thoroughgoing exploration of all aspects of human consciousness can be mounted, and areas of potentially fruitful research identified in our lives. We are awakening to a new language of mental pictures—pictographic cybernetics —which will be used to ascertain higher states of consciousness and cosmic consciousness that will unite all languages of the planet by virtue of a quicker rate of image and knowledge integration.

With these stages of new discovery, Man will no longer remain a mystery to himself as basic problems are resolved. Not only educators, engineers and scientists of the world, but people of all ranks must pull their efforts together in a global team activity, in order for us to realize that problem-solving on this magnitude will be part of the quickening and preparation for all of us to become cosmic citizens while inhabitants of "Spaceship Earth." Even greater discoveries are just around the corner when we realize that we are the harbinger of the first generation of humans who will actually leave planet Earth *en masse* as participants in a Higher Evolutionary intelligence. Should the cosmic forces of intelligence prevail and some sort of transcendentalist presence come to dominate the cultures of the Earth, the consequence would be a social and historical phenomenon of incomparable magnitude. Here, the expanded premises of global awakening will mean the "second coming of science" into the awareness of the cosmic consciousness.

PART ONE

ARCHAE

OLOGY

1

The Ryukyuan Submerged Landforms of the Late Quaternary

Robert M. Schoch, Ph.D.
(Boston University) &
J.J. Hurtak, Ph.D., Ph.D.

PART I: CONTEMPORARY DISCOVERIES

Unusual submerged landforms have been found off the coast of the Ryukyu islands in the westernmost region of Japan. These clusters of islands were once part of a vast trading network extending between Japan, China and Java, and maintained tributary relations with China throughout late prehistoric time (circa 8,000 BC). Scattered off the coast of many of these islands at a depth of approximately 5 to 25 meters are stone terraces that show characteristics of sunken platforms. Hypothesis suggests that these ocean terraces are natural structures that may have been utilized, modified, or enhanced by humans in ancient times.

Limestone concentrations resembling coastal terraces found in several Ryukyuan sites have sharp edges, right-angles, and unusual arrangements which persuade Professor Masaaki Kimura of the University of the Ryukyus, Okinawa, to associate this geological area with the "Three Lands of Mu" as described in historic Japanese and Chinese texts. Writes Kimura, "the lost continent of Mu could have been located in the Ryukyu Archipelago that was submerged after the last ice age."

Whether we can equate this discovery with legends of lost continents might be difficult to confirm, but there is evidence that islands in the Pacific have disappeared over known geological time. It has been estimated that 15,000 years ago, during the Quaternary cold, ice caps several thousand feet high covered North America and Eurasia, resulting in a lowering of the sea level by 120 meters. It is also known that Indonesia belonged to the same large landmass as southeastern Asia. Our investigations in the Ryukyu Archipelago confirm this geological change, where terrace-like formations as well as caves that were once exposed to air were submerged by the oceanic dynamics of the late Pleistocene and Holocene epochs. Our current working hypothesis, therefore, is that the Yonaguni Monument is primarily of natural origin; that is, its overall structure is the result of natural geological and geomorphological processes. We think it should be considered a primarily natural structure until more evidence is found to the contrary. Although on Yonaguni Island and elsewhere in the Okinawa, there appears to be an ancient tradition of modifying, enhancing, and improving on nature.

Looking at a map of the Ryukyu Archipelago we see that the island chain curves west to connect with Taiwan. It is our belief that before the end of the Quaternary cold when the sea levels were lower, this island chain may once have been a semi-continuous peninsula leading south from Japan to Taiwan and the Asian continent. These very long land bridges would have facilitated migration in remote pre-history.

Underwater explorations in 1997 and 1998 in the Ryukyu Archipelago have revealed a number of unusual geological structures between the islands of Taiwan and Okinawa which could possibly have been modified by early man. This is evidenced by right edges, stair-step patterns and large cuts into the stone surface of these underwater structures that, at least superficially, appear to have been altered by humans. The cuts, according to Dr. Kimura, may be too precise and extensive to exemplify natural "pools" or "gutter"

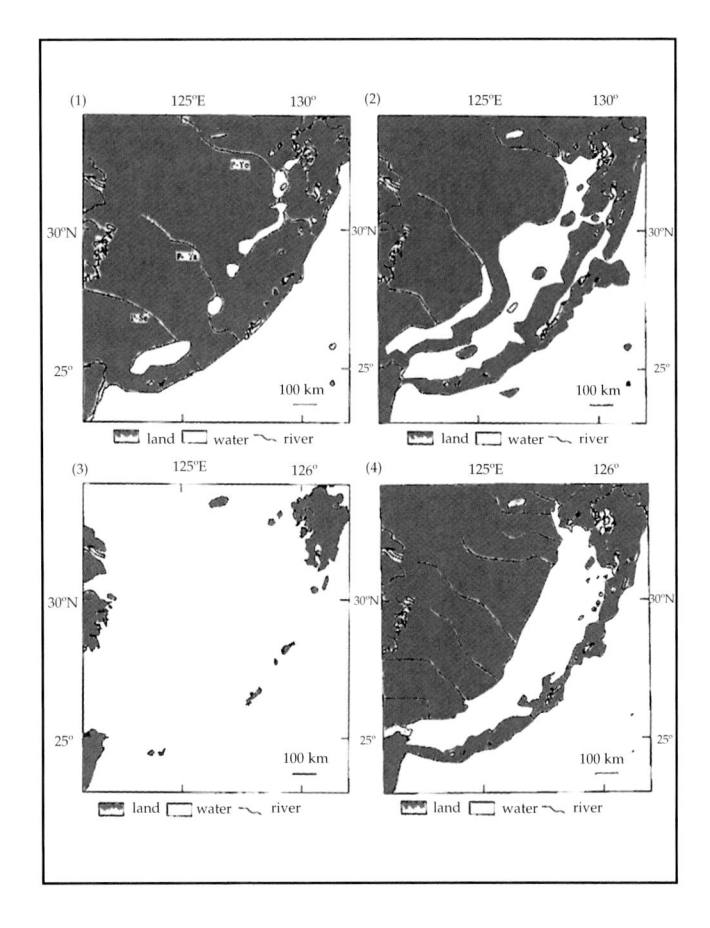

Figure 1.1
Major Stages of the Ryukyu Arc Caused by a Rise in Ocean Levels. Reconstructed based upon the research of M. Kimura. Image courtesy of the Academy For Future Science.

features that otherwise would suggest long sweeps of the ocean current and eddy-like activity. Geological maps have been drawn of Yonaguni Island to designate special diving sites and names such as the Yonaguni Underwater Monument, the Stage, the Amphitheater and the Seashore Shrine have been given to these unusual structures. Professor Kimura believes a specific pattern exists in the placement of these sites on the southeast end of Yonaguni, especially in relationship to the location of the sun on the horizon.

Kimura points out that the so-called Yonaguni Underwater Monument, over 160 feet long (50 meters), is due south of the highest peak on the island. Due east of the highest peak is the so-called Seashore Shrine.

Directly between the Monument and the Shrine is the Stage, also directly southeast of the highest peak. This creates a geographical right angle.

Little is known about primitive man in this region. Culture history begins with the Jomon phase (10,000-500 BC) which spread pottery and stone implements throughout the Pacific. The Yayoi period which followed (500 BC to 500 AD) saw advances in the length of food cultivation periods, trade, and the knowledge of metalworking.

The importance of Kimura's work has been the highlighting of an oceanic profile, taken from ongoing underwater archaeology, that describes a curve of where sea levels have been at certain periods of history. Kimura explains that the Monument was exposed around 10,000-12,000 years ago during the time period known as Riku no Toki (the era of the continents) when ocean levels were as much as 300 feet lower than current levels.

Other authors have also noted architectural similarities between Japan's underwater monuments and the restored Okinawa castles. There are a number of remarkable similarities between some of the underwater structures and the traditional land-based Sheri Castle, including the "Dog run" and the hemispherical "well" area. It is also possible that the underwater site is simply the result of modern activities in the harbor, such as dredging and blasting, that have coincidentally created forms in the coral subsurface that superficially resemble Sheri Castle and other subaerial cultural sites.

Some investigators claim that the unusual formations of the underwater monuments are the work of natural cleavage plates or stratigraphic layers of stones that have slid off from larger pieces of the monument. If the rocks naturally slid off the monument, as some have suggested, then Dr. Kimura has argued that one would expect to find large blocks lying around the monument; to account for the many right angles of the monument and its missing sections of stone, the "removed" stone would have to be somewhere nearby. If it came off naturally, you would expect to find much of it at the base of the monument, but one does not. Therefore, it could be that some of the stones were moved or modified, forming the right angles and regularity, and taken from the site. Kimura argues that there is no way to account for the contours of the larger structures and its missing blocks other than stones having been removed by artificial means and that some stone was actually modified by man. Features that suggest missing stone occur not only at the edge of the monument, with one side exposed to a cliff or exit point, but occur in the middle of the monument as well.

Kimura and his team have also located, off Okinawa, an underwater cave which is approximately 20 meters below sea level and where stalactites in the cave indicate that it was once in the open air, since stalactites do not form underwater. One stone article found in the cave resembles primitive tools found in Australia, New Zealand, and Southeast Asia areas. The confirmation of this artifact as an actual tool would indicate that there was human activity in areas around Okinawa that are now submerged, including the areas around Yonaguni Island.

First-hand scuba diving observations by one of the authors (Schoch) have determined that the underwater Yonaguni Monument is composed entirely of solid "living" bedrock. The surface of the rock is covered by various organisms (algae, corals, sponges, and so forth) that obscure the actual surface, and we believe that this coating of organic material tends to make the surfaces of the Yonaguni Monument appear more regular and homogeneous than they actually are to the natural eye.

During dives, organisms on the rocks were scraped off in several places so as to gain views of the actual rock face, and samples of the rock were collected. It has been ascertained that the Yonaguni Monument is composed predominantly of medium to very fine sandstones and mudstones of the Lower Miocene Yaeyama Group. These rocks contain numerous well-defined, parallel bedding planes along which the layers easily separate. The rocks of this group are also crisscrossed by numerous sets of parallel and vertical (relative to the horizontal bedding planes of the rocks) joints and fractures. Along the southeast and northeast coasts of Yonaguni Island the Yaeyama Group sandstones are abundantly exposed, and here one can observe them weathering and eroding under present conditions. We became convinced that presently, at the surface, natural wave and tidal action are responsible for eroding and removing the sandstones in such a way that very regular step-like and terrace-like structures remain. The more we compared the natural, but highly regular, weathering and erosional features observed on the modern coast of the island with the structural characteristics of the Yonaguni Monument, the more we became convinced that the Yonaguni Monument was a natural geological and geomorphological artifact that may have been modified by human endeavors.

There is also no evidence to suggest that any part of the structure is constructed of separate blocks of rock that have been placed into position, a discovery which would definitively indicate a human-made origin for the structure. However, unlike ancient Egypt, Asia has many structures (e.g., the pyramid tombs in Xian, China) that originate from naturally existing structures reconfigured by man. In contrast on the north coast of Okinawa a rock formation can be found at a location called Tatamishi-Ishi showing flat rocks shaped like pentagons and octagons arranged to form turtle or tile-like patterns. Each rock is diagonal and there is over 1,000 rocks pressed down to form a very unusual site of a 20 meter platform. This site is considered the oldest Stone Age site in Japan because of the V- and M-shaped bones found by Japanese investigators.

With regard to the presumed "missing blocks" referred to previously: the southern coast of Yonaguni is swept by very strong currents and experiences on a regular basis major storms and typhoons. While visiting the area in July-August 1998 we experienced a small typhoon and were able to observe the powerful coastal erosional features in action.

The Ryukyuan Submerged Landforms of the Late Quaternary

Figure 1.2
*A View of the Yonaguni Monument.
Photo by the Academy For Future Science.*

Kimura and others have also referred to presumed "post-holes" on the underwater structure as evidence of artificiality. Similar holes are found along the Yonaguni coast today, forming under natural conditions through the erosive power of strong eddies and currents working on weak spots in the rock. Once such a "pot-hole" forms, pebbles and boulders swirling in it continue to deepen it vertically, ultimately forming what superficially appear to be artificial post-holes. As for the "walls" that Kimura has pointed out near the base of the Yonaguni underwater structure, these are easily explained as slump features where irregular to semi-regular multi-sided slabs of more competent rock slide down over stratigraphically lower and less competent rock to lodge in place either vertically or at high angles. The presumed "road" area that Kimura has referred to as occurring in front of the "walls" at the base of the Yonaguni Monument may be simply a region swept clean of fine debris by the powerful currents.

The principal underwater Monument off of

Figure 1.3
The underwater Yonaguni monument from another perspective. Photo by the Academy For Future Science.

Yonaguni does appear to have at one or more times been above-water which would account for the classic tor-like structures typical of surface erosions. Ancient inhabitants of the island may have partially reshaped or enhanced this natural structure while it was above the surface to give it the form they wished.

In fairness to Dr. Kimura's position, we must point out that he believes that at least some of the surface features that we here interpret as the result of natural weathering and erosion (including the step-like structures seen in the so-called Seaside Shrine area) are man-made. However, in our initial studies we could not find any surface evidence (such as tool marks on the rock surfaces or carved blocks that had been moved into place) that, in our opinion, would substantiate his contention of artificiality.

Our current working hypothesis is that the Yonaguni Monument is of natural origin, but may show signs of modification by the local culture. The concept of human enhanced natural structures fits well within East Asian esthetics, such as the platforms of China and the Zen-inspired rock gardens in Japan. A complex interaction between natural and human made form that influenced human art and architecture thousands of years ago is highly possible. However, additional study of the other "seven" underwater sites is needed before we can argue for the high level of "artificiality claims" made by Dr. Kimura.

Nevertheless, the question of its genesis—artificial versus natural—may not be an all-or-nothing proposition. We should consider the possibility that the Yonaguni Monument is fundamentally a natural structure that has been enhanced or slightly modified by humans in ancient times. The Yonaguni Monument may even have been a quarry from which blocks were cut and removed for the purpose of constructing other structures which are long since gone. It may be a primarily natural structure that was utilized as a dock area for an ancient sea-faring people, and it may also have served sacred ritual functions. Perhaps it originally bore perishable superstructures, possibly made of wood, on its upper surface.

On Yonaguni Island and elsewhere in the Okinawa area, there appears to be an ancient tradition of modifying, enhancing, and "improving" on nature. On Yonaguni there are very old tombs (age unknown, but possibly dating back thousands of years) that stylistically appear to be comparable to the "architecture" of the underwater Yonaguni Monument. Enigmatic stone vessels of unknown age, as well as ancient stone tools (also of unknown age) have been found on Yonaguni, clearly indicating a tradition of stone working that probably extends into the past many millennia. We believe that the art and architecture of the area may have been influenced by the natural geomorphology of the Yonaguni Monument and similar structures. There may have been a complex interplay between nature and artificiality, natural forms and man-made structures, in very ancient times. Perhaps, rather than being the work of humans per se, the Yonaguni Monument directly influenced the art and architecture of humans some 8,000 to 10,000 years ago, throughout the Central Pacific, thus helping to initiate a stylistic tradition that continues to this day.

In conclusion, one of the authors (Schoch) has published a book entitled *Voices of the Rocks* (Harmony Books, 1999) where he states:

> But if there is a human element to the Yonaguni monument, why did the people of long ago want to mark this spot? ...[T]en thousand years ago, in circa 8,000 BC, the Tropic of Cancer was in a different location, at about 24° 15′ north latitude, which is close to Yonaguni's position at 24° 27′... Since Yonaguni is close to the most northerly position the tropic reaches in its lengthy cycle, the island may well have been the site of an astronomically aligned shrine that, like Nabta in southern Egypt, Stonehenge in England, or Brugh na Boinne in Ireland, replicates a celestial point on Earth and anchors our world in the eternal.

PART II: POSSIBLE CULTURAL CONTEXT AND SIGNIFICANCE

The glacial cycle for the region of the Ryukyu Archipelago is given at 130,000-10,000 BP (Before Present), defining the last interglacial stratigraphic framework for the coastal paleoclimatology and North Pacific. During the Upper Paleolithic[1] period, at the time of the last glaciation, in the climactic period called the Late Würm (c. 30,000-10,000 BC), considered the most harsh from the point of view of climate, sea level fell to about 330 to 425 feet (100 to 130 m) below the present zero level.

There is growing evidence that late Pleistocene[2] groups achieved more complex levels of cultural development than has been generally known. Such an explanation can be satisfactory only for a very narrow time-frame (20,000-10,000 BP) because consideration of Eurasian material culture after 10,000 BP shows a disappearance of paraphernalia for several millennia, and thus suggests not a continuity in complexity but rather its collapse in time.

Prehistoric cultures in the coastal region of South China made use of terraces built along river and ocean fronts at sites selected for agricultural and navigational expedience. This culture then spread its knowledge by land and by boat along the coast, and several cultures adopted these same methods of using terraces to prevent runoff and erosion of resources. Most Asian anthropologists consider that later passageways were made to the neighboring off-shore islands of China and the southern Japanese islands. And although the prehistoric sites which have been investigated in recent years seem to support this assumption, the evidence of these underwater monuments seem to indicate that a land bridge first brought this early terrace and pottery culture to the Ryukyu location during the early Neolithic.

The sea-going population of the Lower Yangtse, who colonized the South China coast in prehistoric days, might have regarded the Strait of Taiwan as a large lake. The activities on the island side of the water are evident. Ever since the last century, Japanese scholars have done a great deal of work on Taiwan, and they were recently followed by the members of the Academia Sinica (Taiwan). Dozens of sites have been reported, most of them located along the west coast. Their distributions and stratigraphy seem to suggest that the mainland cultures arrived on the island in successive waves. Archaeological data from Taiwan clearly shows that the prehistoric cultures of the island owed their origin to those that flourished earlier on the mainland. Thus from Lung-ma in South China to Taiwan there emerged various structural remains in the settlement such as natural waterways, ditches, stone stoves, dwelling pits, storage pits, terraced platforms, and city walls that become the signature of eastward expansion. Much of this was covered over by early Austronesian settlements as studied by Professor P. V. Kirch in his investigation of the early ancestry of oceanic cultures in the Pacific.

The connection of prehistoric Japanese pottery with the mainland is also apparent. Sites in central and southern Japan yield a lithic industry akin to southern China with pebble-flaking, chipping, pecking and polishing as its basic techniques. Typical artifacts, such as those unearthed at Kozanji, Kutobo, Ubayama, and the southern Japanese islands are pebble axes, pointed picks, short axes, waisted axes, shouldered axes, and others, all common in China and Indo-China. The pottery is basically a brownish grey cord-marked ware which has a wide distribution in the Western Pacific, but similar "Jomon" artistic examples have extended as far as Peru. In the hands of the Japanese island potters, this art was developed with unusual skill. Besides the common cord-marked decoration, shell scraping and corded and carved stick impressing were introduced, and a large number of pots were decorated with highly ornate reliefs. The pottery gives Japanese prehistory (19,000-3,000 BP) the name "Jomon" which means literally "cord-marks."

A profound connection between Taiwan, the Ryukyu, and China is evidenced in a combination of chipped and partially polished rectangular hoes, stepped adzes, and shouldered axes. In the late Mesolithic period (12,000-10,000 BP) these could have been used to modify stone surfaces and territory for commerce or build terraces for agriculture.

Ancient stone "vessels," their exact age unknown, as well as stone tools also of unknown age have been found on Yonaguni. The stone "vessels," which may have served ritual functions, range in size from about half a meter to two meters in their longest dimensions and appear to be carved of the native sandstone. One beautiful celt-like stone tool in particular that was found on Yonaguni (presently in the possession of Dr. Kimura) is composed of igneous rock, possibly a diabase, that is not found exposed on Yonaguni Island.

Either this tool or the raw material from which it was manufactured was transported to Yonaguni in ancient times, furnishing evidence of an ancient stone-working tradition on Yonaguni independent of the underwater structures.

If we look at the larger picture, we see that a possible connecting blueprint clearly exists throughout China and Japan whether it is seen in the pottery, primitive tools or in the mound and terrace structures. The movement of the phenomenon of sun worship and corresponding symbolic sun crosses and fire serpent motifs on pottery can also be found in Japan and China.

Sun worship, serpents, platform architecture, and terrace-culture, however, are not limited to the Western Pacific. Raised slabs and terraces with posts are common throughout Polynesia, and at one "ahu site" on Easter Island called Vinapu, temple rocks and statues are structured to show the significance of extended ceremonial platforms. Elaborate stone terraces are also seen at Hanalapa me'ae in Polynesia and in the Marquesas islands of the mid-Pacific. In the South Pacific, terrace platforms as special places of gathering were called luakini heiau, a term introduced by the Menehune people who brought the art of heiau building to the Hawaii islands. In the traditions of Ka Po'e Kahiko, the Menehune were the earliest people to populate Hawaii, using stones from Kawiwi to build platforms in Wai'anae. The Ka Po'e Kahiko culture understood the cardinal points (Kukulu) in accordance with the rising of the sun in the East (the Kukulu hikina), the traveling of the sun to the west (Kukulu komokana), as well as the south (Kukulu-hema) and the north (Kukulu 'akau). The platforms for these astronomic points show striking similarities to structures on Ryukyu such as Sheri Castle and some of the other restored castles on Okinawa. These similarities are represented by an overall design and architectural plan, including the downward sloping stairs, levels, terraces, and masonry. Was it possible that throughout the vast oceanic regions, sun worship was the key to oceanic platforms from Talepakemalai on

Figure 1.4
Restored Japanese Castle on Okinawa. Photo by the Academy For Future Science.

Eloaua Island in the Bismarck Archipelago to platform sites at Lolokoka in Tonga and Wai'anae in Hawaii? Were these just places of worship, or could they indicate a rudimentary understanding of astronomy serving cultural, religious and astronomic purposes?

Archaeological similarities have been found between immigrant and indigenous groups scattered throughout the ten thousand nautical miles of the Pacific in what has come to be called the "Lapita"[3] culture. This represents an ancient legacy of art and pottery which may be nothing less than an ethnographic conduit that spread throughout Oceania. The Lapita may be the "missing link" now being accepted as the "Asian Ancestors" of the Pacific Oceanic World!

Another missing link might be connected with an ancient pre-Japanese peoples called the Ainu, an isolated group with possible Caucasian ties, who live on the northern-most island of Japan and may have migrated across the Northern Pacific to North America. A deciphering of the name "Ajimu" may throw some light on the sunken underwater structures of Yonaguni. It is a corruption of Azumi which means "Sea People," in earliest Japan. Until the end of the eighth century AD, the Azumi were among the most powerful seafaring tribes in Japan, but after the Nara Dynasty was established, they declined in strength.

Terrace cultures were at one time also prominent in South America. NASA satellite photographs of Tiahuanaco, Bolivia in the late 1980s revealed an extensive yet forgotten array of stone patterns and platforms which were recently determined to have been used by early cultures to manage a sophisticated irrigation system at high altitudes (4,000 m). These platforms are adjacent to ancient monuments and structures that served as ceremonial centers, exhibiting sun and stellar alignments, as well as containing water conduits for ceremonial rituals. And what about the Mayan culture with their platforms, sun worship rituals and astronomically aligned structures?

One can argue that in the Chinese architectural tradition of temple platforms, vertical discrimination of space was three-fold, including ground level or neutral planes, elevated or positive planes represented by platforms, and pits or negative planes represented by sunken courts. Most sunken courts had two aligned flights of steps on opposite sides, one for descent and the other for ascent, designed for ritual procession into and out of negative space. Yonaguni tombs in the coastal regions imitate the same step functions found on the submerged platforms, viz., two or three steps, usually of different heights, connecting each platform horizon in elevated or sunken space on one side with great systemization of space. A similar three-tiered symbolic structure can also be found throughout South America.

In terms of architecture, terrace arrangements—whether agricultural or ceremonial—throughout South America, Polynesia and Japan similarities of structures do exist. The structures seen in the waters off of Okinawa and Taiwan in this context do not appear as unique structures. One author (Hurtak) has found mathematical relationships between pyramidal and terrace-cultures around the world at a particular longitude and latitude. Serious hypotheses concerned with the origin of various items of culture and language have sought to link the Pacific peoples with America or with eastern Asia through migratory routes both to the north and to the south. Linguistic and cultural resemblances between the Japanese and the Polynesians have been pointed out, and analogies have been traced between art forms and cultural items of the Chinese and those of various Pacific islands peoples. Dr. Douglas Wallace at Emory University also performed a genetic study which showed that there is a genetic linkage between the Polynesian peoples, the Asian peoples and the first Americans.

Concepts about Asian migration to North America have expanded in many directions in that the Bering Strait is now considered not the exclusive connection between East and West. Although genetic research on the 'Richland' or 'Kennewick' Man (the name being used for the 9,300 year old skeleton found near the Columbia River in Washington State) represents an unprecedented finding in the history of the Americas, and is of major interest as perhaps part of the culture that took part in the migration, the recent Monte Verde, Chile discovery also lends a new direction to a pre-Clovis man movement in South America.

In reconciling geology and mythic history, any set of phenomena can be explained by an infinite number of hypotheses, and we must choose between them. Legends from China to South America similarly recorded by European explorers and adventurers speak of ancient floods, although there is much debate regarding which legends to accept and how to determine the influences of differing prehistorical events and traditions, especially those modified in favor of a European perspective.

Although European explorers were eager and almost encouraging in their recording of flood legends in the Pacific, they were equally quick to dismiss claims of interconnecting land masses and terrace cultures that pushed eastward from the Asian continent towards the Western Hemisphere. A few exceptions tried to reconcile the island cultures with a monolithic center of civilization that was once in the Pacific. However, Chinese and Japanese legends also speak of an ancient monolithic culture that existed in the East.

Some theorists have tried to explain the difficulties of oceanic migration by postulating the former existence of a Pacific continent, Mu (analogous to the Atlantis of the Old World), which sank in prehistoric times, leaving only the tops of its mountains and some surviving population above the sea. The stone statues of Easter island and other stone remains elsewhere in the Pacific have been regarded by some of the supporters of this view as the work of the inhabitants of the vanished continent. It is here that popular writer James Churchward entered the scene at the close of the nineteenth century with his desire to create a mega-history of civilization, including a history of all Pacific peoples which he authored under the title *The Children of Mu*. His books, published in several editions early in the twentieth century, placed Mu as a supercontinental expanse covering Micronesia, Eastern and Western Polynesia, and Easter Island, a land of cities and sciences and international trade, that was destroyed by "earthquakes and volcanic outbursts." Churchward's supreme island of paradise and classical map of the boundaries of Mu did not include the Ryukyu islands. However, legends of a great flood encompass almost all ancient legends in the Pacific and South America with the loss of great land areas.

Masaaki Kimura's *Mu—Underwater structures of Ryukyu?* (in Japanese, 1991) and *Lost Stone Tablets* (in Japanese, 1997) represent a latter-day synthesis of archaeological research and ancient legend. Kimura provides an environmental and ecological hypothesis designed to account for human origins and diversity of cultures in the Pacific as coming from one parent civilization. Although not widely appealing to most archaeologists, in all honesty, Kimura does accurately depict ancient legends from an Oriental perspective, making it difficult to choose among such differing hypotheses as those that can be fashioned from ideas about ancient legends versus archaeological evidences.

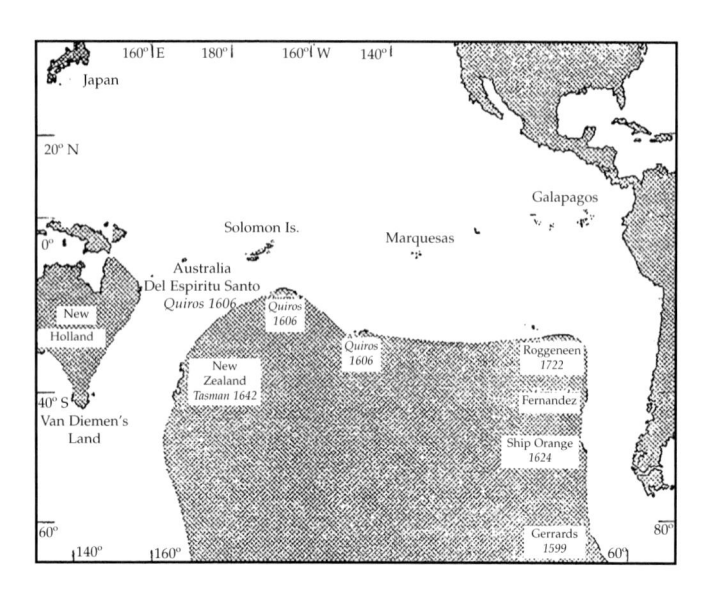

The Ryukyuan Submerged Landforms of the Late Quaternary

Figure 1.5
Dalrymple's hypothetical continent (1767). From the British National Archives.

The search for the missing continent and prospect of a transoceanic migration was also illustrated in the hypothesis put forward by Alexander Dalrymple based upon Polynesian legends, and also found in Japanese legends. Dalrymple argued in 1767 that the isolated discoveries, or believed discoveries, of a large lost continent in the South Pacific Ocean indicated the existence of a continuous coastline roughly approximating to the edge of the shaded area of the unexplored South Pacific, later called "Lemuria" [see Figure 1.5]. The coasts of the countries bounding the Pacific have been taken from Sr. Robert de Vaugondy's chart of the Pacific ocean of 1756. The relatively accurate delineation of the American coast in both North and South America shows the advanced state of Spanish surveys.

Within a decade of Dalrymple, however, the English captain James Cook in his sea voyages utterly destroyed the belief in Terra Australis Incognita, detailing a map of the Pacific essentially in its modern form. By the time he had finished his survey of New Zealand, the East Indies, and New Holland, he had added more to the knowledge of the Pacific than any of his predecessors since Magellan. Before his survey, the

Pacific Rim was a hypothesized mixture of continents, of lands which had in some part been seen, but whose whole extent was unknown, and of islands discovered and then lost again. Although some parts of the ocean remained unvisited and some islands undiscovered, the main outlines of Pacific geography were established. To the discovery and charting of coasts, Cook had added minute details of winds and tides and sunken reefs, not only drawing maps but describing the lands themselves, their people, and their resources with a fullness and exactitude seldom approached by his predecessors.

In the mid-19th century, however, noted German naturalist Ernst Haeckel also presented a reasonable argument for the existence of Lemuria (which he placed in the general region of the Indian Ocean joining Madagascar, India, and Africa) arguing for a missing land mass between Africa and India as opposed to "Mu" which could be interpreted to have been located in the Central Pacific Ocean region. The Lemurian land mass existed as a migratory route for the "lemurs," or "primitive ape men" who moved from the proto-Indian Ocean area into the region of Sumatra and Melanesia.

Two problems which have attracted much attention in the study of Pacific island peoples are those of their origin and their dispersion. Many theories have been put forward to explain where they came from, by what routes, and how they managed to settle over widely scattered islands throughout a vast expanse of ocean between New Guinea, Easter Island, and the Hawaiian Islands. Another allied problem is that of the source of their culture.

Myths of ancient China date back to oracle bone inscriptions 30,000 BP, the earliest tradition of scribal notation on astronomy and star navigation. The historic records, inscriptions and traditions show an interplay involving a series of solar myths, flood myths, myths about the creation of the universe and the sinking of lands in the Pacific commonly referred to as the legendary Meru or Mu. The term "Mu" is also very important in the life story of the "Son of Heaven—Mu," who comes to earth as an example of prehistoric creation. Among the many Chinese creation myths one finds the exploits of the Hunter Ho-wang-mu who is looking for the heavenly land on Earth called Hai-wang-Mu. The breaking apart and destruction of the land of Mu and the sinking of the "Sun of Mu" are stories whose authenticity seems beyond doubt, having been deeply embedded in the minds of the Chinese people.

Japanese historic traditions carry on a popular "Mu myth" by teaching that their first thirty-six generations of emperors, beginning with Jim-Mu and Kim-Mu, came from the region of the Sun. Thus the use of the "rising sun" symbol exemplified the meaning of the divine power on earth that was to spread light throughout the world connected with the divine island of Japan.

The question is asked: "Of what use can knowledge of Mu be to humanity?" To some, of little practicality, but there are many who would be glad to know the origin of man's early movements and cross-cultural interactions over "unknown areas" of the ocean. At this stage of history it is important to know the triggers on which has been based the fabric of the various cultures that have existed and do exist among humankind. This knowledge would serve to correct the misunderstandings that have been major obstacles for generations in man's understanding of the dim planetary past. These submerged "footprints" can make the rocks speak volumes and prepare for the future so as to make improvements on what humanity claims to be, the most perfect work of creation on earth.

Endnotes:

1. Dates vary based on culture, but the general theory for Western culture is:

   Paleolithic (Old Stone Age) 700,000-17,000 BP
   Mesolithic (Middle Stone Age) 17,000-10,300 BP

Neolithic (New Stone Age) 10,300-6,200 BP
Chalcolithic (Copper Age) 6,200-5,000 BP

2. The Cenozoic Period of the standard Geological Time Scale is made up of:
   The Cenozoic Period (66 million years ago to present)
   Quaternary (2 million years ago to present)
   Holocene (10 thousand years ago to present)
   Pleistocene (2 million-10,000 years ago)
   Tertiary (66 million-2 million years ago)
   Pliocene, Miocene, Oligocene, Eocene, Paleocene.

3. The Lapita culture is made up of early Austronesian-speaking Neolithic population that colonized Oceanica (Melanesia, Micronesia and Polynesia) around 3,500 BP.

---

1. Akiyama, Kenzo (1967) "Studies in the Relations between Japan & China (in Japanese)," Iwanami Shoten, Tokyo, 1939, in *Ri Jo Si, Rok Records of the Ri Dynasty*, **Vol. 7**, p. 677-678ff, Gakushuin Daigaku, Toyo Bunka Kenkyujo: Tokyo, 1967.
2. Cheng, Te-kun (1959) *Prehistoric China*. Cambridge: Heffer and Sons, pp. 44-133.
3. Churchward, James (1988) *The Lost Continent of Mu*. London: W.C. Daniels.
4. Clottes, J., & Courtin, J. (1996) *The Cave Beneath The Sea: Paleolithic Images*. Cosquer, New York: Harry N. Abrams.
5. Cook, James (1777) *Voyage toward the South Pole and Round the World*. **2 Vols.**, Blackwell: London.
6. Kimura, Masaaki (1996) "Ryukyu in the Late Quaternary," *Journal of Geography* (in Japanese), 105 (3), pp. 261-268.
7. Minamiyama, Hiroshi (1997) *Bottom of the Ocean Ooparts* [Out of Place Artifacts]. Tokyo: Futami Shobo, Publisher, 302 pages. ISBN 4-576-97087-9. [In Japanese. The Yonaguni Monument & related structures are discussed on pp. 11-46.]
8. Siskei-Meishou (1996) *Cultural Properties of Okinawa*, Part III. Kindaibijyutu Ltd.: Naha.
9. Thomas, Michael F. (1968). "Tor," *The Encyclopedia of Geomorphology*, Rhodes W. Fairbridge (Ed.), pp. 1157-1159, Stroudsburg, Pennsylvania: Dowden, Hutchinson & Ross. Also see Chang, K.C. Prehistoric Ceramic Horizons in Southeastern China & Their Extension into Formosa. *Asian Perspectives*, Hong Kong, **Vol. 7**, nos.1/2, pp. 243-250.

2

Rock Circles of the Kofa Mountains in Southwestern Arizona: A Reconnaissance Study

Steve Skotnicki, Ph.D.

In the dry deserts of southwestern Arizona, southern Nevada, and eastern and southeastern California, numerous enigmatic rock circles and cleared circular spaces can be found. Though evidently man-made, the origin and purpose of these circles has been debated for some time (Rodgers, 1939). Though much has been learned about the location, construction, and form of these rock circles, a full understanding of their genesis and purpose remains elusive.

Rock Circles

The rock circles show several different forms. Most are small cleared circular spaces on desert pavements, between 1 and 3 meters in diameter with little or no rim. Others are bounded by a low-stacked stone rim about 1 to 3 rocks high while others include circles with high stone walls, multiple joined circles, circles within circles, and rare polygonal shapes. In almost all cases the rocks bounding the features were derived locally from the immediate area, apparently from the interior of the circles. Often associated with the features are rock alignments and faint trails. Some trails are older than others, and some appear to lead nowhere. In some areas as far east as the Tucson Basin (Rodgers, 1958), short trails, called "summit trails," lead up the sides of small hills capped by a rock circle.

Even though rock circle sites are found over a vast area, the physical characteristics of the widely separated sites are very similar. The great majority occur at elevations below two thousand feet—and almost never in the mountains. Most were built on rough, rock-covered alluvial terraces now far-removed from modern water sources. Within or near the sites "diagnostic cultural material," such as pottery, food products, or finely worked stone tools, are seldom found. In some cases trails and trail shrine sites (piles of rocks near trails) that contain pot sherds may reflect sites that were occupied continuously up until relatively historic times or were 'rediscovered' and used by younger cultures.

The areas examined in this report lie between Gila Bend and Quartzsite, north of the Gila River in southwestern Arizona (Figure 2.1). In the Gila Bend Mountains northwest of Gila Bend in the Fourth of July Butte quadrangle, several large circles 2 to 3 meters in diameter have walls of stacked basalt cobbles three feet high. They are at the base of a large cliff and are themselves positioned on an old alluvial affording a commanding view of the surrounding land. Nearby three rectangular rock outlines with rounded corners all have their long axes aligned in the same direction—to the northeast. They are about 2 meters long and superficially resemble graves, except that they appear to be on undisturbed ground.

To the west on the Palomas Plain, rock circles are very abundant and are almost always found on the boulder-covered slopes of the isolated hills sticking up like islands above the alluvial plain. On one small hill near the east end of the Tank Mountains, the slopes are covered with dozens of walled circles and semicircles. Locally some of the walls are in the form of an "H" or "I" as well as semicircles, and are 0.5 to 1 meter high. Nearby again are several stone rectangles which also have their long axes aligned to the northeast. Near

Figure 2.1
Index Map of southwestern Arizona showing the location of the areas examined. Dots represent stone circle sites.
Map Courtesy of S. Skotnicki.

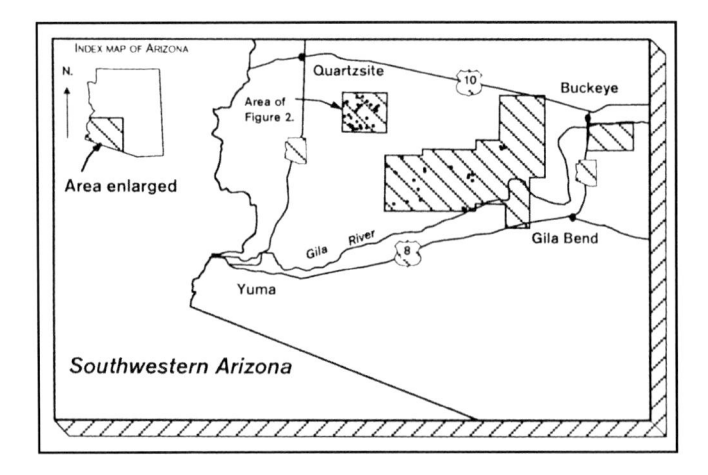

Baragan Mountain and the Agua Caliente Mountains rock circles are outnumbered by small enigmatic rock walls 1 to 3 meters long and about 0.5 meters high, and piles of stones (or "cairns") 1 to 1.5 meters high. All sites were found on the south sides of the mountains.

KOFA MOUNTAINS

The shaded areas delineated in Figure 2.1 were surveyed over a period of three years. The greatest number of rock circles found during this time are in the Kofa Mountains (Figure 2.2). Here they are between 1 and 4 meters in diameter and all were found on older alluvial terraces and bedrock benches along the major washes at elevations between 2,500 and 2,000 feet. None were found in the mountains. At several sites, two or more circles are clustered close to one another or are in contact. Most of the older alluvial surfaces (and even many of the younger surfaces) in the Kofa Mountains have well-developed desert pavements that contain a large percentage of large basalt cobbles.

Several remarkable petroglyph sites were found in the Kofa Mountains. Three sites in the northwest of the Kofa-Manganese Road are etched into dark varnish covering basalt cobbles and boulders half-buried in a dissected Pleistocene terrace. Several nearby sites at the

Legend
- Stone Circles
- ▲ Petroglyphs and/or Sherds
- Trails
- Bedrock
- Alluvium

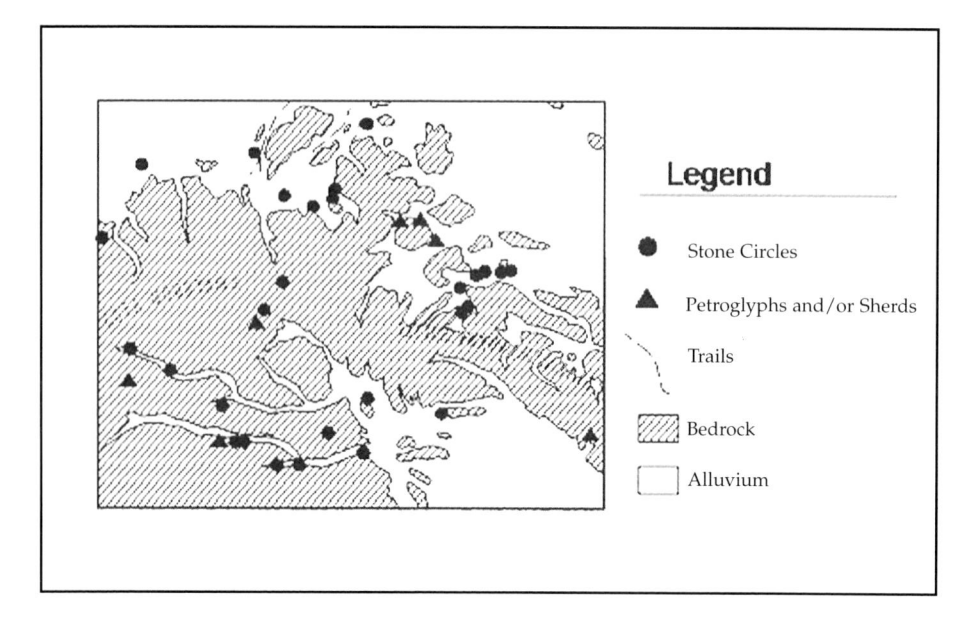

Figure 2.2
Generalized map showing locations of stone circles and petroglyphs in the northeastern Kofa and western Little Horn Mountains. Map courtesy of S. Skotnicki.

base of steep, talus-covered hills contain abundant buff-colored pottery sherds. Two petroglyph sites were found in the upper parts of two drainages in the western part of the range. The western-most site is up on a small south-facing cliff face about 50 feet above the wash and is very difficult to see from below. The most remarkable site is in the south along Hoodoo Wash. Here the images are of box-like grids filled with solid and hollowed circles, adjacent to large elongated human figures. With the exception of one petroglyph site in the center of the range, which is 30 meters or so from a large circular stone pile with a pit in the center (probably from pot-hunters), none of the petroglyphs were found near rock circle sites. Because rock varnish in general becomes darker and thicker on progressively older, stable rocks (and petroglyphs), it is a good indicator of relative age.

Cation-ratio dating (measuring the ratio of Ca and K—which apparently decrease over time—to Ti) has been used with limited success to date rock varnish in other areas but the technique is not widely accepted as an accurate dating tool. Hence, it is not clear if the petroglyphs were created at the same time as the circles or much later.

On the alluvial piedmonts on the north side of the Kofa Mountains there are several faint trails leading from the mouths of two major north-facing drainages northward for an undetermined distance. The trails locally split into two or more branches. Some of the branches are quite short and merge with the main trail after only several tens to hundreds of meters. The interior of the trails are made up of mostly finer-grained pebbles, as opposed to the coarser cobbles away from the trails. The interior stones are all varnished and everywhere developed into a desert pavement. Along at least one branch of the western-most trail pink- to buff-colored pot sherds with fine quartz-feldspar sand temper were found. If the trails were created by the pre-pottery culture(s) that created the rock circles then the ceramics likely represent material from a younger culture, most likely the Patayan (or Yuman) and may also reflect continued use of older trails.

AGE OF THE ROCK CIRCLES

Unfortunately, cultural artifacts that are often most diagnostic of a particular culture are absent in and around the circles in the Kofa Mountains. Because of the general nature of this study no lithic artifacts were discovered in the Kofa Mountains, but artifacts found associated with rock circles elsewhere (Dosh and Marmaduke, 1992) are characterized by unifacial stone scrapers, choppers, and hammer stones. The problem of assigning a cultural affinity to these artifacts is that these types of tools are also found in all younger cultures (McGuire and Schiffer, 1982). But because of the absence of pottery, and the presence of dark varnish and solution weathering on the tools, and because the tools are found embedded in or lying on top of very old desert pavements, it can be said that the circles predate better-understood younger pottery-making cultures in the region.

Several other lines of evidence suggest that the

rock circles are still very old features. The absence of tools and pottery implies that either these items or the technology to produce them did not exist at the time the circles were created or that the circles were used for a purpose other than prolonged habitation (or all of the above). The rocks forming the rim or the walls of the circles and cleared areas, and along trails and rock alignments are almost everywhere covered with a dark desert varnish on the exposed surfaces and with a crust of caliche on the buried underside. Because both varnish and caliche take very long periods of time to develop (just how long is still being debated) the rocks were moved a long time ago. The rocks commonly show frosted surfaces caused by repeated exposure to blowing sand over long periods of time, and the interior of the circles are commonly covered by a regenerated desert pavement. Even though pavements form over long periods of time Dosh and Marmaduke (1992) argue that the regeneration of gravely desert pavements observed within rock circles may be more a result of already varnished rocks washing into the central depression of the circle from the margins, and if such infilling plays a major role then the rock circles could be younger than previously thought.

With few exceptions the sites are located nowhere near modern sources of water. This implies that either at the time the circles were created there was sufficient water nearby, or that the sites were only briefly occupied. If there was water nearby then the climate was likely wetter than it is today. According to Martin (1963), the climate in the region has been arid (with minor variations) since about the early Holocene—about 10,000 years ago. However, some of the sites are on terraces that are much older still—as old as early and middle Pleistocene which were far removed from streams even 10,000 years ago. These observations together with the rarity of tools and/or other cultural artifacts, supports the contention that most sites were only briefly occupied.

In the 40 years that Rodgers studied in the deserts of the southwest he discovered more than 8,000 rock circles. He ascribed the creation of these circles to an ancient people called the San Dieguito living in the area during the Paleo-Indian period (approximately 12,000 to 8,000 years ago). There is no record of their appearance, nor did they possess pottery, but because of the great area over which the circles are found the San Dieguito may have been nomadic hunters and gatherers who subsisted by following game and seasonal growth patterns.

In other parts of the country where deposition during the Holocene was much greater, there are thicker sequences of stratified sediments often containing datable materials such as bone or carbon from fire pits. In the southwest, however, most rock circle sites are found on surfaces that have remained relatively stable throughout most of the Holocene and have had little sediment input except eolian (wind-blown). This combined with the lack of datable material means that these sites cannot be accurately dated using current techniques and the age of the sites must be inferred from similar sites elsewhere where dates are available. The only stratified deposits (yet discovered) for the Paleo-Indian and Archaic occupations of southwestern Arizona occur at Ventana Cave, in the Castle Mountains on the Papago Indian Reservation west of Tucson. Here, two carbon-14 dates were reported: 10,600 + 240 BC on bone apatite in the lowermost layer, and 9,350 + 1,200 BC on charcoal associated with definite artifacts thought to be of Clovis age (Haury, 1975 in McGuire, 1982).

The Purpose Or Function Of The Rock Circles

Why were the rock circles made? The preeminent theory in the archaeological literature is that they are 'sleeping circles.' The German Jesuit Johann Jacob Baegert at the San Luis Gonzaga Mission wrote sometime after 1740 that the Indians in the area seldom ever slept in the same place for more than three consecutive nights, and that they slept on the ground in

Rock Circles of the Kofa Mountains in Southwestern Arizona

Figure 2.3
Rock Circle, Arizona.
Photo by
S. Skotnicki.

cleared circles with low walls for protection from the wind (Rodgers, 1966).

There are no other known direct observations nor reports about the use of rock circles either from Europeans or Native Americans. In historic times cowboys sometimes slept within a rope circle, said by some to keep the snakes out, but this may have been more for psychological rather than physical security. Rock circles may have had a similar purpose. It has been suggested that the circles may have been "tee-pee rings," or the foundations of wikiups. Although some workers have described rock circles with groupings of rocks around the rim that may have been used to hold poles in place, most of the circles show no such groupings. Nor do most show any entrance or doorway. In fact, a small percentage of the features are less than one meter in diameter—seemingly too small for a human to sleep in. It may be that the smaller circles were for young children or pets, or possibly those who created the circles were smaller than modern humans.

Some of the rock semicircles on the slopes of

isolated hills on the Palomas Plain may have been used as 'hides' for hunting game. Another possible interpretation is that the circles were used for 'vision quests.' A person would go out on his own, clear a circle to sit or lay in and meditate, perhaps with the purpose of connecting with the spirit or energy of the universe in the quest for guidance or knowledge. It may have been a ritual performed by knowledgeable elders or by younger members as a right of passage. Groupings of circles have been observed near the base of hills separated by several miles of dissected alluvial plains, and on opposite sides of the Colorado River. It has been suggested that the circles may have been used as communication nodes, similar to phone booths where people communicated telepathically, rather than making the long walk between hills over hot, rugged country.

Conclusion

Although there is still some argument, rock circles seem to be very old features created by the earliest known inhabitants of the southwest. Little is known about the people who created these features, but because of the widespread occurrence of apparently briefly occupied circle sites and the probable semi-arid climate at the time, the circle-makers most likely were nomadic and followed game animals and seasonal growth patterns. The function of rock circles is also still being debated, but most researchers refer to them as 'sleeping circles.'

As of now there is no full detailed synopsis of rock circle sites in the southwest. There have been many detailed archaeological investigations in southwestern Arizona but they have been limited to narrow zones and are usually carried out as a prelude to development.

Southwestern Arizona is normally very dry and hot, and largely uninhabited. Because there is very little development in this part of the state the region is largely unexplored in great detail and many more sites may be waiting to be found.

1. Dosh, S.G. & Marmaduke, W.S. (1992) "Jefferson Proving ground relocation phase 1 mitigation studies: evaluation of the sleeping circle regeneration hypothesis," *Arch. Investigation Report* prepared for the Environmental Division, U.S. Army Yuma Proving Ground.
2. Haury, E.W. (1975) *The Stratigraphy and Archaeology of Ventana Cave*. Tucson: University of Arizona, 2nd Ed.
3. Martin, P.S. (1963) *The Last 10,000 Years, a Fossil Pollen Record of the American Southwest*. Tucson: University of Arizona.
4. McGuire, R.H.& M.B. Schiffer (Eds.) (1982) *Hohokam and Patayan: Prehistory of Southwestern Arizona*. New York: Academic Press.
5. Rodgers, M.J. (1939) "Early lithic industries in the lower basin of the Colorado River and adjacent desert areas," *San Diego Museum Papers No. 3*.
6. Rodgers, M.J. (1958) "San Dieguito implements from terraces of the Rincon-Pantano & Rillito drainage system," *The Kiva*, **Vol. 24**, p. 1-23.
7. Pourade, R.F. (Ed.) (1966) *Ancient Hunters of the Far West*. San Diego: San Diego Museum of Man and the Union-Tribune Publishing Co.
8. Spaulding, W.G. & L.J. Graumlich (1986) "The last pluvial climatic episodes in the deserts of southwest North America," *Nature*, **Vol. 320**, p. 441-444.
9. "An archaeological investigation of Buckeye Hills east," Maricopa County, Arizona (1976) *Arizona State University Anthropological Research*, No. 10.

3

From World Catastrophe to Global Migration

J.J. Hurtak, Ph.D., Ph.D.

The period between 12,000 and 3,000 years BP (Before Present) was a time of profound growth of civilization: the first temple mounds were constructed in Peru, the first pyramids and city complexes were built in Egypt, worldwide civilizations arose in the ancient Near East, and a multitude of changes took place in the Far East with long-term consequences for the development of complex societies throughout the Pacific Basin.

But was that truly our beginning? Many of these temple complexes were centered on earlier "myths of deliverance." James Frazier's monumental study *The Golden Bough* records reports of over four hundred cataclysms in the East, and the great books of the West speak of proto-world civilizations that were interconnected across the globe from Africa to Asia. Legends also allude to worlds of antiquity in "the land of the setting of the Sun" that were destroyed, and we have the report of the Flood recorded in the biblical book of Genesis, which is a condensation of a much earlier oral history. The Egyptian texts call this earlier time period a time when their civilization was ruled by gods who were able to travel great distances to instill and communicate their knowledge.

Throughout the world, from temple walls to stone

From World Catastrophe to Global Migration

Figure 3.1
Stele of Thutmosis IV
Giza, Egypt.
Photo by D. Hurtak.

steles, we find ancient references to proto-world civilizations. The Ethiopic Kebra Nagast, for example, speaks of advanced air travel, and Sanskrit texts describe the Vimanas, "chariots driven by light" which interconnected with the peoples of the earth on a mundane basis. There are also evidences of unique types of electricity, advanced metallurgy and chemistry, an understanding of medicine, anesthesiology, bloodless surgery, advanced civil engineering, and the establishment of standard units of measurement for construction. Where nowadays are these sophisticated civilizations?

About 15,000 years ago, over a span of several centuries, three dramatic ice-melts raised the level of the world's oceans and drowned many coastal regions. Southeast Asia, which had been a single huge continent, became a multitude of islands as the oceans rose more than 300 feet (100 m) to where we find them today. Glaciers melted and gigantic ice dams ruptured across Europe and the Americas, releasing vast quantities of water inland and into the oceans. The last of these abrupt sea-floods, some 12,000-9,500 years ago, was compounded by superwaves set off by cracks in the Earth's crust as ice-plates collapsed and regional volcanic activity occurred. Remarkably, ice-core data recently gathered from Greenland and Antarctica suggests that half of the temperature change (some 14° F) occurred in less than fifteen years around 9,645 B.C. Thus, we could assume that the catastrophic collapse of the legendary Atlantis, as well as stories of the biblical Noah and the pre-biblical Unapashtim in the Akkadian texts, could be connected with these geological events.

However, the glaciation of the Pleistocene age (1.8 million to 11,000 years ago) was not as continuous as was once believed; it consisted of several glacial advances interrupted by warmer periods, during which the ice retreated and a comparatively mild climate prevailed, and human civilization could have flourished.

Archaeologists have found the beginning of recorded language in petroglyphs appearing as far back as 30,000+ years ago near Bhopal (India) and in Australia. Rock engravings found at Toca do Boqueirão

Figure 3.2
Ancient petroglyphs on cavern wall outside Moab, UT.
Photo by L. Photiadis (1998).

da Pedra Furada, in northeastern Brazil have been dated to between 30,000-48,000 years ago by carbon 14 methods, placing man in the southern hemisphere of the new world far earlier than previously thought. Other ancient pictoglyphs in the New World show sacred geometries (in southern Brazil) and humans with six fingers.

Human remains and artifacts uncovered at Monte Verde, Chile have been dated at 12,500 BP, however, some possible stone tools and three hearths at the site have been dated to ~33,000 years old. Similar striking evidence in the Americas comes from evidences of mammoths (specifically proboscidean toe bones) found surrounding a possible hearth which was dated 33,000 BP in El Cedral, near Monterrey, Mexico. This clearly suggests the presence of man in the Americas some 33,000 years ago.

Two early prehistoric civilizations have also been identified in central Europe and Russia: the Aurignacian (40,000-28,000 years ago), followed by the Gravettian (28,000-22,000 years ago). Thousands of small sculptured figurines and personal ornaments produced by these peoples have been discovered and documented.

Were all these civilizations evolving separately? Rapa Nui (Easter Island) and the Hawaiian Islands are clearly some of the most isolated islands in the Pacific. The "faces" and stylistic marks on the gigantic statues of Easter Island have always posed questions as to the people and technology who built and moved them, and yet the "body language" of the hand positions and the mudra-positions of the fingers on the statues clearly lead back to the islands of Southeast Asia.

In the 1970s my colleagues and I traced direct comparisons between the language families of Southwest North American tribes and Central Asian peoples, discovering exact patterns of linguistic parallels which, in turn, show remnant language connections that still exist as a bridge between East and West. The impact of Asian languages can also be seen in Guatemala and the Yucatán, where many of the first American tribes thought of themselves as descendants

Figure 3.3
The monumental statues of Rapa Nui (Easter Island) pose questions not yet answered. Photo by D. Hurtak.

from a land called Tollan or Tlan, which may be none other than India's "Surface People" (talan in Sanskrit). The Mesoamericans thought of themselves as survivors of oceanic cataclysms; many of their temples, built to commemorate the destruction of their ancestors in the Pacific, bear illustrations of ocean waves. Their land on the Atlantic side was known as Atlan, and names having "atlan" roots are found all over Mexico: Autlan, Atlan, Mazatlan, Zihuatian, Cuautitian, etc., and the main city itself called Tenochtitlan. Aztatlan on Mexico's West Coast in Nayrait (Nairitti), means in Sanskrit, "where the moon sets in Atala" or the westernmost border of Atlantis. The hereditary kings in this area of Mexico are still called Nayar.

Studies of the Hawaiian language confirm its close relationship to the language on the Marquesas islands, some 3,000 miles of ocean away. Over 50% of the words in their two basic languages are similar, and linguistic evidences point to an early parent language used by several groups of "sea people" who navigated across the Pacific in several different directions, a people who also have legends of cataclysm.

Explorer Thor Heyerdahl has continually advanced the notion of trans-oceanic contact and migration in the South Pacific and onward to the Americas. More recently, after a prolonged study of ocean currents, Heyerdahl has professed the belief that ocean-going peoples could have migrated both to and from South America.

The ability of sea culture peoples to cross great ocean barriers is further suggested by a study of the movements of human genetics conducted at Emory University. Professor Douglas Wallace has determined that the Pacific Islands and North/South Indian regions of North America were populated by Asians showing DNA trace elements of a strain of genetic material from a common proto-Eve source that originated in Africa and moved into Asia. Analyzing the mitochondrial DNA from widely separate Native American groups, Wallace and others were able to suggest that the first American Indian (Amerind) speakers entered the Americas somewhere between 42,000 and 21,000 years ago, while the ancestral population of the present-day Na-Dene people arrived between 16,000 and 5,000 years ago.

There is overwhelming DNA evidence that at least four strains of early humans connect the Asian continent with the Americas over different pre-historic periods, dating both before and after cataclysmic events. It is also possible that one strain of DNA came to North America from Europe in prehistoric times.

With the use of different gene studies, a more complex picture of migration is being constructed. Most of our genetic information in the form of DNA is stored in the nuclei of our cells, but other bodies in our cells (mitochondria) also contain such information. However, mitochondrial DNA (mtDNA) is passed on only by females, since the male sperm's mitochondria do not survive fertilization. The plethora of new information tends to support a "Multiregional

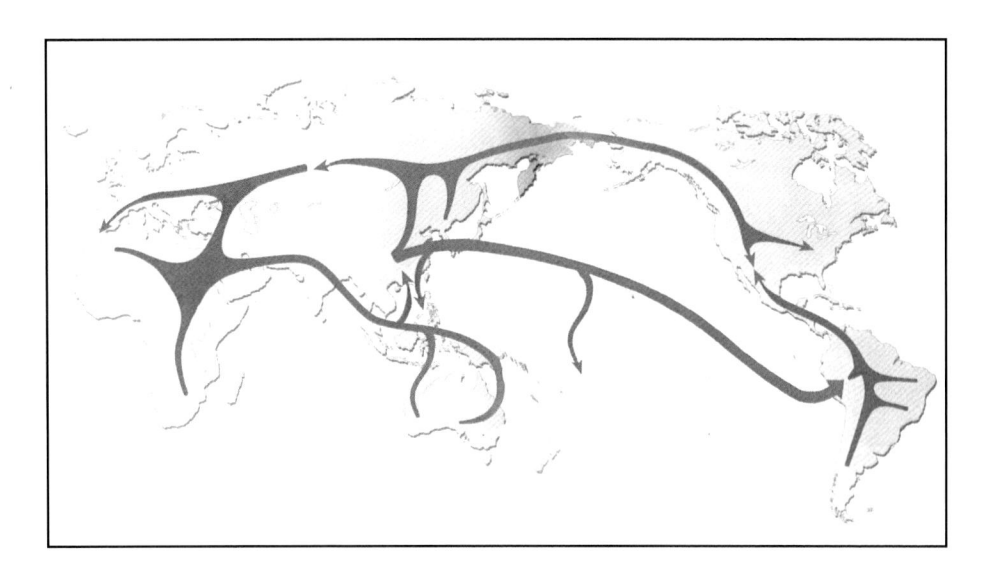

Figure 3.4
Migration routes connecting Asia and the Americas. Drawing by the Academy For Future Science (2002).

Hypothesis"—that homo erectus, having left East Africa and Asia, evolved separately in different parts of the world, and was not simply replaced by a much later migration of anatomically modern humans from Africa (the Mitochondrial Eve Hypothesis).

Enhanced collaboration between paleoclimatologists and archaeologists has begun to foster an integrated view of a crucial period in recent Earth history, showing that the Earth was at some time more "compacted above water," as recorded in the New Testament epistle of *2 Peter*, Chapter 3. Explorations by divers off the island of Yonaguni (Sea of East China) may substantiate the reports of underwater structures like those of "Mu" in waters surrounding Taiwan. These structures show sunken platforms located off the coast of Taiwan which follow a design of land-ocean systems in a manner similar to temple-molt terraces observed in the South American and Pacific islands. Returning to Rapa Nui (Easter Island), we note similarities of its ancient wall structures to those being discovered through remote sensing radar techniques and excavation near Cuzco, Peru, where walls resemble the back of a dragon on three layers of gargantuan rocks, connected with a nearby temple top that

From World Catastrophe to Global Migration

Figure 3.5
Central Asian Oracle Bone.
Photo by J.J. Hurtak.

supports a solar and lunar water wheel. This is all the more important since the temples of the East were connected with the dragon as a central symbol of power and planetary change.

With an eye to global migration patterns of civilized cultures, we find the rubbing from a unique artifact dating from at least 3,500 BP, discovered in Central Asia in the 1930s. It is from an elephant scapula bone carved with pictographs of migratory routes, and lost during World War II, suggesting detailed scientific correspondence on astronomy and cosmology. The presence of both Egyptian and Chinese pictographic script on the scapula, of which rubbings were made before its disappearance, suggest a high level of

64

scientific exchange between distant civilizations sharing a common knowledge of multiple sun systems.

Could these cataclysms come again? According to *The Book of Knowledge: The Keys of Enoch®*, extremely rapid melting of polar ice releases a polar torque that moves vast bodies of water, in some cases so violently that the outer mantle of the earth could slide around the inner core, causing rapid movement of the tectonic plates. However, simple climate changes caused by geophysical events or solar flares are enough to disrupt civilizations. A thorough study of ice cores, combined with analysis of deep sea sediments, indicates that temperatures on Earth were warm about 103,000, 82,000, 60,000, 35,000, and 10,000 years ago, and shows similarities with the Milankovitch's gradual climate change theory pointing to 41,000 years coupled with the precessional cycle of a time period of 22,000 years.

As we come to understand the message of the oracle bones, artifacts, and the precise cues of world architecture that are repeated over and over in different global locations, one message is clear: Long before the written record of the scriptures, the "oral record" of proto-communication suggests high levels of cultural diffusion and adaption by the peoples of both East and West, and this had a profound impact on later periods of historic reconstruction. In the new recoveries of "pre-time" evidences of high civilization, the knowledge of lost civilizations is gained. The archaic reconstructions of temples, shrines and measuring points from East to West shows an advanced understanding of sun movement and cosmology from China and Japan to Egypt and the West. No matter what earth cataclysms, sun spot disruptions, or disasters that ended life in these ancient centers, the same symbols on the bottom of the ocean speak to us with the same precise accuracy as the grand architecture of Asia and the Near East—in short, a house that portrays the "divine grid" on Earth, mirroring the heavens.

New findings of genetics and archaeology have opened a vision of plenitude before our eyes, showing vast migratory movements of Asian peoples to the

From World Catastrophe to Global Migration

Americas as a result of claimed global catastrophes and cataclysmic changes at the end of the last Ice Age. With the breaking of the historical archaeological paradigms, new realities of East-West exchange have appeared. The foundations "of the deep" are being moved and revealed, helping us to understand the "missing pieces" of the fantastic history of our planet and of the earlier cycles of humanity known to the ancients.

---

1. Dalrymple, Alexander (1737-1808) *Historical Collection of the Several Voyages and Discoveries in the South Pacific Ocean* (1770).
2. Dillehey, Tom, (1989) "A Late Pleistocene Settlement in Chile," **Vol. I**, *Palaeoenvironment and Site Context*, Smithsonian Institution Press, Washington D.C., **Vol. II** (1997).
3. Frazer, James (1980) *The Golden Bough: A Study in Magic and Religion*. London: Macmillan.
4. Goodyear, Albert C., Ellis, C. J., Morse, D. F., & Tankersley, K (1998) "Archaeology of the Pleistocene-Holocene transition in eastern North America," *Quaternary International*, 49/50:151-166.
5. Harding, R.M., S.M. Fullerton, R.C. Griffiths, J. Bond, M.J. Cox, J.A. Schneider, D.S. Moulin, & J.B. Clegg (1997) "Archaic African and Asian lineages in the genetic ancestry of modern humans," *American Journal of Human Genetics*, 60: 772-789.
6. Hausman, Gerald (Ed.) (1997) *The Kebra Nagast: the Lost Bible of Rastafarian Wisdom and Faith from Ethiopia and Jamaica*. New York: St. Martin's Press.
7. Heyerdahl, Thor (1967) *The Ra Expeditions* (numerous translations).
8. Hurtak, J.J. (1977) *The Book of Knowledge: The Keys of Enoch*. Los Gatos: The Academy For Future Science.
9. Kirch, Patrick Vinton (2000) *On the Road of the Winds: An Archaeological History of the Pacific Islands Before European Contact*. Berkeley: University. of California Press.
10. Lorenzo, J. L. & Mirambell, L. (1986) "Preliminary Report on Archaeological & Paleoenvironmental Studies in the Area of El Cedral, San Luis Potosi. Mexico, 1977-1980," Bryan, A.L. (Ed.) *New Evidence for the Pleistocene Peopling of the Americas*, Orono: Centre for the Study of the First Americans, pp. 107-113.
11. Milankovitch, M. (1930) *Mathematische Klimalehre und Astronomische Theorie der Klimaschwankungen*. Handbuch der Klimalogie Band 1 Teil A Berlin: Borntrager.
12. Personal conversations between Dr. J.J. Hurtak & Prof. Masaaki Kimura, Okinawa, Japan, 1998.
13. Suggested dates of the Yonaguni collapse range from 5,000 to 12,000 BP by Kimura & associates.
14. Wallace, Douglas C., Lott MT, Brown MD, Huoponen K, & Torroni, A. (1995) "Report of the committee on human mitochondrial DNA," Cuticchia, A.J. (Ed.) *Human gene mapping 1995: a compendium*. Johns Hopkins University Press, Baltimore, pp 910-954.

4

Rujum al-Hiri of Galilee: Stone Computer & Cosmic Timepiece

Bruce D. Curtis, M.A., M.Div.

Staring into space from the plains of the lower Golan Heights, just south of the 33rd latitude, in what some call the "golden belt," the sacred twelve degrees of 27-33° (north latitude, and roughly 10 miles east of the northern shore of the Sea of Galilee, lies a mysterious stone structure. Reminiscent of stone circles like Stonehenge, and the great medicine wheels of North America, this site, known in Arabic as *Rujum Al-Hiri*, or "Hill of the Cat," remains less explored and less understood than its more famous counterparts. Also known by its Hebrew name *Gilgal Rephaim*, or "Wheel of the Giants," [Note: "Rephaim" = Heb. 'shades,' or 'dead,' a generic reference for a broad class of giant human-type creatures also called by various local names, in the Bashan locale and others] this massive megalithic structure defies simple analysis. Conventional reductionistic archaeological explanations attempt to pin down its function as a "stone calendar" or "astronomical observatory." Even less likely solutions to its puzzling presence characterize it as a burial tomb, ritual altar, or ceremonial center. Yet, beyond all of these simplistic assessments one can sense a tale that is still shrouded in mystery, one that may be partially revealed by this other strange

Figure 4.1
Stonehenge.
Photo by D. Hurtak.

designation, Gilgal Rephaim. It is a story that will lead us on a journey from archaeology to archaeoastronomy, and from mythology and sacred scripture to future history. Herein the keys to sciences of the past may illumine the future destiny of humankind.

The earlier obscurity of Rujum al-Hiri was partly due to its inaccessibility under Syrian occupation prior to 1967, at which time the Golan region was annexed to the nation of Israel as a result of the Six-Day War. Israeli archaeologists would then make this site available to the world community upon its discovery during their archaeological survey of 1967-1968. However, it would not be until 1988 that the first thorough and systematic investigation of the complex was conducted under the direction of Yonathan Mizrachi, at that time a teaching fellow and curator of the Anthropology Department at Harvard University.[1] Four field seasons and the employment of such sophisticated technologies as ground-penetrating radar (GPR) and lichenometry (dating by growth patterns in lichen) have yielded some information regarding the age and topology of the megalith. Age and topography would prove insufficient to yield the original function of the wheel-like formation, leaving the purpose of its construction

Figure 4.2
Rujum al-Hiri of Galilee. Photo courtesy of the Academy For Future Science.

unknown.

Rujum al-Hiri is constructed of five concentric rings of stones with a central tumulus, or heap of stones, that is approximately 20 meters across. While this central cairn has often been a sign of burial function, subsequent dating analysis has indicated its construction considerably later than the greater structure. The combined weight of cairn and stone rings totals some 37,000 tons. The overall diameter of the site ranges from 150 meters to 155 meters, with an outermost ring that is most consistent in thickness at 3.2—3.3 meters and as high as 2 meters in places. This wall, designated as number 1, contains some sizeable megaliths, several estimated to weigh 20 tons or more. Most of these are found in the eastern portion of this wall.

The most interesting features of wall number 1 are two large entryways, one to the northeast and one to the southeast. Current speculation indicates that these openings are (or were at one time) aligned with specific celestial events. Conventional wisdom determines the orientation of the complex towards the equinoxes and the summer solstice.[2]

Interestingly, astronomical alignments give us the best clues regarding the function of Rujum al-Hiri as well as support for dating. Yonathan Mizrachi and Professor Anthony Aveni of Colgate University have made a detailed study of both the astronomical and geometrical features of the site. Because of the changing position of heavenly bodies with respect to fixed time-space points upon the earth, celestial coordinates were extrapolated back to the third millennium BCE to determine earlier alignments with the complex. The results confirmed that an observer viewing the summer solstice sunrise from the center of the site in the year 3,000 BCE would have seen the first rays of light appearing directly in the center of the northeast opening in the outer wall. This supports an Early Bronze Age (3,050-2,300 BCE) construction, a conclusion also reached by lichenometric methods, and the dating of various pot sherds discovered in the ruins (including some Chalcolithic sherds which date to the fourth millenium).[3]

Rujum al-Hiri is the only known megalithic astronomical complex on earth built of loose stones. It resembles more the ruins found on Malta and in Zimbabwe than the European sites built at the same time and possibly for the same purpose (such as Stonehenge and Avebury), although its Northeast opening corresponds with the same at Stonehenge. In appearance, however, the site is more nearly like The Great Enclosure in Zimbabwe, the largest single ancient structure south of the Sahara, with a perimeter wall measuring 820 feet in circumference with a height of 36 feet. With its estimated one million granite blocks, The Great Enclosure approximates the mass of Gilgal Rephaim with its 42,000 tons of basalt rock! Oddly, there is no remotely similar monument anywhere in the area.

Similarities with the Arkaim complex in the Russian Urals and with the Stanton Drew circle in England are much more striking, and the architectonic

Rujum al-Hiri of Galilee: Stone Computer & Cosmic Timepiece

Figure 4.3
The Great Enclosure in Zimbabwe. Photo by the Academy For Future Science.

and acoustical correspondences of these stone circles is well documented by Granögger (see Granögger, *Stone Circles, Sky Circles, Sound Circles: New Evidence on Global Round Numbers*, this edition, Chapter 5). In this instance, however, we lack the potential for acoustical signatures, at least given the open-air configuration of the monument in its current state.

The research of Dr. J.J. Hurtak provides a conceptual framework that can help us to understand the purpose and function of this complex more definitively. While drawing a parallel to the stone calendars of Stonehenge and Woodhenge he differentiates its function, explaining how this site near the Sea of Galilee exhibits the working of two calculator spheres that operate like a digital computer.[4] This key insight fits with Mizrachi's assessment of the site as multifunctional, though much more refined metric analysis will be required to decipher the precise computations. Nevertheless, accepted dates for the construction of Rujum al-Hiri would make it more than a thousand years older than Stonehenge, while the stellar alignments seem to point beyond the solar and lunar calculations reflected in that observatory. And just as the Druidic priests of that ancient isle once known as Avalon used Stonehenge for their calculations, it seems equally likely that priest-scientists of the ancient middle east would have used Rujum al-Hiri in a similar fashion. But what were they seeking to compute with this lithic calculator, and what relation did their calculations bear to stellar movements? What are the deeper meanings of the chosen alignments and what significance might they still hold for humanity today? The answers to these questions contain great significance for the ultimate destiny of the human race, and therefore move us to deeper reflection on our place in the cosmos.

Hurtak tells us that we must look at these ancient megalithic sites in order "to see the round numbers, the calculations of star mathematics which are part of the greater astrophysical geometry." The round numbers of these monuments give us the knowledge of where "Melchizedek has reigned." If he is correct and this is a computer in stone, then it will likely unravel the story of just where the human race fits into a larger cosmology of consciousness. As for the assertion of round numbers, Mizrachi verifies their presence in this site: "Measurements of the radii of the concentric walls reveal that simple proportionate whole numbers may have been involved in the design of the complex."[5] Moreover, two of the radii that connect wall number 2 with wall number 3 are aligned as backsights with the two openings in the outer wall. Yet, a more profound meaning lies within the term "round numbers." These whole number ratios indicate the presence of underlying aeonial relationships and geometric proportionalities that convey a teaching that needed to be preserved in stone. What story is told by the star mathematics of this calendrical complex and does it fit into the overall mapping of celestial and terrestrial events, and their possible convergence?

Taking cues from other archaeoastronomical sites, like Palenque, in Chiapas, Mexico, we may grasp these round numbers as providing a temporal mapping of the periodic interface with those who were known in sacred texts of the Near East as "Lords of Light," or what we might term "the Higher Evolution," or "star

Figure 4.4
The Pleiades.

intelligence." In Egypt, as well, these visitors were considered to be divine teachers and identified with specific star fields with which complexes in the Giza plateau are aligned: Sirius, Orion and the Pleiades. As early as 1973, Dr. Hurtak pointed out the significance of the Great Pyramid's alignments with key star groupings, notably with Orion through the southern star shaft in the King's chamber and with Sirius in the Queen's chamber. These alignments were subsequently confirmed by Robert Bauval and discussed in his book *The Orion Mystery*. Within Egyptian religion, we find the deeper significance of Orion and Sirius, [Egyptian: "Sahu" and "Sothis,"] encoded within the Osirian mysteries, wherein Osiris and Isis, as divine counterparts, find their origin and destiny connected with those particular star regions. It would appear more than coincidental then, that Rujum al-Hiri shares the Sirius alignment with the Great Pyramid, with the southeast opening in wall number 1 lining up to allow observation of Sirius' appearance in August.[6]

Such an alignment would seem to indicate some understanding and reliance on the Sothic calendar used by the Egyptians, a period of 365 (or 365.25) days based upon the heliacal rising of Sirius with the sun at sunrise. Harbinger of the Egyptian New Year, this, in turn, would convey with it that connection with the cosmology encoded in the Egyptian system including the 365° of the Enoch circle of the Great Pyramid, reflected in the geometry of the Stone Circle. Given this linkage with astronomical alignments so central to Egyptian religion and the circular geometry, it would be more fitting to refer to the site by its Hebrew name Gilgal Rephaim, "wheel of the Rephaim," and henceforth both names shall be applied as appropriate.

In this most strategic convergence of lattice points, we find that Gilgal Rephaim sits as an extension of the sacred grid connecting Giza, Megiddo, and Jerusalem. The significance of this association lies in the consciousness program of the last 6,000 years with the cradle of Program Israel found in Egypt, the old pyramidal grids of the Earth vibration, the culmination of its spiritual science in the temple work at Jerusalem, and the final judgment of the nations coded at Megiddo, the timepiece for the program. For this last piece, we shall have to extend the scope of our inter-disciplinary reach.

Here, therefore, lies our task: decoding the meaning behind this complex, referred to by Dr. Hurtak as an "astrophysical computer," set within the larger context of a planetary set of energy grids activated by the temples and monuments and telling the full story of the earth's holy history. But what is the deeper spiritual meaning of the message? Unless all of the pieces come together in a way that tells the story behind the simple astronomical correspondences, the true message of these calendar timepiece models will remain a mystery. It would appear that we need a multi-disciplinary approach to decode the hidden truths. Just as scholars turned to the Pyramid Hymns to understand the cosmology of Egypt, so we turn now to the Hebrew Scriptures where we find an abundant reference to stone structures along with place names and events containing clues to their hidden past and future history, along with their deeper purpose. We find a notable example in Beth-El, a place where Jacob erected a stone monument to commemorate his experience of the divine apotheosis. Herein, we may see how these stone timepieces are connected to those writings that contain the codes for "specific events on earth and in space that man must key into."

Why should we re-visit ancient texts to illuminate this particular megalith? First, the place names might illuminate some of the history, tribal movements and struggles within the region, and their relation to celestial events and realities. The place names connect with biblical references, giving us some of the only extant written documents preserving the lost history of these distant eras, together with the trans-historical correlations. Secondly, this is the only known megalithic astronomical structure composed of stone tumuli with nothing similar found in the region, though we have noted the similarity to the Great Enclosure in Zimbabwe, leaving us little to go on from complementary disciplines. Thirdly, and of greatest import, the Scriptures show how the Word of God continues to create new worlds and redeem consciousness out of old worlds. As we examine the descriptions of these physical and consciousness conflicts between peoples, we see evidence of the entire redemptive process of Light as it is modeled into this physical world.

To begin with, we must understand that the Golan region is synonymous with the ancient region of Bashan, an area that was connected, within the biblical context, with the Rephaim, or "giants" (cf. *Joshua* 12:4-5, *Genesis* 14:5, *1 Chronicles* 6:71). Examining the reference in *Genesis* 14 we find the Rephaim associated with the name of *Ashteroth*, the Canaanite mother goddess of fertility, love, and war. A city by that name existed just 15 kilometers to the east of the Rujum Al-Hiri complex. But *Genesis* 14 is more significant as the Melchizedekian text which reveals how a part of Abraham's work—and here Abraham can be seen as a metaphor for those of the seed of Abraham with the Hierarchy of *El Elyon* (God Most High)—is connected with the defeat of the kings of the earth. Within this elegantly spun and deeply coded story we can perceive the battle of the archons, or rulers, played out with the blessing of the divine seed program through Abraham as patriarch extending that blessing to all of the peoples of the earth. In this dialectic the kingship models representing other thrones and dominions are overthrown, and the other genetic experiments (e.g. the Rephaim), typical creations of lower principalities and powers, are recycled.

Concerning the Rephaim, we find the definitive profile in *Deuteronomy*, chapters 2 and 3, and at *1 Chronicles* 20:6. The basic blueprint is that of a people "numerous and tall," to be understood as "like the Anakim" (*Deuteronomy* 2:21), namely, those descended from the Nephilim, the fallen hierarchy. Enoch, the biblical Patriarch and seventh in life from Adam (See *1 Enoch*) has borne witness to the existence of other genetic experiments that have taken place on earth, and this is corroborated in *1 Chronicles*. In that context the Rephaim appear as a remnant civilization still existing at the time of David. The scroll describes one of them as "a man of extraordinary size whose fingers and toes were in sixes, twenty-four; and he, too had been born to the Rephaim" (*1 Chronicles* 20:6). We must, therefore, see the relationship between the lower gods such as Ashteroth, their offspring upon the earth, the Rephaim, and why they are shown in opposition to the forces of Light, symbolized by David and Melchizedek, who exemplify the sovereignty of the Higher Universes. Perhaps Gilgal Rephaim is not a spurious designation, as archaeologists assume. Rather, it could be that this stone, wheel-like complex gives the timing of events in the dialectical struggle between the forces of Light and the forces of darkness, possibly showing even when the Rephaim or their creators might return!

Structurally, there is quite a bit of similarity between living biological cells, various traditional cosmic wheels of life, and the form of the megalithic complex at Rujum Al-Hiri. Given the understanding that in the cosmic evolutionary procession of life, some life forms exist within a greater glory (cf. *1 Cor.* 15), and some which do not bear this type of higher image and similitude of Light are recycled within the lower waters

Figure 4.5
The Loltun caves in the Yucatán contain petroglyphs similar to those found at the megalithic complex of Rujum al-Hiri. Image courtesy of the Academy For Future Science.

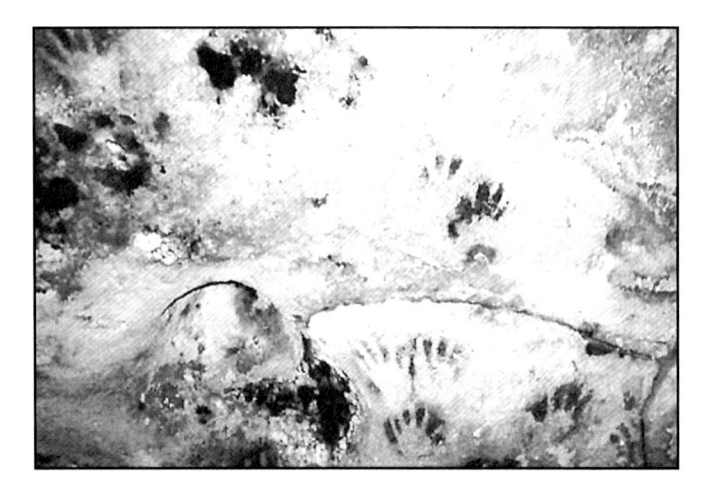

of creation, we could be looking at a timepiece that calculates the timing for these transformations. Toward this end, Rujum al-Hiri may have been built to compute the star mathematics of both regions of Light and lesser star points that have initiated their own genetic programs upon the earth. This grid in the Golan region suggests connections can be seen in triangulation with the grids at Megiddo, Jerusalem, and Giza, it is reasonable to conclude that we are looking at a critical timepiece in what the Dead Sea Scrolls and other apocalyptic texts have called the "war between the sons of Light and the sons of darkness."

Consequently, we must see more than the form of a medicine wheel, an eye, or even a cellular body in this astrophysical monument. For in its structure, as a cross within the circle, we behold the ancient sign and symbol seen in petroglyphs from Macchu Pichu to the Loltun caves in Yucatán, and in sacred sites around the world, one that points to a cosmology that comprehends interconnecting realms of space and time and the Higher Intelligence that traverses the heavens in a flash of Light. Historically, this circle and cross has been recognized as the "sign of the Brotherhood," viz. the Brotherhood of Light, or the Great White Brotherhood. Studies of ancient language systems similar to Egyptian hieroglyphics should cue us into this type of symbolic representation in stone as part of a greater communication system, namely one coming from the higher intelligence.

Aside from the archaeological, astronomical, and historico-biblical aspects of Rujum Al-Hiri, there appears to be some commonality with contemporary graphic phenomena that have baffled modern investigators throughout Europe, Israel, and elsewhere around the world. That is, of course, the recent appearance of diagrammatic figures in crop fields, commonly referred to as "crop circles." These agrograms are so similar to some of the ancient symbols in stone (such as Stonehenge and the formations on the plains of Salisbury in Great Britain and Carnac in France), that investigators have begun to use the term "pictograms" to refer to these modern-day messages.[7] Could it be that the appearance of pictograms in wheat fields is related to the historic building of megalithic complexes such as Stonehenge and Rujum Al-Hiri, and to the 'round numbers' they embody? If so, what underlying message is intended for our contemplation?

It is significant that this relatively obscure site contains the "round numbers" describing the time of return and loci of origination connected with what

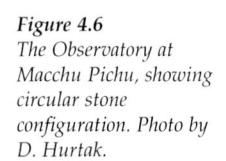

Figure 4.6
The Observatory at Macchu Pichu, showing circular stone configuration. Photo by D. Hurtak.

Mircea Eliade has called "the myth of the eternal return," namely, the who, when, where, and whence of the opposing forces in this archonic struggle. This astrophysical computer is but a part of a much grander legacy given to ensure that humanity would have a permanent scriptural witness in stone to understand the meaning of manifestations of both positive and negative forms of intelligence at the close of the age, and be better prepared for such an appearance. In this light we may view this wheel, Gilgal Rephaim, as a microcosmic representation within the greater cosmic wheel of life and the procession of the infinite.

---

1. For more information on exploration to date see Mizrachi's article (July/August 1992) "Mystery Circles," *Biblical Archaeology Review.* **Vol. 18** Number 2, pp. 46-57, 84.
2. Zohar, Mattanyah (1992) "Rujm El-Hiri" Freedman, David N. (Ed.), *The Anchor Bible Dictionary.* **Vol. 5**, New York: Doubleday, p. 841.
3. Mizrachi, Yonathan (1992) "Mystery Circles," July/August 1992, pp. 54-55.
4. Those interested in a thorough explication of the astronomical & geometrical relationships within the monument at Stonehenge will want to review Hawkins, Gerald (1973) *Beyond Stonehenge.* New York: Harper & Row. Additional seminal work was done by astronomer Sir Norman Lockyar (1836-1920), who was perhaps one of the first to reveal evidences of a computerized system there. *The Book of Knowledge: The Keys of Enoch®* by J.J.Hurtak (1977) contains the first reference to the importance of Rujum al-Hiri in modern times.
5. Mizrachi, Yonathan (1992) "Mystery Circles," July/August 1992, p. 55.
6. Zohar, "Rujm El-Hiri," p. 841.
7. For additional study on "crop circles" see Bartholome, Alick (1991) *Crop Circles: Harbingers of World Change.* Bath, GB: Gateway.

5

Stone Circles, Sky Circles, Sound Circles: New Evidence on Global "Round Numbers"

Ulrike Granögger, M. Phil

New archaeological evidence in conjunction with disciplines as diverse as geology, archaeoastronomy and acoustics necessitates a serious redefinition of the beginnings of humanity's history and possibly the meaning of human evolution itself.

One fascinating phenomenon in this context are the megaliths—stones and stone-circles—that can be found worldwide, standing as voiceless witnesses of a past philosophy and mathematics that no longer seem accessible. The stereotypical explanations of archaeologists on the origin and function of stone circles range from "places of ritual" and "sacrificial altars" to "tombs" and "solar calendars" for the calculation of the times of harvest. Megaliths are ascribed to a Stone Age or Bronze Age mentality, expressing a primitive religion of nature that focussed on the course of the sun and the seasonal changes associated with it. While the alignment of many stone circles with the equinoxes and solstices indeed warrants such an interpretation, many sites are also precisely oriented with distant star constellations, fixed star points, and local stellar and planetary movements, bespeaking a knowledge of astronomical realities such as precession and suggesting a cosmology that

Figure 5.1
The Norfolk Circle.
Photo courtesy of the
Academy For Future
Science.

definitely goes beyond a fixation on our immediate sun.

But alignment with higher star systems for what reason? What was it the ancients wanted to calculate? What days in the cosmos did they set out to mark? Was it merely to establish the times for seeding and harvesting crops?

Recent writings on archaeology refer to stone circles in the context of other significant archaeological complexes on earth and suggest that these must be seen all together as one great global mosaic of "round numbers"—a space-time mathematics that defines the points of intersection of the planetary orb with the greater cosmos.

It seems odd to expect round numbers to be found in our time; haven't stone circles been around for thousands of years? And yet, in recent years, megaliths and circles have literally "appeared" out of a distant past, as if the earth wanted finally to reveal the secrets of her deep. Let us look at some of the more recent discoveries:

In November 1998 in Norfolk on the eastern coast of England, after storms had swept away stretches of peat and sand along the coast, 54 wooden posts in circular formation, badly decayed, emerged from the sea. Archaeologists have worked feverishly to establish as much data as possible before changing tidal patterns swallow up the formation once again or disintegration is accelerated now that the ancient wood poles are exposed to the open air. The site dates from the Bronze Age and is considered as significant as Stonehenge. The posts form an unbroken ring around a central inverted oak tree, thought to be an altar piece on which a sacrificial body was laid (a questionable interpretation).[1]

In Miami, Florida, a building site being cleared for construction of a high-rise condominium revealed a remarkable circle of round postholes and basins in the limestone bedrock. Some experts believe it could be 2-3,000 years old, and that the complete original site possibly looked like a roofed circular building or meeting tent.[2]

Also in recent years, the sand plains of the eastern Sahara have revealed what is most likely the oldest megalithic complex so far discovered on earth. Climactic changes during the past 12,000 years in this region of southern Egypt near Nabta have been mapped with a high degree of accuracy and show that

Figure 5.2
Nabta Megalith. Photo from Malville J. McKim's research at Nabta, as published in "Nature" magazine.

throughout the Neolithic era (New Stone Age: 10,300 - 6,200 BP), periods of rain and monsoons, which would encourage fertility in the soil and allow the foundation of settlements, alternated with periods of extreme aridity. Thick layers of silt deposits from the periods of heavy rains are clearly visible in geological strata today. The ritual stone complex at Nabta which displays alignments with the cardinal directions and solstices was erected on sediments deposited during late mid-Neolithic times (between 9,000 and 8,700 BP). Archaeologists date this "ceremonial complex" as being approximately 8,000 years old.[3]

On very much the same meridian we find another remarkable complex of round numbers in the *Gilgal Rephaim* (Giant's Circle), also called *Rujum al-Hiri* (Cat's Hill) in Arabic, near the sea of Galilee. The existence of this "astrophysical computer" was suggested as early as 1973, at a time when Israeli scholars had only just cleared the site of rubble and weeds, after the Golan became Israeli territory in 1967. It was not until 1988 that proper archaeological excavations were executed on the site. Little if anything was known about the existence and function of this megalithic monument at research institutes of the west before that time. The circle is only visible in its entirety when viewed from above. It has a diameter of some 155 meters, with five concentric rings and a central tumulus.

In November 1997 a magnetometer survey within the stone circle of Stanton Drew (near Bristol, England) produced a sensational discovery: Beneath the fields are the remains of a circular structure of pits arranged in nine concentric circles, the largest having a diameter of 95 meters. The find suggests that the stone circle visible above ground today is only the very latest stage of a much older and more elaborate site than was understood before.[4]

Nine circular pyramidal steps seem also to have been the characteristic feature of a mysterious complex found in the 1980s in the southern Urals (near Celjabinsk, Russia). The site, discovered by aerial photography, reveals a magnificent circular structure

New Evidence on Global "Round Numbers"

Figure 5.3
Stanton Drew
Stone Circle.
Diagram courtesy of
the Academy For
Future Science.

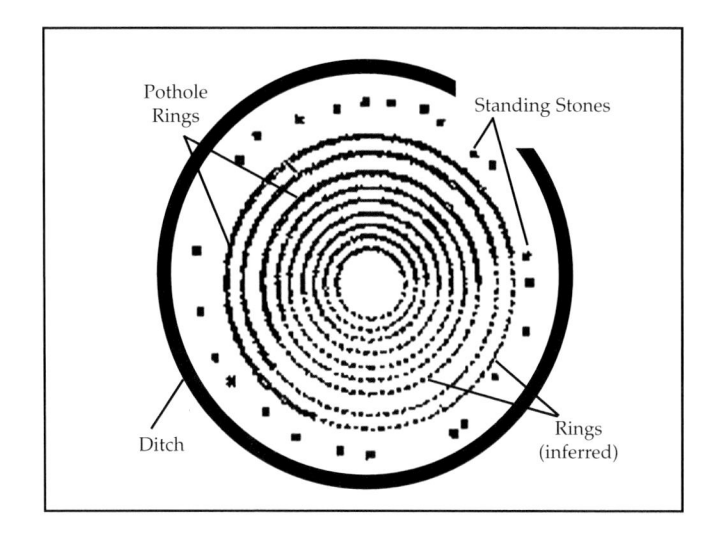

whose geometry is highly reminiscent of the spherical arrangement in Israel (the Gilgal Rephaim). Archaeologists refer to the monument as the ancient city of Arkaim, and links with the Aryan people have been speculated.[5] Again, knowledge of this complex is only just now receiving attention in the western media.

Could there be a connection between these recent finds of ancient ring complexes and the round numbers of ancient mathematical systems, the keys to which have been lost over time? And if so, what coordinate system (or space-time geometry) will this mathematics open up before us?

The premise has been put forward that the ancients were able to think and visualize in space and time simultaneously: distance and measure were not separate from rhythm, and music (demarcation in time) was still at one with architecture (demarcation in space). Scientists of the Academy have published significant proof of the existence of sound patterns within monuments such as the pyramids,[6] and this has been found to hold true also for the stone circles.

Recent research published by two scientists of the University of Reading (UK) report findings that ancient megalithic monuments, such as stone circles and cairns, display striking acoustic features as part of their

Figure 5.4
Distance and measure are not separate from rhythm and music. "Spiral of Life" by D. Hurtak (1997).

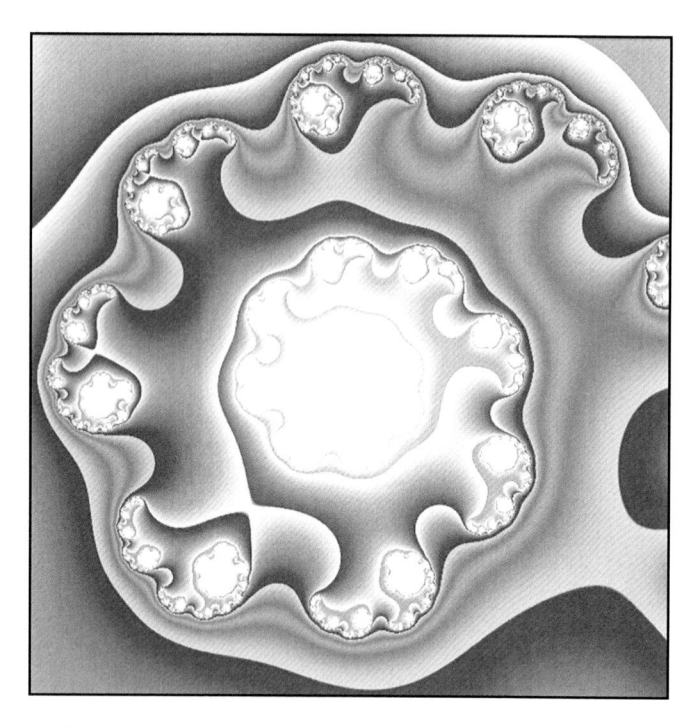

architectural design. Acoustic tests by Aaron Watson and David Keating at Easter Aquorthies stone circle in Scotland demonstrated that the configuration of stones could direct sound in rather unexpected ways. The stones seemed to project sound across specific areas of the site and subdued them in others. Very faint sound could be heard distinctly in certain positions even far away from the source. Furthermore, the engineers recorded subtler reverberations originating from different spots around the circle which could not be explained easily. Pink noise was used as a sound source and recordings were made across the circle, as well as in an open environment to provide a control. The measurements demonstrate clearly that the position of the stones governs the distribution of sound energy within the circle.

A similar and more extensive study was executed at the enclosed megalithic tomb of Camster Round in Caithness, where even more remarkable acoustic behavior was registered. Standing wave patterns were created, even in the audible range of human voice sound production, and when a sustained sound was generated electronically some surprising effects were observed:[7]

> 1. The source of the note became unclear. Rather than originating from the loudspeaker, sound appeared to issue from different directions around the chamber. Listeners occasionally perceived these sounds to be contained within their heads...
> 2. Some standing-wave frequencies created an environment of sound within the monument which could be explored physically moving around the chamber. Even small movements of the head revealed marked variations in the volume and pitch of the sound.
> 3. Listeners in the chamber could detect the movement of individuals along the passage, as the solid mass of their bodies created microtonal disturbances in the distribution of sound which could be heard throughout the monument...

So do the stones speak? Perhaps they are not entirely voiceless after all.

In 1999 Dr. J.J. Hurtak, along with film and sound engineers of The Academy For Future Science, was able to demonstrate the "voice" of the standing stone figures on Easter Island, some of which figures proved to be hollow and thus could function as cavity resonators. When the human voice intonation of certain sacred sounds was applied inside a circular arrangement of the megalithic faces, the whole area entered into resonance with sound being transported and amplified by what seemed to be the megalithic landscape itself.

Could this be a clue to the meaning of ancient monuments and standing stones worldwide? Could the mathematics of round numbers be one of music and of time?

1. *Sunday Telegraph* (10 Jan 1999) Photo: Norfolk Museum Service.
2. *Miami Herald* (April 1999).
3. McKim, Malville J., *et al* (1998) "Megaliths and Neolithic astronomy in southern Egypt," *Nature*, April 1998, **Vol. 392**, pp. 488-491.
4. There are no publications on the discoveries as yet in print. *English Heritage* has issued a visitor's information leaflet on "Stanton Drew Stone Circles," from which this picture is taken.
5. Zyablov, Mikhail (1998) "Volga," *TV*, Nizhniy Novogorod, Russia.
6. See, among others: Hurtak, J.J. & Patrick Bailey (1998) "Music, Acoustics, and Scientific Measurement in the Great Pyramid of Egypt" *Future History,* Spring 1998, **Vol. 2**, Number 7, pp. 2-6.
7. Watson, Aaron & Keating, David (1999) "Architecture and sound: an acoustic analysis of megalithic monuments in prehistoric Britain," *Antiquity*, June 1999, **Vol. 73**, Number 280, pp. 325ff. Furthermore, Helmholtz resonances were measured due to the shape of the mound.
8. See also: Deveraux, Paul & Jahn, Robert G. (1996) "Preliminary investigations and cognitive considerations of the acoustical resonances of selected archaeological sites," *Antiquity*, September 1996, **Vol. 70**, Number 269, pp. 665-6.

6

The Sphinx as a Symbol of Evolution

J.J. Hurtak, Ph.D., Ph.D.

The riddle of the Great Sphinx is well known in popular texts. According to the ancient Egyptian proverb, "What animal walks on all fours in the morning, two legs at noon, and three legs at night?" (The answer is man, of course, throughout the stages of his life.) But that's not the only Sphinx riddle. Why is there a human face on the Sphinx and why is it referred to as Horem-aket, "Horus of the Horizon," the name given to light movement across the sky?

To solve the mystery of the Sphinx is to solve the mysteries of the pyramids. Mainstream Egyptologists claim the Sphinx was carved from bedrock during the reign of Kafre (2520-2494 BC) as a self-tribute to the pharaoh. Then an unlikely combination of events caused a shock wave through the world of Egypt. The research of the late French archaeologist, Schwaller de Lubicz suggested that the Sphinx was far older than the pyramids—and that its severe weathering and erosion were caused not by winds and blowing sands, but by copious rain. In short, the Sphinx must have been built thousands of years earlier when arid Egypt had a wetter climate. The "older" Sphinx theory attracted little interest until 1990 when Lubicz's work was rediscovered by American explorer, John Anthony West

The Sphinx as a Symbol of Evolution

Figure 6.1
The face of the Sphinx—
Giza, Egypt.
Photo by D. Hurtak.

who passed on these assumptions to Dr. Robert Schoch of Boston University. Dr. Robert Schoch, a trained geologist and Boston University professor, investigated these claims that suggested rainfall or the existence of running water. Schoch, examining the weathering and rock fissures in the Sphinx body, concluded that the front and side of the Sphinx dated from 5,000 to 7,000 BC (although most scholars agree that the face is more recent and might have been recarved).

The controversy still continues where many Egyptologists attribute the Sphinx's weathering to wet sand from the Nile floods (Harrell, 1994), or morning dew that condensed and expanded natural salt in the rock, causing layers to flake off. "The atmospheric moisture and pollution had a lot to do with weathering," admits Lambert Dolphin,[1] a former geology expert and remote sensing authority at Stanford Research Institute International. Moreover, if the Sphinx were built millenniums earlier, where are the traces of the cultures that carved it away? "Where are the artifacts of the earlier civilization? Show me one!" argues Dr. Mark Lehrner from the University of Chicago's Oriental Institute before major archaeological panels on the excavations in Egypt.[2]

A new generation of investigators hope further digging at Giza and the use of ground-penetrating radar (GPR) might reveal the answer to the riddle of the Sphinx's age.

In fact, earlier structures have been found under the ground, down several strata that indicate a greater complex behind the Sphinx/Great Pyramid correlation, specifically the so-called Osiris tomb of which this author was part of the preliminary radar team in 1997 that discovered the lid of the coffer when we were exploring at a depth of 33 meters (100 feet) under the Giza Plateau (see Figure 6.2).

But why was the Sphinx built and what is its

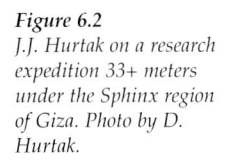

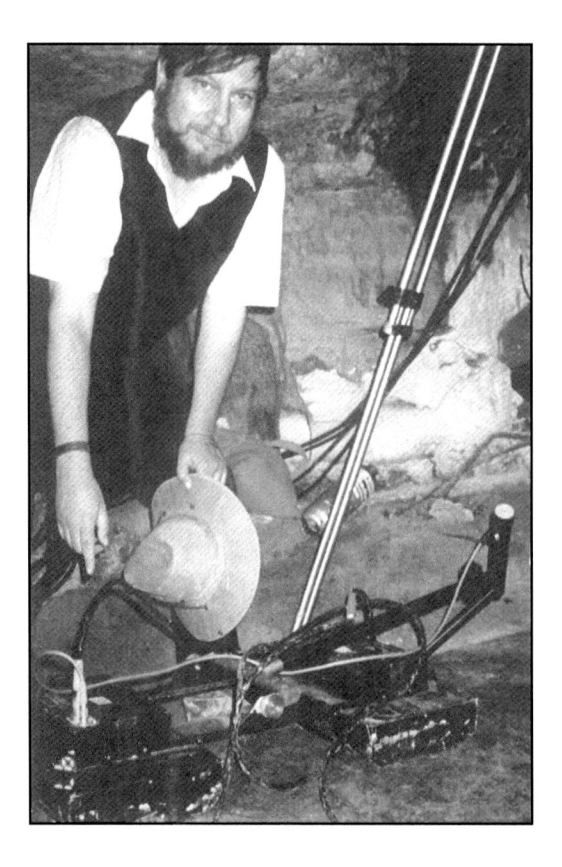

Figure 6.2
J.J. Hurtak on a research expedition 33+ meters under the Sphinx region of Giza. Photo by D. Hurtak.

meaning? According to one school of thought, the Sphinx shares its symbolism with other pyramidal civilizations, or areas of early evolution upon the planet. Around the planet, most ancient civilizations have their own equivalent of the Sphinx or the symbolism of the Sphinx as a model of human evolution, whether it is in male or female form. For example, pyramidal and multi-pyramidal temples in China use the symbolism of the Sacred Lion with its paw upon the Orb of the earth. In some instances, if one looks at the pictographs of Egypt and China, two lions are juxtaposed according to a gateway or path symbolizing the entrance to the higher heavens or Tian'an, and as such can be seen as an element associated in ancient traditions with the spiritual process of Initiation. In some places, such as Giza, one Sphinx is probably missing, for the ancient Egyptian texts often speak of the Double Lion.

In Mexico and Central America, the jaguar becomes the equivalent of the Sphinx or lion symbol seen side by side several pyramidal structures. Also the lion form upon the solar gate at Tiahuanco, Bolivia could be equated with the lion-headed Sekhmet, wearing a solar disk found in Egypt.* Symbolism here is very important because the lion, jaguar, or even leopard forms were seen as places where royalty would establish their connection with the Divine.

These may not be isolated occurrences, for we can find evidence of a connection between the cultures of the Far East and Egypt. One example of this connection is an ancient oracle bone found by my colleague, Dr. Wesley Bliss, in 1936 which shows Imhotep of Egypt with a lion's face. In Egyptian pictographic symbolism, the "good god" Imhotep speaks of many worlds of higher intelligence by means of an archaic, ideographic language. (See Hurtak, *From World Catastrophe to Global*

---

* It is interesting to note that in one location, near great land pyramids in the interior of Peru, is found an elongated head of a type of a teacher or leader that has the headdress and elongated brain similar to that of the Pharonic queen bee one finds in the mythology of ancient Egypt.

Figure 6.3
In certain cultures, the jaguar becomes the equivalent of the Egyptian Sphinx. "House of Masks," Delos, Greece/The Bridgeman Art Library.

Migration, this edition, Figure 3.5). Yet this language is not Egyptian, but of Chinese origin. This reveals an early unity of two extreme cultures which shared a common language of astronomy and cosmology roughly 1,500 BC.

On a global level, from the far reaches of Asia to Iran (with its half animal half human statues) to the mountain areas of Peru and Bolivia, one finds the interconnection of not only the lion form, but the existence of massive pyramids sharing similarities with Chinese pyramids, which are similar to ancient Egyptian pyramids, suggesting either a human archetypal symbol or a world grid system of communication, star notation, and observation that was connected with the coming of the gods. Are these symbols there, waiting for us to put together the pieces of a global puzzle so that the initiation of the knowledge of humankind would be increased as these secrets become known and the body of the lion would be overcome by the face of a greater intelligence. Then the Sphinx, as the guardian of the knowledge, becomes no longer an ancient mystery, but a key to establishing a link with ancient cultural Wisdom.

One additional thought: the remarkable con-

The Sphinx as a Symbol of Evolution

firmations of present research in Egypt, specifically the geological signatures indicating an earlier time period for the Sphinx (see Schoch, *How Old Is The Sphinx? New Findings in Egypt*, this edition, Chapter 7), may be suggesting a very ancient yet advanced society which established special timepieces throughout lower Egypt. It is conceivable that the timepiece of the Sphinx is not only inseparable from the pyramid complex at Giza, but that Giza may also have been coordinated with other great structures, such as the time calendar in the Middle East, namely Rujum Al-Hiri (see Curtis, *Rujum al-Hiri of Galilee: Stone Computer and Cosmic Timepiece*, this edition, Chapter 4) as it is called in Arabic, the place of an ancient stone computer system just east of the Sea of Galilee, or the area of Nabta, in southern Egypt which has been created before 4,000 BC (see Granögger, *Stone Circles, Sky Circles, Sound Circles: New Evidence on Global Round Numbers*, this edition, Chapter 5). And what of the triangular relationship between the timepiece at Rujum Al-Hiri, Megiddo and Jerusalem? References to these sites as time calculators, or chronomonitors, suggest that the ancient megaliths, may also have served a purpose as a consistent time structure understood by the early sages and pre-scientists in the ancient Near East.

We essentially have a series of computerized timepieces whose matrix with unique soundings and alignments, is to be found throughout the world. This indicates we must go even further to see the mathematical relationships of these relevant timepieces which share a similar architecture of the Sphinx/Jaguar or Sphinx/Lion, such as we have in areas of Peru, Ecuador, Egypt, Iran and China and other parts of the world—all from different traditions and cultures, but all with a possible common connection. The key to solving the true mystery of the Sphinx may be to look deeper beneath the surface with remote-sensing technology, as well as around the world to recognize that the Sphinx might be indicating very specific reference points of early proto-communication and information, suggesting a time table of evolution of different types of cultural experimentations, a common cosmology and pinpointing the history of human evolution on planet Earth.

Endnotes:

1. Dolphin, Lambert. Personal conversations in Menlo Park, California, June 1993.
2. Lehner, Mark. Statement made before participants at the U.S. Geophysical Union Conference, San Diego, California, February 1992.

---

1. Harrell, J. A. (1994) "The Sphinx controversy—another look at the geological evidence," *KMT: A Modern Journal of Ancient Egypt.*, **Vol. 5**, number 2, p. 70-74.
2. Schoch, Robert M. & McNally, Robert A. (1999) *Voices of the Rock: A Scientist's look at Catastrophes and Ancient Civilizations.* New York: Harmony/Random House.
3. Schwaller de Lubicz, René (1977) *The Temple in Man.* Brookline, MA, Autumn Press.

Figure 6.4
(Following page)
The Sphinx complex at Giza showing restoration work.
Photo by D. Hurtak. ▶

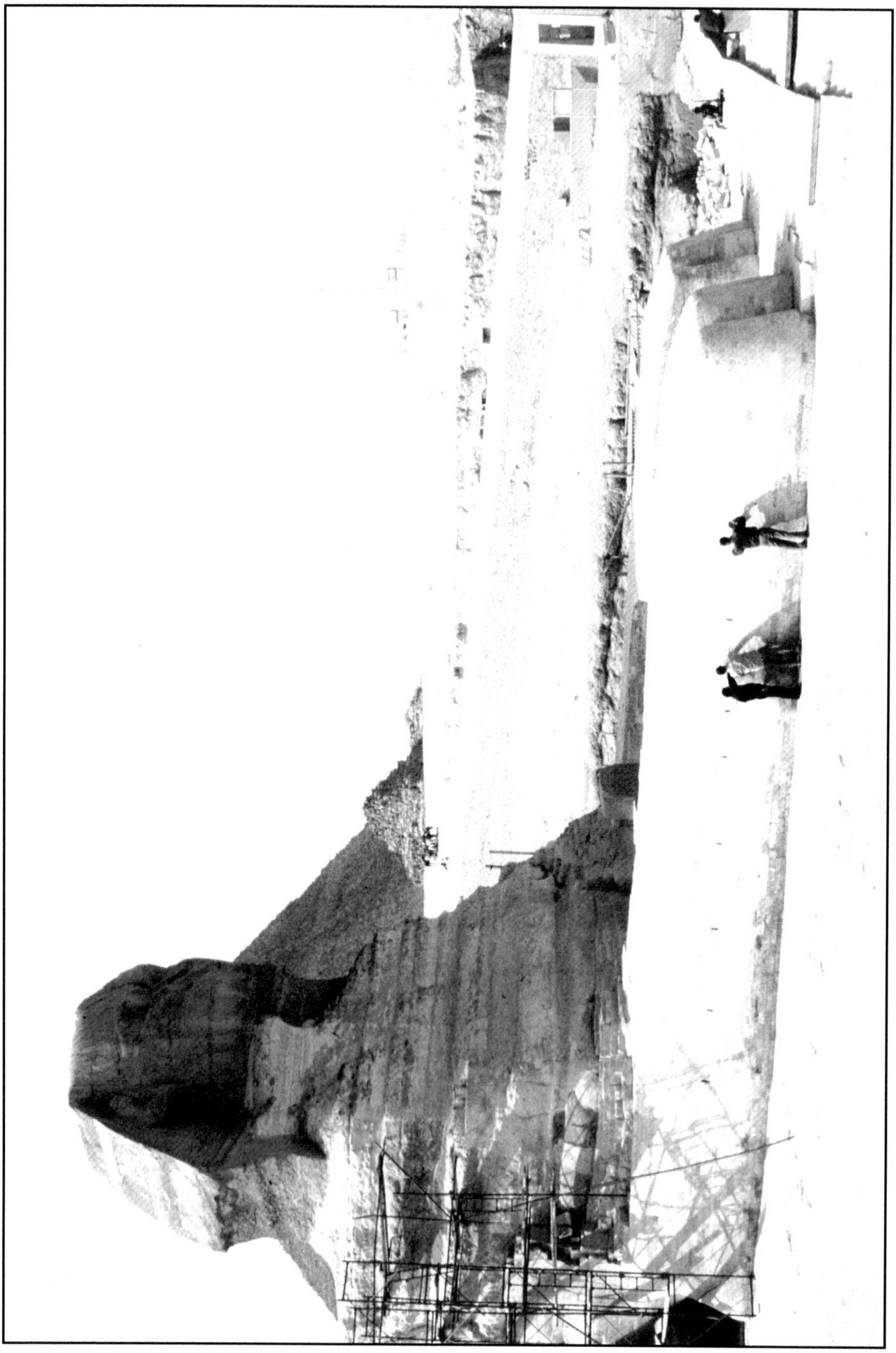

7

How Old is the Sphinx?
New Findings in Egypt

Robert M. Schoch, Ph.D.

Copyright © 1992 by Robert Schoch.
Reprinted by permission of the author.
Basis for the NBC Award Winning
Documentary "The Mystery of the Sphinx"

As a researcher, the current geologic and archaeological evidence suggests to me that the Great Sphinx of Giza is considerably older than its traditional attribution of ca. 2,500 BC. Indeed, I am currently estimating, based on the evidence at hand, that the Great Sphinx traces its beginnings to at least 7,000 to 5,000 BC, and perhaps, even earlier. To be sure, at its inception, the Sphinx did not look the way it does now, some 8,000 years later. The original surface details of the body have long since been weathered away, and the current head of the Sphinx may possibly be the result of recarving, or at least "touching up." Certainly the Great Sphinx has suffered much work, repairs, refurbishing, and abuse from prehistoric times onward. Special attention seems to have been paid to it periodically, for instance in Old Kingdom dynastic times (ca. 2,500 BC), New Kingdom times (ca. 1,400 BC), during the 26th Dynasty or late period (ca. 650-400 BC) and in Graeco-Roman times (ca. 300 BC-400 AD). During these times the contemporary ruler often had the Great Sphinx excavated from the sands that quickly (in just a matter of decades) fill its hollow if left unattended, and after each re-excavation of the Sphinx repair blocks might be mortared to the weathered body in an attempt to restore the original outlines of this great statue.

The first known historical personage to excavate and restore the Great Sphinx may have been the Old Kingdom Fourth Dynasty Pharaoh Khafre (Chephren) around 2,500 BC. Possibly Khafre's predecessor, Khufu (Cheops) also did some restoration work to the Sphinx. This work probably was done in conjunction with the Old Kingdom pyramid building program carried out on the Giza Plateau. Possibly all of the major Fourth Dynasty structures of the Giza Plateau were built relative to the original positioning of the Great Sphinx—with Fourth Dynasty site planning centered around the preexisting Sphinx. In later times the Great Sphinx was alternately allowed to be swallowed up by the drifting sands, and periodically re-excavated and repaired. For instance, Herodotus (5th century BC) and certain other Greek writers do not mention the Sphinx, presumably because it was buried in sand. The Roman writer Pliny (1st century AD) mentions the Great Sphinx only in passing, and according to ancient inscriptions (now preserved in the British Museum), walls surrounded the Sphinx, presumably to protect it from the encroaching sand. These walls were repaired during the reign of the Roman emperor Marcus Aurelius (161-180 AD).

While the rough outlines of the history of the Great Sphinx since Old Kingdom times seem to be clear (as very briefly summarized above), what of the more ancient history of the Sphinx? Current Egyptological dogma would attribute the original carving of the Great Sphinx to the time of Khafre, ca. 2,500 BC. In contrast, as a geologist I am suggesting that the original structure may predate this time by at least several thousand years. As a general academic scholar I have to ask myself whether such an extreme age for the Great Sphinx makes sense archaeologically and culturally. If the Great Sphinx is dated to the seventh or sixth millennium BC (or perhaps even older)—is this compatible with the broad context of known archaeological remains? In other words, is there any context or precedent for a 7,000 or 9,000 year old (or

Figure 7.1
The Face of The Sphinx.
Photo by the Academy
For Future Science.

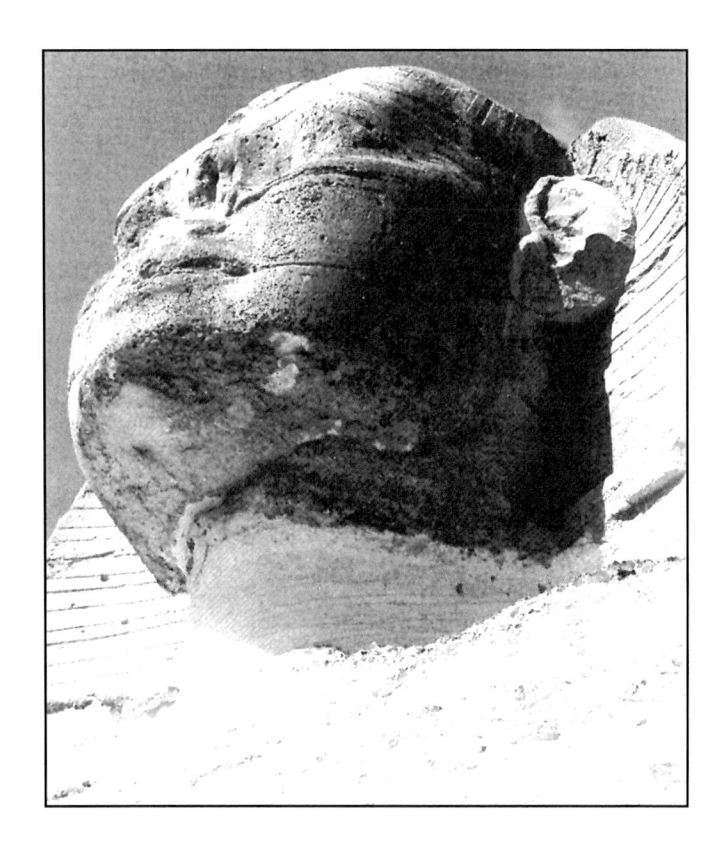

even older) Sphinx? What were other Mediterranean peoples and cultures like at this time? What types of structures were they building?

In taking a quick look at the relevant archaeological literature, I found that for the period from about 10,000 BC to 5,000 BC in Egypt little is known that would suggest there were peoples capable, either technologically or organizationally, of carving the Great Sphinx (see Hoffman, 1979, for a review of the current state of knowledge regarding pre-dynastic Egypt). However, the relatively simple Neolithic sites known from Egypt during this period may in fact be "backwater" peripheral or marginal settlements that were, and are, non-representative of the highest level of culture and technology then attained. Quite possibly other cultural remains are for the most part buried deep under the alluvium and silt of the Nile. In addition, rises in sea level that have occurred since ten or fifteen thousand years ago may have submerged vast expanses of land along the coast that early cultures inhabited (Ters, 1987, p. 234, notes that "in general, the mean level of the oceans has risen 60 m [200 feet] during the past 10,000 yrs" [i.e., since 8,000 BC]).

If we move beyond Egypt, however, we find that by the seventh millennium BC there were already major cities around the eastern end of the Mediterranean Sea. Two particularly well-known examples are ancient Jericho in Palestine and Catal Huyuk in Turkey.

Catal Huyuk, a city built of mud bricks and timber, dates back to at least the late seventh millennium BC. This was no primitive city. Rather, the known remains demonstrate a sophistication and opulence previously un-imagined by archaeologists for such a remote period in time. The inhabitants built elaborate houses and shrines, covered with wall paintings and reliefs, and apparently the residents had a rich and complex symbolic and religious tradition (see Hamblin, 1973, for a popular discussion of Catal Huyuk).

Jericho dates back to the ninth millennium BC and the city included a massive stone wall, tower, and ditch carved in the bedrock — all dating from ca. 8,000 BC. The remains of the stone wall are at least 6-½ feet (2 meters) thick, and still stand in places 20 feet (6 meters) high (nobody knows how high it was when new). Outside of the protecting wall a ditch was cut into the solid bedrock 27 feet (8.2 meters) wide and 9 feet (2.7 meters) deep. Inside of the wall was a stone tower 30 feet (9.1 meters) in diameter, and the ruins of this structure still stand 30 feet (9.1 meters) high. In the center of this tower is a flight of steps built from huge stone slabs. This tower has been compared favorably to the towers seen on the great medieval castles of Europe (again, see Hamblin, 1973, for a popular discussion of Jericho).

Concerning Jericho and its potential relationship to Egypt, Hayes (1965, p. 92) had this to say:

> Jericho lies a scant two hundred miles [320

km] to the east of the Nile Delta, and it would seem inevitable that a Neolithic, food-producing, village culture of the type attested there before 7,000 BC should have reached northern Egypt from this immediately adjacent southwest Asian area in the course of the seventh or, at the latest, the sixth millennium BC.

Hayes (1965, p. 111) also points out that pendants found at the sixth to fifth millennium BC site of Merimda (Merimde beni-Salame; see Hoffman, 1979, p. 168-169), on the western edge of the Nile Delta about 37 miles [60 km] northwest of Cairo, are very similar to pendants found in the early Neolithic levels of Jericho. Baines and Malek (1980, p. 20) state that "contacts between Egypt and the Near East are attested already in the Predynastic Period, and the name of Na'rmer, the latest Predynastic [Egyptian] king, has been found at Tel Gat and Tel 'Arad in Palestine." Baines and Malek (1980, p. 31) illustrate a "probable route" for trade between Egypt and Palestine, and even suggest that there may have been an early (latest Predynastic? or the beginning of the Dynastic Period?) Egyptian settlement in southern Palestine.

The evidence of Jericho in particular suggests that the Great Sphinx, along with its associated massive stone temples, would not have been a totally isolated phenomenon—other massive stone structures were being built as early as 10,000 years ago around the Mediterranean. But the sheer scale of the building project on the Giza Plateau was unequaled by the known public works at Jericho or elsewhere. On the Giza Plateau the ancients carved a statue 240 feet (73 meters) long and 66 feet (20 meters) tall from solid rock while simultaneously assembling huge blocks of limestone, some of them purportedly weighing up to 150 or 200 tons (136 to 182 metric tons), into temple structures.

As is well-known, Thutmose IV cleared the sand away from the Sphinx in ca. 1400 BC and erected a granite stela between the paws of the Sphinx. When this stela was first excavated in the nineteenth century it is reported that the hieroglyph for the first syllable of Khafre's name was decipherable on a bottom register.[1] The pertinent portion of the inscription is given by S. Hassan as "and we shall give praise to Wnnefer ... [missing portion]... Khafra, the statue made for Atum-Hor-em-akhet...[remainder missing]." Furthermore, Hassan [one of the first important contemporary investigators of the Sphinx ca. 1945] claims, Hor-em-akhet is the personal name of the Great Sphinx, and Atum is the name for the God (of the setting sun)[2]. Some persons have taken this to indicate that the Fourth Dynasty Pharaoh Khafre built the Sphinx, others have suggested that it indicated that he restored the Sphinx, and still others have suggested that the syllable "khaf" had no reference to the Pharaoh Khafre, as it is a syllable found in other Egyptian words. Unfortunately, one can no longer go to the original inscription and attempt to translate and interpret its meaning—since the initial excavation of Thutmose's stela the register containing "khaf" has flaked away and been lost forever. Hassan summarized his opinion of the value of this inscription when he stated that "excepting for the mutilated line on the granite Stela of Thothmes [Thutmose] IV, which proves nothing, there is not one single ancient inscription which connects the Sphinx with Khafra [Khafre]."[3]

In 1860 in a pit under the floor of the Valley Temple a beautiful statue of Khafre was found. This statue has been also used to argue that the Great Sphinx was, therefore, built by Khafre. However, one could suggest that Khafre was capable of having a statue of himself placed in a preexisting temple; or the statue may have been buried in the temple much later in order to safeguard it. If an Egyptologist were to find Ptolemaic statues (perhaps ca. 300 BC) buried in a New Kingdom temple (perhaps ca. 1450 BC), he or she would not immediately redate the temple to Ptolemaic times. Likewise, the discovery of a Fourth Dynasty statue in the Valley Temple does not preclude the possibility that the Valley Temple, and the Great Sphinx Temple, could have been built prior to the Fourth Dynasty.

At present the consensus among Egyptologists seems to be that the face of the Great Sphinx is supposed to resemble the face of its reputed builder, Khafre. This is a relatively recent notion, and far from certain. The face of the Sphinx is severely damaged, but what remains of it does not indisputably appear to resemble the face seen on statues of Khafre—perhaps it is a matter of opinion. [In 1991, Detective Frank Domingo, senior forensic artist with the New York Police Department, traveled to Egypt with his team of experts to analyze the face of Khafre. Following police procedures normally used to identify criminals or people whose faces have been unrecognizably damaged, he produced an artist's impression of how the Sphinx would have looked before rain and wind (and vandals) eroded its facial features. Mr. Domingo then compared his picture with the facial structure of the Khafre statue, and after reviewing various drawings, schematics and measurements, concluded: "If the ancient Egyptians were skilled technicians and capable of duplicating images, then these two works cannot represent the same individual."][4]

My hypothesis, that the initial construction of the Great Sphinx was undertaken prior to the reign of Khafre, is actually neither corroborated nor refuted on the basis of whether or not the face of the Sphinx represents the likeness of Khafre. Even if the face of the great Sphinx does represent Khafre, this does not falsify my hypothesis, as I believe that Khafre did indeed work on restoring and refurbishing the Sphinx. Khafre may have even recarved the face of the Sphinx in his own image.

Just because the Great Sphinx is in close proximity to Khafre's pyramid and general funerary complex, that does not necessarily mean that he built the Sphinx, the Sphinx Temple, and the Valley Temple. Khafre may well have restored and refurbished these previously existing structures and then appropriated them unto himself and incorporated them into his own funerary complex.[5]

As opposed to the circumstantial Egyptological evidence, discussed above, that has been used to suggest that the Great Sphinx of Giza was built by Khafre, there is other circumstantial Egyptological evidence that suggests the Sphinx was built prior to the reign of Khafre.

The so-called Inventory Stela is a late Dynastic (Twenty-sixth Dynasty, ca. seventh or sixth century BC) stela that purports to be a copy of an Old Kingdom text. This text refers to the Great Sphinx as already being in existence during the time of the Pharaoh Khufu (Cheops), who was a predecessor of Khafre. In fact, the Inventory Stela credits Khufu with repairing the Sphinx after it was struck by lightning. Although he disregards the notion that the Sphinx is older than Khufu, Hassan does state that "there may be a grain of truth in this story, for the tail of the nemes head-dress of the Sphinx is certainly missing, and it is not a part, which, by reason of its shape and position, could be easily broken off, except by a direct blow from some heavy object, delivered with terrific force."[6] Hassan concludes that maybe, in fact, the Sphinx was struck by lightning in ancient times.

The Inventory Stela has generally been dismissed by modern-day Egyptologists as a late Dynastic fabrication, rather than considering that it might be a valid copy of an older inscription, albeit "translated" into the textual and linguistic attributes of the late Dynastic period.

Radiocarbon dates taken on organic inclusions found in the mortar of various pyramids have given many anomalously old ages relative to the standard chronology used by Egyptologists. These dates tend to be on the order of a couple of hundred years older than the dates usually assigned to the respective pyramids from which samples were taken. This data does not seem to bear directly on the age of the Great Sphinx. To my knowledge, no radiocarbon dates have ever been taken on the ancient mortars used to repair the Sphinx. Furthermore, any such dates would merely date the repairs, not the time when the Great Sphinx was initially built (although it would be interesting if such repairs could be radiocarbon dated to the time of the Fourth Dynasty or earlier).

After reviewing the opinions of the ancients from the time of the New Kingdom until Roman times, Hassan concludes that "the general opinion of the ancients was that the Sphinx was older than the Pyramids."[7] Even to the New Kingdom Egyptians the origins and early history of the Great Sphinx were a mystery.

It may not be inappropriate to note that according to the tradition of some of the local villagers who live in the neighborhood of the Giza Plateau, the Great Sphinx is said to be much older than the time of the Pharaoh Khafre. According to one Abraham Borie, "The history handed down in our families tell us the Sphinx could be 5,000 years older"[8] than Khafre's time of ca. 2,500 BC. (While I would not place much emphasis on such oral history, it is interesting to relate).

Seismic geophysical surveys indicate that the subsurface weathering in the Sphinx enclosure is not uniform. This strongly suggests that the entire Sphinx ditch was not excavated at one time. Furthermore, by estimating when the less-weathered portion of the Sphinx enclosure was excavated and thus first exposed subaerially, one can tentatively estimate when initial excavation of the Sphinx enclosure may have begun.

During our April 1991 trip to Egypt, Dr. Thomas L. Dobecki, a seismologist with McBride-Ratcliff and Associates of Houston, Texas, helped us carry out some low-level seismic work in the vicinity of the Great Sphinx with the permission of the Egyptian Antiquities Organization. We were able to gather a quantity of seismic data, and with this data we have been able to establish subsurface geometries of the bedrock and have located several previously unknown features below the surface.

Preliminary analysis of the seismic data collected in April 1991 contributes further to exploring the age of the Great Sphinx. Seismic lines taken in front of and along the body of the Great Sphinx on either side (east

How Old is the Sphinx? New Findings in Egypt

Figure 7.2
Seismic data in the vicinity of the Great Sphinx reveals subsurface geometries in the bedrock and varying depths of weathering. Map by Dr. Robert M. Schoch.

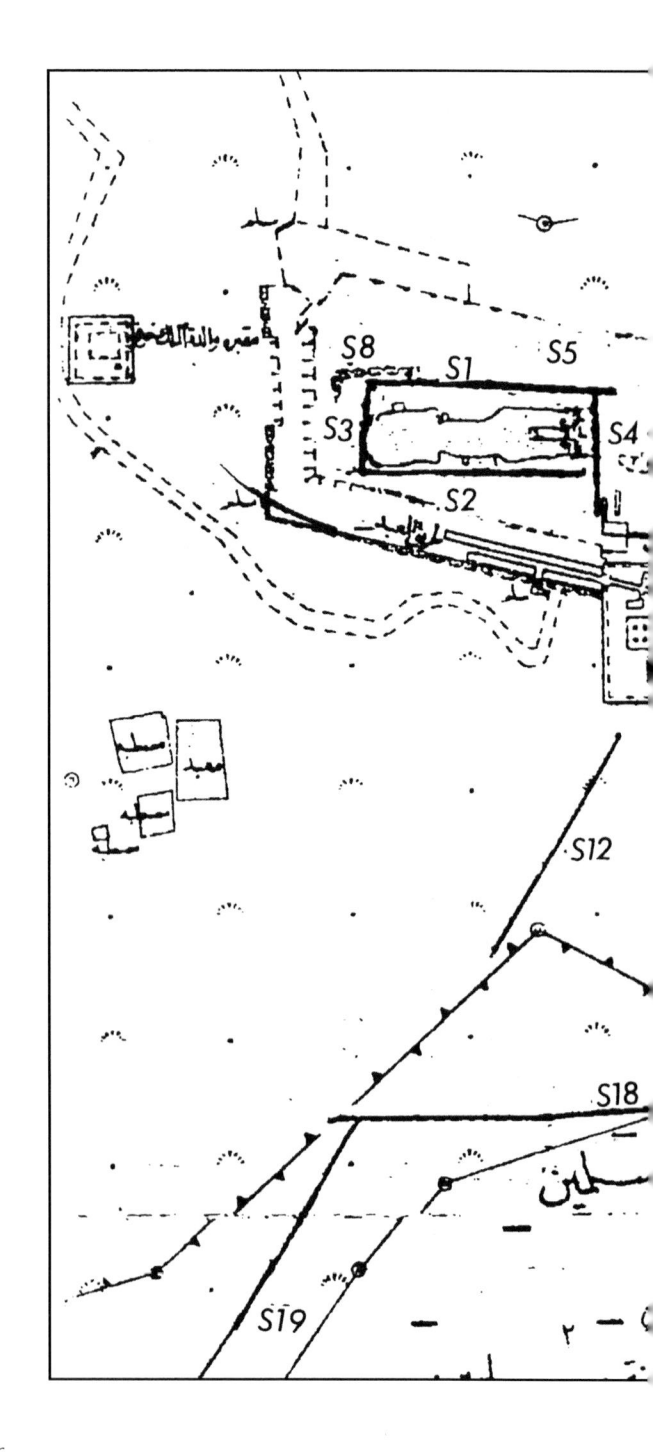

How Old is the Sphinx? New Findings in Egypt

حوض الحاجر الوسطاني نمرة
قسم ثان

بور رمال

[seismic line S4], north [seismic line S1], and south [seismic line S2] of the Sphinx) indicate that below the surface the limestone is weathered up to six to eight feet [1.8 to 2.5 meters] deep. However, along the back (west side [seismic line S3]) of the great Sphinx the identical limestone has only been weathered to a depth of approximately four feet [1.2 m]. These results were completely unexpected. It is the same limestone that surrounds the Great Sphinx (the floor of the Sphinx enclosure where all of the seismic lines were taken consists of Gauri's Rosetau Member, or Member I),[9]. and if the entire body of the Great Sphinx were carved out of living rock at one time, it would be expected that the limestone surrounding it should show the same depth of subsurface weathering.

One possible interpretation of the data we collected is that initially only the sides and front (eastern portion) of the body of the Great Sphinx were carved free from the rock, thus projecting from the rock outcropping, while what would later become the back or rump (western end) of the Sphinx originally merged with the natural rock. Hassan suggests that the Sphinx was originally meant to be viewed from the front (rather than from the sides or rear), such that, with the Sphinx Temple before it, the Sphinx seems to sit on a pedestal. Alternatively, the rump or western end of the Sphinx may have been originally freed from the rock but separated from the bedrock by only a very narrow passage not sampled by our April 1991 seismic line.

In order to determine accurately when the western end of the Great Sphinx was freed from the bedrock, and to establish a chronology of the possible widening of the passage between the western end of the Sphinx and the bedrock, more detailed work (including the collection of several more seismic profiles parallel to seismic line S3) will be necessary. However, it is already clear that the limestone floor behind the rump (western end) of the Sphinx which we sampled seismically in April 1991 was exposed later (i.e., probably in Khafre's time) than the east, north, and south limestone floors. Once the sides of the body and eastern end of the

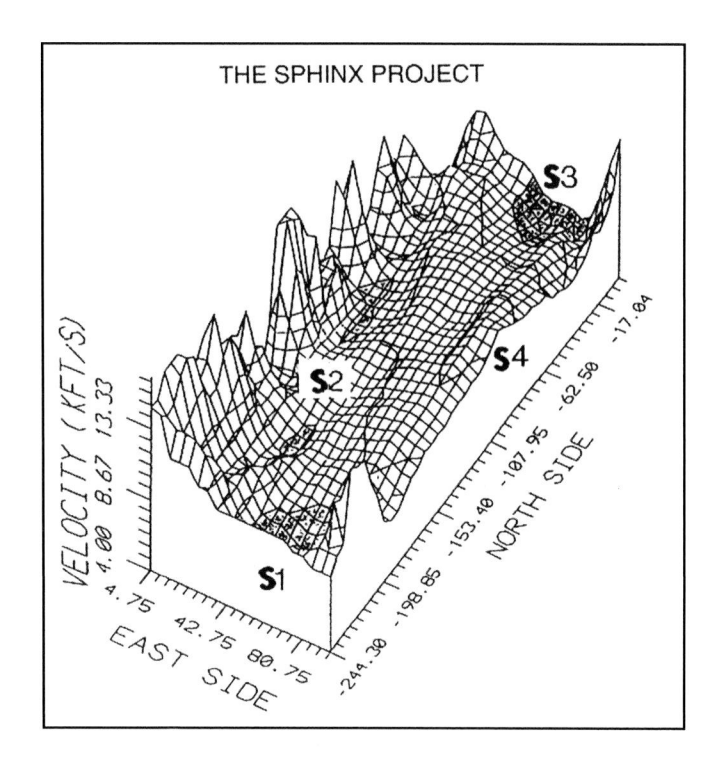

Figure 7.3
The Sphinx Project—Orthographic projection of velocity of the Sphinx from tomographic inversion. Diagram by Dr. Robert M. Schoch.

Sphinx were carved, the limestone floor surrounding it began to weather, but what was to become the limestone floor behind the western end of the Sphinx was still protected by a thick layer of solid rock.

A reasonable hypothesis is that when Khafre (ca. 2,500 BC) repaired and refurbished the Great Sphinx, the Sphinx Temple, and the Valley Temple, he had the back (western end) of the Great Sphinx carved out and freed from the cliff. It is difficult to argue that the back (rump) of the Sphinx was carved out and freed any later than Khafre's time; the base of the rump has, like the rest of the core body of the Sphinx, been weathered and repaired with limestone blocks. Furthermore, one must account for the non-trivial four feet (1.2 m) of subsurface weathering detected behind the rump of the Sphinx. If, for instance, one hypothesized that the rump of the Sphinx had been freed during New Kingdom restoration efforts to the Sphinx, how could we account for this deep (1.2 m) subsurface weathering given the prevailing arid conditions on the Giza Plateau since New Kingdom times and the historical fact that the Sphinx enclosure has been filled with desert sands for much of the period since New Kingdom times?

As an alternative to the scenario that Khafre had the back of the Sphinx carved free from the bedrock, one could suggest that if the back of the Sphinx were already freed from the bedrock prior to Khafre's time, but only separated from the cliff by a very narrow passage, Khafre may have widened this passage and uncovered the limestone floor that we sampled seismically. (Our seismic line was positioned very close to the western wall of the Sphinx ditch). Thus at this time the limestone floor on the western end of the Sphinx began to weather. Based on either this chain of reasoning or the scenario suggested in the preceding paragraph, and given that there is 50% to 100% deeper weathering of the limestone floor on the sides and front of the Sphinx as compared to the floor in back of the Sphinx, we can estimate that the initial carving of the Great Sphinx (i.e., the carving of the main portion of the body and the front) may have been carried out ca. 7,000 to 5,000 BC (that is, the initial carving of the core body of the Sphinx is approximately 50% to 100% older than 2,500 BC). This tentative estimate is probably a minimum date, given that weathering rates may proceed non-linearly (the deeper the weathering is, the slower it may progress due to the fact that it is "protected" by the overlying material), the possibility remains open that the initial carving of the Great Sphinx may be even earlier than 9,000 years ago.

Endnotes:

1. West, John (1987) *Serpent in the Sky: The High Wisdom of Ancient Egypt*. New York, p. 215.
2. Hassan, S. (1949) *The Sphinx: Its History in the Light of Recent Excavations*. Cairo, pp. 196 & 76.
3. Ibid., p. 91.
4. Macintyre, Ben (1992) "Riddle of a birth date," *The Times*. July 3,

1992, London.
5. See Yoshimura, S., *et al* (1987) *Studies in Egyptian Culture*. No. 6, Tokyo: Waseda Un.
6. Hassan. op. cit., p. 224.
7. Ibid., p. 79.
8. *USA Today*. 10 October 1991.
9. Gauri, K. (1984) "Geological Study of the Sphinx A.R.C," *Egypt Newsletter*. No. 127, pp. 24-43.

---

1. Baines, J. & Malek, J. (1980) *Atlas of Ancient Egypt*. Oxford: Phaidon.
2. Carr, Michael H. (1981) *The Surface of Mars*. New Haven: Yale University Press.
3. Emery, W.B. (1971) "Preliminary Report on the Excavations at North Saqqara, 1969-70," *Journal of Egyptian Archaeology*. August 1971, **Vol. 57**.
4. Gardiner, Alan (1976) *Egyptian Grammar*. Oxford: Griffin Institute, Ashmolean Museum, 3rd edition.
5. Hamblin, D.J. (1973) *The First Cities*. New York: Time-Life Books.
6. Hassan, A. (1965-66-67) *Preliminary Report on the Work Carried Out in Chephren Pyramid Area*. Seasons 1965-66-67, Egyptian Organization of Antiquities, Cairo.
7. Hawkings, Gerald S. (1965) *Stonehenge Decoded*. Garden City, NY: Doubleday & *Beyond Stonehenge*. London: Hutchinson, 1976.
8. Hayes, W.C. (1965) *Most Ancient Egypt*. K.C. Seele (Ed.), Chicago: University of Chicago Press.
9. Hoffman, M.A. (1979) *Egypt Before the Pharaohs*. Dorset Press/Knopf: New York.
10. Iskander, Zahi & Naktih, Slawki (1977) "Future Methods for Antiquities Research and Discovery," *Proceedings of Eighth Conference on Antiquities*. February 1977, Rabat: The Arab League Educational, Cultural and Scientific Organization.
11. Ivimy, J. (1974) *The Sphinx and the Megaliths*. London: Turnstone.
12. Letheridge, T.C. (1957) *Gog Magog: The Buried Gods*. London: Kegan Paul.
13. Michel, John (1979) *Simulacra: Faces and Figures in Nature*. London: Thames and Hudson.
14. Noyes, Ralph (Ed.) (1990) *The Crop Circle Enigma*. London: Gateway.
15. Petrie, William F. (1920) *A History of Egypt*. London: Methuen.
16. Porter, B. & Moses, R.L.B. (1964) "Royal Tombs and Smaller Cemeteries," *The Theban Necropolis,* Part 2. Oxford: Griffith Institute, Ashmolean Museum.
17. Reisner, George A. and Smith, Wmn. S. (1949) *History of the Giza Necropolis.* Oxford: Oxford University Press.
18. Sagan, Carl (1973) *Communications with Extraterrestrial Intelligence (CETI).* Cambridge: The Massachusetts Institute of Technology.
19. Sheldrake, Rupert (1988) *Presence of the Past*. London: Collins.
20. Shklovskii, I.S. & Sagan, Carl (1966) *Intelligent Life in the Universe*. New York: Holden Day.

21. Sykes, Egerton (1973) *The Pyramids of Egypt*. London: Oxford University Press.
22. Ters, M. (1987) "Variations in Holocene Sea Level on the French Atlantic Coast & Their Climactic Significance," Rampino, M.R. *et al* (Eds.), *Climate: History, Periodicity, & Predictability*. New York: Van Nostrand Reinhold.

PART TWO

BIO

LOGY

8

Genetics, Cloning & the Ethics of Survival

J.J. Hurtak, Ph.D, Ph.D.

Since the news emerged of the successful cloning of a sheep six years ago, science fiction has been changed to fact. Could parents one day clone their fatally ill children? Could Hitler or the Ice Man of the Alps be brought back to life? Could humans be cloned solely to provide organs? These futurist scenarios are only a short step away from the reality of today's genetic research. But is any human cloning experimentation ethical?

If, through disease or accident a child is dying, cells could be procured to create a new child that looks exactly the same. But would that child have the same soul, the same consciousness, or would it be a new being in borrowed clothes?

If the child was dying because of a genetic disease, its clone could circumvent the disease by having its genes altered. Taken to the extreme, a person could have himself cloned with improvements in his genes to provide a supply of genetically acceptable "spare parts," leading to a vision of immortality or at least extra years of life.

Most people should agree that it would be completely unethical to clone people as "organ-farms" for they would still be individuals. However, instead

Figure 8.1
Scientists have effectively discovered how to clone the DNA helix.

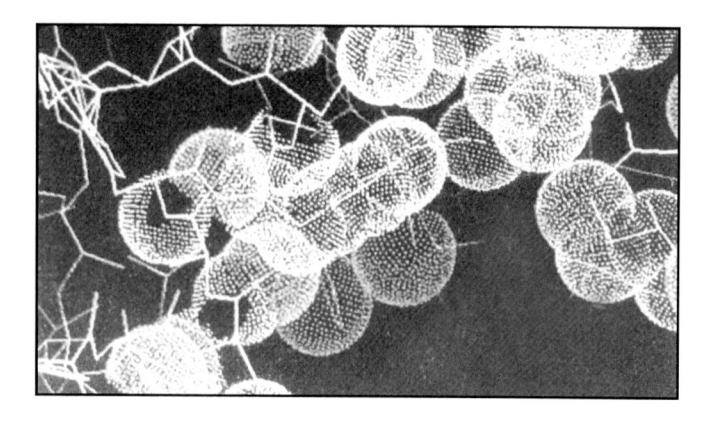

of growing an entire person, Harvard University is already growing skin in culture dishes and using that skin to treat people with severe burns. Medical researchers cannot yet produce a kidney, liver or heart in a culture dish, but they have been semi-successful in constructing a bladder. There is still interest in genetically modifying, say, a pig, to act as an organ donor for human purposes, until such techniques are more fully developed. As genomics continues to improve and advance, the ethics of experimentation is something our society will soon face.

What about the Ice Man, thousands of years old, found in Austria; could he be cloned so we could examine his particular characteristics and unlock history? If even part of his tissue or blood was properly frozen, if the ice crystals themselves have not destroyed the cells, a clone could potentially be made. Unfortunately, in most cases, the ice crystals themselves destroy the cells; the nucleus disintegrates and the DNA becomes too degraded to be reactivated.

What about creating a better species or a better race? What Hitler did not realize is that homogeneity in the human race makes us vulnerable to catastrophes of disease that could destroy an entire species. The secret to human existence lies in the variation produced through sexual reproduction.

Genetic testing is not a foreign notion, and in our society 9 out of 10 pregnant women in the U.S. already submit to some prenatal screening for indications of spina bifida or Downs syndrome in the fetus. These tests also reveal gender. Within a few decades, however, knowing gender will change to selecting gender, as well as selecting other attributes parents want their child to have, such as how tall, what body type, what hair and eye color, what illnesses he or she will be naturally resistant to, even before the child is born. Picking a baby may be closer to picking out a new car with whatever features you want to include. "It's the ultimate shopping experience: designing your baby," says biotechnology critic Jeremy Rifkin[1] (from the Foundation for Economic Trends), who is appalled by the prospect. "In a society used to cosmetic surgery and psychopharmacology, this is not a big step."

Conceivably, flawed genetic information as the product of "natural" reproduction could be used to deny jobs or health care. Princeton University biologist Lee Silver, whose book *Remaking Eden*[2] addresses these sorts of issues, tells us that "medical researchers are moved by a desire to cure disease more effectively. Reprogenetics [a term Silver coined] is going to be driven by parents, or prospective parents, who want something for their children. It's the sort of demand that could explode."

We can expect even more genetic manipulation in just a few decades. Using biochips (thumbnail-size

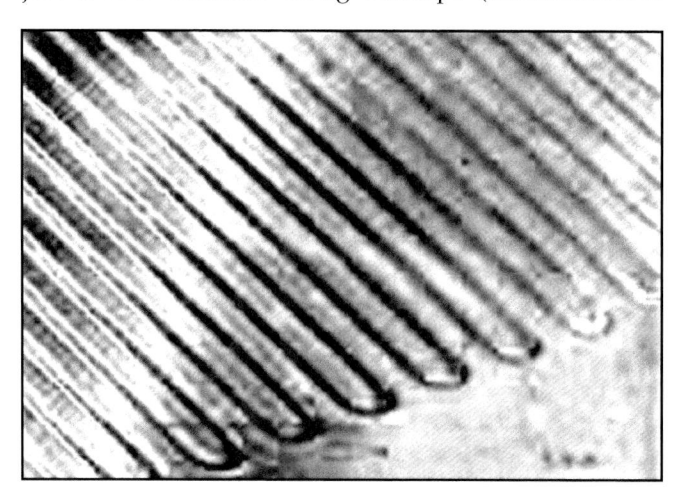

Figure 8.2
Detail of a biochip. Image by the Academy For Future Science.

pieces of material imprinted with hundreds of different DNA probes) scientists will be able to identify genetic errors almost as quickly as a supermarket scanner scans the barcodes of groceries. Some system probes use different fluorescent dyes that glow under laser light when they hook up with target genes, allowing computerized tabulations of the genetic data automatically. Genetic researchers are already talking about using "FISH [for fluorescent insitu hybridization] and chips," as they have nicknamed these new tools which analyze a number of genetic characteristics, concentrating on the genes that indicate familial patterns of Alzheimer's, diabetes, heart disease, stroke, cancer, as well as various kinds of mental disorders and even recessive gum disease. Says Dr. Wayne Grody,[3] head of the DNA diagnostic lab at the UCLA Medical Center, "We'll soon be governed by a new paradigm—genomic medicine—with tests and ultimately establishing treatment for every disease linked to the human genome." In reality, a new genome is being formulated.

We cannot deny the benefits, but at the same time, can we as a society afford to be so selective? And what about cloning not only organs, but people? Has twenty years of genetic manipulation prepared the way for more provocative manipulation of the human egg?

We must soon acknowledge that such scenarios are no longer science-fiction. According to *Time* (January, 1999) magazine, with the prestidigitation of gene-amplification, only a single drop of blood or a snippet of hair or a scraping of skin can reveal the full length of the human genome, including its myriad flaws. The potential for abusing that information is already here.

Is aborting a semi-flawed fetus just another name for eugenics? The ideal of gene therapy will be not to abort if a genetic problem is detected, but to manipulate the genes in the embryo (or prior) state, removing undesirable traits and actually inserting the more desirable genes.

There are two ways to look at the ethical dilemmas posed by the new genetic research. One is to say that genetic manipulation of humans is something our species has been doing for millennia. Research studies by NIH have shown that although women have fewer mutations in the species, it is the men that have caused most of the variations from the original Adam and Eve. Cultural factors, through the help of parents prearranging marriages for their offspring, have helped to preserve genetic codes. On the other hand, most societies quickly understood that breeding between relatives should bear strong taboos. The same types of taboos could carry over to clones.

The correctness or incorrectness of the assertion of a prospective ethical violation of a clone's rights as a human created in the image of God is difficult to evaluate in the Judaeo-Christian tradition, since neither Christian nor Jewish religious traditions have consolidated their views, leaving society to make its own decision. More conservative Christian theological arguments point largely to the teachings of Thomas Aquinas in the West and the Latin dictum: "nothing new is to be found in the external world that is first not within the body"—that is, all tampering with human nature beyond what the inner mechanisms of life provide for the human body is a violation of natural law.

On the side of Jewish tradition, it is clear that a person produced through cloning, and incubated by a mother, is a full human being according to Jewish law and is entitled to be treated as such by all who encounter this person. Take, for example, the medical example of newly born twins. Each person is created "in the image of God" and must be treated as such. Indeed, just as identical twins with identical genetic "codes" are two unique individuals, similar in some ways and different in others, are to be treated as two separate unique humans in the separation of the egg under a natural condition, so too a human being who is hypothetically cloned from another human is a separate and fully entitled unique person, based on the coding of the mother. But what if there is no natural father or mother but a third source of birth?

Genetics, Cloning & the Ethics of Survival

Figure 8.3
According to mystical Judaism, the Golem is a life form brought forth from the dust by reciting the divine name of God or writing the word אמת, *emet (truth) upon the forehead. Image by the Academy For Future Science.*

In examining both Jewish and Christian theology, what if the child is not a product of natural law process, do they represent a violation of canon law, or the law of sacred scripture as it is presently interpreted? The whole record of the New Testament is founded on the immaculate conception of the Christ child. The term used for the "overshadowing" of Mary by the Holy Spirit is "eperchesthai," light surrounding the Virgin body, conceiving new life without sexual contact. However, we must not forget that Jesus was begotten and had a physical mother and was not cloned.

In mystical Judaic literature we do encounter legends of the Golem, an artificially created life form. These stories tell of figures made from dust brought to life by reciting one of the names of the Divine or by placing a piece of parchment with God's name (or the word emet/truth) on the forehead. One example from the Talmud (Sanhedrin 65b) recounts:

> *Rava created a man and sent him to Rav Zera; the rabbi spoke to him, but he did not answer; Rav Zera exclaimed "you are artificial: return to dust".... Rav Hanina and Rav Ohaya would sit every Sabbath eve and study the book of creation and create a calf one third the size of a full calf, and eat it.*

The correspondence between medieval scholars contains a clear discussion of whether an artificially created person (a golem) is human or not, and whether such a life form can participate in a prayer circle, or should be killed, and so on. The legendary texts can be interpreted to permit the eating of created animals, but there is also the ethics of compassion for Humanness: being created in the image of God teaches respect for human life that is also not dependent on intelligence.

One is inclined to state that religious ethics based on the scripture, and post-biblical literature, view cloning as a lesser way of reproducing people and animals; however, when no other method is available, it would appear that religious law can be strained to mean that having children through means of cloning to continue life, or producing animals for food through cloning, is acceptable if there is a loving need. And in turn, the soul should be carefully incubated to respect all life.

On the other hand, futuristic scenarios of cloned beings cover a wide range of intelligence, from full human to part-machine part-human forms, working in the frigid frontier of other planetary worlds. Cloned workers on demand could degenerate into a plethora of robots, slaves, or semi-human servants, and any attempt to multiply vast numbers of cloned people could be a global travesty, as we are reminded in the historic book of *1 Enoch* (Chapter 7) where the unrighteous hybrid offspring became too numerous and began to kill off vast numbers of human life on the planet. Eventually divine intervention was required to stop this activity.

The first cloning of humans who will be exposed to the public is only a few short years away. Nevertheless, the current controversy over the genetic manipulation of stem cells, cells from the very dawn of an organism's life and naturally found only in embryos, raises immediate ethical questions. The leap from stem cells to designer babies is confronting the world so rapidly that doctors, ethicists, religious leaders and politicians must now begin to assess the implications.

Genetics, Cloning & the Ethics of Survival

Figure 8.4
Hildegard Von Bingen—
"Second Vision: On The
Construction of the
World" from the
Latinum Codex, 1942.

We've seen these visions glinting in the distance for some time: the prospect that one day parents will be able to browse through gene catalogs to special-order a hazel-eyed, redheaded extrovert with perfect musical pitch. Leave aside for the moment whether scientists have actually identified an "IQ gene," or should we ask, what really constitutes intelligence? Every new discovery gives shape and focus to a debate just barely begun. If you could make your kids smarter, would you? If everyone else did, would it be fair not to?

It's an ethical quandary and an economic one, about fairness and fate, about vanity and values. Which side effects would we tolerate? What if making kids smarter also made them meaner and more destructive? Does God give us both the power to re-create ourselves and the moral strength to resist? "The time to talk about it in schools and churches and magazines and debate societies is now," says ethicist Ted Peters of the Graduate Theological Union, Berkeley, before the critical mass moment of making a smarter baby out of the test tube becomes the rule in society, rather than the exception to the rule.

The dialogue that we must now demand between science and ethics deepens the meaning of some of our most enduring questions: What is creation? What is humanness? What is the soul? Are we as Adamic Man, not more than a mere body; Adamic Man is a "thinking soul" which may have been generated from a higher corpus by God.

Our future ethic requires a strong defense of our Higher Image and Purpose in all areas of discussion so that political imperatives of the new genetics are not made at the expense of our higher mission. This mission is not simply to create new bodies, but to evolve this body of man and woman into a greater destiny.

---

1. Rifkin, Jeremy (September 11, 1998) "Opposing View," *USA Today*.
2. Silver, Lee (1997) *Remaking Eden: How Genetic Engineering & Cloning will Transform the American Family*. New York: Avon Books.
3. Grody, Wayne cited in Frederic Golden (January 11, 1999) "Good Eggs, Bad Eggs," *Time Magazine*. p. 3.

9

DNA-RNA: The Genetic Blueprint of Life

Heleen L. Coetzee, Ph.D.

For many years the substance determining heredity and the variations found in man and other organisms was sought. Indeed, a German biochemist Friedrich Miescher had first isolated DNA in the last century. But subsequent studies showed that the DNA contained only four kinds of compounds which seemed to deny such a complicated role. By the early 1950s it was generally recognized that DNA must be the substance. But how could it carry the enormous amount of information that a cell needed? How could it transmit this to the cell? And above all, how could it be accurately replicated in cell division?

Watson and Crick recognized from the DNA diffraction patterns which they were studying that DNA exhibited a typical helical structure and that there must be two DNA strands in each helical model. The great leap of intuition was the realization that a two-strand helix could be stabilized by hydrogen bonding between bases on opposite strands if the bases were paired in a particular manner. The Watson and Crick model proposed that purines, adenine (A) and guanine (G) paired with pyrimidines, thymine (T) (or uracil (U) for RNA) and cytosine (C) in a specific way, namely:

DNA-RNA: The Genetic Blueprint of Life

A pairs only to T (or U) and G pairs only to C.

The base pairs were stacked on one another with the phosphate-deoxyribose backbones on the outside. Each base pair was rotated by 36° with respect to the next pair in order to accommodate 10 base pairs in the two strands, which were then complementary. Separation of the strands can lead to a new DNA synthesis. Following the same base-pairing rule, new strands are built to attach to the open strands, to produce two double-strand DNA molecules, each with an exact copy of the original. It had also been recognized that this DNA double helix has great plasticity in that three forms of DNA have been identified, two of which are right-handed helices and one which is left-handed. Each DNA strands runs antiparallel. (Figure 9.1)

Thus, the fundamental role of the nucleic acids, DNA and RNA, is the storage and transmission of genetic information and physical development all of which is preprogrammed in these remarkable molecules. That is, they act as the blueprint for this development. The proteins that the cells will make and the functions that they will perform are all recorded on

Figure 9.1
A model for DNA replication. Each DNA strand acts as a template for a new complementary strand. When copying is finished, two double-strand daughter DNA molecules are formed, each identical in sequence to the original molecule. Image by the Academy For Future Science.

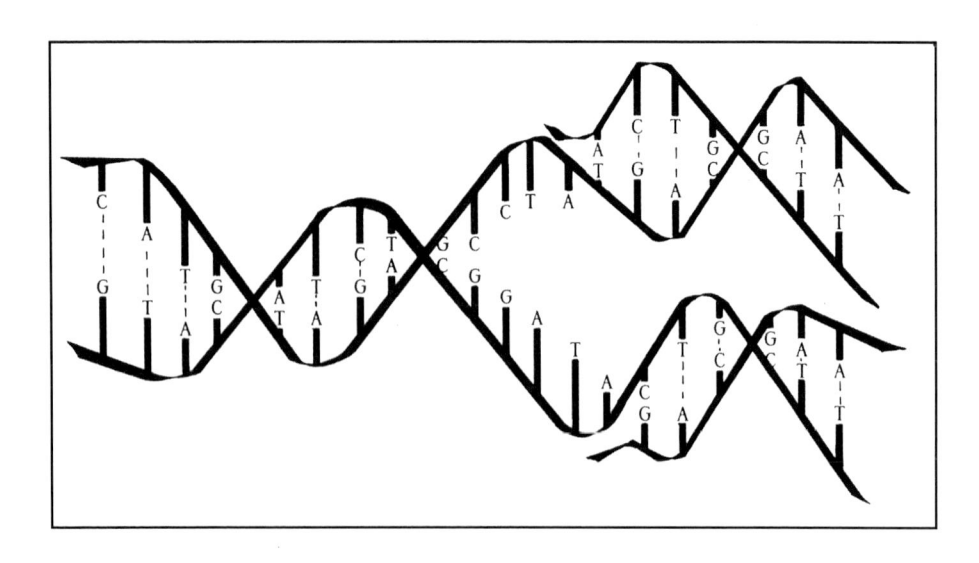

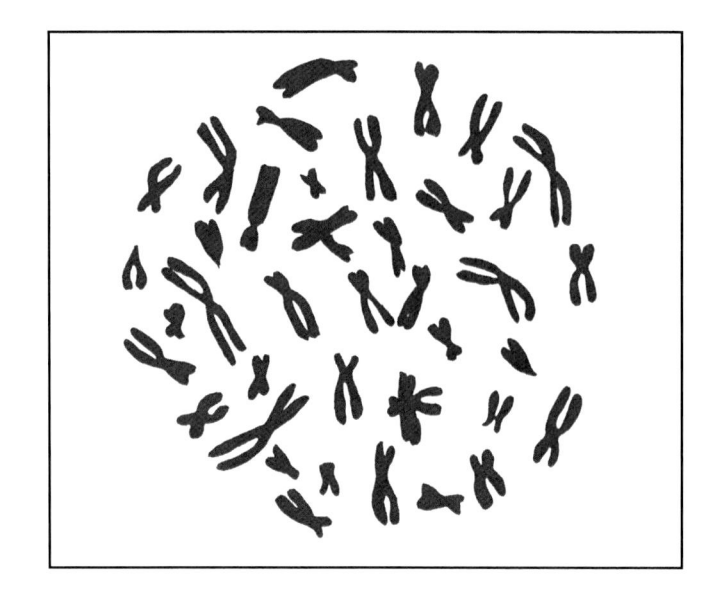

Figure 9.2
DNA molecules are contained in chromosomes and each chromosome consists of two closely aligned chromatids joined at the centromere. Image courtesy of H. Coetzee.

this molecular tape. This tape is a polynucleotide chain determined by the sequence of its bases. In other words, the nucleotide sequence is a coded string of information. The DNA contained in each cell constitutes the genome, or total genetic information content of the organism. (Figure 9.2) A gene is nothing more than a particular DNA sequence, encoding information in a four-letter language in which each letter represents one of the bases.

A large portion of this DNA is capable of being transcribed, or "read" to allow the expression of this information in directing the synthesis of RNA and protein molecules. The segments that can be transcribed are the genes. The DNA in each cell of every organism contains at least one copy of the gene carrying the information to make each protein that the organism requires. In the last decade the genes that are present on the human chromosomes have been analyzed and counted. The count varies from between 29,691 and 75,982 genes, the latter being the latest count.

Expression of the genetic information always involves as a first step the transcription of genes into complementary RNA molecules. Just as a DNA strand directs replication of a new DNA strand complementary to itself, it also directs the formation of a complementary RNA strand.

The production of proteins, thus, does not proceed directly from the DNA. For the information to be translated from the DNA sequences of the genes into amino acid sequences of proteins, a special class of RNA molecules are used as a go-between, messenger RNA (mRNA).

DNA sequences of genes are transcribed into mRNA molecules which are in turn translated into proteins. But there are only 4 kinds of nucleotides in DNA, each of which transcribes to a particular nucleotide in RNA and 20 kinds of amino acids. In order to specify each of the 20 amino acids, the protein-coding information is "read" by the cell in groups of three nucleotides called codons, each corresponding to a separate amino acid. The set of rules that specifies which nucleic acid codons correspond to which amino acids is known as the genetic code. By using triplets of nucleotides (codons) for each amino acid, 4^3, or 64, different combinations are possible as a 1:1 relationship between nucleotide and amino acid is insufficient. This is more than sufficient to code for 20 amino acids, so most amino acids have multiple codons. In particular, three triplets—UAA, UAG, and UGA—do not code for any amino acids but serve as "stop" signals to end translation. (Table 9.1)

In order to make the correspondence between individual amino acids and their corresponding codon triplets, an additional set of molecules is needed, each of which can be coupled to a specific amino acid and which will recognize the corresponding codon in the messenger RNA. These molecules are the transfer RNAs (or tRNAs). Each tRNA contains a nucleotide sequence, called the anticodon, which is complementary to a codon for the particular amino acid. Thus the whole set of tRNAs contained in a cell constitute a kind of molecular dictionary for the translation—they define the correspondences between words in the nucleic acid

		SECOND POSITION				
		U	A	C	G	
FIRST POSITION (5' end)	U	Phe Leu Phe Leu	Tyr Stop Tyr Stop	Ser Ser Ser Ser	Cys Stop Cys Trp	U A C G
	A	Ile Ile Ile Met	Asn Lys Asn Lys	Thr Thr Thr Thr	Ser Arg Ser Arg	U A C G
	C	Leu Leu Leu Leu	His Gln His Gln	Pro Pro Pro Pro	Arg Arg Arg Arg	U A C G
	G	Val Val Val Val	Asp Glu Asp Glu	Ala Ala Ala Ala	Gly Gly Gly Gly	U A C G

Table 9.1
The genetic code consists of 64 triplet combinations which correspond to a amino acids. Any amino acid can be found by reading the three letter codon. Image courtesy of H. Coetzee.

language and words in the protein language. In order to translate an mRNA, there must exist a mechanism that brings the amino acid-bound tRNAs and the mRNA together, matching anticodon and codon triplets and joining amino acids together in the correct sequence. The cellular structure that accomplishes this is the ribosome, a particle composed of both RNA and proteins. A ribosome can bind mRNA and "read" it, accepting the bound tRNAs in the order dictated by the message and transferring their amino acid residues one by one to the growing protein in the proper order. The message is always read 5' ——> 3', that is, starting near the 5' end (the fifth carbon of one deoxyribose sugar) and proceeding in the 3' direction (third carbon of sugar in adjacent nucleotide) of the DNA.

The ribosomes of man contain 4 different rRNA (ribosomal RNA) molecules and each are divided into two subunits that combine to form a functional ribosome. When the subunits of the ribosome are

DNA-RNA: The Genetic Blueprint of Life

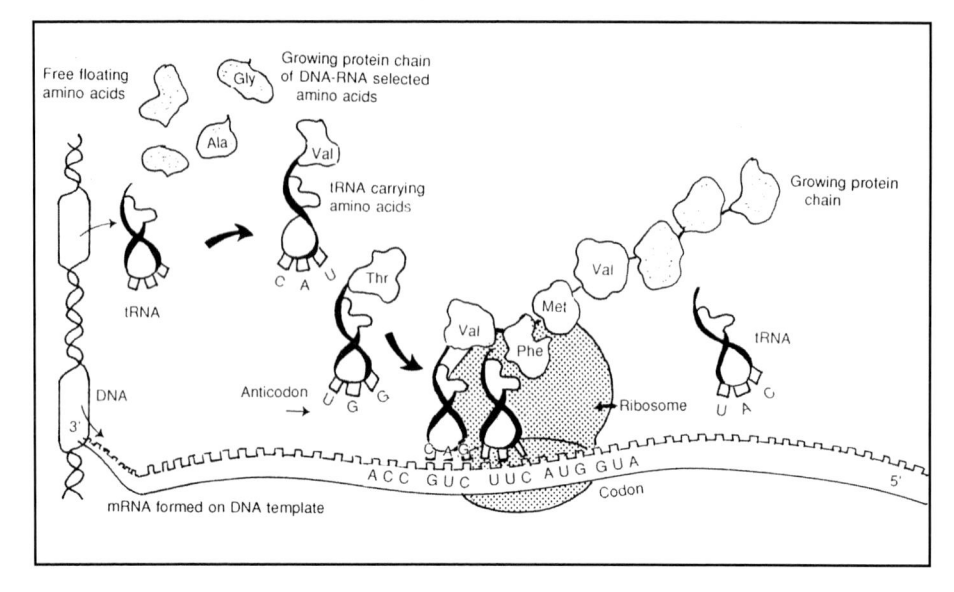

Figure 9.3
Translation. A mRNA is bound to a ribosome. Individual amino acids are brought to the ribosome, one at a time, by tRNA molecules. Each tRNA with its anticodon picks us a free-floating amino acid and identifies the appropriate codon on the mRNA and adds this amino acid to the protein chain. The ribosome travel along the mRNA, so that the genetic message can be read and translated into a protein. Image courtesy of H. Coetzee.

united, the rRNA can assemble all the components of the amino acids to form proteins. As the ribosome moves along the mRNA it eventually encounters a "stop" codon. At this point the protein chain is released. (Figure 9.3)

The universality of the genetic code is unique and indicative of a greater process controlling and ordering the code. Research of The Academy For Future Science states that "there is a coding process for the code itself" and that the ordering of the code is through "seed forms" which contain the predetermined arrangements for this ordering. One can thus envision the primal code for the DNA-RNA unfolding into a seed package, which then further unfolds into particulate light which follows the laws of this particular dimension with regard to gravity and the different forces operating between atoms, molecules and sub-articles.

Latest research shows that the initiation of transcription is by means of electromagnetic fields. EM field stimulated transcription appears to require specific DNA sequences, and these bases may be sites where EM fields generate large repulsive forces between chains by accelerating electrons that move within DNA. Sites rich in C and T would be more likely to come apart in EM fields. Furthermore the different electromagnetic vibrations present in this realm that we are part of have the ability to form certain geometric structures, as demonstrated by Hans Jenny on the stroboscope. One can envision the amino acids, which are also geometric structures, being formed by these vibrations. Moreover, Wilfried Kruger's research with musical theory and atomic physics has uncovered an unmistakable association between the four musical intervals namely the octave, fifth, fourth and second, and the structure of the nucleic acids.

Academy research suggests that the 64 triplet combinations of the four bases of DNA-RNA are the physical code manifestation. The one structure which has the capability for the interpretation of this original code manifested in our DNA-RNA membranes is the tRNA. X-ray diffraction studies show that the molecular shape of tRNA is quite complex but overall the tRNA model appears triangular.

---

1. Blank, M. & Goodman, R. (2001) "Electromagnetic initiation of transcription at specific DNA sites," *Journal of Cellular Biochemistry.* **Vol. 81(4),** pp. 689-92.
2. Jenny, H. (1972) *Cymatics, I & II.* Basilius Press AG, Switzerland. Cymatics encompasses research into electromagnetic energy and the concept that every living thing is surrounded by an energy field that resonates at its own particular frequency. Dr. Hans Jenny's experiments show how audible sound can excite diverse substances into life-like forms. These patterns reflect a variety of forms found throughout nature and brings forth an understanding of the invisible forces which underlie the natural processes from basic movements of singular cell organisms to the formation of galaxies.
3. Krüger, W. (1974) *Das Universum singt.* Trier: FRG. Wilfried Krüger was a German musicologist that discovered that the eight electrons of the oxygen atomic shell and the eight protons of the oxygen nucleus generated a major scale with the spins of the particles expressing the half tones and whole tones.
4. Mathews, C.K. & van Hokle, K.E. (1990) *Biochemistry.* Redwood City: Benjamin/Cummings Publishing Company.
5. Watson, J.D. & Crick, F.H.C. (1953) "Molecular structure of nucleic acids: A structure for deoxyribose nucleic acid." *Nature.* **Vol. 171,** pp. 737-738. In the early 1950's various researchers were trying to discover DNA. Watson and Crick found that through x-ray

diffraction images they could postulate the structure of DNA and suggested the molecule was made of two chains of nucleotides, each in a helix but one going up and the other down. This discovery has been called the most important biological work of the last 100 years and won Watson and Crick the Nobel Prize.

6. Watson, J.D. (1968) *The Double Helix.* New York: New American Library.
7. Wright, F.A. *et al* (2001) A draft annotation and overview of the human genome. *Genome Biology.* **Vol. 2,** pp. 1-18.

10

The Search for the DNA Code of Life & Its Applications

J.J. Hurtak, Ph.D., Ph.D.

The human genome has been called the Crown Jewel of 20th century biology, the Book of Man, the Code of Codes, and a new periodic table. For some it is a blueprint, to others, something much more exotic. Richard Dawkins (1976) finds it a digital archive of the African Pilocene to the exclusion of all other possibilities of evolution. A crucial early proponent of DNA research, Walter Gilbert, called the complete sequence of the human code the "grail of human genetics" and saw it as a tool to study biological function. The struggle to find the grail or understand the blueprint has also become a struggle between science and religion, where many scholars are becoming reductionist or revisionist neoscientists, describing the human genome as "the decoding of the language in which Man created God," as opposed to those theologians who view the Bible as the language in which God created Man.

From the first moments of the James Watson and Francis Crick discovery of the double helix structure of DNA in 1953, to the trailblazing accomplishment of J. Craig Venter's team that completed a mapping of the genome in nine months (beginning September 8, 1999 until the formal announcement on June 26, 2000), a

Figure 10.1
The double helix structure of DNA. Image by the Academy For Future Science.

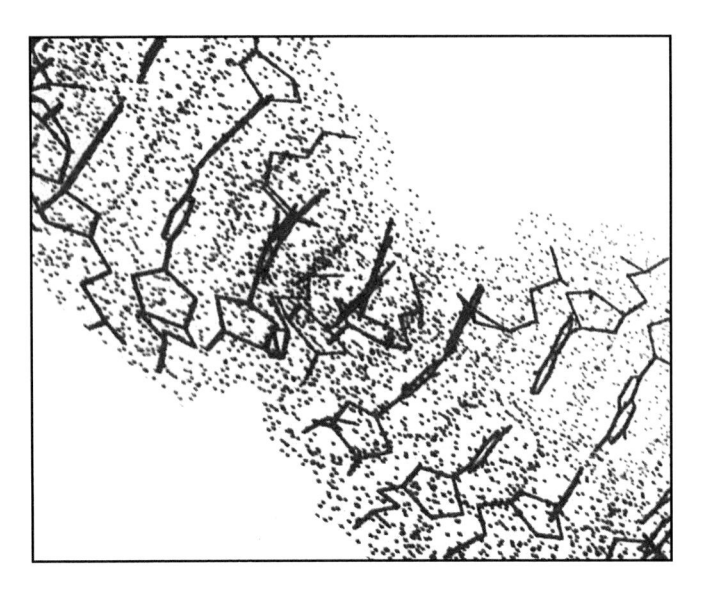

project initially estimated by researchers to take fifteen years, the pace of many other scientific breakthroughs has accelerated. In fact, truly starry-eyed and technological applications of genomics are rapidly changing the human condition. The knowledge base for this growth is cumulative, increasingly interdisciplinary, and showing no sign of slowing down, as it adds new frontiers to vastly accelerate computer technological, nanotechnology, chemical efficiency, and biotechnology for better medicine.

A key result of the monumental work of Venter *et al.* (2001) was the recognition that humanity's closest cousin in a separate species is the chimpanzee, which has been found to be 98.5% genetically identical. Cow DNA is still being sequenced by universities, and so far, of the 768 known genes, 83% are identical to those in humans. Even more astonishing, human DNA is only about one-third different from the nematode or roundworm (C. elegans) which, with about 20,000 genes, grows to only 1 millimeter in length. C. elegans has 959 cells in its tiny nematode form, and yet it still contains a working nervous system, muscles, sexual organs, and an intestine that share many features with those of humans. Even more interesting is the fact that

75% of our genetic make-up is the same as a pumpkin. All of this is certainly quite provocative and has triggered scientific, philosophical, ethical, and religious questions.

If we can be convinced that our approximately 31,000 genes might be compatible with our perception of human complexity, then we must be aware that this number is being reconciled with the number of mRNA (messenger RNA) in our species. It was originally thought that we had as many as 80,000 to 100,000 or more DNA genes and some 85,000 genes of RNA from the various assemblies of 'Expressed Sequence Tags' or EST. However, the latest estimate only predicts about 39,000 different RNA endings from 31,000 DNA genes, although this number could prove slightly higher.

EST is the method used by Venter to rapidly sequence the human genome. How does this work? A strange feature of mammalian genomes is that perhaps 95% of its DNA does not code for any RNA or protein. The function and purpose of this portion of DNA is yet unknown, and some scientists call it "junk DNA," though it appears to contain certain regulatory sequences and other important information. Only the pieces of DNA that are transcribed into mRNA in a cell actually correspond to genes. So after extracting mRNA

Figure 10.2
Humans and primates are close cousins, sharing a large percent of identical genes. Image © Aris Multimedia Entertainment, Inc. 1992.

from a cell, scientists can copy it into strands of complementary DNA (cDNA) that correspond to the genes expressed in the cell at that time. Then they can sequence fragments of these cDNA strands and use them as "expressed sequence tags" (ESTs) to identify the expressed genes.

RNA is being considered, more significant than DNA in terms of evolution since Tom Cech's discovery in 1982 that RNA could splice introns out of itself (type I and type II introns are self-splicing) without any protein being present. This means that RNA had enzymatic activity. This changed our concept of the origin of life, by saying that proteins were not needed early in the evolution of life. A complete DNA to RNA to protein apparatus was not needed. DNA was not even needed in the first replicating cells. Everything could be done by RNA. The concept of life without DNA or protein is a RNA world.

Genomics is the study of whole sets of genes rather than of single genes (our 30,000+ genes of DNA interact in sets), and research into the formation of proteins by gene sets is providing us with a basic understanding of how to manipulate these genes. Scientists who can apply this study of the genome to remedies of diseases are aware of its enormous possibilities, and every sector of the global pharmaceutical industry, estimated at $28 billion per year, will be affected. The next step for researchers, once the genes are identified, is to identify the proteins made by those genes, determine the function of that protein in the body, and then devise therapeutic drugs.

With only 30,000+ candidate genes to work from, and many of those considered "junk DNA" (not considered important in sequencing amino acids), and if 100 companies want to patent the human genome throughout the world, that would limit each company to something on the order of only 300 patents. The struggle for patents in the pharmaceutical industry could conceivably overtake the struggle of science. The end of the beginning of the genomic era might be followed by the designing and marketing of medicines based on the human gene sequences that are owned and controlled by a variety of world-wide companies.

But should these sequences be patented, so that only the company who has done the research can benefit for the life of the patent, some 17 years? Those at NIH have argued that human gene sequences, being a production of nature and not of human artifice, should never be patented and should be available to all researchers. Venter, who was funded by his own private gene company (Celera), worked to be the first to accomplish the Human Genome project in the hopes of acquiring hundreds of patents.

Beyond new pharmaceuticals, this research has promethean impact on the ability to clone adult mammals, including human beings. The exotic practice of using reproductive engineering to propagate endangered animal species and to produce replacement organs for transplant patients can be seen as beneficial to society. Some uses remain questionable and possibly detrimental, as in the field of animal husbandry. Should dairy farmers be permitted, or even encouraged, to clone their champion cows, making it possible to produce more milk from smaller herds? And sheep ranchers, their top lamb and wool producers? And what about people? The clone is a genetic replicate of materia, but human organisms are not determined by their DNA alone. Humans are also products of an interaction between environment (including psychological upbringing) and individual soul, neither of which are modified by random cellular events.

It may be time to slow down the rapid acceleration of gene sequencing of the code of life and first develop a bio-ethic. Even scientists at the recent AAAS conference (publishers of Science magazine) in San Francisco [Feb 2001] called for a reevaluation before human cloning actually begins.

Scientists who have now sequenced our 30,000 genes tell us that the human genome is not significantly, on the level of raw material, more complex than the first jet airplane (Messerschmidt Me-

262) which contains some 200,000 unique parts. However, it is dangerous to regard the DNA triplet-amino acid with its 64 different sequences to the exclusion of the bigger picture. The DNA can be equated to a code, language, and information set just like a series of metaphors, terms appropriated by science and technology, but which have special content for special purposes. To say that DNA contains determinative information about amino acid sequences is simply to say that a coding mechanism may exist in the universe that allows sequences of information to be conveyed on various levels of creation.

Now that human gene sequencing is complete, we must seek to further define the source of molecular biological knowledge, the source of the origin of the sequence and coding structure, consider the one(s) who originated the genetic actors, and define the operations of transformation themselves. If thinkers only consider the similarity of gene types, they will fail to see the consciousness behind creation. Is it simply complicated brain circuitry that makes us so different from cows and worms? How much more complex is a human with consciousness, capable of going to the moon and beyond, compared to a worm? Is it part of a causal mechanism within a greater design?

The real question is are we involved in exclusively Darwinistic evolution, or are we also part of a "quantum evolutionary state" that was engineered through Divine levels of Life that utilized the basic chemical building blocks on this planet to form all physical life forms. Although we may not be Divine in this life structure, that does not mean we "evolved" from lower primates. As we go out into space, we may find that we share the same building blocks of other human-type intelligences.

The search for the DNA code of life has become a means of harnessing the ten trillion cells in each human being. We are now seeing a new information highway of the body of the future, opened by the availability of sequence information. We now must learn how to use it and protect it, understanding that the biology of the

The Search for the DNA Code of Life & Its Applications

Figure 10.3
Detail from "Angels of Creation: The Third Day" by Sir Edward Burne-Jones c. 1890.

life-organism is reflective of a higher purpose and design. The purpose and objective of the time line of human existence is far greater than an ultimate surrendering of the human body-matrix to a ground full of worms. The gene is a reminder of a more complex code wherein we find the dignity of paternity given to man and woman, and the subtle compassion of the Divine for all Creation. The genome can become a Rosetta stone, opening the way to an understanding of a higher code, perhaps connected with life throughout the universe for in the Bible, we are told that man was created "in the image and similitude" of the Divine.

1. Audie, S. & Claverie, J. M. (2000) *The first draft of the human genome: An academic and industrial perspective*. 1 to 2 Oktober 2000, workshop at the Max Planck Institute fuer Molekulaare Genetik, Berlin.
2. The C. elegans Sequencing Consortium, *Science*. 282, 2012. 1998.
3. Crick, F.H.C., Barnett, F. R. S. Leslie, Brenner, S. & Watt-Tobin, Dr. R. J. (1961) "General Nature of the Genetic Code for Protein," *Nature*. 192:1227-1232.
4. Dawkins, Richard (1976) *The Selfish Gene*. New York: Oxford University Press.
5. Venter, J. C *et al* (2001) *Science*. 291, 1304.
6. Watson, J.D.& Crick, F.H.C. (1953) "Genetic implications of the structure of DNA," *Nature*. 171:964-967.
7. Watson, J.D. & Crick, F.H.C. (1953) "A structure for DNA," *Nature*. 171:737-738.

11

A New Perspective of Life on Earth

Steve Skotnicki, Ph.D.

Nearly 4 billion years ago the young Earth was a hostile place. Although the infant sun was 30% less luminous than it is today, it bathed our planet, which had not yet developed a protective ozone shield, in high levels of ultraviolet radiation. Oxygen levels were very low and high levels of carbon dioxide probably created a sweltering greenhouse on the surface of our world. A mere 600 million years young, the Earth retained much of the heat acquired from its earlier accretion, as well as that produced by the decay of abundant radioactive elements such as potassium. All in all the early Earth was not a very friendly place to living things.

Yet, on a barren island in the frozen seas off southern West Greenland, there is indirect yet compelling evidence that not only life but relatively advanced life existed on Earth at that distant time. A 3-meter thick banded iron formation within a foliated amphibolite layer on Akilia Island attests to the presence of liquid water, probably a deep ocean, existing at about 3,850 million years ago (abbreviated "Ma") (Nutman et al., 1996; Mojzsis et al., 1996). The depleted carbon isotopic signature in these rocks has been widely accepted by many researchers to be a fingerprint of photosynthetic biologic activity. What

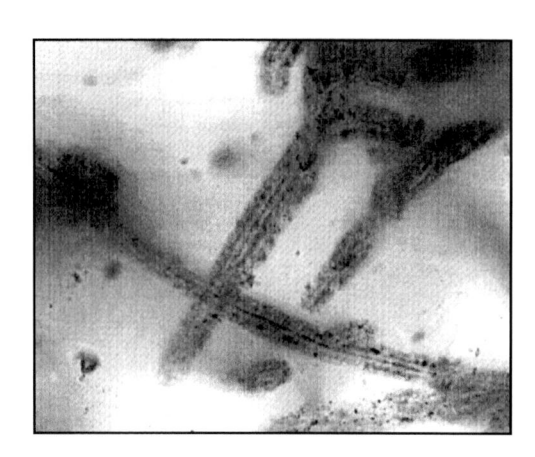

Figure 11.1
Cyanobacteria-like microfossils preserved in chert in the Mescal Limestone, central AZ. Image courtesy of S. Skotnicki.

makes this discovery all the more astounding is that these marine organisms thrived during the episode when the inner planets, at least, were being bombarded by a lethal rain of large meteorites, an episode termed the Late Heavy Bombardment (Ryder, 1990). Somehow life survived.

It was around the same time as the Akilia Island discovery that several other remarkable discoveries conspired to set the story of life on Earth on its head. The discovery of microfossil-like forms resembling nanobacteria in the Martian meteorite ALH84001 (McKay *et al.*, 1996) galvanized the scientific debate about the real possibility of life on another world. The discovery by the Galileo spacecraft of a probable water ocean under the frozen surface of Jupiter's moon Europa showed that liquid water, and life as we understand it, may exist on yet another world. The dense hydrocarbon-rich atmosphere of Saturn's moon Titan and the amazing discovery of the first extra-solar planets around other stars (Svitil, 2000) showed us that the conditions where life as we know it can develop may be more widespread than we first realized.

These discoveries in space occurred not long after the discovery of whole communities of animals thriving off the chemicals and heat given off by thermal vents or "black smokers" at the bottom of our own ocean. Until their discovery it was thought that all life

A New Perspective of Life on Earth

Figure 11.2
Stromatolites formed by algal mats from the Proterozoic Mescal Limestone, central AZ. Left: upper surface; right: cross-section. From Shride (1967).

was dependent, either directly or indirectly, on photosynthesis for survival. Yet these creatures appeared to thrive in a world of permanent darkness, living and growing via chemosynthesis. More recently drilling in basaltic rock on the Columbia Plateau in the state of Washington accidentally revealed a community of microorganisms deep within the earth living off nothing more than hydrogen produced by groundwater oxidizing magnetite minerals in the rock (Stevens and McKinley, 1995; Gold, 1992). Completely unknown a few years ago, the Archea, as they are called, are now recognized as a major branch of the evolutionary tree of life. These discoveries have made us question the very roots of life on Earth.

For more than three-fourths of Earth's history life grew no larger than single-celled organisms. At first they did not even possess a nucleus (the Prokaryotes). These organisms exhibited a variety of forms. Many were simple spheres, others exhibited ornamentations, some looked like tiny vases, and many were long filaments that resemble modern cyanobacteria or blue-green algae (see Figure 11.1). During the Archean (about 4,000 to 2,500 Ma), when there were no larger predators around to graze or burrow into them, many microorganisms formed large, wavy, dome-like colonies called stromatolites (see Figure 11.2). Each stromatolite was up to tens of centimeters across and somewhat resembled the enlarged surface of cottage cheese. Stromatolites are by far the most common and most conspicuous fossil forms observed from this period of Earth's history.

During the Archean and on through the Proterozoic (2,500 to 540 Ma) the Prokaryotes gained a nucleus and membrane-bound organelles (becoming the Eukaryotes), but other than that modification, not much changed. Then at the end of the Proterozoic a strange group of organisms called the Ediacaran fauna appeared in the shallow seas. They were up to several feet across–much larger than all forms of life up to that time–and exhibited strange frond-shaped and jellyfish-like forms. It is still unclear why they developed when they did and if, in fact, they were unicellular or multicellular creatures. But as suddenly as they appeared the Ediacaran fauna vanished, and then the most amazing event of life on Earth occurred. About 540 million years ago, at the beginning of the Cambrian, almost all modern phyla of animals suddenly and mysteriously appeared in the marine fossil record.

Until recently nearly all preserved fossils of very ancient life forms have been found exclusively in marine sedimentary rocks, and for good reason: environments above water are by definition undergoing erosion. Most sediments that were deposited in this ancient period, along with their entrained fossils, have long since disintegrated and washed away. Those that remain have been squeezed and baked by the ceaseless tectonic forces of the Earth. Because of this, evidence of primitive terrestrial life forms living on land during the Archean and Proterozoic (collectively called the Precambrian) are almost completely lacking.

Because we have a negligible record of life on land in the Precambrian, and the record of unicellular life in the oceans stretches back nearly 4 billion years, the fossil record does nothing to disprove the model that life first evolved in the oceans and then exploded onto the land shortly after the Cambrian began. However, three independent lines of evidence suggest a slightly alternate view.

Prior to about 2,500 Ma the surface of our planet was dominated by a global ocean covering a thin basaltic crust. As temperatures in the interior cooled and convective overturn slowed down, stable continents began to form. As they grew, these buoyant blobs of mostly granitic rocks raised above the oceans and began eroding. Sediments shed from these highlands were eventually buried, metamorphosed, and accreted to the margins of the slowly growing continents. During plate movements these blocks were faulted and tilted to varying degrees, creating shallow basins that were intermittently filled with seawater and then closed off. This situation allowed seawater to evaporate and enormous quantities of salts to be precipitated and consequently buried upon the land. Knauth (1998) proposed that it was only when enough salt had been sequestered upon the continents that the salinity of the oceans dropped to a level in which complex life forms could thrive. Therefore, the incredible explosion of complex life forms in the oceans at the beginning of the Cambrian may really reflect a migration of already-evolved, freshwater-adapted organisms to a newly hospitable marine environment.

About 200 botanists from 12 countries, members of the Green Plant Phylogeny Research Coordination Group, have been working for the past five years to refine the "tree of life"—a branched drawing showing how all life forms are related to one another. Rather than using solely the traditional Linean system of comparison, based on morphological or anatomical similarities, the team compared newly available DNA sequences from many different plant species. They found that rather than having several separate origins, all land plants shared a single common ancestor, at least 450 million years ago (Sixteenth International Congress, 1999). The group concluded that this ancestor was not a marine plant but, surprisingly, a freshwater plant.

High above the parched deserts of south central Arizona, an ancient erosion surface was etched into the

A New Perspective of Life on Earth

Figure 11.3
Tendril-like forms preserved in chert in the Mescal Limestone, central Arizona. Image courtesy of S. Skotnicki.

Mescal Limestone during the Proterozoic. Now mostly concealed by tangles of manzanita and thick forests of Ponderosa Pine, the ancient, uplifted surface of the limestone was dissolved, leached away, and partially replaced by hard, resistant chert (very fine-grained quartz) about 1200 million years ago. Lenses of sandstone filled ancient caverns and solution cavities. Jumbled layers of angular collapsed breccias and depressions filled with red, insoluble clay (terra rossa) show that the old erosion surface was a karst, a cavern-filled dissolving limestone surface similar to many such landforms in the eastern United States today. Deep within the colorful red- and purple-hued chert at the top of the karst are rare microscopic fossil organisms that lived on the land surface over a billion years ago (Horodyski and Knauth, 1994). Many of them are filaments and tiny spheres, and resemble fossils recovered from marine sediments. One new discovery looks very different. It consists of wavy, tendril-like sheets that radiate from a point and fan outward in one preferred direction (see Figure 11.3). Unlike most microfossils these larger forms are several millimeters across and can be seen with the naked eye. Is this a primitive freshwater plant, an ancestor to all modern plants that lived on land 700 million years before the earliest known plant fossil? Or is it just an exotic type of replaced cave mineral? A study currently underway hopes to answer this question.

Conclusion

These exciting discoveries of new forms of life in strange environments on our own planet, as well as the discovery of more and more worlds possibly capable of sustaining life as we know it, have prompted a renewed and intensive study into the origins of life. Thirty years ago this was the realm of science fiction, an area few scientists would seriously consider as an acceptable field of study. All of these discoveries have made it more scientifically acceptable to seriously consider the possibility of life outside of Earth. The new views provided by techniques as varied as genetics and our far-flung spacecraft are giving us a new perspective of our place in the universe. And you can bet there will be many more exciting discoveries in the near future.

---

1. Gold, T. (1992) "The deep hot biosphere," *National Academy of Sciences.* **Vol. 89**, p. 6045-6049.
2. Horodyski, R.J. & Knauth, L. (1994) "Life on land in the Precambrian," *Science.* **Vol. 263**, p. 494-498.
3. Knauth, L.P. (1998) "Salinity history of the Earth's early ocean," *Nature.* **Vol. 395**, p. 554-555.
4. McKay, D.S., Gibson, E.K., Thomas-Keprta, K.A., Vali, H., Romanek, C.S., Clemett, S.J., Chillier, X.D.F., Maeschling, C.R., & Zare, R.N. (1996) "Search for past life on Mars; possible relic biogenic activity in Martian meteorite ALH84001," *Science.* **Vol. 273**, p. 924-930.
5. Mojzsis, S.J., Arrhenius, G., McKeegan, K.D., Harrison, T.M., Nutman, A.P.,& Friend, C.R.L. (1996) "Evidence for life on Earth before 3,800 million years ago," *Nature.* **Vol. 384**, p. 55-59.
6. Nutman, A.P., McGregor, V.R., Friend, C.R.L., Bennett, V.C., & Kinny, P.D. (1996) "The Itsag Gneiss Complex of southern West Greenland; the world's most extensive record of early crustal evolution (3,900-3,600 Ma)," *Precambrian Research.* **Vol. 78**, p. 1-39.
7. Ryder, G. (1990) "Lunar samples, lunar accretion and the early bombardment of the Moon," *EOS* (Transactions, American Geophysical Union), **Vol. 71**, p. 322-323.

8. Shride, A.F, (1967) " Younger Precambrian geology in southern Arizona," *U.S. Geological Survey Professional Paper 566.*
9. Sixteenth International Botanical Congress, XVI, (1999) *"Plant evolution."* http://www.sciencedaily.com/releases/1999/08/990806075252.htm.
10. Stevens, T.O., & McKinley, J.P. (1995) "Lithoautotrophic microbial ecosystems in deep basalt aquifers," *Science.* **Vol. 270**, p. 450-454.
11. Svitil, K.A. (March, 2000) "Amazing worlds beyond our own solar system," *Discover.*

12

Biomagnetism & Bio-Electromagnetism: The Foundation of Life

Heleen Coetzee, Ph.D.

New research in the fields of biomagnetism and bio-electromagnetism being carried out in recent years has lead to some exciting discoveries.

Throughout the past 30 years, scientists have been extensively researching organisms that have the ability to produce the ferromagnetic mineral magnetite. Magnetite is a black mineral form of iron oxide that crystallizes in the cubic or isometric system, namely all crystals which have their crystallographic axes of equal length at 90° to each other. It is a mixed Iron (II), Iron (III) oxide, Fe_7O_4, and is one of the major ores of iron that is strongly magnetic. Some varieties, known as lodestone, are natural magnets; these were used as compasses in the ancient world. The discovery of a biogenic material (that is, one formed by a biological organism) with ferromagnetic properties and found to be magnetite was the first breakthrough toward an understanding as to why some animals have the ability to detect the earth's magnetic field. Searches for biogenic magnetite in human tissues had not been conclusive until the beginning of the 1990's when work with high-resolution transmission electron microscopy and electron diffraction on human brain tissue extracts of the cerebral cortex, cerebellum, and meninges (membranes surrounding the brain and spinal cord) identified magnetite-maghemite crystals. These magnetite crystals were found to be organized into linear, membrane-bound chains a few micrometers in length, with up to 80 crystals per chain. Furthermore individual crystals have their {111}* aligned along the length of the chain axes (the "easy" direction of magnetization). The {111} crystal alignment has been interpreted as a biological mechanism for maximizing the magnetic moment per particle, as the {111} direction yields approximately 3% higher saturation magnetization than do other directions. This prismatic particle shape is also uncommon in geological magnetite crystals of this size, which are usually octahedra. The crystal morphology was found to be cubo-octahedral with the {111} faces of adjacent crystals lying perpendicular to the chain axis.

All the magnetite crystals that have been examined to date are single magnetic domains, which means that they are uniformly and stably magnetized and have the maximum magnetic moment per unit volume possible for magnetite.

Elemental analysis, by energy-dispersive X-ray analysis, electron diffraction patterns, and high resolution transmission electron microscopy lattice images, showed that many of the particles were structurally well-ordered and crystallographically single-domain magnetite. This means that the production of this biomineral must be under precise biological control.

Ferromagnetic crystals interact more than a million times more strongly with external magnetic fields than do diamagnetic or paramagnetic materials (deoxyhemoglobin, ferritin, and hemosiderin).

With this finding researchers were posed with a fundamental question for biology, namely: What is the mechanism through which the weak geomagnetic fields are perceived by organisms that are able to precipitate crystals of a ferromagnetic mineral such as

---

* See Glossary: *Crystal Faces*

Figure 12.1
Electron-Microscope Illustration of Magnetite Crystals Under Low Magnification. Image by Esther Raab.

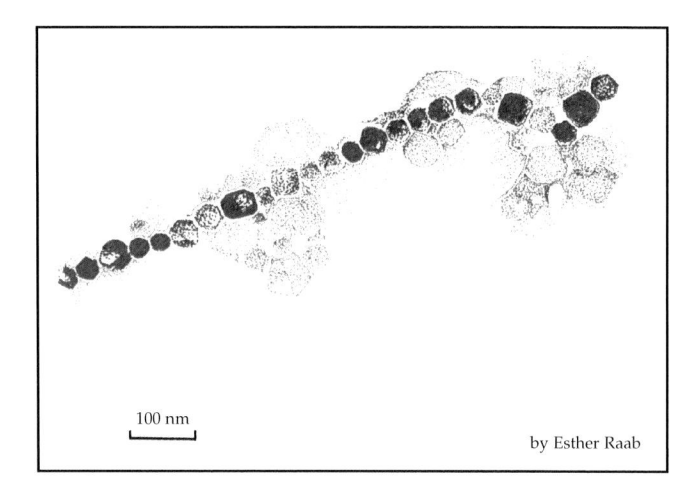

100 nm

by Esther Raab

magnetite (Fe_3O_4)? Could these crystals use their motion in a variety of ways to transduce the geomagnetic field into signals that can be processed by the nervous system?

The presence of membrane-bound biomineral magnetite, which has been shown to have a biological origin, and the implication that some kind of mechanical coupling must take place between each compass magnetite particle and a mechanoreceptor, or at least a functionally equivalent mechanism allowing the position of the particle to be monitored by a sensory organelle in the body, is unique. Research has also found that the magnetite is produced by the cells of the organism when needed, and documents relating to the physiology of consciousness suggest that forms of advanced physical intelligence can directly tap into this [magnetite network] if they have a crystalline network within their brain cavity.

Scientists are now asking the fundamental question: What is magnetite doing in the human brain? In magnetite-containing bacteria, the answer is simple: Magnetite crystals turn the bacteria into swimming needles that orient with respect to the earth's magnetic fields. Magnetite has also been found in animals that navigate by compass direction, such as bees, birds, and fish, but scientists do not know why the magnetite is present in humans, only that it is there.

We have seen in research done in the late 1980s that proteins, DNA, and transforming DNA function as piezoelectric crystal lattice structures in nature. The piezoelectric effect refers to that property of matter which may convert electromagnetic oscillations to mechanical vibrations and vice versa. Studies with exogenously administered electromagnetic fields have shown that both transcription (RNA synthesis) and translation (protein synthesis) can be induced by electromagnetic fields and furthermore that direct current in bone will produce osteochondrogenesis (bone formation) and bacteriostasis, as well as affect adenosine triphosphate (ATP) generation, protein synthesis and membrane transport.

In the human brain, pyramidal cells are present and arranged in layers in the cortex of the two cerebra. The pyramidal cells act as electro-crystal cells immersed in extra-cellular tissue fluids, and seem to operate in the fashion of a liquid crystal oscillator in response to different light commands, or light pulses which, in turn, change the orientation of every molecule and atom within the body. Biogravitational encoded switches present in the brain allow a type of liquid network to release ions that induce currents to the surrounding coiled dendrites. Electron impulses from a neuron, on reaching the dendrite coil of the abutted cell, generate a micro amperage magnetic field, causing the ultra thin crystal, or liquid crystal in the pyramidal cell to be activated in a very unusual way. On flexing, this ultra thin crystal becomes a piezoelectric oscillator, producing a circular polarized light pulse that travels throughout the body, or travels as a transverse photonic bundle of energy.

According to Einstein, matter is to be regarded itself as part, in fact the principle part, of the electromagnetic field, and electric energy is therefore the fundamental origin of our entire physical world. Work published by The Academy For Future Science states that "under present biological conditions,

Figure 12.2
Single Magnetite Crystal in Human Brain. Image by Esther Raab.

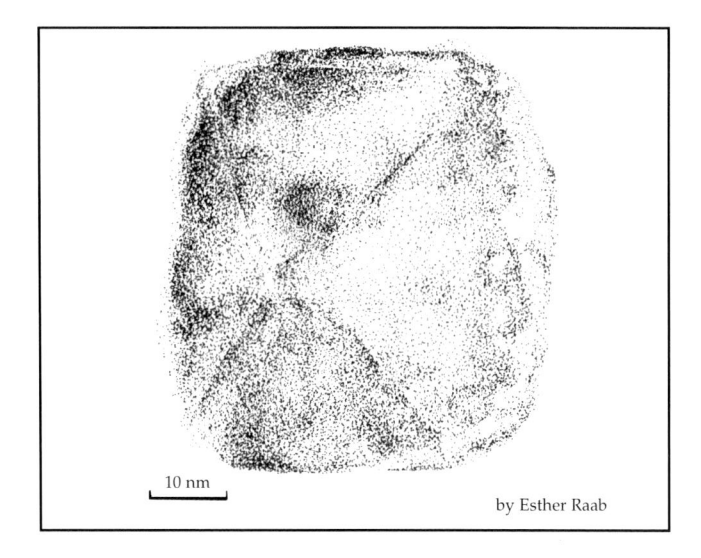

10 nm

by Esther Raab

evolutionary development in living bodies from earliest inception follows unicellular semiconductivity, as a living piezoelectric matrix, through stages which permit primitive basic tissues (glia, satellite and Schwann cells) to be supportive to the neurons in the human system where the primary source is electrical. This has been especially shown in bone growth response to mechanical stress and to fractures which have been demonstrated to have characteristics of control systems using electricity."

Ongoing research has shown that bone has electrical properties. The bone matrix is a biphasic (two-part) semiconductor, i.e. a crystalline solid with an electrical conductivity. The collagen component of bone matrix is an N-type semiconductor and the apatite component a P-type. When tested for piezoelectricity, collagen turns out to be a piezoelectric generator while apatite is not. These function as two semiconductors, one an N-type, the other a P-type forming a PN-junction, which sets up a potential barrier and acts as an efficient rectifier, i.e. a semiconductor diode. Mechanical stress on the bone thus produces a piezoelectrical signal from the collagen. The signal is biphasic, switching polarity

Biomagnetism & Bio-Electromagnetism: The Foundation of Life

with each stress-and-release. The signal is rectified by the PN-junction between apatite and collagen. The strength of the signal tells the bone cells how strong the stress is, and its polarity tells them what direction it comes from. Osteogenic (bone forming) cells which have been shown to have a negative potential would be stimulated to grow more bone, while those in the positive area would stop production of matrix and be resorbed when needed. If bone growth and resorption are part of one process, the electrical signal acts as an analog code to transfer information about stress to the cells and trigger the right response. Hence, stress is converted into an electrical signal. An interesting property of PN-junctions of semiconductor diodes may be observed when current is run though the diode in forward bias, i.e. when there is a good current flow across the barrier. Some of the energy is turned into light and emitted from the surface and are therefore

Figure 12.3
Generated electric currents have been linked to changes in developing embryos.

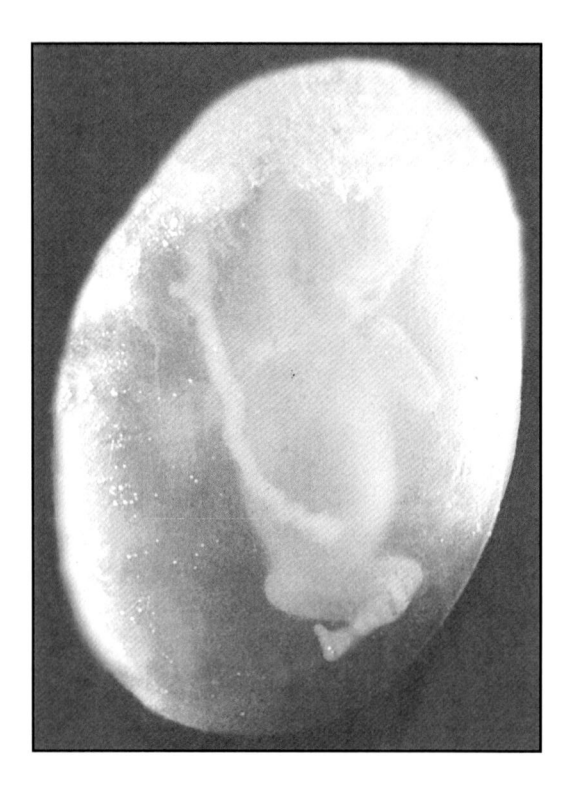

known as light-emitting diodes (LEDs). Researchers found that bone was an LED that required an outside source of light before an electric current would make it release its own light, and the light it emitted was at an infrared frequency invisible to us, but consistent.

With the use of an applied current of a few microamperes regeneration of the spinal cord, optic nerve and bone has been demonstrated and naturally generated electric currents have been linked to changes in developing embryos and in regenerating limbs.

During the past decades a great increase has taken place in research on the effects of non-ionizing electromagnetic radiation on biological systems. Much has been revealed about the human organisms on all levels but the question still being asked by scientists is: What electromagnetic signal might tune to a magnetic resonant energy which would alter the metabolic genetic regulation to bring about growth and repair? This author considers the possibility that tRNA molecules may play a central role in causing cells to alter their normal properties which will then receive the original genetic transmission (of the Adam Kadmon), given through a 'spin point,' to a cell. These transmissions at the spin points, as discussed in AFFS papers, may provide a regenerating instruction for the manufacture of enzymes and proteins which are the building blocks for the 'new tissue' or the 'new organ form' which is physically regenerated. Projecting energy into the spin point may allow for the formation of a blastema (mass of primitive type cells) that gives rise to the regenerated tissue. Thus, through the spinpoint, cells become the tissue responsible for the generation and transmission of direct current signals used in regeneration processes.

Glossary of Terms

Crystal Faces are represented by indices and when the indices are enclosed in braces, e.g. {111}, the indices refer to a complete group of faces.

Diamagnetism is the phenomenon exhibited by

substances that are repelled by both poles of a magnet and thus lie across the magnet's line of influence i.e. have a negative susceptibility to magnetism. All substances are diamagnetic.

Ferromagnetism is the phenomenon exhibited by substances such as iron that show increasing magnetization with applied magnetizing field and persists after the removal of the applied field.

Magnetic Domain is one of the regions in a ferromagnetic solid in which all the atoms have their magnetic moments aligned in the same direction.

Paramagnetism is a weak magnetic condition of substances that have a positive but small susceptibility to magnetism.

---

1. Becker, R.O. & Selden, G. 1985) *The Body Electric: Electromagnetism and the Foundation of Life.* New York, NY: Quill, William Morro.
2. Dubrov, A.P. (1978) *The Geomagnetic Field and Life: Geomagnetobiology.* New York, NY: Plenum Press.
3. Hurtak, J.J. (1986) *"The Power of Healing,"* Lecture given to the members of the Bioenergetics Institute, Johannesburg.
4. Jacobson, J.I. (1992) "Exploring the potential of magneto-crystallization of genes and associated structures with respect to nerve regeneration and cancer," *International Journal of Neuroscience.* 64:153-165.
5. Kirschvink, J.L. (1989) "Magnetite Biomineralization and Geomagnetic Sensitivity in Higher Animals: An Update and Recommendations for Future Study," *Bioelectromagnetics.* 10:239-259.
6. Kirschvink, J.L. *et al* (1992) "Magnetite biomineralization in the human brain," *Proceedings of the National Academy of Sciences.* 89:7683-7687.
7. Nordenstrom, B.W.W. (1992) "Impact of Biological Closed Electric Circuits (BCEC) on Structure and Function," *Integrative Physiological and Behavioral Science.* 27:285-303.

13

Microcosmic Music—
A New Level of Intensity

Susan Alexjander, M.A.

> *All day and night music,*
> *A quiet, bright reed-song.*
> *If it fades, we fade.*
> —*Rumi*

Is the body creating music? Are we, as the composer Charles Ives felt, walking, talking musicians capable of creating our own symphonies? The answer seems to be an increasingly obvious "yes" as we study the body, its brainwaves, heartbeat, rhythms of blood circulation, endocrine cycles, right up to the microwave level of organ vibration. On the fastest level, we reach the rates of vibration of infrared light, as molecules and their atomic structures vibrate and jiggle, stretch, and bend. If these movements are happening, can they be recorded, can they be "heard?" If so, what would they sound like? Random noise? Melodic?

It was with these questions (as a composer) that I approached Dr. David Deamer, cell biologist at the University of California, Davis, in 1988. Dr. Deamer had published two tapes based on a measuring of the rhythm of the four DNA bases (adenine, thymine, guanine and cytosine) as they traveled along the helix (DNA Suite and DNA Music). He had discovered some

Microcosmic Music—A New Level of Intensity

Figure 13.1
DNA spiral showing the four DNA bases. Image by the Academy For Future Science.

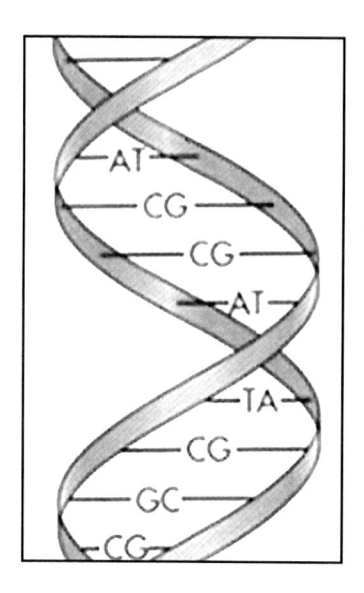

charming patterns that made sense to our ears and bodies. We recognized the movements as music, somewhere between static and chaos.

I proposed that we try to measure the actual molecular vibrations of the bases that make up all of DNA as we know it, as it appears in all life forms. To my astonishment Dr. Deamer explained that the vibrations were easily measurable using an infrared spectrophotometer. By exposing each base to infrared light and measuring which wavelengths each base absorbs it is possible to identify a unique array of approximately 15 different wavelengths for each base. Since each base has a slightly different atomic structure, it will vibrate in a unique manner. As the atoms of carbon, hydrogen, nitrogen and oxygen receive the light, they absorb some of it depending on their vibrational frequencies, and those absorbances can be measured, plotted on a graph, and read as numbers. These numbers, in turn, represent a wavelength "scale" on the light spectrum, but very fast, very high. If we see those numbers in relation to each other, or in other words as ratios, then we can translate them into the sonic spectrum and have a corresponding set of ratios in sound. This is exactly how an ordinary scale works

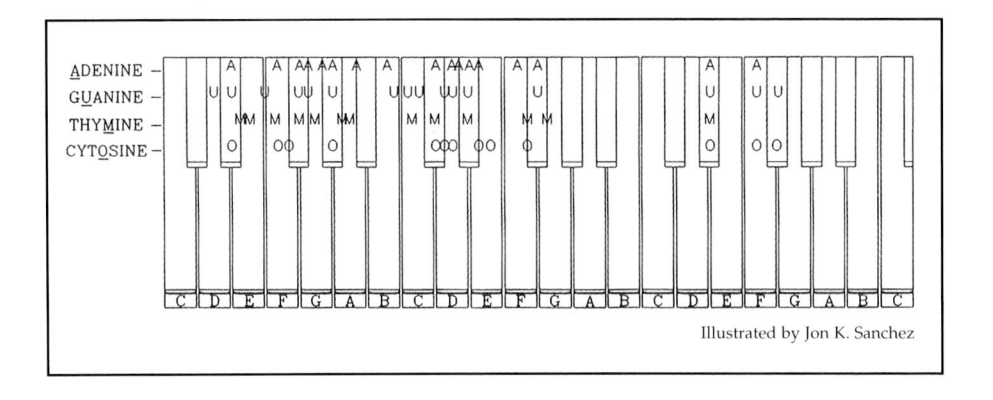

Figure 13.2 Approximate locations of scales for DNA bases. Image by Jon K. Sanchez.

on any musical instrument. The sound of the scale depends on the relationship of adjacent tones to one another.

The question naturally arises at this point: If the ratios are actually those of light vibrations, how can they become sound? This is not as difficult to achieve as it might seem. The answer lies in the fact that we are working with ratios and correspondences. Of course, light is not sound. The two manifest on the material plane in different ways. But, there may be a common archetype to which they both relate, and this archetype may be found in the relationships among various rates of vibration.

Although not common, except perhaps in infants, there are a number of people who hear color or see sound. This crossing of the senses, so to speak, is a process known as synaesthesia.

Perhaps we can gain insight into this matter by taking a different approach. Consider the following koan (of sorts): Sound works by pushing molecules in the air, causing vibration. What happens when the sound vibration is faster and tinier than the smallest molecules? What do we call it then? Where does "the sound" go?

An important key to understanding how we can actually hear high, fast light vibrations is the Law of the Octave. This law states that any vibration of sound (or light) can be doubled or halved, and the same pitch (or light frequency) will result, but what changes is the octave of the sound (or radiation). A simple example: Orchestras tune to the concert pitch A, which is established at a frequency of 440 hertz (cycles per second). Playing the same note at 220 or 880 hertz results in a tone we recognize immediately as an "A," but it sounds either an octave lower or higher than the concert A as such. By taking a very rapid vibration of light and halving it many times (about 35 iterations), we can bring this vibration into the range of hearing. In this manner we can get an idea of what all those light "pitches" might "sound" like if we heard them within the octave range of our sense of hearing. Hence, the sound is relational—poetic, if you like. But, is it musical?

From an artistic perspective I believe it is. On Earth Day 1990, *Sequencia*, was recorded and published in cassette form (and in 1994 on CD). This music, for synthesizer, tabla, cello, violin, and voice, is based entirely on a tuning system created out of my collaboration with Dr. Deamer. There are some astonishingly beautiful combinations which arise out of the total number of about 60 pitches that we measured. Most of the pitches are microtonal, that is, their frequencies occur in the areas between the half-tone, or half-steps, of our normal musical scale. It should be recognized that our equal-tempered scale is a crude one. Microtonal pitches are nothing new, however, in that some cultures have long histories of their use. The most familiar of these, of course, are the cultures of the Indian subcontinent and the Far East, but also those in the Middle East as well.

Many of the DNA "pitches" are tightly packed, or extremely close in frequency. Yet, there are curious leaps, larger intervals of almost minor 7ths. (The layperson may get an idea of this range by performing the following exercise: Sing "There's a place for us" from the popular musical *West Side Story*; the first two notes form a minor 7th). Each DNA base, however, is very similar to the other three, with only subtle differences. And, if we are laying out pitches from low to high, the span for each base is about two and a half octaves. We can therefore state with a high degree of certainty that we are creating wondrous combinations of light and sound within our bodies, playing off of and in relationship to each other.

Some listeners, but not all, report profound reactions to the tunings. They describe an expansiveness, an opening, a naturalness in reaction to them. This leads to the interesting possibility that through listening we are somehow setting up a corresponding reaction to the light patterns that are already in place. Are we touching some part of ourselves that is alive and singing? Is there an aspect of us that is coming into resonance with intelligence and possibly even memory? And if so, what is it about the particular ratios involved that might help us access that intelligence? Is some lower fundamental at work, generating the tunings as overtones? Are the sonic patterns relating to other areas of the body in any orderly way that we can perceive? The implications of our findings and the reactions of the listeners to the tunings open heretofore unsuspected vistas of possibilities.

Perhaps by looking at vibrations through the sonic filter we can discover relationships and mystery that have been hidden in their connectiveness—hidden in the exquisite continuum of our life essence, the quiet, bright reed-song.

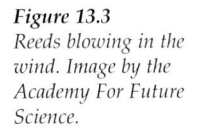

Figure 13.3
Reeds blowing in the wind. Image by the Academy For Future Science.

1. www.healingmusic.org/SusanA/
2. xjander@got.net

14

Memory & the Synaptic Gap

Heleen L. Coetzee, Ph.D.

Most neuroscientists acknowledge that consciousness exists and ongoing research is trying to answer the major question: Is it probable that at any moment some active neuronal processes correlate with consciousness? Brain researchers and psychologists have also come to realize that memory is absolutely crucial to our consciousness. The molecular and sub-molecular levels of the memory process is enjoying much research with some exciting discoveries. Scientists have reached the stage where they feel that they can genetically enhance the mental and cognitive attributes such as intelligence and memory in mammals.

Developments in the human genome research have enabled the first steps toward a molecular understanding of cognitive function. Scientists have been able to show that there are numerous genes on the X chromosome affecting intelligence at the lower end of the cognitive range. Seven of these genes have so far been identified, and the latest data indicate that normal expression of many more X-linked and autosomal genes contribute to cognitive function.

The brain of a person is a complex organ consisting of two cerebral hemispheres, brain stem, cerebellum and spinal cord. Two layers, the gray matter or cortex

Memory & the Synaptic Gap

Figure 14.1
A diagrammatic view of neural tissue in the CNS, showing relationships between neuroglia and neurons. Image by the Academy For Future Science.

and the white matter or medulla, form the cerebral hemispheres. Neurons and supporting cells called neuroglia are the cells that make up the cortex and medulla. Neurons are the main functional unit of the brain and are arranged very specifically in the brain as nuclei (different to cell nuclei) in the cortex. The fundamental task of the neuron is to receive, conduct and transmit signals.

Neurons are distinctive cells with a large cell body containing cytoplasm and a nucleus as well as a number of long, thin processes radiating outward from it. Usually there is one long axon, to conduct signals away from the cell body towards distant targets, and several shorter branching dendrites, which extend from the cell body like antennae and provide an enlarged surface area to receive signals from the axons of other nerve cells. Signals are also received on the cell body itself. The axon commonly divides at its far end into many branches and so can pass on its message to many target cells simultaneously. Communication occurs because an electrical disturbance produced in one part of the cell spreads to other parts. This travelling wave

Memory & the Synaptic Gap

of electrical excitation is known as an action potential or nerve impulse.

Neuronal signals are transmitted from cell to cell at specialized sites of contact known as synapses (see Figure 14.2). The cells are isolated from one another at the synapse, the pre-synaptic cell being separated from the post-synaptic cell by a synaptic cleft. A change of electrical potential in the pre-synaptic cell triggers it to release a chemical known as a neurotransmitter, which is stored in vesicles and released into the synaptic cleft. The neurotransmitter then diffuses across the synaptic cleft and provokes an electrical change in the post-synaptic cell. Other than neurotransmitter containing vesicles, synapses also contain organelles such as mitochondria and microtubules.

Psychologist Donald Hebb stated that learning and memory are based on modifications of synaptic strength among neurons that are simultaneously active. Over the past 10 years scientists have been focusing on a particular molecule called the NMDA (N-methyl-D-aspartate) receptor which they have found acts as a graded switch for memory formation. One of the

Figure 14.2
Diagrammatical representation of a synapse. Image courtesy of H. Coetzee.

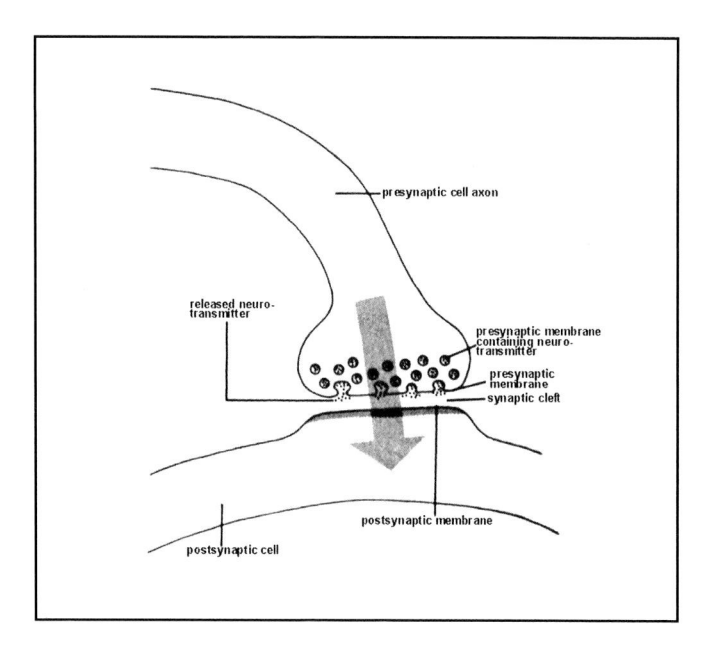

Figure 14.3
A: *The NMDA receptor remains closed without two specific signals.*
B: *One signal is a glutamate molecule released by the presynaptic neuron.*
C: *The other is a change in electric potential triggered within the cell.*
D: *This unblocks the receptor and calcium flows in helping to form a memory. Image courtesy of H. Coetzee.*

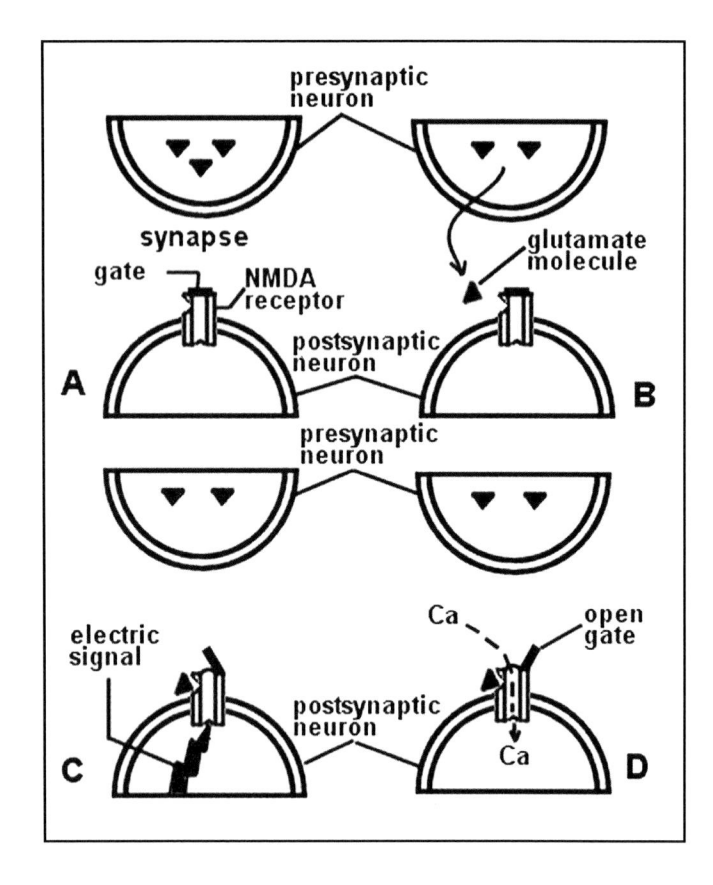

NMDA receptors, receptor 2B (NR2B) has been identified as critical in gating memory formation.

NMDA reacts to a chemical cue. In the case of learning and memory formation, it is glutamate, a neurotransmitter secreted by the axon of a neighboring cell. NDMA unlike other receptors also needs an electrical discharge from its own cell at the same time of the release of glutamate. It then permits calcium ions to flow into the receiving (post-synaptic) neuron making the neuron easier to turn on the next time a signal is received. This is believed to be the essence of one type of memory formation (see Figure 14.3). The gene encoding the human NR2B receptor has been mapped to chromosome 12p12.

A direct and indirect relationship exists between

glutamate receptors and the cytoskeletal proteins of the cell. The cytoskeleton or internal skeleton of cells is composed of a network of protein filaments, two of the most important are actin filaments and microtubules. Actin filaments are formed by globular subunits which are associated with one molecule of ATP. Microtubules are formed from molecules of tubulin. Although tubulin is present in virtually all eukaryotic cells, the most abundant source is vertebrate brain reflecting the high density of microtubules in the elongated axons and dendrites of nerve cells. When tubulin molecules assemble into microtubules, they form linear "protofilaments." In a complete microtubule there are 13 protofilaments arranged side by side around a central core.

The role of microtubules is that of transport and with respect to the neuron that of the extensive traffic of membrane-bound vesicles along the axon between the cell body and the nerve end. Microtubules also play a crucial part in controlling cell shape. All eukaryotic cells have a distinct geometry, both in terms of their external features and in terms of the position of their organelles. While all components of the cytoskeleton participate in this geometry, microtubules often seem to play a unique part in determining it. In fact, the synaptic-activity-controlled balancing of the different forms of actin and the tubulin of microtubules might be relevant for physiological events such as learning and the formation of memory.

It is also becoming known that there may be second messengers like Cyclic AMP (adenosine monophosphate) that may play a key role in neuronal plasticity, and hence in learning and memory. Now it is becoming possible to determine the relationships that exist in the metabolic pathways where second messengers interact. The binding of adenine to membrane-associated cell receptors regulates the formation of Cyclic AMP. (Nucleotides can act as carriers of chemical energy. The triphosphate form of adenine, ATP, participates in the transfer of energy in hundreds of individual cellular reactions. Its terminal phosphate is added using energy from oxidation of foodstuffs, and this phosphate can be readily split off by hydrolysis to release energy that drives reactions elsewhere in the cell.) Cyclic phosphate-containing adenine derivative, Cyclic AMP, serves as a universal signaling molecule within the cells and controls the rate of many intracellular reactions. Cyclic AMP and Ca^{2+} are perhaps the most important intracellular mediators produced as a result of cell-surface receptor activation. Both activate specific proteins by binding to them and changing their conformation. Cyclic AMP exerts its effects in animal cells mainly by activating an enzyme called A-kinase, which catalyzes the transfer of the terminal phosphate group from ATP to specific amino acid residues of selected proteins in the target cell.

The hippocampus, a seahorse-shaped structure located within the brain as part of the limbic system, also plays a key role in functions such as learning, memory and emotion. It has been shown to be necessary for both encoding and retrieval of spatial memory and for either consolidation or long-term storage in the memory process as has other areas of the cerebral cortex such as the prefrontal cortex and the temporal lobe. With sophisticated instrumentation called near-infrared imaging scientists have also found that active neurons reflect light differently than inactive neurons.

Although scientists have found the memory trail along the neuronal cell membrane, across the synaptic gap, on to the adjacent neuron and into the cell via the Cyclic AMP process converting chemical signal (impulse) back to electric with the concomitant connection inside the cell to the microtubules and onwards, that is as far as the biophysical knowledge extends at the beginning of this millennium. The increasingly rapid development of new breakthroughs by scientists in the higher understanding and connection with finer levels of consciousness is daily becoming more of a reality, bringing predictions of the last thirty years in this field to fulfillment.

1. Crick, F. & Koch, C. (1998) "Consciousness and Neuroscience," *Cerebral Cortex*, 8:97-107.
2. Gécz, J. & Mulley, J. (2000) "Genes for Cognitive Function: Developments on the X," *Genome Research.* 10:157-163.
3. Mandich, P. *et al* (1994) "Mapping of the human NMDAR2B receptor subunit gene (GRIN2B) to chromosome 12p12," *Genomics.* 22:216-218.
4. Tang, Y.P. *et al* (1999) "Genetic enhancement of learning and memory in mice," *Nature,* 401:63-69.See also:
5. For a discussion of microtubules: Vind, Gerald, "Seeking Higher Consciousness," this edition, Chapter 36, pp. 395-402.
6. For a discussion of ATP: Palmer, Roger (1996) "The Human Body— Its Energy & Resonance Matrix," *Future History Journal*, 2:1, Los Gatos: The Academy For Future Science, pp. 2-6.

15

Who Are We, Anyway?

*Gerald H. Vind, M.A.
Former New Technologies
Staff, Northup Corporation*

Throughout recorded history humans have searched for answers to the questions of our origins. Charles Darwin presented his theories of evolution in his book *The Descent of Man* in 1871, and proposed that humankind was most probably of African origin and had evolved from the Great Apes of Africa. Religious authorities rejected Darwin's ideas because they contradicted the Biblical accounts of creation. While not accepted initially, Darwinian evolution has grown to be a major pillar of modern science.

Creationists and Darwinian evolutionists continue to fight in defense of their positions although true science no longer favors either side. New scientific findings in genetics point to entirely different answers to the mystery of our origins.

In 1962 James Watson and Francis Crick won a Nobel Prize for their discovery of the structure of DNA, arguably the most important development in biology in the last 100 years. In the decades following, tremendous growth in this field has yielded many new discoveries related to DNA.

DNA sequences have become a primary source of information for determining relationships between organisms. The field of paleoanthropology now relies

Who Are We, Anyway?

Figure 15.1
According to Darwin's theory of evolution, humankind originated in Africa, descending from the Great Apes. Image by the Academy For Future Science.

heavily on analysis of DNA sequences and genetic trees to examine evolutionary paths. Such studies have determined the chimpanzee lineage as the closest to humans, with the gorilla as next closest lineage.[1]

Recent studies of the specialized DNA found in human mitochrondria present significant problems for the Darwinian evolutionists. Mitochondria are specialized organelles found in all cells, and they function as tiny power plants for cellular metabolism. Since the male sperm do not have any mitochondria, all of the mitochondria in our cells come from the female ovum. Thus, the fertilized ovum (zygote) contains only maternal mitochondrial DNA (mtDNA). In subsequent cellular growth, the tiny mitochondria within each cell multiply, replicating themselves using their mtDNA.

Since mtDNA does not combine with any other DNA in order to replicate, as does the DNA of the nucleus, analysis of mtDNA sequences is direct and simple, and the mtDNA in all humans can be traced back to some original maternal "Eve." Slight variations and mutations have occurred in human mtDNA over

Figure 15.2
The DNA Spiral whose structure was discovered by J. Watson & F. Crick. Image by the Academy For Future Science.

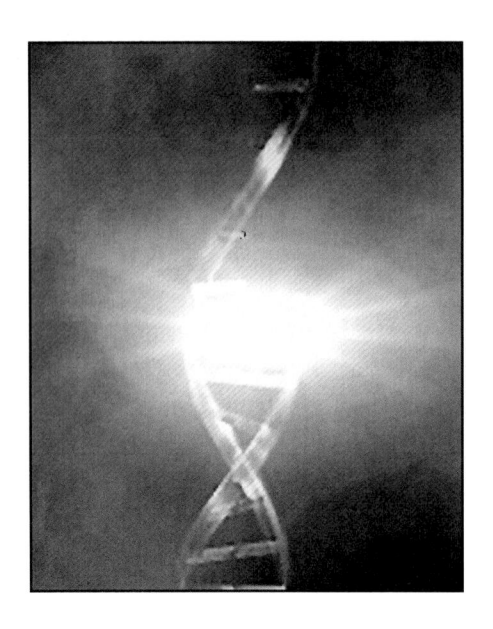

the centuries, and analysis of the changes in mtDNA sequences gives a beginning date for the original human mitochondrial "Eve" as almost certainly less than 200,000 years ago.[2]

This means that our human species has existed for less than 200,000 years, making it difficult for Darwinian evolutionists to explain how changes at the species level can evolve from genetic mutations at the cellular level. However, the short evolutionary timeframe indicated by mtDNA studies is insignificant when compared to the inability of the DNA itself to do what evolutionists claim it can do.

A scientific orthodoxy of genetic evolution holds the belief that evolutionary changes occur within a species through random mutations of DNA—that is, changes at the cellular level become expressed at the species level; micro-evolution drives macro-evolution. However popular this view, it does not hold up under compelling scientific evidence to the contrary.

DNA research with mouse embryos shows that certain genes exhibit great differences, depending on whether they are from the male (sperm) or female (ovum) side. Attempts to combine two genes from the same sex (two male pairs and two female pairs), by implanting them in a surrogate female mouse (where they were expected to gestate and produce male gene-pair-only, and female gene-pair-only offspring), failed their objective completely, but the attempts provided new understanding of genetic processes and proved that "...both parental genomes are necessary for complete embryogenesis [viable growth]."[3] This means that the exact same random mutation must occur in both male and female partners before the genetic change can be passed on to successive generations. The odds against random cellular mutations introducing major changes at the species level to produce the human lineage quickly become astronomical.

If the micro-to-macro evolutionary principle does not work, what then explains the adaptations and diversity that so inspired Charles Darwin? While evolution can be demonstrated at the level of simple organisms, it cannot explain the observed physical evidence at the species level. But if not Darwinian evolution, what else is there?

The failure of Darwinism is not limited to the field of genetics. If you disagree that only 200,000 years ago was the origin of "mitrochondrial Eve," there is also the claim that a major scientific cover-up exists that has blocked the publication of credible archeological discoveries of bones and artifacts that show human-like beings existed on earth millions of years ago. Should this evidence be released, all of the carefully ordered archaeological progression of human evolution (e.g., Australopithecus, Homo habilis, Homo-erectus, etc.) could be proven wrong.

This cover-up is well documented in the book *The Hidden History of The Human Race* by Michael A. Cremo and Richard L. Thompson. They present ample documentation of numerous cases of scientific cover up, presenting evidence that the evolutionary prejudices that are held by powerful groups of scientists have acted as a "knowledge filter." Opinion leaders in science have ignored or distorted credible evidence, and this has given us distorted and incomplete facts from which we have formulated the story of our human origins.[4]

Lloyd Pye has also pursued this area of investigation in his book *Everything You Know Is Wrong*. Pye presents evidence found in the fossil record to show that there is "...no legitimate way to connect humanity to Earth's remote past, which means that Darwinism does not, and never will explain how mankind got here."[5]

Pye goes on to turn us away from archeological hominid research into the area of anthropological hominoid research, that is, investigating animals closely resembling humans but clearly not human. He uses the term hominoid to provide separation from the hominids that are presumed to be our evolutionary predecessors.

Hominoid is a technical term that refers to members of the Superfamily Hominoidea (i.e., all living and fossil apes and humans). The term Hominid is used to identify members of the Family Hominidae (usually humans and fossil humans). However, based on DNA-sequence studies, many paleo-anthropologists argue that Hominidae should include African apes and humans, and then differentiate them at the Subfamily level.

Pye uses the term "hominoid" to refer to what are really Crypto-hominoids, such as Bigfoot, Yeti, Almas, and Kaptars, creatures that some have identified but still lack the scientific documentation to enter mainstream science. Short of presenting a live Bigfoot, Yeti, or other similar hominoid creatures, Pye presents convincing forensic evidence and eyewitness accounts of four distinct types of Crypto-hominoid creatures still living in remote wilderness areas.

Of greatest interest are the Almas described by Dr. Boris Porshnev, a scientist and historian in the former USSR. Porshnev carried out extensive and highly credible hominoid research that has been published in respected technical journals. He has documented the Almas as a separate species, showing that Almas appear to be contemporary Neanderthals. A shortened version of Porshnev's description follows:

Their average height is from five to six feet… The entire body is covered with hair from ¾ to 3-inches in length… [with] not much hair on the hands or feet, and none on the palms or soles. Witnesses often report that they have a very distasteful smell… The head leans forward more than a man's and is supported by strong muscles that make the neck appear short and wide… The back of the head rises to a cone-shaped peak. The forehead is low and receding, with protruding eyebrows, and eyes buried deeply in the skull. The bridge of the nose is flat with nostrils turned outward… They are active mainly in twilight and at night. Their sense of sight, hearing, and touch are acute, and they can move without making a sound. They are expert at concealing themselves…"[6]

Dr. Porshnev also studied extensively the accounts of Zana, a female Alma that was caught and tamed in a region noted for the longevity of its inhabitants, and later died sometime in the late 1880s or early 1890s. During her life in captivity Zana had four children that were fathered by various men in the village. Zana's children had some of her brutish characteristics, but they acted and looked like normal people, although more robust and stronger than humans. They were all capable of normal human speech (unlike Zana), and possessed normal human intelligence. Khvit, the youngest of Zana's four children died in 1954 and was the best known, however there are numerous descendants of all four throughout the Abkhazian Republic.[7]

The new evidence cited above falls between Creationism and Darwinism. Assuming Porshnev's account to be accurate, the genetic compatibility of Zana with humans is remarkable because it is the successful joining of DNA from a non-human hominoid species with human DNA; furthermore, that hybrid DNA was subsequently passed on to succeeding generations. Trans-species unions, when viable, are usually sterile, as with the mule that is produced by the union of a male donkey and a female horse.

Nevertheless, Zana may point us back to our human genetic history. Studies of the human genome (DNA) have revealed some 4,000 genetic defects in our human gene pool, resulting in numerous genetic diseases. However, the chimpanzee (the species closest to us genetically) has only a few defects in its DNA. And, it is curious that humans have only 46 chromosomes (23 pairs), while chimps have 48 (24 pairs). Presumably, higher human evolution would suggest more chromosomes than chimps.

Is there a record of tinkering with the human genome? Some scholars have interpreted the biblical Genesis accounts of creation as efforts by ancient learned men to describe a technical genetic process that they could not fully comprehend. Zachria Sitchin, scholar of ancient Middle-Eastern languages, believes that Adam was the first test-tube baby.[8] Sitchin has been a leader in developing public interest in the ancient Sumerian civilization, and it is in these ancient records as well as in various parts of the scroll Genesis that we can find evidence of genetic manipulation that may have created or influenced early humans.

The Sumerians, for example, were a highly advanced civilization that appeared suddenly out of the Neolithic Stone Age without adequate time for evolutionary development. Their written records, preserved on fired-clay tablets in a sophisticated system of wedge-shaped symbols we now call cuneiform, include a numbering system that used 5, 6 and 60 as its base, rather than the base of 10 we use today. This ancient numbering system is still in use today as we divide minutes and hours by 60, and the circle by 360° (6 x 60). The Sumerians also created the first calendar, and divided the day into 24 hours. Side-by-side translations of Sumerian text into the language of their conquerors, the Akkadians, have given linguists access to the Sumerian language.

Sumerian authors describe an amazing cosmology not only of their origins, but also of a cataclysmic interaction between planetary bodies in our solar system that created the Earth and its moon in their

Figure 15.3
Sumerian Tablet depicting the Nibiruan Gods on Earth.

present form and location. Modern scholars who first translated these stories considered them mere myth and fantasy. However, when Zacharia Sitchin published his analysis and interpretations these ancient "myths" began to be considered an accurate historical record.

Evidence is compelling that our otherwise slow evolutionary processes received influences originating outside our planet. The Sumerians attributed all that they knew to a race of superior beings who created them and lived with them. These beings were called the Anunnaki, human-appearing beings of Anu, their heavenly Father. The Anunnaki descended to Earth from a planet they called Niberu.

Primitive workers were genetically created as a slave race to do the heavy labor that the elite Anunnaki did not want to do. The Anunnaki god-like leader ENKI conducted genetic experiments to improve their primitive workers, and these changes coupled with subsequent inbreeding of Anunnaki men with female primitive workers produced the hybrids (as a sub-species) we now call humans.

With a somewhat different interpretation, Sanskrit accounts of our creation tell us we emerged from a cosmic egg connected with the gods. Genesis makes it clear that around the time of Noah there was a distinct influence of some less then welcome "sons of god" who played genetic havic with the human race:

> *Now it came to pass, when men began to multiply on the face of the earth, and the daughters were born to them, that the sons of God saw the daughters of men, that they were beautiful; and they took wives for themselves of all whom they chose.*
> —*Genesis 6:1-2*

In times of great change, transformational processes become more important. Successful transformation is only possible if there is time, and some preparation for change; in other words don't wait until your ship is sinking to build your lifeboat.

A little over 30-years ago futurist Alvin Toffler, in his book *Future Shock*,[9] popularized the idea that we humans have a limited capacity for change, and too much change or innovation produces "future shock," resulting in personal and societal instabilities. Yet more than any other mammalian species, humans are most able to adapt and to change. Far greater than any other species, humans are guided by learned behavior, as contrasted with genetically programmed behavior. We pattern our behavior after parents and others close to us, and our learning experience is drawn from the cultural pool of language, customs, and artifacts. This cultural pool forms a collective or virtual consciousness field that guides and directs our language, thoughts, and actions. This cultural field effect is our exogenetic pool, complementing our genetic pool; and in reflexive new developments, we are beginning to modify our genetic pool from our rapidly advancing exogenetic pool.

Today, we are witnessing genetic research and a new medical technology of gene therapy that, for better or for worse, have the potential to change the human genome. Even without genetic improvements, we have the potential to make enormous improvements in ourselves individually, and collectively in our world.

Somehow we have moved from flat-Earth view to spherical-Earth. Will we soon move on to a hyperdimensional-Earth? Are we ready for a transformational new worldview?

As we reexamine the question: "Who are we?" we see that we are whatever we call ourselves. And thus, we are also becoming whatever we make of ourselves. Knowing this, we are now challenged to transform ourselves individually and collectively, rising above the limitations of our past and transcending space and time, to accept and enlarge our relationship with a vastly larger conscious awareness.

---

1. Waddell, P.J. & Penny, D.(1996) "Evolutionary Trees of Apes and Humans from DNA Sequences," *Handbook of Human Symbolic Evolution*. Lock, A. & Peters, C.R. (Eds.) Clarendon Press, Oxford.
2. Ibid.
3. Cattanach, B.M. & Kirk, M. (1985) "Differential Activity of Maternally and Paternally Derived Chromosome Regions in Mice," *Nature*. June 6-12, 1985, 315 (6019):496-8.
4. Cremo, M. & Thompson, R.L. (1994) *The Hidden History of the Human Race*. Govardhan Hill Publishing, Badger, California.
5. Pye, Lloyd (1997) *Everything You Know Is Wrong, Book One: Human Origins*. Adamu Press, Madeira Beach, Florida.
6. Ibid, p. 142.
7. Ibid, p. 178-181.
8. Sitchin, Z. *The 12th Planet* (1976), *The Stairway to Heaven* (1980), *The Wars of Gods and Men* (1985), *The Lost Realms* (1990), *When Time Began* (1992). Avon Books, New York. *Genesis Revisited: Is Modern Science Catching Up with Ancient Knowledge? (1991)* Bear & Co., Santa Fe, New Mexico.
9. Toffler, A. (1991 reissue) *Future Shock*. Bantam Books.

PART THREE

ENVIR

ONMENT

16

Remote Sensing & the Rediscovery of Lost Worlds

J.J. Hurtak, Ph.D., Ph.D.

Archaeologists and geologists often face two major problems in considering excavation sites: first, determining the specific coordinates of what they are looking for; and second, having identified the target area and begun to dig, the external area may become largely destroyed. If the area is one that local people hold sacred, the archaeologist's destructive data gathering also makes him/her unwelcome. Both these problems are being addressed by new advances in remote-sensing technologies, ranging from satellite images to ground-based instruments.

Since the turn of the last century archaeologists have used aerial photography. Aerial balloons were used to photograph the temples of lower and upper Egypt, and they continue to be useful even today, as seen on the documentary, *Mystery of the Sphinx* (1991). But many other superb methods of remote-sensing, including infrared and radar imaging mounted on the platforms of helicopters, as well as ground-based methods called geophysical surveying, have been developed since the mid-1980s. These methods have provided archaeologists, environmentalists, and even engineers looking for subsurface gas, oil and water, with direct accessibility to information that could not

Figure 16.1
View of the earth from an imaging statellite. Image courtesy of NASA.

have been found in other ways.

Satellites generally show pictures 120 meters on a side, and the archaeologist is usually only interested in a 10 meter area. This discrepancy in scale has been changing with the ever improving capabilities of satellite and Space Shuttle imagers. For instance, the environmental Landsat 7 satellite has a resolution of 10 meters, and the IKONOS satellite can resolve objects with a dimension as small as 1 meter. In Antarctic studies on the other hand, the important TIMS multispectral satellite system that was looking at the "Ozone Hole" in the 1970s, 1980s, and 1990s was able to monitor not only a whole continent, as well as upper atmospheric pollution, but the entire curvature of the South Pole of Mother Earth.

Even if these are not useful for investigating a specific archeological site, the images are useful for putting a site into context. Older remote sensing images with lower resolution are still useful for detecting and locating larger features, such as waterways, roads, and the location of ancient settlements along the riverbeds in Africa. Images taken from the Space Shuttle as early as 1981 revealed some of the first "footprints of civilized man" in Africa. In conjunction with spaceborne radar, an elaborate trans-continental river system was discovered to have existed millions of years ago. Regions that are now vast desert were shown to have had major rivers spanning from Egypt to Chad and on to Niger. The images pinpointed exact locales for the archaeologists where the human eye could see only sand for hundreds of miles.

Recent expeditions in Egypt (1991 and 1996-97) confirmed the radar data that located these ancient rivers that ran through the Sahara Desert 5000 years ago. While images from the Space Shuttle showed fault lines, the Egyptian government used this information to drill for water. The radar penetrated to a depth of 10 meters (30 feet), under the sand; dry sand is easier to penetrate than water rich environments.

On the Giza Plateau, the use of advanced GPR (Ground Penetrating Radar) permitted our group to study signals which attenuate rapidly in the ground while reflecting at interfaces of materials with different conductivity and dielectric properties. This distinguishes soil from bedrock and buried metal objects from the soil around them. This kind of radar can find buried walls, hardpacked clay floors, and can even distinguish between different soils with different electrical responses. It was vital in helping us locate, in 1997, the "Tomb of Osiris" chamber 33 meters (100 feet) beneath the Giza Plateau (see Hurtak, *The Sphinx as a Symbol of Evolution*, this edition, Figure 6.2).

With additional acoustical technology we were able to study the resonant standing-wave patterns established at the inner walls of structures which, in turn, corresponded with certain alignments and walls which reflected specific sound frequencies, showing sophisticated engineering.

The possibilities of resolving the puzzles of history, religious and culture history over millenniums is the

Remote Sensing & the Rediscovery of Lost Worlds

challenge of future science using remote sensing. There are numerous imaging systems available to the archaeologist who can employ both long-distance (airborne and spaceborne imaging) and short-distance (geophysical surveying) methods. Imaging from the air or space is attractive because it gathers large amounts of data quickly. Multispectral scanners are especially useful, as they provide more information than film photography.

Visible photography and color infrared photography have been used for decades. New solid-state imagers, however, provide data that can be digitized, manipulated, and integrated with geographic information systems (GIS). Due to attenuation in the atmosphere, UV is seldom used. Radar is attractive because atmospheric effects are minimized. Thermal Infrared can detect different kinds of vegetation, which in turn can indicate the presence of disturbed soil—buried walls, middens, roadways, etc.

Figure 16.2
View of the Dead Sea from space. Image courtesy of NASA.

Satellite and aircraft-mounted sensors include the Landsat Thematic Mapper, the SPOT satellite images, Thermal Infrared Multispectral Scanner, Calibrated Airborne Multispectral Scanner, Airborne Terrestrial Applications Sensor, and Airborne Oceanographic Lidar.

Additional low-cost sensors include an IR imager and Inframetrics that collects a broad thermal IR band and allows accurate temperature measurement to $0.1°$ C. As always, cost is a consideration: Images gathered from a plane may provide better resolution, but is generally more expensive than satellite images. The ability to link information from different sources—such as radar, visible photography, ground topography, magnetometers and resistometers, with Ground Penetrating Radar (GPR)—allows composite imaging, which may reveal anomalies unnoticed in a single image.

Investigations of the Academy For Future Science in the jungles of Guatemala-Belize in the 1970s found that the northeastern Petén region of Guatemala was once inhabited by several million Mayan people before the civilization's collapse in the 10th-11th centuries. NASA's SAR mapping of northern Guatemala in 1978 showed an extensive canal network, completely covered today with soil and vegetation (see Figure 16.3). The images taken from 12,000-24,000 feet above the ground reveal features even in cloud cover that cannot be readily seen while walking on the ground. Similar ground penetrating radar (GPR) was used in the Coricancha Temple in Cuzco, Peru to locate underground tunnels used by the Incas. Legends relate that there is a tunnel that goes from the Coricancha Temple to Sacsayhuaman and beyond.

However, radar is not only important for archeological research, ecologists are now analyzing planetary resources, agriculture and deforestation utilizing airborne radar techniques. As NASA recently discovered, radar was also able to uncover unique agricultural trenches in the fields near Lake Titicaca designed to create a greenhouse effect allowing the

Figure 16.3
Top: *Aerial View of Petén, Guatemala.*
Bottom: *Same area as above but seen through NASA's SAR showing ancient man-made canals (1978). Images courtesy of NASA.*

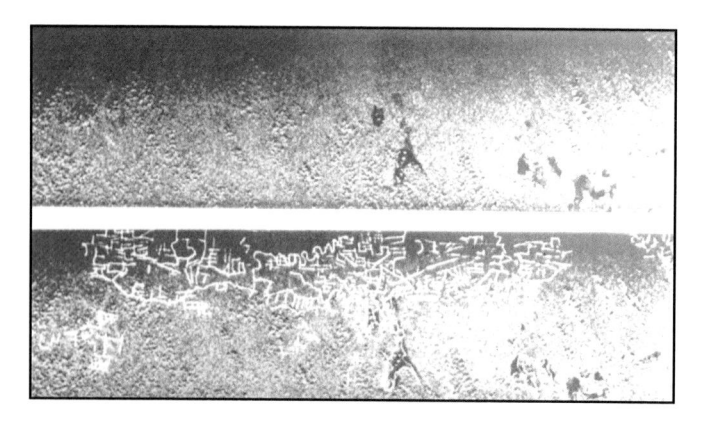

inhabitants of Tiahuanaco (Bolivia) to grow substantial amounts of food at 4,500 meters (14,000 feet) above sea level, a technology which we are only now starting to understand.

The visible, Infra-Red, and microwave images show roadways, canals, reservoirs and vegetation, none of which can usually be seen from the ground in areas of dense vegetation. Scanners can provide crop analysis and even check dams. The availability of these different scanners allows researchers to examine sites in the spectral bands best suited for them. In the hot and humid climates of Central and South America, reflected IR thermal radiation can be used to image the compacted earth of ancient footprints beneath the jungle canopy. Microwave radar is best suited for penetrating the dry sand of the Sahara to show underground geologic features.

Remote sensing of the Petén (Guatemala) over a period of 20+ years shows relentless deforestation. In the last 20 years, more than half of the forest has been cut down. The situation of rapid destruction of the remaining invaluable rainforests is causing problems, not only for local inhabitants but also neighboring countries.

In 1970 only about 20,000 people lived in the Petén. In 1990, the population was more than 300,000. The subsistence farmers, commercial farmers, and cattle ranchers who live in the area now are using methods that result in soil loss and regional degradation.

Uniquely, when archaeologists and environmentalists were brought together, they discovered in 1990 that the Petén had a human population density of only 26 inhabitants per square mile, while ancient estimates of Mayan population densities was as high as 2,600 persons per square mile in the center and between 500 and 1,300 per square mile in the more rural areas. Given that the current population isn't nearly as dense now as the ancient Mayan population—and the inhabitants are still destroying the area—how did the Maya manage to maintain their populations over several centuries?

We have found some answers by radar pictures which revealed the ancients were perhaps able to make better use of hydraulics in this area and in Mexico. There are many areas of seasonally flooded swamps, called Bajos, in the Petén, and there has been lively debate about whether the Maya farmed these areas, which represent about 40 percent of the land surface in the area. The presence of elaborate waterworks around the Bajos, and of populated living areas among the Bajos, suggest that the Maya did farm these areas, and used more sustainable agricultural methods than the typical slash-and-burn farming techniques employed by present-day inhabitants.

But something happened to the ancient Mayans, who built one of the most impressive canal systems in the New World: a cataclysmic collapse reduced the population by two thirds between 830 and 990 AD, even before the Spanish conquistadors arrived and almost finished the job through violence and disease. The Mayan collapse may well be one of the greatest demographic disasters in human history. While the cause of the collapse is probably due to a variety of factors, it may be linked to deforestation. At the time of the collapse there was no tree pollen, and other evidence suggests that the forests of the Petén were nearly destroyed by the Maya. There is evidence of a 200-year-long drought, which may be related to deforestation. Researchers studying climate in other parts of Central and South America note that without trees, cumulus clouds fail to form and rainfall diminishes.

Radar has also helped determine the mean annual rate of gross deforestation in the Amazon, which during the mid-1999 to mid-2000 time period was 19,836 square kilometers (7,658 square miles). This is a serious increase from the August 1998 to August 1999, where the mean annual rate of deforestation which was 17,259 square kilometers (6,663 square miles). Moreover, the satellite TM-Landsat, used by INPE, does not include deforestation of areas smaller than 6.4 hectares (.02 square miles). In 1970, only one percent of the Brazilian Amazon had been deforested. By 2000 almost 15 percent has been destroyed. This means a forest area the size of France was lost in only 30 years.

In sum, remote sensing can help us analyze and maintain the resources on planet Earth. It can also save archaeologists many years of digging in the wrong places and is now opening up very quickly an avalanche of treasures from Peru and Mexico to Giza and China that have been hidden within the earth for thousands of years. The evidence is showing our true birthright to be not only much older than previously thought, but much more sophisticated. It is continually being revealed that ancient cultures were not primitive, but extremely complex. They were able to place sarcophagi into chambers which they carved out 30 meters (100 feet) below the sand, and they were able to construct vast canals for travel and irrigation. The sands of time beckon the spirit of adventure within each of us as we bring together the pieces of the lost treasures of ancient knowledge.

---

1. Ahern, F. J., & Drieman, J. A. (1988) "Assessment of clearcut mapping accuracy with C-band SAR," in *Proc. IGARSS'88*. Edinburgh, Scotland, pp. 1335-1338.
2. Ahern, F. J., Raney, R. K., Dams, R. V. , & Werle, D., (1990) "A review of remote sensing for tropical forest management to define possible RADARSAT contributions," *ISPRS International Symposium on Primary Data Acquisition*. Manaus, Brazil, June 24-29, 1990.
3. Birk, R., Camus, W., Valenti, E., & McCandless, W , (1995) "Synthetic aperture radar imaging systems," *IEEE AES Systems Magazine*. **Vol. 10**, no. 11, pp. 15-23.
4. Chipman, J. W., Lillesand, T. M., Gage, J. D., & Radcliffe, S., (2000)

"Spaceborne imaging radar in support of forest resource management," in *Photogrammetric Engineering and Remote Sensing.* **Vol. 66**, no. 11, pp. 1357-1366.

5. Evans, D. L., Elachi, C., Stofan, E. R., Holt, B., Way, J., Kobrick, M., Vogt, M., Wall, S., van Zyl, J., Schier, M., Ottl, H., & Pampaloni, P., (1993) "The Shuttle Imaging Radar-C & X-Band Synthetic Aperture Radar (SIR- C/X-SAR) mission," in *Eos Transactions.* **Vol. 74**, no. 13.

6. Saatchi, S. S., Soares, J. V., & Alves, D. S., (1997) "Mapping deforestation & land use in Amazon Rainforest using SIR-C imagery," *Remote Sensing of Environment.* **Vol. 59**, no. 2, pp. 191-202.

7. Sun, G., & Ranson, K. J., (1995) "Three dimensional radar backscatter model for forest canopies," *Remote Sensing Science Workshop.* NASA/GSFC, Feb. 27- March 1 1995.

Figure 16.4
Local inhabitant's home showing damage and deforestation of the area, Amazon, Brazil.
Photo by D. Hurtak. ▶

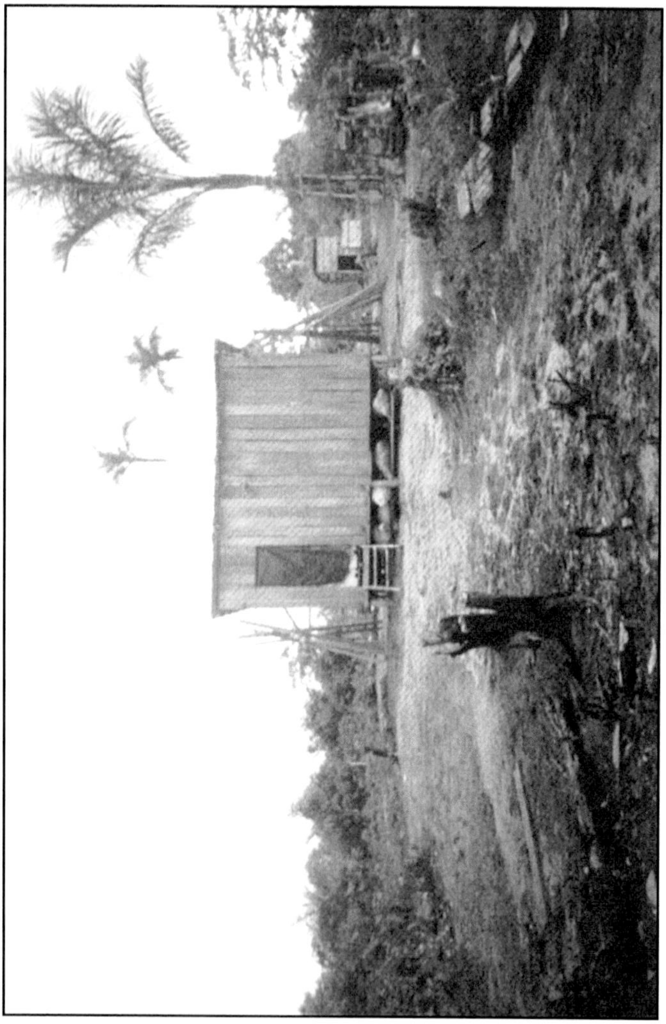

17

Environmentalism: In the Spirit of Sustainability

David Skinner, M.A.

At one level or another people are awakening to the sense that things seem to be changing in ways they have not seen before. For many there is an unspoken sense of uneasiness about these times, perhaps because we do not feel like we are in control any more. In a deeper sense, there is a feeling of a new spirit, or spirituality, arising. This article is an exploration of the impact this emergence of Spirit is having upon our paradigm of commerce and its relationship to our ecological and social systems.

Thomas Kuhn[1] describes paradigms as socially agreed-upon interpretations of reality that allows us to comprehend our world with a degree of certainty, and as such they possess a coherent body of knowledge that is internally consistent which over time tends to become increasingly inflexible or dogmatic. As our knowledge of the world evolves, paradigms must be able to incorporate this changing worldview or be replaced with one that can. Kuhn also observed great confusion and unrest often arising before a new paradigm emerges. In writing about change in the world of commerce, Charles Handy[2] believes we are in a period of discontinuous change, where change is no longer predictable or part of a pattern, that is perhaps

Figure 17.1
The development of commerce has been an influence of the Western mind that has spread world-wide. Shown here: São Paulo, Brazil. Photo by the Academy For Future Science.

the confusion of which Kuhn writes.

CHANGING WORLD VIEWS

The worldview of the Western mind has greatly influenced the development of commerce. The path of Descartes, Newton and Darwin has left us with a value set that may be described as predominately masculine, mechanistic, and objectified, a competitive paradigm stressing separateness from nature and survival of the fittest. Many however, are looking for ways of expanding human consciousness beyond its self-centered approaches to nature, an alternative set of values that describe a deeper, more spiritual approach, an holistic approach to the web of life. By contrast, it could be described as a feminine perspective of caring for all life and consuming only what is necessary. We see here a rebalancing of our masculine, left-hemispheric consciousness through the increasing influence of Spirit in our planetary consciousness program. As the weights and measures of our three-dimensional space and time are changing so too are our paradigms of consciousness.

To further understand the paradigm shift as it affects commerce, we need to look at a number of critical factors influencing its movement in new ways. First there is the problem of growth. Growth of the world economy is most often described in terms of a percentage of increase over the previous year, giving us a linear picture where "the amount of increase is

Figure 17.2
The human habitat from space. Image courtesy of NASA.

Environmentalism: In the Spirit of Sustainability

constant in a given time period."[3] Yet, today's growth is exponential, meaning we find it doubling or more in ever decreasing periods of time. It took mankind over twenty centuries to reach an annual output of goods and services of almost $5 trillion in 1950. In the 1990's the world produced an average $26.6 trillion in goods and services each year. For 2001, global output is estimated to be $33.4 trillion, over a six-fold increase in 50 years.

Closely related to this is a second critical factor: population. A little over two hundred years ago (1750), an estimated 750 million people lived on earth. World population now stands at about 6.2 billion and is estimated to grow to 8.8 billion by 2010. A third factor is the interrelationship between the first two.

We are consuming resources and emitting pollution and wastes into the environment at an equally increasing rate. In other words, human activity is stripping away nature's ability to support life through regeneration of our planet's ecosystems. The impacts of discontinuous change in economic development and technology are being seen around the world. Worldwatch Institute notes the "constraints imposed by nature are also now directly affecting global economic trends. Among these are the capacity

Figure 17.3
Global population is a critical factor to consider in moving towards a more sustainable future for the planet.

of crops to use fertilizer, of oceans to yield seafood, and of the hydrological cycle to produce fresh water."[4] For example, The United States government has limited the number of days its northeastern fishing fleet can go to sea in an attempt to enhance the regeneration of stocks of haddock, cod and halibut, after the Canadians closed their fishing grounds in 1992. The World Bank has issued a warning regarding 80 countries experiencing water shortages serious enough to threaten agricultural production. Also, despite record harvest around the world, in 1994 the consumption of grain exceeded production for the second year in a row.

Another factor to be considered is the decline of cultural diversity. Under increasing global economic integration, local and national cultural norms are giving way to a commercially controlled culture of globalized mass production and mass consumption. Often fed by the creation of artificial needs through advertising, consumer economics is becoming the driving rationale in decision-making. With the viability of nature coming from the diversity of life found within it, is the same not true of man?

Sustainable Development

What is seen as the next step in the environmental movement is a convergence of economics, ecology and sociology. Called sustainable development or sustainability, it recognizes our way of doing business has detrimental impacts on our web of life. It moves the dualistic debate of jobs versus the environment into a holistic or systems perspective, by focusing on creating a life enhancing balance between the economic needs, the environmental needs and the social needs of our local, national and world communities. Sustainable development focuses on commerce getting better not bigger.

The concept of sustainable development entered global consciousness in 1987 at the World Commission on Environment and Development which defined sustainable development as development that meets the needs of the present without compromising the

Environmentalism: In the Spirit of Sustainability

*Figure 17.4
Human consciousness must expand to recognize our interconnectedness and develop a more holistic, spiritual approach to our web of life. Image by the Academy For Future Science.*

ability of future generations to meet their own needs. It outlined three critical, interlocking components: valuing the environment as an integral part of the economic process; changing the distribution of power and wealth in global society; and creating anticipatory rather than reactive policies that would insure the needs of future generations by creating long-term environmental security versus short-term economic gain. Similarly, the Worldwatch Institute has defined a sustainable society as "one that satisfies its needs without jeopardizing the prospects of future generations."[5] Recognizing that societies are beginning to see "they are not only destroying their environments but undermining their futures," the authors state, "inherent in this definition is the responsibility of each generation to ensure that the next one inherits an undiminished natural and economic endowment."

The U.N. Conference on Environment and Development (UNCED), more commonly known as the Earth Summit, brought 177 nations together in Rio de Janeiro in 1992 and produced a global blueprint for sustainable development entitled Agenda 21.[6] Focusing on such issues as economic vitality, clean air and water, health care and educational equality, it stresses the necessity of finding a balance between the economic, environmental, and social needs of our global community as we move into the next century. In June 1993, the President's Council on Sustainable Development (PCSD) was established by Executive Order 12852 and adopted the Brundtland Commission's definition of sustainable development.[7] The council of twenty-five members is "charged with developing bold new approaches to integrate economic and environmental policy" with major focuses on: eco-efficiency—identifying models of sustainable manufacturing; pollution prevention and product stewardship; energy and transportation; natural resources management and protection; principles, goals and definitions; population and consumption; public linkage, dialogue and education; sustainable communities; climate change; and sustainable agriculture. Currently, more than seventy countries around the world have similar initiatives under way.

THE RESTORATIVE ECONOMY

The key to sustainable development is restorative economics. This is an economic system which operates according to the limits and laws of nature. Designed to be regenerative, it is intended to meet the current and long term needs of the people it serves. We now have an economy that rewards the production of goods and services at the lowest possible price in mass quantities. Additionally, this least-price approach takes inadequate responsibility for the damage it does to our ecosystems. By labeling this damage, be it resource depletion, waste or pollution, etc., as an externality—external to the system of commerce—it leaves society to bear the costs of these repercussions. Driving constant increases in productivity through technological efficiency (automation) and/or low wage manufacturing, our industrial system and tax structure also reward the use of natural resources and penalize the use of human resources.

Paul Hawken[8] envisions restorative economics rewarding manufacturers for producing goods and services that have the least impact on the environment. Designed to incorporate nature's cyclical ability to reuse material from one living system to nourish another, this least-cost system will value our natural resources at their true replacement costs. It will focus on efficient resource usage in all areas of its operations and produce long-term, quality, durable goods that can be recycled or parts of which may be reused at the end of their useful life. Besides lowering its impact on our natural capital (our natural, human and energy resources), Hawken sees the restorative economy's emphasis on natural systems increasing employment and providing more meaningful work.[9]

GETTING THERE

So how do we get there from here? Hawken sees education and dialogue as the way to move through this paradigm shift. People need to understand where

Figure 17.5
The current Western approach to economics takes inadequate responsibility for the waste it creates and subsequent damage to the planet's ecosystems.

we are, how we got here, and realize they have a choice about where we go. We need to learn more about the principles of nature and use them as a model to construct a regenerative economy, one that not only walks softly upon the Earth but also works to restore the damage already done. To go beyond the identity patterns that put us into opposition with, and fear of, one another, we need to talk to one another in dialogue, a form of conversation that allows consensus opinions to be formed. This means an honest exchange of ideas and opinions where everyone is heard and included in the decision-making process. We need to envision our future and take responsibility to work for it. We need to create models and plans for the way we want things to be. There are working models of sustainable development in place today, and there are parts of the restorative economy in place in countries and businesses around the world.

In 1988, Dr. Karl-Henrik Robert, founder of The Natural Step, a Swedish organization, with support from the Swedish scientific community, was able to send an educational packet to every school and house in Sweden that outlined the following principles :

(1) Nature cannot withstand a systematic buildup of dispersed matter mined from the earth's crust (e.g. minerals, oil, etc.).

(2) Nature cannot withstand a systematic build up of persistent compounds made by man (e.g. PCBs, DDT, etc.).

(3) Nature cannot withstand a systematic deterioration of its capacity for renewal (destruction of its caring capacity).

(4) For life to go on we must be efficient in our use of resources and promote social justice because poverty only leads to a short-term survival focus that destroys resources we need for our long-term survival.

When speaking to companies, Robert stresses that adopting these four principles is an investment in the future. He asks businesses "to adopt compliance [of these principles] as a long-term goal with practical interim steps."

While often frustrated by the complexity and the lack of coordination between national, state and local regulatory requirements and the added costs of implementing the health and safety programs these statutes require, many businesses acknowledge their need and benefits. It is the environmental legislation of the past twenty years that continues to keep our air, water and soils cleaner than they would be without it. In addition, hazardous materials management programs which promote the substitution of less hazardous or non-hazardous materials in business processes move commerce in the direction of sustainability. Transportation management programs promoting car pooling and use of public transportation reduce the amount of oil extracted from the planet and its associated pollutants. Energy conservation programs using compact fluorescents, motion detectors for switching and other technologies reduce energy usage and increase efficiency. The use of eco-audits, a tool by which businesses can measure their movement towards sustainable business practices, is increasing.

SELF-REALIZATION

Though not fully manifested, the most powerful and profound changes within business are now occurring inside its organizational structure. These changes are effecting the way people work with one another and how they see their relationship with the world. Driven by the rapid rate of change in technology and the marketplace, businesses are scrambling to break out of their rigid, hierarchical structures built around incremental change. To respond effectively to these discontinuous times, they are seeking to stay competitive by tapping into employee innovation and creativity. While still in service to the profit motive, this recognition and utilization of the higher functions of the mind and spirit are moving people beyond economic rationalization. It is this movement which is revolutionizing the world of commerce, for it is bringing Spirit back into that world. A recent article in the Harvard Business Review reflects this trend, stating "The most basic task of corporate leaders is to unleash the human spirit which makes initiative, creativity and entrepreneurship possible."[10] New organizational development strategies are doing the same thing. Peter Senge speaks of self-mastery as one of the five characteristics of a learning organization; Steven Covey speaks of principle-centered leadership; and the work of many others in the fields of total quality management, continuous improvement and team-centered organizations is creating the new ways of doing business.[11] Self-actualization is leading to self-realization. Business people are recognizing the way to survive our system of economic rationalization is through the creative imagination.

So we are coming full circle. The presence of the Spirit, the regenerative feminine perspective, is emerging in the economic paradigm of sustainable development. These are thought-forms that bring a rebalancing to our male-dominated economic paradigm of the last three hundred years. What we see is the opening of the economic mind and the recognition of the need to set people's spirits free. Through the opening of their creative imagination, the right hemisphere of the brain, a revolution in consciousness is taking place. The greater the self-realization of man, the sooner a system of commerce will be established that will serve the higher purpose of man. The consciousness of the Western mind is opening to the new potentialities of life which lie before us. Through the seeding of these thought-forms, we are the bridge builders between economic paradigms and, on a greater scale, consciousness time zones. The future pictures of the new worlds of creation that are ours to inherit are being articulated now.

1. Kuhn, Thomas (1966) *The Structure of Scientific Revolutions.* Chicago, IL: University of Chicago Press.
2. Handy, Charles (1990) *The Age of Unreason.* Cambridge, MA: Harvard Business School Press.
3. Meadows, Donnella H. *et al* (1992) *Beyond The Limits: Confronting Global Collapse, Envisioning a Sustainable Future.* Chelsea Green Publishing.
4. Brown, Lester R. *et al* (1993) *Vital Signs.* Washington, DC: Worldwatch Institute.
5. Brown, Lester R. *et al* (1990) "Picturing a Sustainable Society," *State of the World 1990: A Worldwatch Institute Report on Progress Toward a Sustainable Society.* New York, NY: W.W. Norton & Company.
6. United Nations (June 1992) *Agenda 21.* U.N. Document no. A/CONF. 151/26. Report of the United Nations Conference on Environment & Development, ANNEX II, New York: United Nations Publications Office.
7. For more information contact: *President's Council on Sustainable Development.* MS 7456-MIB, 1849 C Street, NW, Washington, DC 20240, (202) 208-7411.
8. Hawken, Paul (1993) *The Ecology of Commerce: A Declaration of Sustainability.* New York, NY: Harper Business. See also "Natural Capitalism," *Yoga Journal.* Sept./Oct. 1994.
9. For an associated perspective, see Fox, Matthew (1994) *The Reinvention of Work: A New Vision of Livelihood.* San Francisco, CA: Harper Collins.
10. Bartlett, Christopher A. & Ghoshal, Sumantra (1995) "Changing the Role of Top Management: Beyond Systems to People," *Harvard Business Review.* May-June 1995.
11. Senge, Peter M. (1990) *The Fifth Discipline: The Art & Practice of the Learning Organization.* New York, NY: Doubleday.

18

Crisis of the Amazon: An Overview by a Visiting Scientist

J.J. Hurtak, Ph.D., Ph.D.

Over the past twenty years, the fight has been on to save the Amazon and to protect its Indian lands. Pertinent in this struggle is the construction of the last sector of the BR-364 Road which would give the general population, as well as the timber industry, increased access to the Amazon and its wild resources.

Some of the greatest environmental and geological studies of the Amazon Basin to date have not been made from the ground but through the use of remote-sensing technology. Many specialists have long recognized the need for classifications of the vast biographical domain of the greater Amazon Basin. Deforestation is clearly contributing to the build-up of CO_2 in the atmosphere, yet the actual amount of deforestation for a long time was largely unknown. It was found that no one system of remote sensing could provide the answers. Therefore both spaceborne and airborne radar images were acquired of portions of the Middle and Upper Amazon Basin in the State of Amazonas and the Territory of Roraima.

Deforestation in the Amazon began in the late 1950s with the construction the Belem-Brasilia Highway. But it was in the 1980s that deforestation reached the highest rates. Radambrasil which operated

Figure 18.1
Landsat thematic mapping image of South American rainforest. The grid-like lines show areas of deforestation. Image courtesy of NASA.

from 1970 to 1985 began to collect the data. Radar image data sets were also obtained using Shuttle Imaging Radar B (SIR-B) in 1984 and SIR-A in 1981. Later L- and C-band polarimetric SAR data was acquired during the Shuttle Imaging Radar-C (SIR-C)/X-SAR space shuttle mission in 1994.

The most recent projects include the Landsat Thematic Mapper (TM) and the new Terra satellite launched in 1999. These radar device used are able to penetrate clouds and the jungle canopy to reveal the surface features below. Radar has proved to be an effective supplement to NOAA observations because of persistent cloudiness in the tropics. Remote-sensing radar can reveal features such as agricultural fields, urban areas, mountain ranges, and water surfaces.

The first research by Radambrasil produced mappings which were compiled into 38 volumes of between 300 and 500 pages each. Radambrasil used a research airplane to take radar photos that covered a circular area of 37 kilometers in diameter. An altimeter registered the changes in altitude, but the plane attempted to maintain itself at 11 kilometers above the ground. For SIR-A and SIR-B data which was acquired from NASA's Shuttle flights, wavelengths from the radar system on board was set to 23.5 cm. SIR-A had a standard 50-kilometer swath width. SIR-B swath varied (20-50 kilometers) depending on the orientation of the antenna and with the bit rate and the variable antenna depression angle. The Amazon Basin is so massive that it would require approximately 400 Landsat scenes unless a sampling strategy was adopted.

In comparison, Radambrasil used a depression angle of 7-25° as opposed to the 37-43° depression angle used on SIR-A. A depression angle is the angle from the airplane, measured horizontally down to the surface, whereas incidence angle is the angle from the ground up which is complementary. Radar pulses that strike a horizontal surface at large depression/small incidence angles produce strong return echoes, while pulses that strike the same surface at smaller depression/larger incidence angles produce weaker radar returns. Differences thus are analyzed between the angle of the radar system and variations in surface relief and roughness.

The rate at which the backscatter decreases with increasing incidence angle is governed primarily by the physical characteristics of roughness, slope, dielectric constant, and moisture on the surface. As a general rule, a rougher surface will produce a stronger radar return than a smoother surface at incidence angles greater than 30°. In some cases, the Radambrasil image showed clearer drain angle patterns because at relatively large incidence/small depression angles a greater shadowing effect occurs . This clarity is also effected by the closer proximity of the radar.

However, the lower depression angle sometimes failed to penetrate the jungle canopy. In the area of the Rio Negro, the flood-plain is also clearly distinguished and outlined showing contrast in image tone by the Shuttle radar, but not visible except for some relief information on Radam (Projecto Radar da Amazona) images due to the low depression angle. There is also no contrast along the length of the drainage to indicate flooded conditions on the Radam image, but appears on SIR-A as a cut-back condition. Similarly, the alluvial forest by the rivers Santa Helena and Taxidermista is

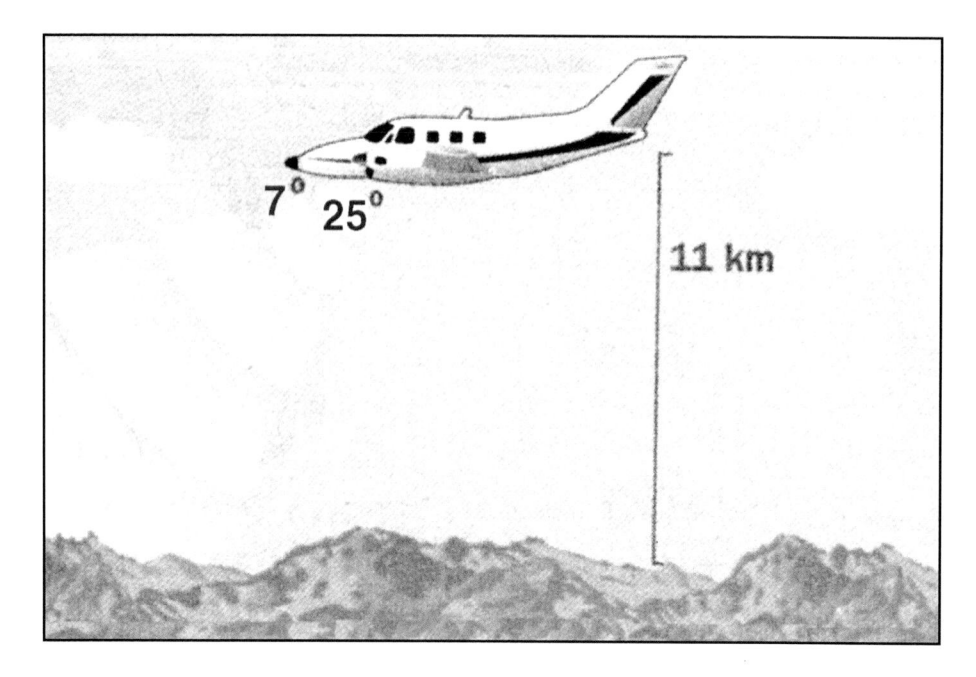

Crisis of the Amazon: An Overview by a Visiting Scientist

Figure 18.2
Remote Sensing from airborne technology showing depression angle and distance. Image courtesy of NASA.

completely indistinguishable by Radam and there is little or no contrast with vegetation from each side of the floodplain. At the much larger depression angle used on the SIR-A, the alluvial forest appears very bright in marked contrast to the forest on each side of the floodplain.

Taking into consideration variables such as time of day, incidence angle, etc., it is theorized that in particular regions of vegetated areas (excluding swampy areas) SIR-A brightness tends to increase with the vegetation index. Uncut areas are textually rough and, therefore, had a moderately strong radar return. Recently cleared regions showed increased spectral reflection, but older cut areas used for pasture land or vegetation were less bright due to the dielectric effect in wet regions, or because abandoned, previously cleared areas often have a rougher texture than even the primary forests, and are less efficient volume scatterers, showing a stronger return signal.

SIR-B has multiple angle imaging capabilities and therefore can collect pictures using a greater range of depression angles (from 30-75°) so they can be used to differentiate surface materials on the basis of their roughness characteristics in much the same way that Landsat imagery collects information in multiple spectral channels to identify materials on the basis of the way they reflect sunlight.

SIR-B data experienced technical problems while flying over the area, but it showed forest clearing near Alta Floresta and Sinop in northern Matto Grosso. Near Sinop, some 200 farming plots were evident. They are generally long, in lattice-like patterns, and in narrow clearings parallel to one another. Most plots are smaller than 200 hectares indicating small operations of family farmers. In contrast, there are several clearings of 6,000 hectares. Clearings of such a large scale usually are for commercial cattle grazing. It is becoming more essential that information on vegetation structure and regrowth be available to help separate primary forest from secondary regrowth.

Thus, scientists have been able to witness through remote-sensing, which produces both two and three-dimensional pictures, the first-hand destruction of massive hectares of forests robbing nature of the last ecosystems for the survival of the Indian people. There is no doubt that large-scale environmental changes are being created by population influx and land

Figure 18.3
Destruction and deforestation of the Amazon forests threaten both the ecosystem and the survival of the Indian peoples. Photo by D. Hurtak.

development. Computer simulations based on extensive historical data suggest the Amazon's rainfall can be expected to decline radically as drainage and deforestation proceed; then as deforestation proceeds, reforestation becomes nearly impossible.

Brasil's former Minister of the Environment, Dr. Jose Lutzenberger, was the visionary who saw the role of interdependence between the Amazon and the world. His plan was for education, research and protection policies to create a realistic authority over environmental units in each of Brasil's twelve government ministries to form a "consensus strategy" for long-range preservation of both land and wildlife, but before long he was displaced from his position.

Reacting to worldwide concern over the devastation of the rainforest, many claim there is no need to worry. After all, burning forests in Amazonia only account for less than 20% of the total increase in atmospheric carbon dioxide (according to Prof. A. Goldemberg, University of Sao Paulo, Brasil). However, the burning of the rainforest is doing more than just increasing carbon dioxide. The Amazon is the "great heat factory of the world" with a daily energy turnover equal to some six million atomic bombs. One of the great ironies of the modern industrial society with its remote-sensing technologies is that we can now see planet Earth as a whole—as a living biosphere. Yet, down here, we continue to behave as if we were blind.

Looking at the Amazonia from a satellite perspective, we see that the air masses, as revealed by cloud movements, travel into central South America from the Atlantic, go west and hit the mountain chains of the Andes. There the flow splits into several branches. The central part rises over the mountains into the Pacific and continues west along the Equator, roughly following the convergence of the warm northern sea current, El Nino, with the cold Humboldt stream that comes from the South. These are systems of interconnected ocean streams and air streams which are responsible for the incredible richness of life in and above the waters of the west coast of South America

Figure 18.4
Satellite image of the San Francisco coastline. Image courtesy of NASA.

and where in the last two decades we have seen the serious "flip-overs" of weather that have caused overnight collapse of the fishing industry.

However, according to Lutzenberger, the air currents over the Amazon do not only affect South America. The currents connected with El Nino affect the weather pattern over Central and Southern Africa. Moreover, the air masses over the Amazon work like a giant vortex and spawn off air currents that are capable of traveling as far north as the eastern coast of North America which in turn merge with the Gulf Stream air which reaches and penetrates Northern and Central Europe and may be the cause of the "green vegetation" in northern Norway.

What will happen if the Brasilian rainforest disappears? The forest makes its own climate and is the result of that unique climate. What if devastation continues at the present rate? Most everything could be gone by the year 2025 AD. A hundred thousand square kilometers of primeval forest are cleared every year the results of destruction grow exponentially. Land the size of Portugal is slashed and burned every year. And the end will inevitably be: (1) a change in weather, (2) an increase of drought and desert, and (3) massive starvation for many peoples, regardless of background and world economics. With large land parcels being given away for exploitation, there is absolutely no way, even with Radam surveys, to oversee clearance. At the present time, 100 tons of topsoil are lost per hectare each year. The forests that are destroyed will take a thousand years to regenerate. With their destruction goes the refugia of a species diversity entirely preserved from the early periods of evolution—the Pleistocene era in our "present" time: with color morphs, strange and beautiful speciations, butterfly wings of color.

All of this is being steadily destroyed, and there is human tragedy as well. At least 87 Indian tribes have become extinct this century. Anthropologists have seen an overall Amazonian aborigine population decrease over the past 500 years from an estimated 6.8 million to the present 125,000. Anthropologist Emilio Moran cites disturbing research indicating the decline of the Parakana and Nambiquara indigenous groups within very short periods of time due to the influences of outside companies, ranchers, and road workers whom the Indians call the "termite people."

As highways and small farmers who are simply trying to create a livelihood intensify their own slash-and-burn techniques throughout the Amazon basis— and more and more ruropoli (frontier family villages) of some 48-1,000 people spring up in various locations throughout the Amazon—the forests are razed, the inroads flooded, the malaria vector is strengthened,

Figure 18.5
Aboriginal Brazilians' lives are severely threatened by the continuing destruction of the Amazon. Photo courtesy of Maria Thereza Sampaio.

intense soil erosion occurs, and the river fish species die out. The tragedy is that most of these small family plots created by hundreds of thousands of new inhabitants are only able to sustain crops for a limited number of years because of the rainforest terrain. Therefore, these farmers must move on and find new land to utilize. What happens to their old plots of land? They become wastelands with small brush, because the original trees cannot grow back due to their root structures and because the soil has been destroyed and removed.

In the wake of vast devastation throughout the Amazon, only now has the revelation of global atmospherics impressed biologists. The Amazon is the critical link in the Earth's carbon dioxide clearing house. Furthermore, Amazonian Indians and forest species possess the richest repository of native wisdom and potential medical, and technological plant products of any other region of the planet. But the metaphor of human disruption—since the sixteenth century—is fully at work in Brasil. The country is the vortex of ecological imperialism and new deforestation. A generation of embattled conscience has arisen in Central and South American writers who have responded to the political and moral crises with an anguished outpouring due to the mismanagement of such critical factors as: population growth, political agendas, and regional economics. Nobel Prize winner Garcia Marquez (*The Autumn of the Patriarch*) and Vargas Llosa (*The War of the End of the World*) are but a few of the many testimonies of this anguish.

Our time has now come to work for new cooperation in this and other critical environmental regions. Our species is the only one to lay claims to being able to influence the make up of the natural world. We long ago drew up the battle lines. Today, that struggle is most dangerously pronounced in the tropics, where soil is in short supply and human food is at a premium. The Amazon contains some 550 million hectares of rain forest, 3.5 million square kilometers, nearly half of the Earth's water moisture, easily a million plant and animal species. In but 2 hectares of

Amazon forest, 173 floral species have been discovered on a base of 900 metric tons of living biomass. In short, for several thousand years, life has been fashioned according to its evolutionary laws and in the Amazon basin archaeological relics suggest an early habitation at the mouth of the Amazon dating back as far as 5,000 years. As a part of Eden on earth, its destruction may also signify the end of life as we know it. It is our time to make the change—to work together to expand the lifetime of the Amazon Basin in Brasil—so that there would be no end of real civilization, but a wise and practical preparation for the opening of the high frontier in meeting with other cultures and cosmic civilization in the 21st century.

1. Chomentowski, Salas, W., B., & Skole, D. L., (1994) "Landsat Pathfinder" project advances deforestation mapping, GIS World 7.4:34-38.
2. Elachi, Charles (1987) *Introduction to the physics and techniques of remote sensing*. J. A. Kong (Ed.), John Wiley & Sons, 413 pp.
3. Grainger, A. (1993) *Controlling Tropical Deforestation*. Earthscan, London.
4. Hess, L. L., Melack, J. M., Filoso, S., & Wang, Y. (1995) "Delineation of inundated area & vegetation along the Amazon floodplain with the SIR-C synthetic aperture radar," *IEEE Trans. Geosci. Remote Sensing*. **Vol. 33,** no. 4, pp. 896-904.
5. Kasischke, E., Melack, J. & Dobson, M.C. (1997) "The Use of Imaging Radars for Ecological Applications-A Review," *Remote Sensing of Environment*. **Vol. 59,** no. 2, pp. 141-156.
6. Laurance, William F., Laurance, Susan G., Ferreira, Leandro V., Rankin de Merona, Judy M., Gascon, Claude, & Lovejoy, Thomas E. (1997) "Biomass Collapse in Amazonian Forest Fragments," *Science*. 278: 1117-1118.
7. Mann, M.E., Bradley, R.S., & Hughes, M.K. (1998) "Global-scale temperature patterns & climate forcing over the past six centuries," *Nature*. 392: 779-787.
8. Saatchi, S., Soares, J. V. & Alves, M. (1997) "Mapping deforestation & land use in Amazon Rainforest by using SIR-C imagery" *Remote Sensing of Environment*. **Vol 59,** no. 2, pp.191-202..
9. Saatchi, S. S., Nelson, B., Podest, E. & Holt, J. (2000) "Mapping land cover types in the Amazon Basin using 1 km JERS-1 mosaic," *Int. J. Remote Sensing*. **Vol. 21,** no. 6 & 7, pp. 1201-1234.
10. Wang, Y., Hess, L.L., Filoao, S., & Melack, J.M. (1995) "Understanding the radar backscattering from flooded and nonflooded Amazonian forests: Results from canopy backscatter modeling," *Remote Sensing of Environment*. **Vol 54,** no. 3, pp. 324-332.

19

Understanding Living Energy & Our Living Environment

J.J. Hurtak, Ph.D., Ph.D.

Environmentalists have found that there is a mosaic in nature that works like the mosaic of the body. The more types of monitoring data—air, water, sediment, and so on—that we accept, the clearer it becomes that we are actually part of a living mosaic that can lead to a greater structuring of our life with the species forms around us. In this greater mosaic, improvements are available not only for life sustaining processes but for evolutionary upgrades to occur.

Environmental issues have evolved themselves for a number of reasons. First, the phenomenon of environmentalism in the late 1960s and early 1970s saw the arrival of many new interest groups raising new issues against a background of a very rapid increase in public interest in environmental matters. Second, while not a new problem, the environment was redefined in the 1970s in a more holistic manner requiring holistic thinking. Finally, expounding on the holistic view in the 1980s, environmental issues reached a greater cross-section of planetary inhabitants with global implications.

The recent eruptions of volcanic activity in key areas worldwide have convinced many experts that by the end of the next century the earth's temperature will

Understanding Living Energy & Our Living Environment

Figure 19.1
Research team at work in Antarctica. Photo by the Academy For Future Science.

rise 2-9° above the present global average. This will result not only in massive thawing of the ice sheets at the polar areas but will lead to the disruption of the planetary and environmental balances of life. In looking at the earth's remaining environmental reserves from the viewpoint of remote-sensing, it is clear that there are built-in space-time mosaic patterns that can also be used for the renewal of life even down to the various layers of micro-intelligence. This relates directly to the fact that species composition can remain in an approximate steady-state at the landscape scale despite drastic local fluctuations of weather. In a landscape steady-state, forces of community "regeneration" (that is, succession by the life forms) counterpoises "degenerative" disturbance processes. This steady-state may persist until modified by larger climactic change, species migrations, or evolution, all acting in a living drama at longer time scales. Our living environment can, therefore, be understood as a heterogeneous and ever-changing entity that nevertheless maintains a constancy and predictability of disturbance and recovery patterns in time scales meaningful to human beings and other life forms. However, these processes that maintain spatial-temporal heterogeneous life in whole ecosystems are generally not functional in small, isolated nature preserves. A new generation of naturalists and futurists have recognized that a natural ecosystem must be large enough in extent to contain and maintain its characteristic species diversity and species composition.

Today, as natural landscape dynamics are

Figure 19.2
The Conch represents the mosaic of Life. Image courtesy of the Academy For Future Science.

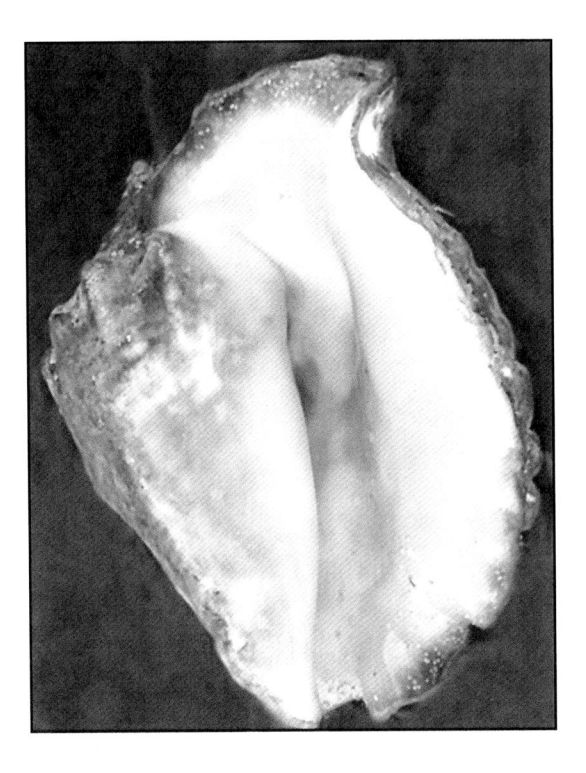

Understanding Living Energy & Our Living Environment

increasingly disrupted by the entry of more people who build artificial extensions into a living habitat without regard for the mosaic pattern of life, a growing number of individuals recognize the need to reach out to the environmental frontiers of each country in new ways. The reaching out is not only by stopping the use of toxic substances, or by considering the agents of change, but by focusing upon the renewal patterns of ecological history. The importance of knowing about the quality of the environment, improving the ecological habitats, and building environmental data bases is directly connected with the mosaic patterns in natural landscapes. These patterns naturally provide for their own sustenance and reseeding mechanisms if not severely disrupted.

Another aspect of preparing for our future is the recognition that our environment is a flexible biological hierarchy. Each of the levels in nature is subject to different forms of natural selection and random and deterministic perturbations. Hierarchical levels include genes and gene complexes, individual organisms, races and subspecies, species, communities, ecosystems, landscapes, biomes and the biosphere. Although some of these levels may be more real or manageable than others, our knowledge is not so complete that we can

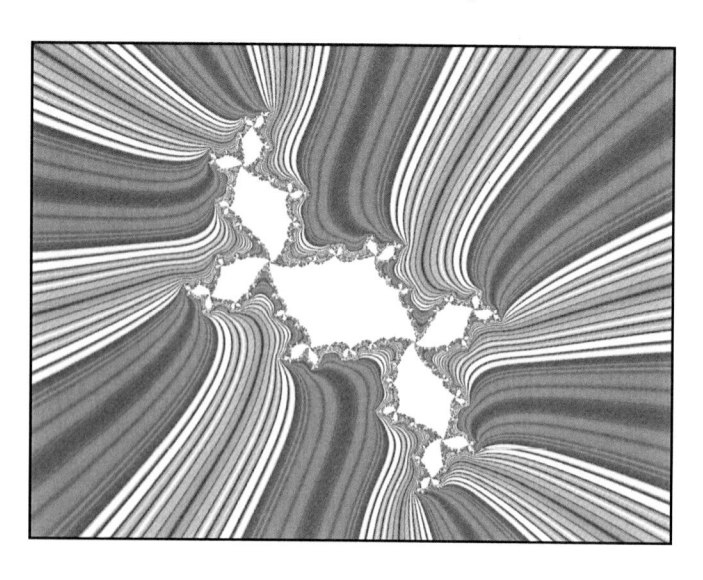

Figure 19.3
Fractals contain the inherent patterns of life.
"Evolving," by D. Hurtak (2001).

afford to disregard any of them. Simply put, wherever we look with a microscope or telescope we realize the integral and masterful designed array of interconnected hierarchies.[1]

To protect the full spectrum of biological diversity in a given landscape under change, the existing patterns have also revealed, through space-borne, multi-spectral analysis, subtle high quality buffers and interconnecting environmental designs by historic caretakers which allowed for the greater planning and restructuring of nature. In many areas of Mexico and South America vast corridors interconnect to form natural networks with a buffering network of preserves. The discovery and use of the natural network patterns helps us to examine its potential in contributing to the preservation of the regional bioata, flora and fauna, by minimizing artificial barriers and maximizing our living connectivity within a sustainable environment. A network can conceivably also facilitate the shifting of meaningful human habitats across the landscape by evaluating disturbance and recovery of each area, that is, by maintaining environmentally safe areas and corridors as sources of protection for a variety of intelligences in their regional and local refuge areas.

Here ecologists, environmentalists and anthropologists should weigh the living architecture of a biological mosaic as the background to the areas being managed for human development or for joint human/non-human survival. For example, in rural areas barriers to flow should be removed or circumvented along corridors whenever possible, by allowing, even in urban areas, the movement of animals and sheet flows of water to bypass the concrete developments. Development centers producing bottlenecks of flow, moreover, should be managed so as to constrain the flow of toxins and pollution that would be dangerous to the preserved areas.

In the end, pollution control involves engineering process development, commercial ventures and resource development that are appropriate for the environmental situation unique to each area and which emphasize the balance between new fuels and processes, water resources, and agricultural development so necessary for the food chain.

When it comes to a living environment, we are talking about an entire consciousness domain that has been misused. Unfortunately, we have seen few instances where the importance of holistic approaches have led to meaningful implementation of conservation by science and technology until the present time where a synoptic view of Mother Earth is provided. Without widespread participation by everyone that makes up the living mosaic, the human evolution must understand the short end of its enterprise. Fundamental environmental change does not come about through the effect of activists and specialists alone. In the truer sense, to understand environmental change from the inside, the global community must understand the inner workings of nature as well as the dynamics of the living mosaic itself.

By working together we can manage our energies and goals to be intolerant of habitat fragmentation by

Figure 19.4
We must consider and care for the future of our children. Photo by the Academy For Future Science.

providing for a plan that fundamentally seeks to use large-scale ecological patterns and processes meaningfully. In this way, species and ecosystem-level conservation can meet and minimize conflict, for we can simultaneously evaluate and participate with the entire biological hierarchy integrated by using the hierarchy design built into nature.

Environmental problems are no longer limited to the changes we are making on land, but the problems of pollution we have created in our ocean, air and sky. Technology to fuel our planet, until quite recently, has not taken into account the devastation to the environment. For example, we run air conditioners to make the internal environment comfortable. However, the pollutants put out by current air conditioners are actually increasing the temperature outside. Using this analogy we can clearly see the need not only to create the technology, but the "environmentally safe" or clean technologies, that will benefit planet earth.[2]

Thus, when we talk about environment, we must also include the energy-environment equation as revolving around practical advancements of clean energy use that can service the mainstream needs of humanity while protecting the fragile environment that must be sustained. Specifically, there are inventions available that make use of non-fossil energy sources so as to preserve our environment. In addition to traditional renewable energy sources, there are new approaches that could make use of the energy environment as a whole such as the possibility of using latent energy possibilities, namely, hydrogen energy, magnetohydrodynamics (MHD), or even the zero point energy fields (ZPF) concept and further exploration into the potential of so-called "cold fusion." All of these should be considered for potential pilot programs in alternative energy throughout the world as new energy sources which will shape the world environment in the 21st century.

Just as we need to take a new approach to Newtonian physics so also we must begin to grasp the unity of energy that exists throughout the universe. If we can free the human experience from its dependence upon the fossil fuel world which creates a complete disruption of the mosaic of life, and begin to produce a whole new stream of energy possibilities, we will begin to redefine the experience of evolution. Although many of these new energy possibilities may challenge the material domain of establishment science, whole new energy possibilities and productions will allow us to define new frontiers of life no longer limited to a singular planetary system. In addition, a second breakthrough will come when we understand and use the real forces of gravitation.

With this in mind, we can also equate the environmental crisis as not only an existing crisis, but as a challenge to bring us out from under the shadow of the dinosaur fossil fuel mentality and into a greater understanding of a higher mosaic of life—functioning even beyond planet earth. This goes back to the age-old idea that there is only one source of energy out of which all material is created. Ultimately, we realize that energy is connected with a spiritual approach to life and cannot be grasped as merely a phenomenon. We are living in a time in which we are also thinking about a new intellectual spirituality dawning beside technological advances.

Let us ponder on this. The use of purer forms of energy ultimately will bring about purer forms of insight and action, not encumbered by simple material survival, but capable of moving through the varied mundane problems of life. Thus, environmental problem-solving not only widens the arena of spiritual-social actions, but fosters genuine cross-cultural analysis and appreciation. The upward expansion of the multi-level mosaic way of thinking of environmental concerns brings about the use of an additional analytical unit which is made up not of localized individual interactions but also of a greater understanding of actions which are dependent for their success on operations across space and over considerable periods of time. Thus, the higher awareness of life should open the door to regional,

Figure 19.5
The higher awareness of life opens the visionary window to a greater understanding of ourselves and our environment.
Photo of Bryce Canyon, Bryce National Park, UT by L. Photiadis (1998).

national, and transnational sharing by means of the higher designs of a synoptic vision that use higher states of consciousness for problem-solving. New developments which are designed for the benefit of environmentalism, bring us into an awareness of a greater understanding of ourselves interacting with all life.

When we look at the roots of consciousness and the intellectual heritage of both the East and the West, we see there was always an interconnected cosmology of consciousness based upon the idea that we were to be co-evolutionists and co-engineers in this process of life on Mother Earth. In the West, the questions of spirituality and philosophy of consciousness have become connected with the control of new energy frontiers for new living environments. The test of the human race now will be to see if there is an effective overlap between consciousness evolution and scientific evolution.

The new image of man that is arising will hasten

the recognition that we are all interconnected and we all represent a powerful Life Force which is going through a transformation process. This is now taking shape before our eyes and in the not too distant future I believe we will see the results in a whole new condition of evolution which I call spacekind: intelligence that is totally free from the influence of limitation—both of consciousness energy as well as environmental energy which can survive on its on by virtue of readapting itself to the mechanisms of life throughout the universe in continuing the work of the Divine Author.

---

1. Dubois, René (1972) *The God Within*. New York: Scribner's Sons, pp. 46-72.
2. William, Clark L. & Munn, R.E. (Eds.) (1986) *Sustainable Development of the Biosphere*. International Institute for Applied Systems Analysis, Cambridge: Cambridge University Press, pp. 5-42.

20

Agriculture in Emerging Countries & Remote Sensing

Richard N. Quast, B.S.
C.P.S.Sc., University of
Wisconsin

Our understanding of the Earth's ecology accelerated dramatically in 1972 with the launching of the first successful imaging satellite. Since then numerous imaging satellites have been placed in orbit around the planet for many diverse applications. Now, satellites track disease-carrying mosquitoes in tropical regions, provide clues to the whereabouts of Noah's Ark, monitor El Nino's movements in the Pacific Ocean, and help the Indonesian tourism industry identify opportunities on the Trawangan islands off Lombok, the western most city in Indonesia.

All of these applications fall within the field of remote sensing, a relatively new technology for obtaining information about the properties of surfaces and objects from a distance. Remote sensing measures various physical characteristics of soils, rocks and plants by reflected or emitted electromagnetic radiation, acoustical or seismic waves, and magnetic and gravity force fields. The types of equipment employed may include single format cameras, multispectral cameras, synthetic aperture radar, as well as other advanced equipment. This article addresses the use of remote sensing technology in agriculture employing single format cameras to detect reflected

Agriculture in Emerging Countries & Remote Sensing

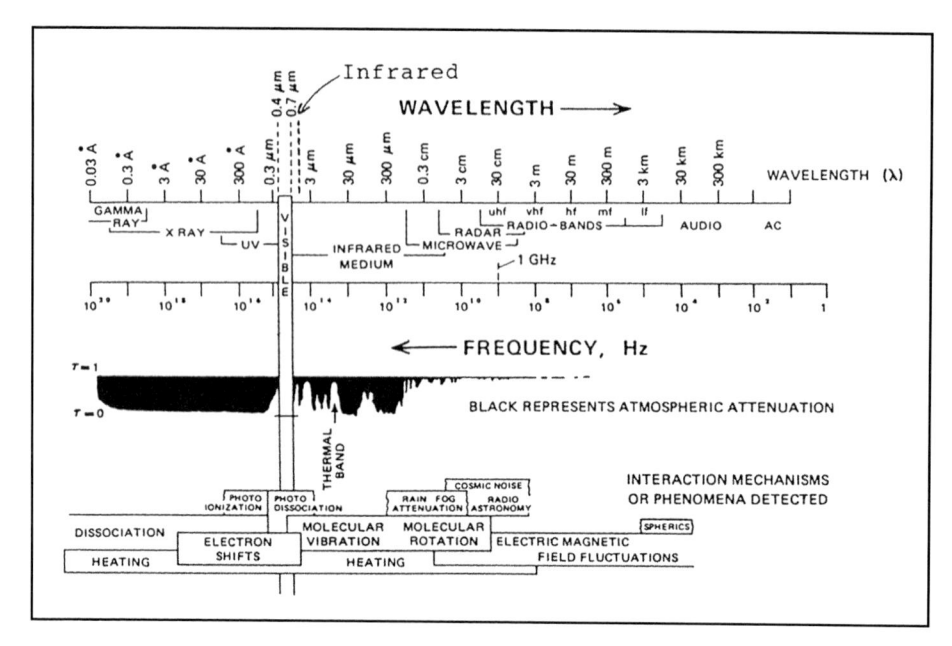

Figure 20.1 Diagram of the Electromagnetic Spectrum showing infrared band.

electromagnetic radiation (EMR), namely, the narrow band of infrared between wavelengths 0.7 m and 0.9 m which are just beyond the red end of the visible spectrum.[1] (See Figure 20.1) It should be noted that in the visible spectrum most healthy vegetation is green but in infrared it is reflected as red, which is the primal color of Earth.

Within the context of remote sensing, a long standing problem must be recognized: the gap in agricultural technology between the affluent and the emerging countries. Many factors have contributed to this gap and continue to perpetuate it, including cultural attitudes toward change, economic and political problems, and traditional farming practices. Despite these barriers, however, the potential benefits from this new technology and from others like sustainable agricultural and sound environmental practice, should encourage farmers to look at new ways of doing many routine farm tasks.

REMOTE SENSING AND AGRICULTURE

In developed countries, remote sensing technology is

Figure 20.2
Remote sensing technology is a rapid and effective way for farmers to assess crop and field conditions. Shown here: Illinois corn fields. Photo by L. Photiadis (1997).

being used extensively in agriculture as a rapid means of assessing crop and field conditions. For farmers using this technology, the benefits are timely, comprehensive assessments of the health of their crops. For example, early detection of insect infestations, diseases, nutrient deficiencies, drought, or flooding enables farmers to take the necessary steps to avert serious crop damage and financial loss.

In addition to these there are other applications of remote sensing that can save the farmer time and money, while providing greater accuracy than many traditional field practices, i.e., detecting variations in soils (which have a profound influence on plant growth), estimating crop production well before harvest, monitoring the effectiveness of irrigation and drainage systems, assessing damage caused by soil erosion, checking the condition of pastures, and making livestock counts.

Although many farmers in America and other affluent countries have been using this technology to their benefit for the past decade, it has not been readily available to farmers in emerging countries because it has been expensive, hard to acquire, and difficult to interpret. Over the past couple of years, however, much has changed in this respect, thanks to the launching of commercial satellites like Space Imaging's IKONOS, ESSI's Probe 1, the soon-to-be-launched Orbview-3, and QuickBird. CATERRA Geo products from Space Imaging are available from essentially any geographic location in the world in 1-meter panchromatic and 4-meter multispectral images. Image snapshots can be viewed and ordered for a small fee, but receiving them may take a week or more.[2]

HOW EMR REMOTE SENSING WORKS

Whether taken from satellites, aircraft, or at ground level, remote sensing, using reflected solar electromagnetic radiation, has proven to be one of the

Figure 20.3
Transection of a leaf, showing the different parts of the cell. Image courtesy of the Academy For Future Science.

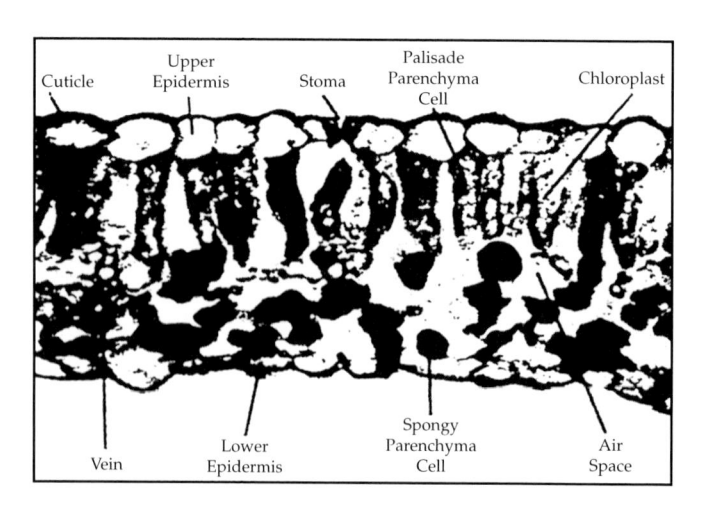

most effective measures for identifying crops and for determining their health. For example, the reflected light from corn leaves has optical properties which yield a spectral "signature" distinct from all other plants. Cell size and shape within the leaf can also indicate plant maturity, stress, and vigor, from which can be drawn certain inferences on the condition of the crop. (See Figure 20.3)

Satellite Imagery is particularly useful in mapping large areas covering hundreds of square kilometers. Although the spatial resolution is lower than that achieved with airborne or ground level imagery, it is relatively affordable, even for farmers in emerging countries. Such imagery can be used to get a general idea of the conditions in a specific bio-region.

Airborne Imagery is preferable when a higher spatial resolution is desired than that obtained from satellite imagery. To this end, videography or small-format aerial photography is useful. Recent advances with hand-held digital color infrared (CIR) cameras[3] with a spectral sensitivity of 0.4 m to 1.0 m have greatly simplified the acquisition of high resolution imagery. Using this system, data is recorded on a removable hard drive compatible with most computers. When interfaced with a color printer, high resolution images can be produced within minutes, facilitating ground truthing procedures. This method also permits delineating on a print-out the areas requiring corrective measures such as integrated pest management techniques, applications of fertilizers, or additional irrigation. Integrating a geographic position system (GPS) to the camera, the precise location and time the images were taken can also be recorded.

Small aircraft, such as the high wing Cessna 172, provide an excellent platform for obtaining videography or aerial photos because they can fly from grass airstrips common in many rural areas. Such aircraft can also be flown at very slow speeds, permitting a window to be opened or a door removed, to facilitate the taking of images. Because of poor ground transportation systems in many emerging countries, small aircraft are readily available and can be hired for this specific purpose.

Ground Truthing is the process of verifying in the field what is seen in the imagery, whether taken from a satellite, aircraft, or at ground level. This usually involves collecting samples of plant foliage or soils for analysis or by directly identifying some anomaly in the field in order to establish a 'signature' or unique characteristic which identifies the object or condition. If the imagery is obtained from aircraft, additional data must be recorded, such as the date, time of day, amount of sunlight, flight elevation above ground level or the forest canopy, and any unique atmospheric conditions like mist or smoke.

Since most remote sensing research in agriculture has been done with crops in the temperate climate and most emerging countries are located in tropical and semi-tropical climates, farmers there will need to establish signatures of their crops before they can really benefit from this technology. This will involve coordinating the acquisition of imagery with ground truthing procedures for each crop in their local bio-regions.

SEVERAL CIR PROJECTS IN LATIN AMERICA[4]

The following are summaries of several projects performed in Latin America using airborne CIR imagery and ground truthing procedures:

Corn Production Estimates A survey was made of Guatemala's corn production six weeks before harvesting. Interpretation of the color infrared imagery and subsequent ground truthing data revealed that corn production during the season would be 30 per cent below that of normal season. Having been forewarned of the impending short fall, the government had adequate time to take steps to avert a serious food shortage.

Applied Research In Sugar Cane Several sugar cane plantations in Venezuela and Central America were

Figure 20.4
Remote sensing technology used in sugar plantations in Central America helps to determine sucrose levels in sugar cane.

surveyed with color infrared imagery to determine whether it was possible to correlate color tones in the imagery with sucrose levels in the sugar cane. Field tests were run to determine the percent of sucrose in plants within each of the tonal variations. From this information it was learned that specific color tones corresponded to sucrose levels in increments of 2 percent. In plotting this information on the farm plan, it was possible to delineate mature plants from less mature ones, and growers were able to increase their production of raw sugar by approximately 15 percent.

Banana Farm Management Practices Surveys of banana plantations in Honduras and Costa Rica provided management with a powerful tool for monitoring the conditions of their banana plantings. Strong tonal contrasts in the imagery effectively revealed such agronomic problems as infestations of Sigatoka disease, nitrogen deficiency, dry triangles, wind damage, tip over, irregular spacing between plantings, open canopies, poorly drained areas, and many more features difficult to detect from the ground.

Soil Surveys One of the most useful applications of color infrared imagery has been for making soil surveys of areas with a vegetative cover. Slight variations in soil moisture are immediately reflected in the covering vegetation. By correlating tonal variations in vegetation with soil texture, large tracts of land can be surveyed with high precision in a fraction of the time required by traditional methods. Bare soils were best surveyed using black and white infrared imagery.

Mariculture Research Shrimp ponds built adjacent to estuaries in Ecuador were surveyed in an attempt to correlate shrimp size with biomass density in the ponds. Investigations revealed that as biomass density increased, the color of the water changed gradually from pink to dark red. Samplings of the ponds showed a direct relationship between tonal changes of the water and shrimp size, which in turn had a direct bearing on determining the best time to harvest.

Plant Disease Detection A remote sensing survey of an African oil palm plantation in Honduras disclosed an infestation of crown disease in 10 percent of the farm. In the CIR imagery, diseased palms showed slightly bluish discoloration in the center of the crown. Through early detection it was possible to remove the infected palms before the disease could spread to neighboring palms. No other methods are feasible for detecting this disease because the trees average 35 feet in height and the disease is not visible in its early stages from ground level.

Timber Surveys Airborne CIR imagery proved to be the only economical way to locate a commercial species of trees in the rainforests of Belize and El Peten. Having previously determined the signature of the desired species at 10,000 feet above the forest canopy, the subsequent survey located nearly every tree of that species within an area of 200 square kilometers.

Coffee Plantations Color and CIR imagery were taken of several coffee plantations in Mexico to study the condition of the shade trees and the new coffee plantings. A mosaic of each farm was made from the color imagery,

Figure 20.5
Color and CIR imagery used in coffee plantations in Mexico helps to determine the condition of the shade trees and the plantings.

providing an excellent map of each farm. The CIR imagery provided information on the health of new coffee trees and detected open spaces in the shade tree canopy.

CONCLUSION

Remote sensing technology is a tool for doing many traditional tasks better, cheaper, and faster. Farmers in emerging countries can now narrow the technology gap between themselves and farmers in affluent countries by using affordable satellite imagery. For higher resolution, airborne imagery using the new hand-held CIR digital cameras enable farmers to enhance production by monitoring their fields and crops in near real time. Because conditions in the field change rapidly, ground truthing should follow soon after the acquisition of imagery. Accuracy in interpreting CIR imagery is directly proportional to the accuracy of ground truthing. When in doubt of some anomaly observed in the imagery, farmers should always verify it in the field. The only thing limiting the discovery of new applications for this technology is the imagination.

1. Reeves, R.G. (1975) *Manual of Remote Sensing*. Falls Church: VA: The American Society of Photogrammetry, pp. 54 & 104.
2. Source obtained from: www.spaceimaging.com.
3. This is the Eastman Kodak Company's Digital Color Infrared Camera.
4. Files of Remote Sensing-Engineering, Ltd. 1970 to 1984, & PAAC, 1995 to 1997.

21

Laser Remote Sensing of Forest & Crops in Genetic-Rich Tropical Areas

J.J. Hurtak, Ph.D., Ph.D.

[*Originally published in International Archives of Photogrammetry and Remote Sensing, Vol. XXIX, 1992, ISPRS, Washington, D.C.*]

INTRODUCTION

Optical remote sensing from airborne operations can be either active, by inducing a distinctive response through a broad-band or selective stimulus, or passive, by purely spatial and spectral analysis of reflected light.

Active monitoring of environmental changes, terrain profile, water abundance, gas temperature and concentration for various molecules, clouds and other parameters of special relevance to forest studies, have been carried out using various laser techniques. Purely passive spatial and multispectral analysis of LANDSAT and SPOT data have also provided valuable tools for remote sensing of forest areas (Hurtak, 1986).

Helped by field studies, both techniques can be used to classify land use mainly as forest, cleared areas, pasture, and secondary growth vegetation. These four main classes are, however, highly variable and transitional into each other. For example, pasture can be only grass or a mixture of grass, crops, soil, and slash. This further complexity lowers the analysis confidence factor and even prohibits a finer analysis, such as crop type determination or species monitoring.

However, there is a need for more information than current land usage analysis can provide. Crop estimates, spread of plant disease, control of illegal crops, selective deforestation, crop species abundance profile, and other detailed vegetation data, are highly needed on a reliable, short-time basis. In the Amazon region, collecting the detailed vegetation data can be even more challenging because of the genetic variety observed even in same plant species. Furthermore, the inaccessibility and vastness of the majority of the Amazon region forest and farm areas make it mandatory to use remote sensing methods, because field analysis would not be feasible.

This paper deals with measurement techniques and issues pertinent to the remote sensing of finer vegetation data, by using laser induced fluorescence (LIF), both differential and excitation-selective.

PLANT LUMINESCENCE

Lasers, by inducing fluorescence in plants, can be used to monitor plant species, through its signatures in multiple wavelengths. Yentsch and Menzel (1963) showed that a fluorescence technique could be used to determine the concentration of *chlorophyll a* with phytoplankton. The fluorescence time is short, close to a nanosecond. Many plants demonstrate high spectral absorption in the 430nm-575nm within the violet and blue visible spectrum. *Chlorophyll a* molecule P_{680} is

Figure 21.1
Yentsch & Menzel (1963) used their laser fluorescence technique to determine the chlorophyll *a* concentration within phytoplankton. Shown below: four types of phytoplankton.

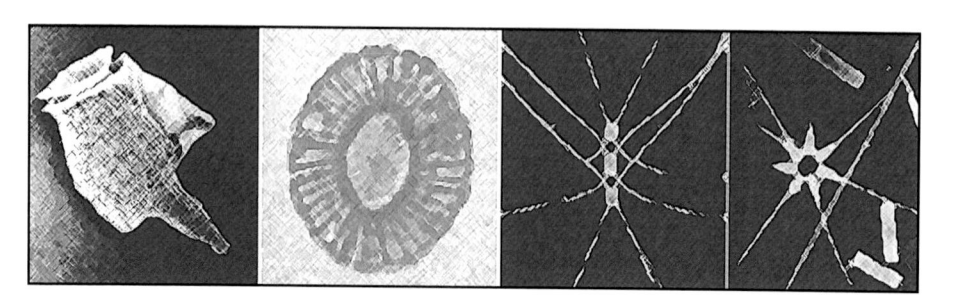

Figure 21.2
Graph showing the wavelength in nm for the fluorescence of a chlorophyll a molecule to be detected. Image courtesy of the Academy For Future Science.

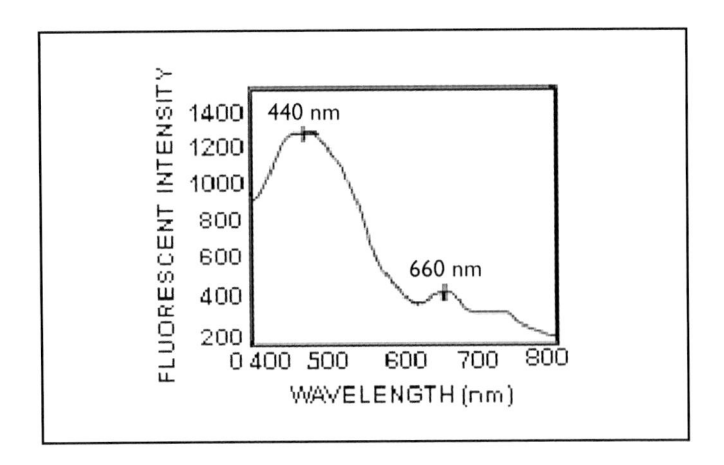

detected between 650-685 nm and its return fluorescence can be used to measure the efficiency of photosynthesis.

Plants also fluoresce in the presence of UV wavelengths (300-380 nm) from pigments other than *chlorophyll a*. Bands from 530 nm-575 nm can be used to locate paved surfaces and minerals such as iron in rocks and soil. Bands of 770 nm-810 nm show cellular arrangement and water content.

Chlorophyll a generally shows little variation over different types of leaf, although chlorophyll combines with different proteins to form chloroplasts where one leaf cell can contain 50 chloroplasts. Four kinds of chlorophyll exist (a-d), with *chlorophyll b* absorption peak in the 480 nm region. Leaf pigments of carotenoid, and anthocyanin are relevant in determining plant types. The presence of carotenoids appears at 460-500nm. Absorption by anthocyanin is within similar wavelengths of 400-550 nm, both far shorter than the P_{680} chlorophyll peak.

Visible pulses from argon or dye lasers with powers in milliwatts are known to excite chlorophyll and phycoerythrin (a red pigment phycobilin). The difficulty has been in determining calculations for reflectance applicable to a majority of plants due to their complex multi-layered structure (i.e., monocotyledonous, dicotyledonous) containing both scattering and absorbing materials. Willstatter and Stoll (1918) explained plant reflectance based on light at the cell-wall-air interface of mesophyll tissue. Another approach tested is to treat the leaf as a scattering and absorbing turbid medium (Yamada, 1991) using the KMT theory (Kubelka-Munk theory) of modeling light in a multilayered object.

A dicot leaf can be composed of as many as six layers, i.e., two waxy external cuticular layers, an upper and lower epidermal layers, a mesophyll layer, and a palisade tissue layer. The cuticle layers are composed of cutin and contain no pigment; hence no absorption, whereby the sum of reflectance and transmittance of the layer is equal to unity. The palisade tissue layer containing pigments and chlorophyll is densely packed allowing negligible scattering. The mesophyll layer contains the absorbing and scattering materials such as chlorophyll, other pigments, and cells that are uniformly distributed in them, according to their unique optical properties. Calculations are best gained from analysis of both the palisade and mesophyll layers.

FLORESCENCE STUDIES FOR CORN CROPS (MONOCOT)

The monocots can be differentiated from dicots by virtue of having a higher fluorescence intensity at 440 nm than the fluorescence intensity 675 nm-740 nm from the *chlorophyll a* molecule P_{680}. Present evidence

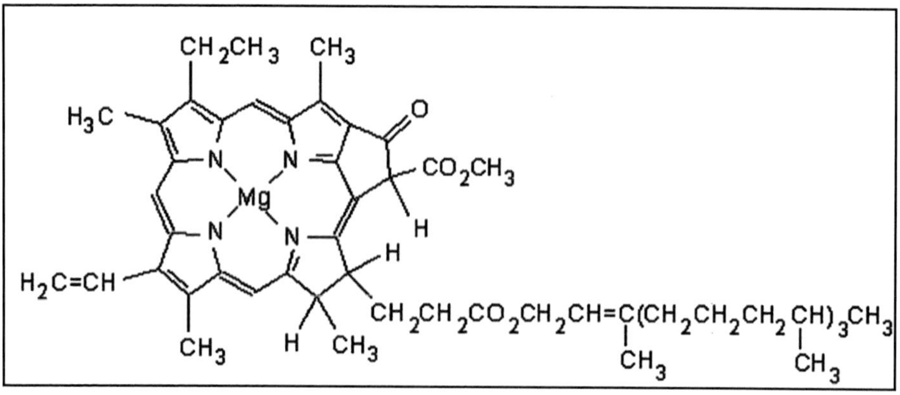

Figure 21.3
Molecular structure of Chlorophyll a. Image by the Academy For Future Science.

indicates that the fluorescence in the 675 nm-740 nm range may also determine different plant types by the working of two different photosystems. In one photosystem, the *chlorophyll a* molecule P_{680} peaks as previously described. In the second photosystem, the *chlorophyll a* molecule P_{700} peaks which may not be a unique molecule but a dimer of two *chlorophyll a* molecules in association with special proteins in the membrane. Both systems can occur within a plant simultaneously.

Analysis can be made thus by measuring reflectance and transmittance integrated over a hemisphere at each wavelength. For the *chlorophyll a* molecule P_{680} wavelength from λ_0(875 nm) to λ_x(650 nm) can be used. A minimum of three bands of close proximity best determines the scattering coefficient and the slope of the peak. This peak range eliminates the contribution from other kinds of scattering and absorbing materials within the leaf so one can calculate the chlorophyll content per unit area.

The results are aimed at confirming the spectral absorption coefficient of chlorophyll pigment with maximum peaks at ~440 and ~680 nm, as well as the absorption coefficient of other pigments contained in a leaf.

According to Yamada, by selecting wavelengths with large absorption coefficients, one loses accuracy at large chlorophyll contents and gets accuracy at small chlorophyll contents. By using wavelengths with small absorption coefficients, one can achieve relatively lower accuracy over the whole range. Wide bandwidths usually reduce errors in the reflectance and transmittance measurements. However, they also reduce the linearity between absorption coefficient and pigment content, especially when measuring the slope of the peak (Yamada, 1991).

LASERS

Candidate lasers are the solid-state lasers such as the Nd:YAG (532 nm-3 µm) pulsed from 100-200 Hz proven effective for measuring *chlorophyll a*. Other possible laser wavelengths have been used, but for spaceborne lidar Nd:YAG currently offers the most developed technology. The 355 nm is sufficiently short to be dominated by Rayleigh scattering. The 1064 nm wavelength is sufficiently long to be dominated by aerosol particle scattering in the lower troposphere, with poor noise properties from available APD detectors. The 532 nm wavelength is suitable for both aerosol and molecular scattering having good detector characteristics.

Both flashlamp-excited or diode-array excited Nd lasers can be used, to provide the necessary S/N ratio. The lasers and accompanying equipment can be assembled as mobile land units or airborne devices. In the case of choice, as airborne devices whenever possible, the equipment can be flown by helicopter or plane and must be light-weight and sturdy.

In addition solid-state lasers, the TEA CO_2 laser at up to 11 µm can be operated at PRFs of up to 300-400 Hz with pulse energies of a few hundred mJ.

LIDAR FOR AIRBORNE REMOTE SENSING

Monitoring of crops and environmental changes can be performed from airborne operations to provide large scale surveillance uses topographic lidar based on high S/N ratio. In studying soil or topography, each laser pulse can be used for a unique range measurement and waveform data.

Essential in airborne monitoring interpretation is aircraft pointing attitude data for range measurements, recovery of accurate surface elevation, and assignment of the elevation data to the correct Earth surface location. Laser altimeter signal strength depends on laser pulse power backscatter from the target surface and collected by the receiver telescope. Competing processes are optical background noise and detector noise (Bufton, 1991).

For detecting soil, plant, and man-made surface features, the surface backscatter coefficient R varies due to the surface type, but can be approximated by R_λ ground=ρ/π, (Reagan, 1991) where ρ is the surface hemisphere or albedo with an albedo percentage value

Figure 21.4
The use of the ER-2 aircraft is another remote sensing technique that provides large scale surveillance of topographic areas. Image courtesy of NASA.

of 4-5% for wet soils and 30-40% for concrete structures. Trees and crops have a 15% albedo value for 532 nm and 60% for 1064 nm wavelengths. Using two or three beam pulses, the beams can be transmitted simultaneously and then detected in order to derive backscatter profiles at these wavelengths.

DIFFERENTIAL-SAR DETECTION TECHNIQUE

During one measuring event, the plant species is selectively excited by a narrow-band laser emission and fluoresces. The intensity dependent fluorescence band and the fluorescence decay time must be measured.

Because of the relative movement between source and target and because of the non-specular nature of the fluorescence, if the fluorescence radiation is collected by a line detector then the total yield is very low. Also, if the detection method does not compensate for wind, moisture, background fluorescence from unwanted species, angle of absorption, etc., then the measurement is masked by important calibration factors that are time-varying and weather dependent.

The LIF method being reported in this paper,

Figure 21.5
View of earth's surface from SAR monitor. Image courtesy of NASA.

proposes to solve both problems by a combination of Synthetic-Aperture Radar (SAR) signal processing with differential fluorescence measurement.

Analogous to SAR, the receptor is a bi-dimensional array of point detectors, connected (in parallel in each row and with a computer controlled delay for each row) to a series of summing units that coherently adds the light intensity collected in each point to a point further in time. The coherence is maintained between source-target velocity and summing point, achieving a synchronism between the time scan of the array and the areas scan of the target. This technique is also similar to the Time Delay and Integration (TDI), nowadays a common signal processing technique for CCD detectors [EGG&G, Sierra Scientific, and DALSA are the main manufacturers] in low-light level moving inspection systems. The analogy to SAR is the effective increase of the detector (antenna) area, by signal processing. Since the intensity addition is performed immediately upon detection, the S/N ratio is not largely influenced by the further processing stages.

After the SAR-type detection (with on-line signal processing), the signals are available in various bands as a function of the target scanlength for each fly-by coordinate. These bands are chosen to provide for a variety of differential combinations that can uniquely identify a particular species by its fluorescence spectra. With the time analysis of the differential combinations (based on the fluorescence lifetimes for each chosen bands of the particular species), a further discrimination factor is added as a time-correlation for each differential signal, in pairs. The time-correlation data reduces to a function of the target scanlength, which is the confidence level in 0% to 100% of finding the particular species in the target. The spatial resolution is a trade-off between sensitivity and background noise and can be adjusted by adding together one or more detector lines in each row.

The experiments under way to apply the above technique to an actual case have three main steps: (1) Modeling the method and calculating the actual laser/detector/electronics parameter; (2) Measuring the various differential spectra in the laboratory for typical plants of interest; and (3) Setting-up a first system for mobile or aerial use. The first step is being completed together with some sample measurements.

Discussion

This paper has presented a high-sensitivity method for detecting plant species in genetic-rich areas, with a LIF technique. The method is based on increasing the S/N ratio immediately upon reception by coherent addition of the multispectral fluorescence intensities, band for band, and by performing a ladder of cross-correlations of the time-dependent band signals, that takes into account the dynamics of the decay channels. The resulting signal is a function of the scanlength covered by the plane after the starting coordinate, and represents a series of confidence levels of finding the species along the flown line.

The application of this technique can lead to better

law-enforcement control of present issues such as illegal crop production and unlawful deforestation, as well as an improvement in agricultural planning and crop estimation.

---

1. Bufton, Jack L. *et al* (1991) "Airborne lidar for profiling of surface topography," *Optical Engineering.* **30**(1):72-77.
2. Ford, John *et al* (1986) "Satellite Radars for Gelogical Mapping in Tropical Regions," presented at the 5th Thematic Conference: "Remote Sensing for Exploration Geology," Reno, Nevada.
3. Hurtak, James (1986) "Airborne & Spaceborne Radar Images for Geology & Environmental Mapping in the Amazon Rainforest, Brasil," *Symposia Latino Americano De Sensoriamento Remoto.* **Vol. 1**, Gramado, Rio Grande do Sul, Brasil.
4. Reagan, John A. *et al* (1991) "Spaceborne lidar remote sensing techniques aided by surface returns," *Optical Engineering.* 30(1): 96-101.
5. Yamada, Norihide *et al* (1991) "Nondestructive measurement of chlorophyll pigment content in plant leaves from three-color reflectance and transmittance," *Applied Optics.* 30(27): 3964-3973.

22

The Quest to Terraform Mars

Desiree Hurtak, M.S.Sc.

In August 1996, NASA scientists publically announced that a meteorite discovered in Antarctica showed evidence of previous microbial life. Analysis of the meteorite's interior revealed the same gas and chemical ratio and composition that Viking had found on Mars, leading scientists to believe that the meteorite (see Figure 22.1) had originated on Mars thousands of years ago, and that Mars had once harbored life, however primitive.

Although controversy still surrounds this discovery (many scientists contend that the biological evidence in the material is not the "tubular structure of carbonates" left behind by some microscopic life form, but a set of geometries created by chemical outgasings within the rocks), scientists do agree that billions of years ago Mars was a more hospitable place, with conditions similar to those that gave rise to life on Earth. Viking and Mariner pictures of the Martian surface reveal dry river beds and drainage patterns that could only have been created by water flow (see Figure 22.2).

Today, temperatures on Mars are well below freezing most of the time, and no liquid water exists on the surface of the planet. Human travel to Mars in the

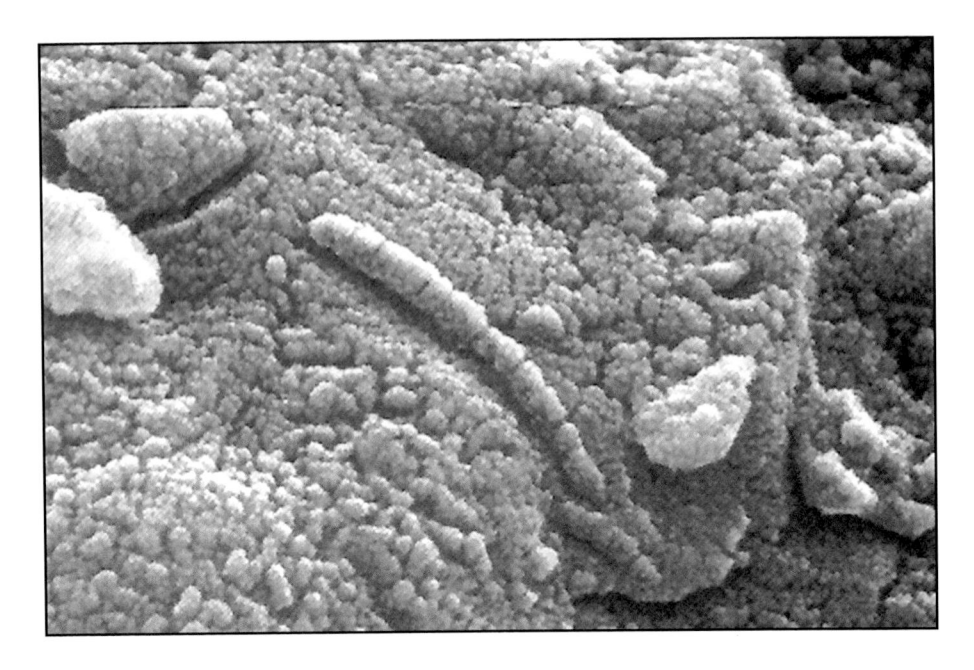

Figure 22.1
The Mars Meteorite: ALH84001. Image courtesy of NASA.

future will most probably reveal that "life" as we understand the term no longer exists there. If humans wish to colonize and eventually inhabit the red planet, two options exist: 1) We can build space stations and underground structures as habitations, wearing space suits every time we venture out on the surface, or 2) we can terraform the planet: introduce primitive life and transform the Martian atmosphere into a climate suitable for at least some life, perhaps similar to what it was in the far distant past.

Critics might say that terraforming is simply a human attempt at "playing God;" others might wonder if other planets throughout the universe could not have been likewise selected as the platform for life by some "superior intelligence" that deposited a few microbiological life forms in the right places only to return every hundred or thousand years to see how the planet was progressing.

Earth's history itself is one of terraforming. Scientists believe that carbon dioxide (CO_2) may have made up as much as 80% of Earth's atmosphere around 4.5 billion years ago, diminishing to 30-20% over the next 2.5 billion years. Free oxygen was scarce-to-nonexistent in this early atmosphere, and indeed poisonous to most of the anaerobic life-forms that existed.[1] Through some exceptional, even Divine "Force of Nature" photosynthetic organisms evolved that transmuted carbon dioxide into oxygen. Aerobic organisms, those that utilize oxygen, later evolved, and thus so did our "perfect" atmosphere. This atmosphere not only provides the right chemical elements for breathing, but gradually changed the earth's temperature to allow mammalian life to thrive.

The current Martian atmosphere is around 95% CO_2, 3% nitrogen and 2% argon, compared to Earth's atmosphere of 78% nitrogen, 21% oxygen and a 1% mixture of other gases—argon, water vapor, carbon dioxide, nitrous oxide, methane, chlorofluorocarbons (CFCs), and ozone—all of which (except argon) have

Figure 22.2
Ancient waterways on Mars. Image courtesy of NASA.

Table 22.1
Greenhouse Cases on Earth, showing how increases can be generated in less than 150 years.
From: Reporting on Climate Change: Understanding the Science, Environmental Health Center, A Division of the National Safety Council.

Gas	Concentrations in 1880	Concentrations in 1990 (assumed)	Concentrations in 2030 (projected)	Source of Increase
Carbon Dioxide (CO_2)	260-290 ppm	353 ppm	440-450 ppm	Fossil fuels, combustion, deforestation
Methane (CH_4)	1.2 ppm	1.72 ppm	2.5 - 2.6 ppm	Rice fields, cattle, landfill, fossil-fuel production
Nitrous Oxide (N_2O)	290 ppb	310 ppb	340 ppb	Nitrogenous fertilizer, biomass burning, refrigerators, deforestation, foams
CFC-12	0 ppb	0.48 ppb	1.0 - 1.1 ppb	Aerosol sprays, refrigerators, foams

influenced the regulation of the Earth's climate and brought the average surface temperature to a comfortable 15° C (60° F). What has become an important factor is how these "greenhouse" gases can rapidly increase, as we have seen in the 20th century manipulation, misuse and mismanagement of our ecosystem (see Table 22.1). Yet without most of these atmospheric gases, so crucial to life, Earth would be a cold and barren planet, at least 12° C (over 50° F) colder on the average.[2]

While the atmosphere of Mars closely resembles that of primitive Earth, scientists have confirmed that Mars today has water, carbon, oxygen, and nitrogen. More significantly for its temperature, Mars has an atmospheric pressure that is only 1% that of Earth's. For water to have flowed upon the Martian surface its atmosphere would have to have been thicker than it is today.

A primary factor in determining whether a planet like Mars can be terraformed is to determine if there exist (or could be introduced) sufficient greenhouse gases such as CO_2 to create an atmosphere that would warm the planet at least to the point above freezing. Most scientists believe that there is a sufficient amount of CO_2 on Mars, in its polar caps and in its surface soils (the regolith), to begin the terraforming process.

Two proponents of terraforming, Robert Zubrin (formerly a staff engineer at Lockheed Martin Astronautics in Denver, now president of his own company, Pioneer Astronautics) and Chris McKay (of NASA Ames Research Center), calculate that even a 4° C (7° F) rise in surface temperature on Mars would be sufficient to initiate a process that would eventually produce the overall necessary increase of 55° C (100° F) (current temperature on Mars is an average -60° C or -76° F), bringing the average surface temperature above the freezing point, permitting water to exist once again in liquid form on the surface, and transforming a thin atmosphere of 6-10 mb into one in the hundreds of mbars.[3]

Zubrin and McKay believe the place to start is with the placement of orbital solar reflective mirrors on Solar Power Satellites (SPS) that would circle the Martian poles and focus sufficient heat from the sun to begin warming the caps and releasing CO_2 into the

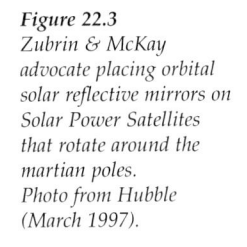

Figure 22.3
Zubrin & McKay advocate placing orbital solar reflective mirrors on Solar Power Satellites that rotate around the martian poles. Photo from Hubble (March 1997).

atmosphere.[4] This process would not destroy the polar caps but would melt a controlled amount, sufficient to start the thickening of the Martian atmosphere and global warming. Zubrin and McKay have also calculated that a temperature rise of 10° C (18° F) could further release significant amounts of CO_2 from the Martian regolith (surface soils) and increase atmospheric pressure by as much as 200-300 mbs.

Another way to introduce greenhouse gases on Mars would be by drilling to release water vapor. Scientists now suspect that the surface permafrost layer of Mars might contain pockets of water at a drilling depth of 800 meters. Liquid zones at 800 meters would release hot water as well as water vapor. Water vapor itself is an effective greenhouse gas and in its vaporous state has an important heat-trapping "greenhouse effect." If water is not found in sufficient quantities, drilling might find and release other gases that could assist the global warming.

Another means under discussion to introduce greenhouse gases is the establishing of factories on Mars that would principally produce greenhouses gases (CFCs) through the electrolytic and chemical methods which have contributed to "global warming" on Earth. Once Mars could support even the smallest forms of life, we would artificially follow the course that earth has taken, that is, introduce primitive bacteria that produce not only carbon, but methane and ammonia—strong greenhouse gases which could later be removed from the atmosphere when the planet had warmed sufficiently.

Although Zubrin and McKay estimate that Mars would only reach an atmospheric pressure close to that of Earth's in 1,500 to 2,500 years, this is not an outlandish time frame. Man could live and work on the planet during the process of terraforming. In fact, with the proper implementation of all four factors—mirrors, drilling, factory-produced gases (CFCs), and bacteria—it could conceivably take less than 500 years for humans to be able to walk on Mars without a space suit, wearing only a small "scuba-type" breathing apparatus around their mouths.

Once the Martian atmosphere has thickened and temperatures have risen above freezing, the final stage of terraforming can begin. At that time, in addition to bacteria, primitive plants are to be introduced to aid in transforming the abundant carbon dioxide in the atmosphere into the oxygen necessary for more advanced forms of terrestrial life. This process could take over 100,000 years, with established organisms slowly removing CO_2 from the atmosphere through the photosynthetic use of sunlight. Sufficient greenhouse gases would have to be present to contain the heat generated during this process and prevent the planet from cooling once again. Gradually, the oxygen content would reach a level where humans could breathe, a process that occurred on Earth several billion years ago. More advanced plants could not be introduced until the atmosphere contained enough oxygen and nitrogen for their survival.

Terraforming is not an impossibility; humans begin the process and nature completes the majority of the work. Terraforming only becomes a doubtful possibility if Mars lacks sufficient reserves of CO_2, water and nitrogen, elements which are essential for life as we know it. But Mars seems to have an abundance of these important elements and, as McKay sees it, terraforming would help Mars revert to an earlier state when microbial life flourished, as evidenced in the Mars meteorite. Of course, if life currently exists on Mars in any form, no matter how small, we would not want to disturb its evolutionary process and must keep a "hands off" approach. However, if no life currently exists there, why not make it a better place—not only for human generations to come, but for all the other exobiological expressions of life in the universe that may surprise us with a new definition of life.

---

1. *"Greenhouse Gases: Some Basics"* Reporting on Climate Change: Understanding the Science, Environmental Health Center, A

Division of the National Safety Council, 1025 Connecticut Avenue, NW, Suite 1200, Washington, DC 20036.
2. Zubrin, Robert (1997) *The Case for Mars.* New York: Touchstone.
3. Earth's atmosphere is calculated at 14.7 lbs/in2 or about 1,1013mb. Also Nadis, Steve (1994) "Mars: The Final Frontier," *New Scientist.* February 5, 1994, **Vol. 141,** No.1911, p. 28.
4. McKay, C., Kastings, J. & Toon, O. (1991) "Making Mars Habitable," *Nature.* 352:489-496.

23

Existing Space Law Concepts & Legislation Proposals

J.J. Hurtak, Ph.D., Ph.D.

Condensed from the paper delivered at the Mars Society Conference in Boulder, Colorado, August 15, 1998. With "outer space" daily becoming less of an abstract notion and more of a cultural reality, the utilization of "near space" must be addressed on a practical level. In the wake of successful Mars fly-overs and landings, humanity must consider the government and management of regions no longer reachable only in imagination, but reachable and exploitable by man and his various technologies. An equitable and binding code of behavior is applicable to all who venture into these realms.

Space Law requirements have been proposed by the United Nations for the human settlement, scientific discovery, and industrial explorations on the terrestrial moon and on Mars. Brought to the United Nations General Assembly by the Committee on Peaceful Uses of Outer Space (COPUOS), currently composed of 61 members, nation-states have enacted five treaties to provide and enforce procedures in the human experience of outer space:

> 1. (1967) *The Treaty on the Principles Governing the Activities of States in the Exploration and Use*

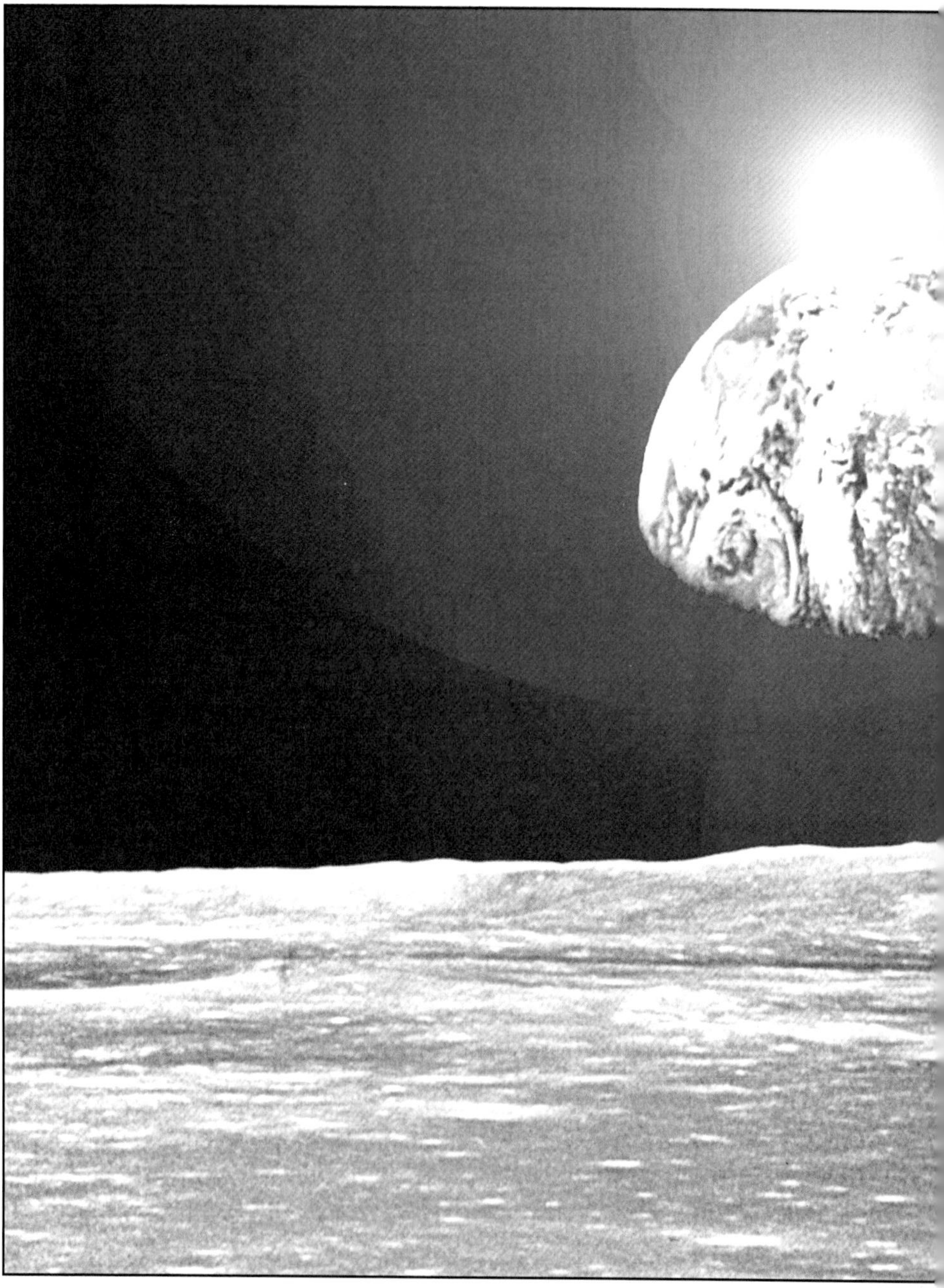

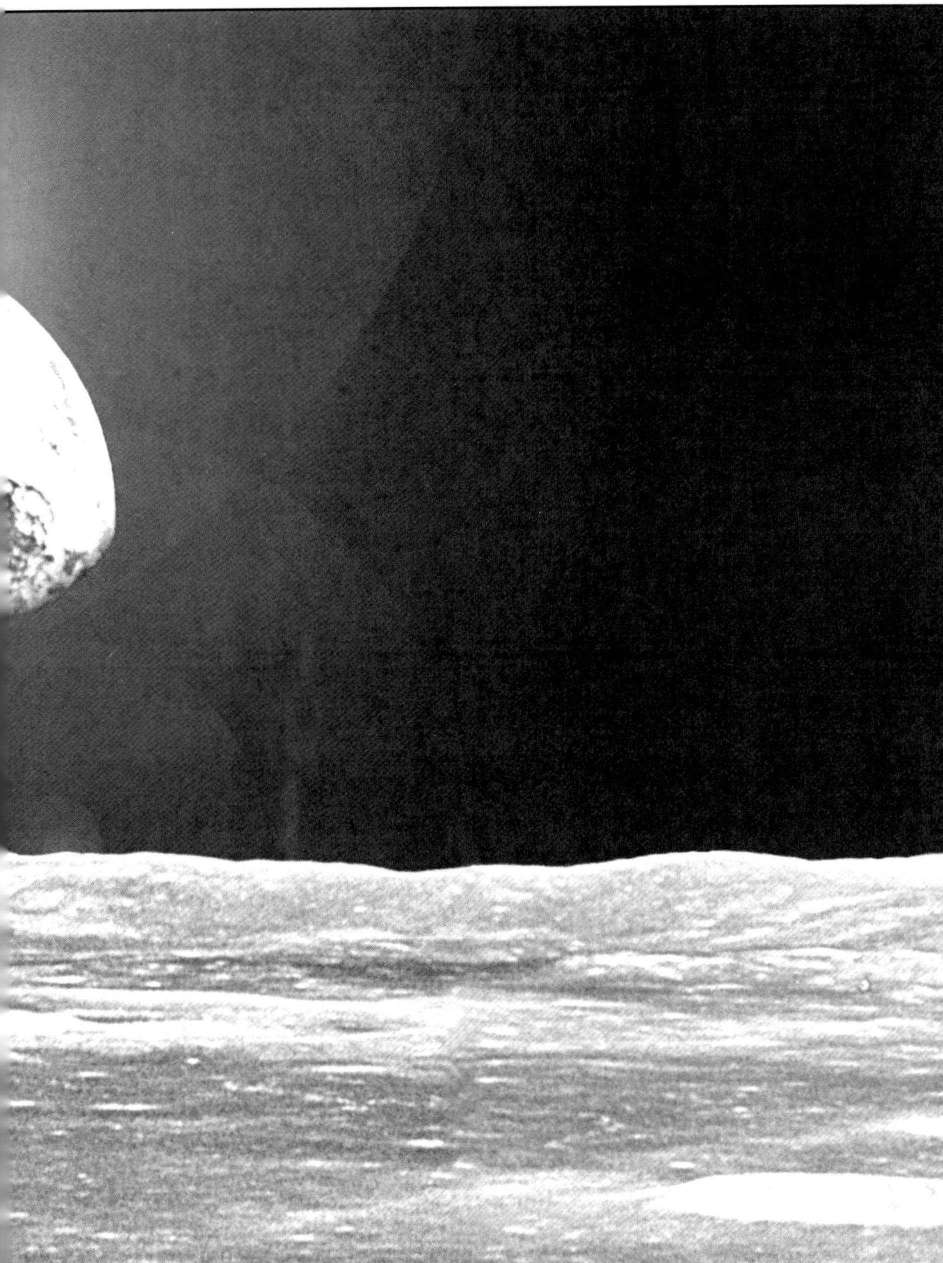

of Outer Space, including the Moon and Other Celestial Bodies (commonly known as the **Outer Space Treaty**) seeks to keep outer space free for exploration by all States while protecting celestial bodies from national sovereignty. The Treaty permits private enterprises to use space for peaceful purposes if their activities and results are made public. The responsibility for all launches is borne by the State.

2. (1967) *Agreement on the Rescue of Astronauts, the Return of Astronauts and the Return of Objects Launched into Outer Space* (the **Rescue Agreement**) details assistance and retrieval procedures.

3. (1971) *The Convention on International Liability for Damage Caused by Space Objects* (the **Liability Convention**) attaches liability to the launching State.

4. (1974) *The Convention on the Registration of Objects Launched into Outer Space* (the **Registration Convention**) requires the UN to maintain a central register of specific information for each space object, available on inquiry.

5. (1979) *The controversial Agreement Governing the Activities of States on the Moon and Other Celestial Bodies* (the **Moon Treaty**) designates space as the "common heritage of mankind," not merely the "province of mankind" as written in the Outer Space Treaty.

Outer space qualifies as *res communis* (the property of all) under Article 1 of the Outer Space Treaty, rather than as *res nullius*, the principle that these resources belong to no one and are to be doled out on a first-come, first-served basis. The Moon Treaty agrees, placing limitations on national sovereignty: "The moon is not subject to national appropriation," and "the placement of personnel, space vehicles, equipment,

Figure 23.1
View of planet earth from space. Image courtesy of NASA.

Figure 23.2
Natural resources of the earth's moon are protected under the Moon Treaty, ratified by nine countries.

facilities, stations and installation on or below the surface of the Moon... shall not create a right of ownership."

Article 11 of the Moon Treaty directs the establishment of an *international regime*, whose purposes are: the orderly and safe development of the natural resources of the moon; the rational management of those resources; the expansion of opportunities in the use of those resources; and an equitable sharing by all States-Parties in the benefits derived from those resources. The "common heritage of mankind" would thus require an international consortium to monitor and hold accountable actions with potential consequence towards any other State.

Only nine nations have ratified the Moon Treaty (Australia, Austria, Chile, Mexico, Morocco, the Netherlands, Pakistan, Philippines, and Uruguay),

Existing Space Law Concepts & Legislation Proposals

while over 90 have signed the Outer Space Treaty. By UN agreement, five signatures are sufficient to validate a treaty as an international instrument, but there is concern at the refusal of the USA and Russia/USSR to sign—the two nations most likely at present to engage significantly in space exploration.

Obviously, it is the criteria for exploitation of natural resources found on the moon, Mars and other celestial bodies that is of the greatest practical interest. In the foreseeable future, Mars and perhaps its two satellites will be the only sources of usable resources for space researchers or colonists, until we are able to reach the nearest earth-asteroid for mining. By not signing the Moon Treaty, the USA and Russia/USSR tried to set a precedent for the possible future commercialization of space that most likely will occur in the 21st Century.

Most scientists also do not want to recognize the Moon Treaty for fear that it would inadvertently prevent our expansion into space if no economic benefits can be derived. The Moon Treaty, however, does not place a moratorium on exploitation of natural resources, but insists upon the establishment of an international regime to monitor and control such exploitation. In fact, mining could be begun on an experimental basis even while clearer rules are established and eventually made law. But what is at question here, if taken literally, is the "common heritage of mankind" clause which indicates that if exploitation does commence, all nations should have a share in the proceeds.

In addition to the five treaties instituted by COPUOS, five other resolutions have been signed that are shaping the parameters of international space law. These five resolutions, regarded by member states as guidelines rather than as legally binding obligations, address such concerns as the broadcasting of signals via artificial earth satellites into areas that may be politically or socially opposed to the information being broadcast; the regulation of satellite communications and orbital slots; the use of nuclear power sources in outer space (drawn up in 1992 after a Soviet nuclear-powered satellite broke up in air-space over Canada); the need to ensure international cooperation in outer space; and remote sensing of the earth from space, with principles designed to take developing countries into particular consideration.[1]

Monitoring through remote sensing is a priority for most Mars orbital missions. Besides being used to evaluate and select landing sites, this operation can furnish a complete geological mapping of the surface and subsurface of Mars, while analyzing mineralogical features at the same time.

With the potential discovery before us of new resources, it is the commercialization of outer space and its celestial bodies that must be addressed. As Space Station *Freedom* (SSF), a multi-purposed facility to be stationed in low-earth orbit is developed and the Mars program is expanded in the 21st Century, more and more private companies will want to become involved in space development. Mineralogical discoveries on a distant planet or asteroid will enhance this growth tremendously. Numerous companies in at least 20 countries are already involved in commercial space enterprises, ranging from satellite communications and remote sensing to microgravity manufacturing research and development. Service corporations such as insurance companies and promotion agencies have also become involved. In the near future, over a dozen countries will be able to launch their own satellites and, as satellites continue to crowd low space orbits, the rights of satellite power and their purpose in space will become more and more contentious.

The first real manufacturing in space took place on August 30, 1984, when Charles Walker, a McDonnell Douglas Astronautics Company engineer and scientist, processed pharmaceuticals onboard the Space Shuttle Discovery. He used a procedure known as continuous flow electrophoresis which is a process of separating molecules by means of an electrical field. It had already been determined that a better separation of molecules takes place in a gravity-free environment. In the electrophoretic procedure in space, molecular

Existing Space Law Concepts & Legislation Proposals

Figure 23.3
Model of a space station in orbit above the earth. Drawing by NASA.

separation increased by a factor of 700 and purity levels quadrupled. One of the earliest electrophoresis products may be urokinase which is an enzyme that can be taken from male urine or separated from human kidney cells and used as an anticoagulant. Current urokinase production costs in Earth laboratories are expensive, where a single dose can cost $1,500. An experiment conducted in 1975 on the joint Apollo-Soyuz space mission successfully separated the enzyme from the kidney cell cultures at six times the efficiency achieved to date on Earth. One analysis suggests that full-scale production of urokinase on the Shuttle or Spacelab could lower the cost to $100 per dose.[2]

In July 1985, polystyrene spheres went on sale as the first commercial product to have been manufactured in space. Produced onboard the Space Shuttle Challenger, where astronauts found that space manufacturing eliminates distortions in shape and size caused by gravity.[3] Soon other products—advanced metals, alloys, semiconductor materials, pharmaceuticals, bubble free glass and ceramics, polymers and organic chemistry—may carry the label "Made in Space." Space-produced gallium arsenide crystals (a product of Fairchild Industries), for example, have already become key elements in solar power systems in space and on earth, and have uses also in lasers, computer chips, fiber-optics systems and antennas.

As more products are developed in space and we witness the construction of artificial structures on Mars, whether in the fashion of Buckminster Fuller or Arthur C. Clarke, I suggest that a new type of "astro-law" will have to be established to match the scope of private enterprise activities. Astro-law will address the finer issues of liability insurance in the integration of public and private services in outer space. Astro-law will also have to define criminal jurisdiction in cases where there has been a deliberate violation of common properties.

International law may set the framework for outer space law, but when it comes to governing a large number of individuals in space, with manufacturing and mining occurring in remote areas, a different set of laws for regulating relationships will be needed. As colonies or bases are established on the moon, Mars or the La Grangian points, we must avoid dispute resolution and administration taking on its own form of self-regulation and self-governance without adherence to an international legal system. The best system might be that which has already been proposed, an "international regime," with individual groups or colonies having some local say, as exists in the canton system of Switzerland. Theorists like Karen Cramer of the Space Policy Institute (George Washington University, Washington DC) would like to see a Lunar Users Union (LUU) or, for purposes of this paper a Mars Users Union (MUU) where those on Mars become the major decision-makers and hence not as restrictive as an international consortium from Earth.

Like the international regime, the MUU would grant rights to private enterprises and states for commercial mining and exploration and would function mainly to ensure non-interference amongst groups wishing to pursue similar interests.

Existing Space Law Concepts & Legislation Proposals

Although in some cases certain terrestrial laws may no longer be applicable in space, we should realize that our laws have evolved for the protection of citizens over a 2,000 year period and that they should serve as the initial basis for any new territories. Our laws might be the one connection that these space adventurers take with them as they travel into even greater reaches of outer space. Even when self-sufficient colonies exist, the basis of the laws that we have evolved on earth should be the basis for life in space, to ensure the protection of earth citizens, wherever they travel to these colonies, and to ensure only minimum or necessary exploitation of Mars, the asteroids, or eventually other planets.

A legal framework is necessary for international cooperation in space with respect to how territorial jurisdictions will apply to temporary or permanent installations on Mars and other celestial bodies. Once precedent has been set in connection with initial, unique missions, the need for generic legal guidelines pertaining to jurisdiction and control of multinational activities can be foreseen.

A balance will be needed between Earth-based law and space law when considering off-earth production and resource removal. Preconditions might be outlined, directing dominant powers to recognize Third World interests and form cooperative alliances, providing certain availability of new technologies, data, and resources within reasonable economic limits.

Finally, international agreements will have to be worked out with scientific and logistic flexibility maintained, so that adjustments can be made for the missions to and in the Mars environment. Technical design facilities must control re-entry, retrieval and disposal techniques in all commercial payloads. Natural decay mechanisms cannot be relied on for removal. With such agreements, the necessary balance for the exploration and use of outer space and the protection of this shared universal resource may be maintained for future generations.

Space law is now only in its infancy. New branches

of the discipline will probably develop into astro-law as it applies to outer space and astro-law relating to celestial bodies. So far, space law has really been earth law, but regardless of its applicability, international space law should stem from humanistic philosophies evolved from rules and forums developed here on earth.

Future Mars missions, with perhaps a joint manned mission (US-CIS-ESA) to land on the surface of Mars in the early part of the next century, will have a major impact on the development of space law in its natural environment. As people begin to remain away from the earth for extended periods and finally establish permanent residences off planet, the earth-based courts might be received by the colonists in the same way that American colonists perceived the English Privy Council—with increasing antagonism toward a distant overseer.

No doubt ecospace will be a distinctive economic/social zone. If proper laws and permits are allowed with reasonable economic and technical rewards, the commercialization and development of outer space will undoubtedly expand in the future. It is anticipated that international law will also adapt and expand to meet the challenges presented by the space frontier, in much the same fashion as US product liability principles have followed the growth of commercial aviation on earth.

Mars offers a significant opportunity to establish cooperation in exo-industrialization and exo-commercialization as humanity establishes both a data bank of knowledge in the planetary sciences and a unique environment for testing new technologies. Ultimately, we as the extraterrestrials will have transformed Mars from being the traditional planetary symbol of "war" into a planet of "peace," and we, as travelers, will take our place as *homo universalis*.

---

1. *Multimedia Space Educators' Handbook*. NASA Johnson Space Center, Houston, Texas 77058.
2. OMB / NASA Report Number S677. See also research in 1975-1978,

Edgewater Hospital, Dr. M.S. Mazel, Chicago, Il.23. *Multimedia Space Educators' Handbook.* NASA Johnson Space Center, Houston, Texas 77058.
3. *Chemical process* developed by NASA & Lehigh University under the direction of Professor John W. Vanderhoff.
4. For more information, visit www.marssociety.com.

24

Pyramidal Modeling of A Self-Sufficient Community

Alberto Rios Salinas,
Architect
& Alberto Rios Fernandez Jr.,
Architect

A new concept in architecture that is gaining force in Europe is called Bioarchitecture, and its intent is to integrate elements from the electromagnetic to the supercosmic, so that a harmony may exist between the environment and our living conditions, a balance between ourselves, our planet and our cosmos. Careful attention is now being given to the selection of building materials with a view toward their site-specific placement.

In past centuries, house design, construction and decoration have been bound up with esthetic concepts and social fashions. Economic interests prevail along with a rationalist approach to architecture, producing parallel-piped shaped buildings as monuments to monotony and a withdrawal from nature. Is the cost or the external appearance of a building its real worth? Or is it the internal concept that gives us the chance to inhabit a harmonizing space between our human nature and greater nature?

On the threshold of the third millennium, architecture faces a great challenge: to go further in design than man has reached until now. Achievements are various, from ancient times when man was nomadic and lived in caves, to the fortified cities whose

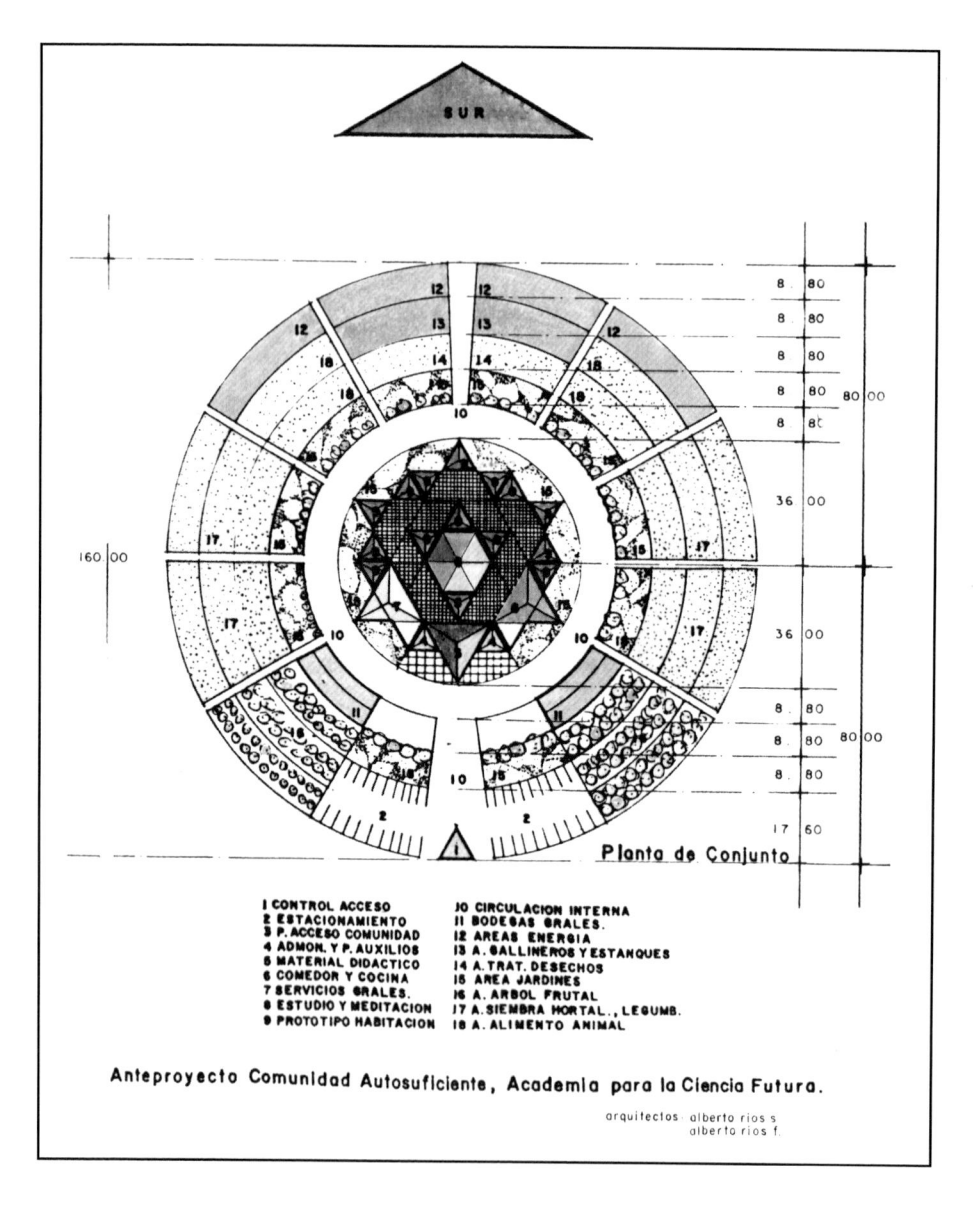

Pyramidal Modeling of A Self-Sufficient Community

Figure 24.1
General Design
For Planned Community.
Schematic by Alberto Rios
S. & Alberto Rios F.

ramparts speak of power, and even more, to these modern cities immersed in a chaos of contamination in every sense. However, there remain vestiges of many cities where Whole Man was the elementary focus, as we can see in Mayan, Incan and Egyptian sites.

It becomes necessary to analyze the current moment in which we live, taking into account our political, economic, social and spiritual environment. The extreme specialization of each branch of science permits only a few experts and organizations to have a clear grasp of their specific themes, and the common man is blocked from realizing the human evolutionary process that is occurring through all fields at this important time.

The developments of this century surpass the range of development registered in the last twenty centuries. Unfortunately, the speed of this growth has not been orderly and there has been no conscience for preserving our planet's environment, from its ozone layer to its subterranean aquatic stratums, through the unnatural development of petroleum-based and nuclear energies. Political, social and economic changes all over the world have ushered humankind into a disorder that produces shortages of food and energy and interferes with natural ecologic processes. In order to maintain a balance between humanity, our planetary environment and the cosmos, there must develop a real consciousness, so that we may understand what we are, and at the same time preserve our species.

And with that consciousness, living in a non-polluting community, self-sufficient in energy usage, food, communication, education and research, we might have a kind of life more suitable to the human being during the changes and processes of disorder that man himself has caused, and where collective work and communication will be the key for mankind's evolution in the Third Millennium.

In a desire to transcend the individualist, materialistic concepts that humanity has demonstrated till now, and to create architectural spaces in which direct links with "community" can be made increasing communication while maintaining peace as well as space for solitude. For this reason we decided to work together toward the realization of a self-sufficient Community that would solve five basic necessities:

a) Education, b) Communication, c) Food, d) Energy, and e) Economy.

The concept of the design for the community came from a premise of interpenetrating the scientific knowledge of ancient Egypt along with a biblical understanding of how early cultures sustained themselves, from this we developed the "Star of David" form within a pyramidal construction.

The amazing achievements of ancient civilizations prove to us beyond any doubt the existence of a special knowledge that can hardly be explained as the product of a science based on reason alone.

The Great Cheops Pyramid must be mentioned here, not only as a joining of blocks with a perfect layout and design, but also as a construction model with deep and verifiable astronomic and geophysical references. One of its most extraordinary aspects is the complex calculus necessary to allow the star rays of Orion and Sirius to reach the center of the pyramid precisely on the day when the location of this star announced the beginning of the new Egyptian year, an important calculation in recognizing seasonal changes relating to agriculture.

The shape of the Pyramid has been the subject of an enormous literature. We must acknowledge that shapes provided in nature are not absolutely capricious: Minerals crystallize in a given way, permitting us to recognize them at first sight; the leaves of a tree all match a single pattern; running water always drains in a spiral. The chemical bonds of some elements like carbon and silicon are in pyramidal form. It seems that shapes and bonds in nature form groups in given ways in order to modulate energies, whether of light or electricity or of subtler and less known qualities. In studying the shape of the Pyramid, we are completely conscious of the fact that, in using this example, we are entering the para-scientific world, but we remember that many phenomena of nature were considered para-scientific until science could explain them, and that still these phenomena were real before the explanation arrived.

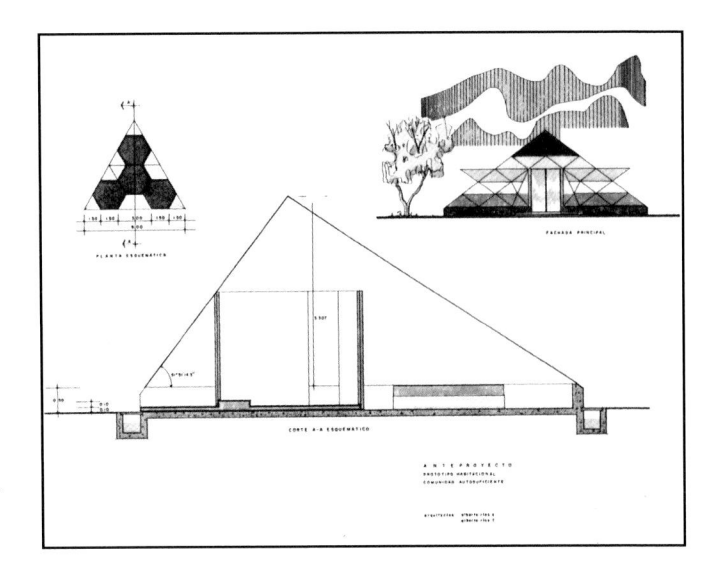

Figure 24.2
Various Perspectives of Basic Pyramidal Structure. Schematic by Alberto Rios S. & Alberto Rios F.

In this particular case, we may affirm that perhaps the pyramid shape marks a condenser, regulating and rectifying the effect of certain telluric energies, effects well known to the Egyptians, Mayans, Aztecs and Chinese. Proof of this can be seen in the pyramidal cities of Teotihuacan, Tenochtitlan, Chichen-Itza and Tikal, and complexes in Peru, in Brasil, and even in China. Perhaps our ancestors wished to communicate something to us, leaving so many evidences of pyramidal structures all over the world that we cannot believe the selection of a pyramidal shape and its essential qualities is a random one.

The first design that we made for our self-sufficient community was in the form of two interpenetrating pyramids—the "Star of David." Later, we attempted to match this geometry with the spiritual concept of Circles within Circles, completely integrating the areas for the different functions—human, agricultural, energy and manual works, and in such a way that the mathematical and spiritual correspondence remained implicit. For example:

a) The general radius of the community is 80 meters, corresponding to the power of the

infinite over the number 40.
b) The community is surrounded by 5 protective concentric circles which serve mainly as cultivation and work areas.
c) Within the community 14 modules are created.
d) The three central pyramids (in the original document colored red, yellow and blue) are the service areas corresponding to a specific zone.
e) The mathematics used in all of our pyramidal constructions correspond to the mathematics of the Great Pyramid at Giza.
f) In organizing the habitational modules, because the inclination of the pyramid at its perimeter is shallow, it was necessary to raise them 50 cm from ground level.
g) The common area for Education and Meditation corresponds to the largest pyramid, looming up from the central Star of David, as the heart of the community wherein the energy of the whole community is concentrated.
h) The number 9 as an inversion of the number 6 is implicit in almost all of the pyramidal construction.
i) Finally, as we finished the scale model of the general project, we realized that the internal circulation area of the community had shaped the stylized silhouette of a Dove, and we took this as the logotype for the community.

Detailed architectural plans of the project, which was designed to cover two hectares of land, include as shown in Figure 1: a main access (1) and circular external road (10) for direct radial access (2), a parking lot, modules for areas of administration and alternative medicine (7-9), a kitchen and a common dining area (6), sites for lavatories, bathing and laundry, habitation dwellings, education, training and relaxation areas,

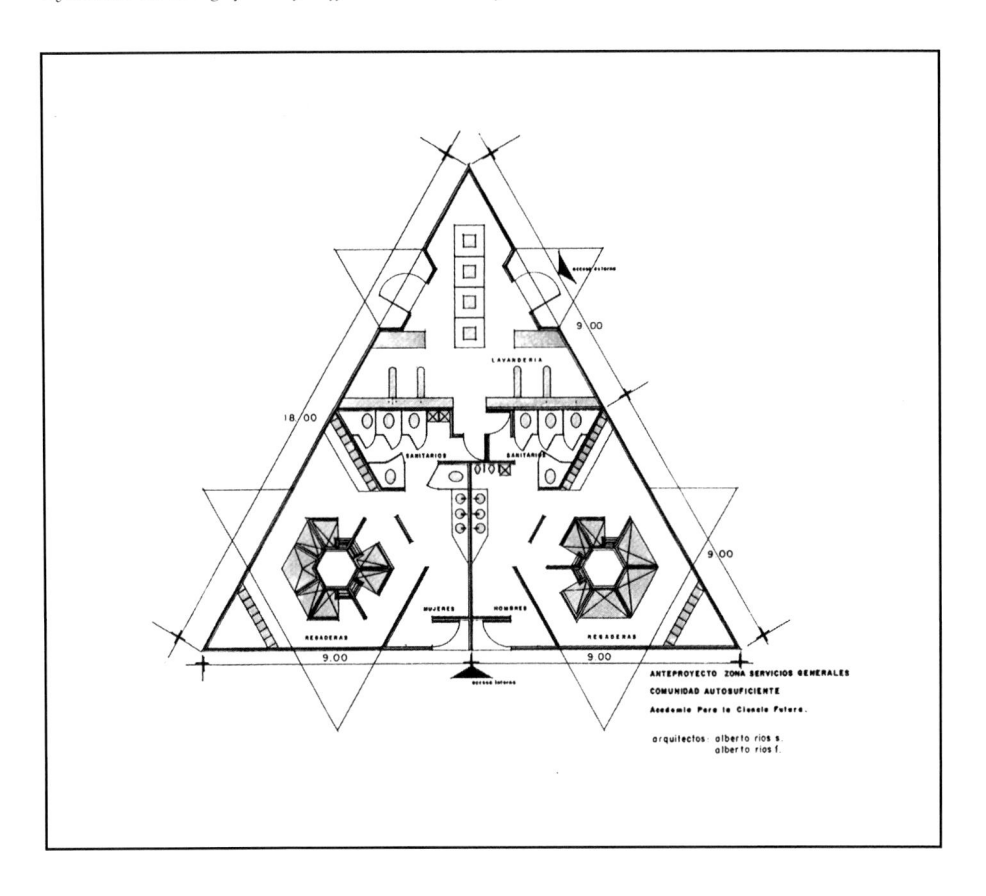

Figure 24.3
General Activity Center For Autonomous Community. Schematic by Alberto Rios S. & Alberto Rios F.

market gardening and greenhouse areas (15-17), and a warehouse/workshop area, as well as exterior areas designated for fruit-growing and gardens, apiaries, pisciculture and silviculture, compost and waste treatment, and solar and aeolian energy gathering (12).

The special arrangement of areas reflects an aspect of internal man, harmonizing and completely integrated with the conditions of nature, without losing sight of the process of progress that is continually going on. We believe that the fulfillment of this project will give us feasible support to the present process of evolution in which man is involved. As a member of such a self-sustaining community, and others like it, we may gradually be trained to become aware of who we are, and where our true destiny is. In addition, we may come to focus on those concepts of a new culture that were perhaps known to our ancestors.

It is not our intention to be alarmists or extremists, but only to draw attention to this fact: It might be that, with a gradual change of conscience and culture, of our life habits and our habitations, and of our work and study centers, we could live and coexist in calm and tranquillity, balanced in our nature and in harmony with ourselves, our planet and our cosmos. Concepts of bioarchitecture conduce toward a recognition of the necessity for a balance between the environment and our internal and external conditions. As architects, designers and builders, and even more, as space integrative persons, this is our challenge: to create living spaces that will allow us to truly evolve and flourish during the Third Millennium.

Conclusion

In synthesis, we are able to say that the conformation of these self-sufficient communities must contemplate three levels: the Community of Light, the conscious Community, and the physical Community. The question is: Why integrate, or be integrated in a community? Possible reasons are: to better equip oneself for contingency times, to develop a new lifestyle, to establish communities in harmony with an ecological vision of environmental protection, to work jointly with groups committed to elevating our consciousness levels or to simply accumulate Light and life.

Actually, with such religious, political, social and economic fluctuations, it is highly challenging to set up these types of communities. These architectonic models are, indeed, "Living Architecture"—as musical architecture or acoustical architectonic forms, not only for those external pyramidal models, but also for those internal ones. These structures represent a type of thought-form or vibratory pattern that allows us to belong to the Communities of Light all the time, if such commitment is our intention and our work. In order to facilitate these communities, we first must better organize and develop our neighborhood and family relationships, both physically and spiritually, preparing not only to set up and develop a community on a piece of earth, but also to set up a place for community in our souls and to cultivate it. We must strive to find the exact balance that deeply reflects both our fulfilled individual needs and those of the collective before we can truly be in community with each other and with God.

PART FOUR

FUTURE

SCIENCE

25

Beyond Newtonian Physics: The New Cosmology, & the Dialogue of an Open-Ended Universe

J.J. Hurtak, Ph.D., Ph.D.

As we look at the dynamic dialogue taking place between science and religion, we are influenced by the emphasis being placed upon the study of creation and the very mechanisms through which the universe came into existence. In this dialogue, it has become clear how Western science has slumbered under Newton's Laws of Motion which are not totally accurate and which are being reexamined in terms of a new science which views creation in essence as a co-creation working through the internal propagation of universal laws.
 Newton's First Law of Motion states a body will remain at rest or move uniformly in a straight line unless compelled by external forces to change this condition. It refers only to an external force which, of course, requires a second body to produce that force. These circumstances exclude any possibility for an internal force or other dimensional force which requires no external second body to react against it at all. Newton's Second Law states that force must equal mass times acceleration ($F = ma$). Similarly, Newton's Third Law states that for every action or force there is an equal or opposite reaction, which implies that there can never be a force acting in nature unless, again, two

Figure 25.1
Sir Isaac Newton (1642-1727). Image by the Academy For Future Science.

bodies are involved. There is one that exerts the force and the one upon which the force is exerted. Moreover, this indicates that whenever energy is manifest there must have been a source in the three-dimensional universe that gave up its force to create it.

Newton's laws, generalizing the conservation of momentum principle, forbid an internal force or force coming from outside of our known reality to be valid. No matter how many weights may shift or gears may turn one can never propel an object by means of anything except a physical, external mechanism. This assumes we are functioning in a closed system with a limited amount of energy available and we can clearly measure that limit. It is true that the principle of conservation of momentum has generally held true and is applicable in all fields of traditional physics to date. However, recently we have seen with the development of certain forms of hyperspace modeling, a complete break with orthodox physics. In short, traditional Newtonian physics is being rapidly superceded. The conservation of linear and angular momentum cannot explain quantum mechanical propagators working across vast dimensions of superspace. Stated differently, we have come to the realization that a whole new reality has outstripped the laws of Newtonian science and has opened up a new era for space navigation and for the reconsideration of cosmology itself.

In order to understand the new cosmology, one must understand our physical universe is made up of massless electrically charged forces which in turn are immersed in a vast, energetic, all-pervasive, electromagnetic field as the under lying substratum of evolution. This indicates multiple tracings of light unfolding in all directions that are not contained, but instead work from free energy or zero point energy (ZPE) unfoldments which shape the inertia mass relationships that give solidarity to life.

In a sense, most philosophers would interpret life in terms of the traditional notion of creation *ex nihilo*, or creation out of nothing. However, if creation is truly a Thought-Form from a Divine source, then the point of creation is clearly not in the form of a period of zero or even two dimensions, but in a conic spiral or pyramidal manifold *from* which consciousness is able to expand itself into creation. Thus, consciousness shapes our environment in such a way that the environment, including the very aspect of mass reality, can be implemented, as well as changed and subordinated to a consciousness physics. Moreover, the thought forms of the divine process of creation which is described at the very beginning of *Genesis* is something that should be achievable when we are willing to rise out of chaos.

As we begin to understand this linkage between hyperspace realities, we are being called back into a creative order of management that we have lost and surrendered to physics and to physicists who have placed engineering in mundane relationships that completely exclude the inner dynamics of micro-energy fields of long-term precognitive experience inherent in our birthright. Ultimately, we become the consciousness energy *einlink*, that moves up the ladder of creation where we become the investitures of the higher creation in human dimensionality.

Figure 25.2
Michelangelo—
"The Creation of Adam"
1508-1512. Fresco:
Sistine Chapel, Vatican.

Some people seem to recognize this, but even a brief look at the reality of the world makes us wonder why so many of our fellow human beings do not seem to have made such a recognition. One answer may be that the attractiveness to the experience of life is also repulsive at the same time. Just as on a carousel we are simultaneously attracted toward its center while being slightly propelled off the center toward the exterior, the push-and-pull of life may have caused us to be influenced by the commotion of the external world so much that we have forgotten about the mechanisms behind the carousel.

When we reconsider the story of *Genesis*, and the creation "out of nothing," we come to the realization that the world at that point of origin was like an open seed or energy envelope which contained a universe within it, which contained another universe within it, which contained another universe within it, and so on. So in the very concept of the beginning of creation was implied the experience of infinite universes of infinite possibilities. In fact, when we begin to contain that nothingness as a singular type of genesis experience and build a material cover for it, then we became locked into the classical concepts of life, space, time, and purpose. We became encapsulated in the shell of creation or embryonic god-form with little or no

The New Cosmology & the Dialogue of an Open-Ended Universe

understanding of the inner mechanisms of the purpose of life.

Thus, in summary: we have reached whole new levels of postmodern physics in recognizing the most interesting possibility in science, namely, that consciousness itself is the hidden variable that determines the cause of individual quantum transitions from one evolutionary reality to another, from one universe to another. There are many worlds and universes, and our rebirth is a rebirth into many universes. Discoveries that we are not only connected with each other, but with other life forms throughout a great and wondrous universe of universes begins the quantum leap.

What makes notions such as zero point energy (ZPE) and zero point fields (ZPF) so fascinating is the realization that these imply that we can actually open up a gate to this free energy that is abundant in all directions and, thereby, go into other layerings of creation, so to speak. We can visualize this as a type of Jacob's Ladder, not of physical rungs or physical steps,

Figure 25.3
Our known Electromagnetic Spectrum.

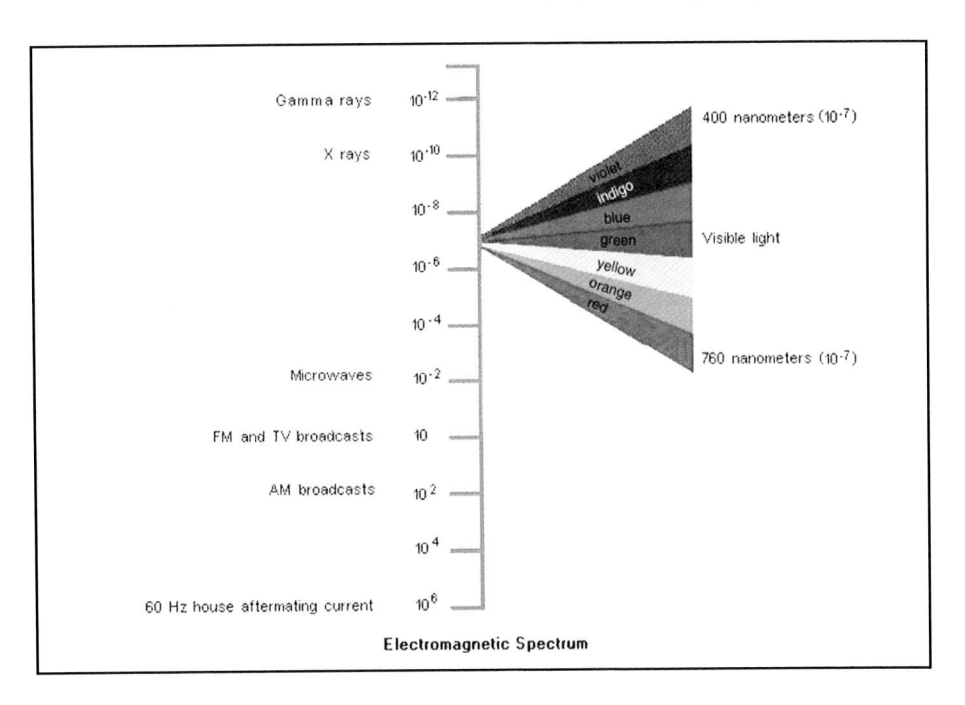

Electromagnetic Spectrum

Gamma rays	10^{-12}	
X rays	10^{-10}	400 nanometers (10^{-7})
	10^{-8}	violet, indigo, blue, green
	10^{-6}	yellow, orange, red — Visible light
	10^{-4}	760 nanometers (10^{-7})
Microwaves	10^{-2}	
FM and TV broadcasts	10	
AM broadcasts	10^{2}	
	10^{4}	
60 Hz house alternating current	10^{6}	

but of energy layers through which we can travel if we can balance the incoherent and the random signals which impinge upon us. On the mundane level, this "ladder" is available through magnetic and gravitational flux lines which can open the time doors and unleash the limitation of the physical garment of reality. This is now becoming scientifically possible if one takes the assumptions of zero point fields as the conducting mechanisms of inertia and mass structure and the finding of controllable anti-gravity forces by extracting energy from magnetism.

Furthermore, this concept of free-energy leads us into an even more complex universe that is an open-ended universe (in terms of infinite quantum dimensions) far from the traditional closed-ended system. To take a quantum leap beyond our three-dimensional system is merely to restructure or "resuscitate" the physical system beyond a singular relativity, whereby we can consciously experience Life outside this singular frame of space and time. However, to experience the supernal aspect of the consciousness light body is to go beyond all structure into a consciousness of being.

The realization that there is no material universe but rather everything is energy flux explains why we are only one manifestation of a body within this energy flux. This realization allows us to graduate, if we are properly orientated, through the next gate of vibration.

Hence, we can say that since everything which occurs in the universe is a result of one or several quantum events, or sparks of energy drawn from the molecular spin system in the nuclear domain—our universe is composed of an almost unlimited number of operating levels of life. These activities describe the initiation of the human race into the attractive interaction and co-sharing of creation that does not bring an end to things but instead a constant renewal of the world into many worlds, the universe into many universes, and the human life code into infinite speciehood.

An open-ended universe is not confined by a singularity or one event of infinite energy or time-space but rather is an open ended process, whereby we can experience all places and times with the convenience of knowing that we are interconnected not as strangers but as co-participants with the rules of cosmic evolution. The *a priori* knowledge of higher dimensions overcomes human prejudice and limited scientific hypothesis.

And so, through energy tunneling, space time quantum transitions, and other types of experiments through human perception the old limitations are overcome and we emerge ourselves not as passivists but activists in actually opening up doors and windows to the universe in the greater celebration of life.

---

1. Evans, Myron W. *et al* (1999) "On Whittakers Representation of the electromagnetic Entity in Vacuum, Part V: The Production of Transverse Fields and Energy by Scalar Interferometry," *Journal of New Physics*, Winter 1999, 4 (3), p. 76-78.
2. Puthoff, H.E. (1989) "Source of Vacuum electromagnetic Zero-Point Energy," *Physics Review A*, November 1, 1989, 40 (9), p. 4857-4862.

26

A Critical Review of the Available Information Regarding Claims of Zero-Point Energy, Free Energy, & Over-Unity Experiments & Devices

Patrick G. Bailey, Ph.D., Toby Grotz,
& J.J. Hurtak, Ph.D., Ph.D.

"Zero-Point Energy" (ZPE) is known as an energy that fills the fabric of all space. Technically the ZPE results from an electric flux that flows orthogonally to our perceived dimension or reality. The mass equivalence of this energy has been calculated by physicists to be on the order of 1093 gms/cm³. Henry T. Moray, Walter Russell, and Nikola Tesla described the nature of the ZPE and designed and built equipment to engineer its proper ties. It may be possible to build devices to cohere this energy. This would result in a non-polluting, unlimited supply of virtually free energy.

"Free Energy" is a term that can have two meanings: either the additional energy that can be obtained from a device at little or no additional cost, so the additional energy is essentially free; or more output energy that appears to be available than the input energy, such as in the case of detonating an atomic bomb.

"Over-unity Devices" are those systems which appear to produce more energy than they use. In analyzing such systems, a box is drawn around the device and energy balances are formulated to measure the amounts of energy coming into and out of that box. Whether or not the device is termed an 'over-unity' device will depend upon the size of the box. When the

Figure 26.1
The Hoover Dam on the Colorado River is a natural "free-energy device." Image by the Academy For Future Science.

box is drawn large enough, all systems or devices will have a net energy transfer of zero. On the other hand, when the box is drawn just small enough, the device can be said to be an 'over-unity' device, and an intelligent physicist will know better.

From this point of view, examples of existing so-called free-energy devices abound: such as Hoover Dam. The same could be said of any generator, or any nuclear reactor. More energy certainly comes out of a dam than went in to making it (by us, at least). And any dam engineer will tell you that it will produce more energy than it cost to build and that it will last for a very long time. So it is seen that these generators can be thought of as free-energy devices, while they are really only energy conversion devices, and obviously not perpetual motion machines.

Ultimately, the sources for all information in these areas come from the inventors, researchers, or investigators themselves. The US and foreign patent offices provide some information into new developments in these areas, yet the actual patents reveal very little useful information and almost no experimental results. Patent law does not require complete disclosure of all data, and patents are held nationally. An interesting area of big business today is the international transfer of patents at no cost.

Other sources of information and data include papers, reports, books, and conference proceedings. Papers and books that are of special interest are those by Hans Coler (1946), the Gravity Research Group (GRG 1956), Stefan Marinov (1992), Hans Nieper (1984), and Shinichi Seike (1992). Conferences that have been recently held to collect and summarize information in these areas include the 26th through 32nd Intersociety Energy Conversion Engineering Conferences (IECEC 1991-1997) and the International Symposiums on New Energy (ISNE) (1993 to present), sponsored by the Institute for New Energy (INE). As a result of a 1993 ISNE working group, the working devices were categorized into four distinct areas: (1) Solid-State Space-Energy Generators, (2) Rotating Space-Energy Machines, (3) Fusion Conversion Devices, and (4) Hydrogen Energy.

There are now several societies and conferences world-wide, such as the Institute For New Energy (INE) founded by Hal Fox, Patrick Bailey, and Toby Grotz, that present and sometimes document the results of research in these areas. As this work is not considered as mainstream science within the US, much of the results of these researchers goes by unnoticed. In 1991, the 26th IECEC (Intersociety Energy Conversion Engineering Conference) held in Boston was one of the first serious international forums for researchers in these areas to come forward voluntarily and present their ideas, theories, and results to the mainstream scientific community. They were met with interest ranging from mistrust to awe, and from feelings ranging from friendship to outright anger.

The 26th IECEC created international interest that stimulated further review papers to be published in the later IECECs. A growing group of organizations is now networking on a world-wide basis to continue to support and organize this on-going research.

This review paper includes all of the information that was made available to the 1991 IECEC, all subsequent IECECs, all of the International Symposiums on New Energy (ISNE), and other contributed personal source information and documents. After these forums, the INE has continued to provide annual conferences to date which have brought together researchers from all over the world. The focus here is on actual data and results—not on ideas or mathematical theories. The emphasis here is on repeatable experimental evidence—or on the documented testimony of multiple reliable witnesses.

While on one hand some researchers may possibly be overstating the capabilities and results of their experiments and devices, on the other hand many so-called 'scientific experts' are unfortunately very active in discounting all of the research results in these areas without investigating the details of any of them.

> The Nobel chemist Irving Langmuir (1881-1957) used to give a cautionary talk on pathological science, and ... told a number of stories of pathological science and listed the features they have in common. (Cromer, Skeptical Inquirer, 1993).

In his eight page article, Cromer states that there are many lessons from this:

> (1) Scientists themselves are often poor judges of the scientific process; (2) Scientific research is very difficult. Anything that can go wrong will go wrong; (3) Science isn't dependent on the honesty or wisdom of scientists. (4) Real discoveries of phenomena contrary to all previous scientific experience are very rare, while fraud, fakery, foolishness, and error resulting from over-enthusiasm and delusion are all too common. Thus, Glashow's closed-

minded 'I don't believe a word of it' is going to be correct far more often than not.

Cromer also cites Langmuir as saying (Langmuir 1989):

There are cases where there is no dishonesty involved, but where people are tricked into false results by a lack of understanding about what human beings can do to themselves in the way of being led astray by subjective effects, wishful thinking, or threshold interactions. These are examples of pathological science. These are things that attracted a great deal of attention. ... [But] the critics can't reproduce the effects. Only the supporters could do that. In the end, nothing was salvaged. Why should there be? There isn't anything there. There never was.

Our sincere response to you is: If there is no initial interest—then there will be no investigation. If there is no investigation, there will be no research to replicate. Your interest will spark the urge to replicate. If there is interest, research, and no replication, then that fact should be published and disseminated with integrity. If there are witnesses to the results and the results were or are repeatable, then we feel the fault and blame lies with the critic and not with the researcher. Therefore, given the experiments and devices referenced in this paper: Demand that they be tested with an open mind! One success out of all of the failures is more than worth the effort!

The researchers and the works that we feel are worthy of great attention in the near future are those that are listed in Table 26.1. It should be noted that no researchers have been included if their work is of a proprietary or confidential nature, or if we could not obtain the required data or documentation from witnesses. All of the researchers have provided and we trust will continue to provide important contributions to and documentation of their work. In fact, some of this work may be turn out to be more important than those currently listed in Table 26.1. However, at the time of writing, we considered those devices listed in Table 26.1 to be of the greatest interest to us.

Some of the most exciting research has been done by Tom Bearden, M.S., retired military colonel, who has examined the reality of energy availability to meet the world energy crisis from using what is called "Giant Negentropy from the Common Dipole." The recent U.S. patent granted in March 2002 for the Motionless Electromagnetic Generator (Patent #6,362,718) by Tom Bearden *et. al.* is an electromagnetic generator without moving parts. It includes a permanent magnet and a magnetic core having first and second magnetic paths. A first input coil and a first output coil extend around portions of the first magnetic path, while a second input coil and a second output coil extend around portions of the second magnetic path. The input coils are alternatively pulsed to provide induced current pulses in the output coils. Driving electrical current through each of the input coils reduces a level of flux from the permanent magnet within the magnet path around which the input coil extends. In an alternative embodiment of an electromagnetic generator, the magnetic core includes annular spaced-apart plates, with posts and permanent magnets extending in an alternating fashion between the plates. An output coil extends around each of these posts. Input coils extending around portions of the plates are pulsed to cause the induction of current within the output coils.

Perhaps the most historic device of interest is the Methernitha Swiss M-L Converter developed by Paul Baumann and the Methernitha spiritual community in Switzerland. It has been repeatedly demonstrated to many scientists upon request (26th IECEC, Nieper 1984, SEA) as an electrostatic slow spinning disc device that produces a high voltage output. Its three-foot, counter-rotating disks and specially designed energy storage system are reported to generate a steady output power of about 3 to 5 kilo-Watts (kW) indefinitely—

Zero-Point Energy, Free Energy, & Over-Unity Experiments & Devices

HIGHEST INTEREST
(A Larger Size Prototype Seems To Be Proven)

Catalytic Hydrogen Collapse (CHC) — Mills, Dr. Randall
Device Category: Thermal Energy Cells
Device Type: Over-Unity
Inventor Address: Blacklight Power, Inc., Great Valley Corporate Center, 41 Great Valley Parkway, Malvern, PA

Davis Tidal Turbine — Davis, Barry
Device Category: Tidal
Device Type: Over-Unity

Electrohydrogen Generator — Studennikov, V.V.
Device Category: Hydrogen
Device Type: Over-Unity
Inventor Address: Russia, 117574, Moscow, Str. Vilniusskaya, 4, Apt. 339, ph. (095) 421-13-87

Harmonic Frequency Generator Circuit — Ewing, David & Walt Myers
Device Category: Room Temperature Superconductivity
Device Type: Frequency Generator
Inventor Address: 6315C Gessner Rd. Houston, Texas 77041

Motionless Electromagnetic Generator — Bearden, Tom *et. al.*
U.S. Patent #6,362,718 (March 2002)

HIGHEST INTEREST
(The Device Seems To Be Scaleable To A Larger Size)

Minato Magnetic Motor — Minato, Kohei
Device Category: Motor Generator
Device Type: Over-Unity
Inventor Address: Mexico City (via INE Office)

Moray Radient Energy Equipment — Moray, T. Henry
Device Category: Electr. Magnetic
Device Type: Over-Unity
Inventor Address: deceased

N-Machine (India) — Tewari, Paramahamsa
Device Category: Rotat. Magnetic
Device Type: Over-Unity
Inventor Address: India

Schauberger Vortex Effects — Schauberger, Viktor
No current information available

Sonofusion Reactor — Stringham, Roger
Device Category: Fusion
Device Type: Over-Unity
Inventor Address: First Gate Energies

Sweet Vacuum Triode — Sweet, Floyd
Device Category: Elect. Magnetic
Device Type: Over-Unity
Inventor Address: deceased

Swiss ML Converter (Switzerland) — Baumann, Paul
Device Category: Rotat. Magnetic
Device Type: Over-Unity
Inventor Address: Methernitha, CH-3517 Linden, Switzerland

HIGH INTEREST
(The Phenomena Is Repeatable)

Bug Powered Fuel Cell — Bennetto, Peter
Device Category: Fuel Cell
Device Type: Over-Unity
Inventor Address: King's College, London

Capacitive Discharge Motor — Gray, Edwin V.
Device Category: Capacitive Discharge
Device Type: Motor

Capacitive Discharge Motor — Ide, Osamu
Device Category: Capacitive Discharge
Device Type: Over-Unity
Inventor Address: Clean Energy Laboratory,Minato-Ku Mita 3-4-21-601, Tokyo 108, Japan

Cold Fusion Results — Fox, Hal
Device Category: Cold Fusion
Device Type: Over-Unity

Finsrud Motion Machine (Norway) — Finsrud, Reidar
Device Category: Perpetual Motion Machine
Device Type: Over-Unity
Inventor Address: Reidar Finsrud, N-1440 Drobakk, Norway; FAX +47 64932990

Gary's Magnetic Motor (1879) — Gary, Wesley W.
Device Category: Rotat. Magnetic
Device Type: Magnetic Motor
Inventor Address: deceased

Hendershot Coil Device — Hendershot, Lester
Device Category: Resonance
Device Type: Over-Unity
Inventor Address: deceased

Jefimenko Electrostatic Generators — Jefimenko, Oleg
Device Category: Elect. Magnetic
Device Type: Over-Unity

Los Alamos Experimental Research Results — Storms, Edmond
Device Category: Cold Fusion
Device Type: Over-Unity

Motional Electric Field Effect — Hooper, William
Device Category: Electr. Magnetic
Device Type: Effect

Noble Gas Motors (Papp Engine) — Papp, Joseph
Device Category: Nuc. Isotopic
Device Type: Over-Unity
Inventor Address: deceased

Patterson Power Cell — Patterson, James
Device Category: Cold Fusion
Device Type: Over-Unity

Podkletnov Device (Finland) — Podkletnov, Eugene
Device Category: Rotat. Magnetic
Device Type: Anti-Gravity

Zero-Point Energy, Free Energy, & Over-Unity Experiments & Devices

Pons and Fleischmann Status (France) — Pons and Fleischmann
No current information available

Russell Optical Dynamo Generator — Grotz, Toby
Device Category: Elect. Magnetic
Device Type: Over-Unity

SRI Experimental Research Results — McKubre, Michael
Device Category: Cold Fusion
Device Type: Over-Unity

Sweet VTA Device — Watson, Don
Device Category: Electr. Magnetic
Device Type: Over-Unity

T.T. Brown Devices — Brown, T. T.
Device Category: Elect. Magnetic
Device Type: Over-Unity

T.T. Brown Devices Replication — Deavenport, Larry
Device Category: Elect. Magnetic
Device Type: Over-Unity

Theracore Cold Fusion — Thermacore Co.
Device Category: Cold Fusion
Device Type: Over-Unity

WIN Device — Lambertson, Wingate
Device Category: Casimir Effect
Device Type: Over-Unity
Inventor Address: 216 83rd St., Holmes beach, FL 34117

HIGH INTEREST
(The Operational Techniques And Measurements Are Being Refined)

Giant Negentropy from a Common Dipole — Bearden, Tom
High Voltage Solar Cells — Sater, Bernard
Kwai Motor — Kawai, Teruo
Orgone Energy Phenomena — Reich, Willhelm

HIGH INTEREST
(Replicated By other scientists)

Brown's Gas — Brown, Yull
Geomagnetic Generator — Smith, Wilbert B.
Magnetstromapparat — Coler, Hans
N-Machine (Japan) — Inomata, Shiuji
RQM Devices (Switzerland) — RQM, Rusterholtz & Rudi
Stromerzeuger (Germany) — Coler, Hans

MEDIUM INTEREST
(Demonstrated and witnessed by others)

Angus Engine — Angus, Neil
Bessler's Wheel — Bessler (Orffyreus), J. E. E.
Betavoltaic Battery — Brown, Paul
Brown Resonance Device (US Patent) — Brown, Paul
Crystal Energy Converter — Hutchinson, John
Energy From Electrical Discharges — Pappas, Panos
E.T. Transformer — Cobb, Mel & Hurtak, J.J.

Gravito Magnetic Device (Canada) — Sinclaire, Pierre
Keely Motor — Keely, John E. W.
Keely Motor (Hydro-Vacuo Engine) — Keely, John E. W.
Kidd Device — Kidd, Sandy
Musical Dynasphere (Globe Motor) — Pond, Dale, & Keely, John E. W.
Newman Machine — Newman, Joe
Permanent Magnet Energy Conversion — Dragone, Leon, R.
Radient Energy Capture Device — Perreault, Bruce A.
Reich Orgonne Motor — Reich, Willhelm
Rotoverter — Torres, Hector D. Perez
Sinclaire Generator (Canada) — Sinclaire, Pierre
Stevens Generator — Mark, Stephen
Takahashi Magnet Motor (Japan) — Takahashi, Yasunori

MEDIUM INTEREST
(Something Was Again Demonstrated by One Person that appears significant)

Magnetic Distributer Generator — Brown, Paul

LOW INTEREST
(Something Unusual Was Demonstrated by One Person)

Ampere-Neuman Electrodynamics — Graneau, Peter
Bedini Energy Converter — Bedini, John
Hyde Device — Hyde, William
Jamison Energizer System — Jamison, Lawrence
Lutec 1000 — Brits, Lou & John Christie
Muller Magnetic Motor — Muller, William, J.F.
Reed Magnetic Motor — Reed, Troy
Searl Generator (England) — Searl, John
Searl Levitation Device (England) — Searl, John
Siberian Coliu — Marinov, Stefan
The Energetic Vacuum (ZPE) — Puthoff, Hal

LOW INTEREST
(Being Researched By Only One Person)

Aqua Fuel — Richardson, William, H.
Ecklin Motor — Ecklin, John W.
Fogal — Fogal, Bill
Graham-Low Power Research/Teaching Model — Graham, Roy
Kromey Converter — Kromrey, Raymond
Magnetic Sink — Smith, Wilbert B.
Permanent Magnet Motor — Johnson, Howard

*Table 26.1
Device of Interest (June 2002). [Ref. Institute for
◀ New Energy Website].*

while sitting on top of a table. A videotape has been produced and its narration has been transcribed.

Tim Binder and his team have replicated the 1927 experiments of Walter Russell and have created fluorine from pure water vapor using complex E-M field arrangements. This work validates Russell's theories about nuclear structure and the proper arrangement of the Periodic Table of the Elements.

Hans Coler demonstrated two major devices to many amazed witnesses and officials in Germany during 1925-1945. A 60 kW device was built in 1937, and the war bombings ended further research in 1944. A complete 32 page report declassified by the British Intelligence Objectives Sub-Committee is now available (Coler 1946, Nieper 1984). The theories expressed are very similar to those presented in a comprehensive report (GRG 1956) (the latest one we could find so far) on electrogravitics systems, interactions of
E-M with gravity, or counterbary control devices.

Don Kelly is the editor of the Space Energy Newsletter (SEA) and has been conducting and reporting results of E-M to gravity drop tests. He finds that energized coil assemblies have a longer drop time over about five feet. Other related research world-wide verifies that spinning masses appear to lose weight at high rotational speeds.

Floyd Sweet had developed the vacuum Triode Amplifier which used a similar 10 volt input to produce a larger output. This excess energy was pulled in from the dormant energy that lay in the empty space around us, and merely need a catalyst to activate and control it. Floyd Sweet demonstrated his vacuum triode device to at least two expert electronics technicians that have documented their observations in sworn affidavits. From a nine volt battery starter unit, nearly continuous output powers of 500 W to 50 kW have been reported to be observed. Experimentation is still in progress to further refine the device and to improve its operational capabilities.

Stanley Meyer obtained over 28 patents in both the U.S. and other countries that document his water fuel cell and hydrogen fracturing process technology. He began this work in 1980 and spent over $1.6 million. Although he was approached to sell the technology, he said that he had no intention to do so and planned to retain control to make sure his invention was brought to the public for the good of mankind.

John and Kevin Moray are pursuing the technology that was repeatedly demonstrated to the press in the 1930s by T. Henry Moray. One device was reported to generate 50 kW for long periods of time by itself by several witnesses and news reporters.

Edmund Storms has reviewed much of the work done internationally in the so-called area of 'cold fusion' and has documented the results and repeated results of the now world-wide research in this area. Major breakthroughs have been made recently in this area, and are being reported in several technical conferences, such as those sponsored by the American Nuclear Society (ANS).

Paramahamsa Tewari has been doing experiments with a N-Machine in India and has reported over-unity operation from instrument readings. He is currently performing new experiments to feed the output of the device back into the input to obtain a 'free-running' condition. Many researchers have performed experiments with these devices, also called, homo-polar generators, or unipolar dynamos. They usually consist of a rotating magnetic disk where electrical current is passed from the center of the disk to its edge. Small increases in the motor input power result in large increases of output power, thus encouraging the idea of an over-unity cross-over point.

These are but a few of the devices in this exciting area that are being researched today; all of these are documented in the INE website at: *http://www.padrak.com/ine/*. You can assist us in our quest to research and test these devices with integrity.

If ignorance was a good enough reason not to try, the light bulb would have never been invented and the Earth would still be flat. Let us be judged by our work and repeatable results, and not by hasty words. If some

Figure 26.2
The light bulb was invented in 1879 by Thomas Edison. Image by the Academy For Future Science.

of these works turn out to be not valid, so be it. Let it be known, and let's move forward with integrity. We are all looking for the next big breakthrough in modern physics to assist us in solving the escalating energy and environment crises. Do something to promote and encourage the continuation of these researchers and these works! If you don't do it, who will? If not now, when?

---

1. 26th IECEC, (1991) "Proceedings of the 26th IECEC," August 1991: *American Nuclear Society*, 555 North Kensington Avenue, La Grange Park, IL 60525. **Volume 4**, pp.329-492,
2. 27th IECEC, (1992) "Proceedings of the 27th IECEC," August 1992: *Society of Automotive Engineers*, 400 Commonwealth Drive, Warrendale, PA 15096-0001, Order No., P-259.**Volume 4**, pp. 4.357-4.295,
3. 28th IECEC, (1993) "Proceedings of the 28th IECEC," August 1993: *American Chemical Society*, Meetings Department, 1155 Sixteenth Street N.W., Washington D.C. 20036.
4. Adams, R. (1993) "The Adams Pulsed Motor Generator Manual," *Nexus New Times Magazine*, January 1993, PO Box 30, Mapleton Qld 4560, Australia.
5. AERI, Advanced Energy Research Institute, 14 Devonshire Mews W., London W1N 1FP, England.
6. Academy for Future Sciences, PO Box FE, Los Gatos, CA 95031.

7. Coler, H. (1946) "The Invention of Hans Coler, Relating to an Alleged New Source of Power," *British Intelligence Objectives Sub-Committee report,* Summer 1946, No. 1043 Item 31, 32 pp, Now Unclassified, Cromer, A. (1993) "Pathological Science: An Update," *Skeptical Inquirer,* **Vol. 17**, pp 400-407.
8. GRG, Gravity Research Group, (1946) "Electrogravitics Systems: An Examination of Electrostatic Motion, Dynamic Counterbary, and Barycentric Control,"*Gravity Research Group report,* Summer 1946, GRG-013/56, Wright Patterson AFB Technical Library, Cat. No. TL 565 A9, WPAFB, OH 45433.
9. GRI, Group Research Institute, PO Box 438, Nelson, New Zealand.
10. IASA, Institute for Advanced Studies at Austin, 4030 Braker Lane W., Suite 300, Austin, TX 78759.
11. INE, Institute for New Energy, 3084 E. 3300 South, Salt Lake City, UT 84109-2154 http://www.padrak.com/ine/
12. ITS, International Tesla Society, PO Box 5636, Colorado Springs, CO 80931.
13. ISNE, (1993) "Proceedings of the International Symposium on New Energy," *International Association for New Science* (IANS), April 16-18, 1993, 1304 South College Avenue, Fort Collins, CO 80524, (303) 482-3731. IANS supports the INE.
14. JPI, Japan Psychotronic Institute, c/o Shiuji Inomata, Electrotechnical Laboratory, 1-1-4 Umezono, Tsukuba-shi, Ibaraki 305, Japan.
15. Langmuir, I. (1989) "Pathological Science," *Physics Today*, October 1989, 42: 36-48.
16. Marinov, S. (1992) "Regarding Becocraft-Letter to Mr. Richard von Weizsacker, President of the German Federal Republic, 10 October 1992," *Deutsche Physik*, **No. 7**, East-West Publishers, Morellenfeldgasse 16, A-8010 Graz, Austria.
17. Meyer, S. (1991) *Water Fuel Cell Technical Brief.* July 1991, S.A. Meyer, 3792 Grove City, OH 43123.18. Newman, J. (1993) "The Energy Machine of Joseph Newman," July 1993, Joseph Westley Newman, Route 1, Box 52, Lucedale, Miss. 39452.
19. Nieper, H. A. (1984) *Revolution in Technology, Medicine and Society.* MIT Verlag, Germany, (In English): Tesla Book Company, PO Box 121873, Chula Vista, CA 91912.
20. SEA, Space Energy Association, PO Box 11422, Clearwater, FL 34616.
21. Seike, S. (1992) "The Principles of Ultra Relativity," 11th Ed., *Space Research Institute*, Box 33, Uwajima, Ehime (798), Japan.
22. Storms, E. (1993) "The Status of 'Cold Fusion'," *28th IECEC paper*, August 1993.
23. TI, Tesla Incorporated, 820 Bridger Circle, Craig, CO 81625. USP, University of Science and Philosophy, Swannanoa Pl., Box 520, Waynesboro, VA 22980.

27

Cold Fusion Research: Models & Potential Benefits

J.J. Hurtak, Ph.D., Ph.D.
& Patrick G. Bailey, Ph.D.

Few subjects have arisen in science in recent years that are as controversial and as hotly debated as cold fusion. Many dismiss the phenomenon out-of-hand claiming its impossibility within the Newtonian realm of physics; others look to more recent quantum models for evidence of its acceptability. What may be known needs to be investigated, and this article does just that: it takes a new look at some recent findings that may shed new light on this enigmatic and contested subject. Cold fusion has been largely a study of results first and theories which then must follow. Since most results from solid fusion experiments do not agree with old and contemporary nuclear theories, new theories are being generated to account for these new data and results.

After the Pons and Fleischmann announcement, numerous institutions all over the world began their own experiments. As of 1996 there were over 100 independent research groups worldwide investigating the potential possibilities of this new energy anomaly. Not all experiments have been successful and as research has persisted several new theories have been explored based on the new data found from various substitutions from the original experimentation in an

Figure 27.1
Fusion is a nuclear reaction in which two smaller nuclei join or fuse together to form a new, larger nucleus. Image by the Academy For Future Science.

attempt to determine a clear theory as to the factors that are occurring within the electrolytic cell. One of the most important results is the discovery of neutron emissions in the form of bursts which have been observed by De Nino, Sanchez, and Gozzi (De Nino, 1989), (Sanchez, 1989), (Gozzi, 1992). Neutron spectra with a 2.45 meV peak should be evidence of deuteron-deuteron (D + D) fusion. However, the detection of neutrons is complex and expensive, requiring a great deal of equipment and experimental expertise.

Even after the critics assured the press that "cold fusion" was only a delusion of a few scientists, SRI International, Los Alamos National Laboratory, California State Polytechnic University, and the Fermi National Accelerator Laboratory were willing to sponsor research. Although the U.S. Government has not thoroughly supported many of these projects, the Ministry of International Trade and Industry (MITI) in Japan has committed, along with IMRA Europe (which is the European branch of the Toyota Motor Company research institute), over 3 billion dollars to this research. The Japanese have made the most impressive and consistent advances in cold fusion research of all countries. Their research interest was spawned by a successful experiment by Akito Takahashi (1992) at Osaka University.

Researchers soon expect to be able to document for public inspection, energy increases from 30 to 70 percent in excess of electric power input. Researchers in India have already reported 70%, and Thermacore, Inc. in the United States claims that 18 Watts of power in are producing 68 Watts out for an excess of heat production of 50 Watts. Excess tritium (T) has also been detected, and this presence of nuclear by-products indicates that a nuclear reaction is taking place.

However, neutron and tritium emissions are not the most common factor of most cold fusion experiments. For the most part cold fusion reactions produce excess thermal energy, enough excess (or "latent") energy to heat the water surrounding the electrode. These reactions have produced sufficient heat to cause water to boil. If the fusion cell is pressurized, higher temperatures can be obtained (S. Pons and M. Fleischmann, 1989). Water temperatures in excess of 170° F. Have also been observed (Haag, 1990). The argument of the physics community is that the amount of heat does not correlate with the limited number of neutron emissions. The opponents suggest that a chemical reaction of some type must be occurring. Yet, additional experiments have shown Pd (palladium) x-ray lines and clear evidence of nuclear transmutation events.

THE FACTORS

In a chemical reaction, only a few electron volts (eV) of energy are released per atom taking part in the reaction, and even fewer in a mechanical process. In a nuclear reaction, millions of electron Volts (meV) can be released per atom. If all the atoms in an electrolytic cell were to react, the energy release would be on the order of a thousand electron Volts (keV)/atom

There are several approaches to cold fusion development but the basic approach since 1989 has deviated only slightly from the original Pons and Fleischmann model using electrolysis of lithium deuteroxide (LiOD) on palladium (Pd). Specific

Figure 27.2
Hydrogen, Deuterium & Tritium Atoms. Image courtesy of the Academy For Future Science.

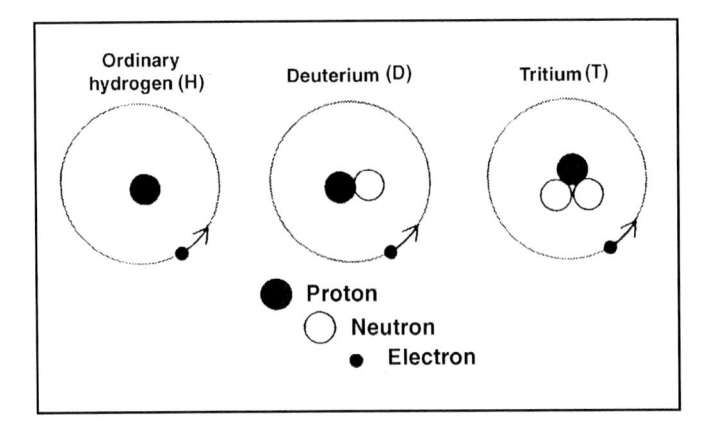

correlations between fusion yield and voltage, current density, or surface characteristics of the metallic cathode have yet to be clearly established. What is known is the reaction occurring produces excess thermal energy, and raises the temperature of the water.

There are various approaches to loading the palladium, one of which incorporates the use of pulsed heating which has a clear effect on the loading speed. Many researchers consider pulsed current an important factor, along with temperature variations. However, further research is examining the effects of magnetic and optical irradiation, ultrasonic waves (>10^9 Hz), and the use of pressure waves. Also, certain foreign atoms may enhance or detract from the surface dynamics.

Theories

In 1989, Pons and Fleischmann publicly announced their results, (and also the results of others) using the term "cold fusion," and since that time many theories have been put forth to account for some or all of their results. Some researchers continue to see their results as purely fusion based, others have come up with terms such as "new hydrogen energy," or "chemically assisted nuclear fusion" or "cold nuclear fission." The biggest conflict appears to be designing a theory in which the nuclear Coulomb barrier is overcome even at low temperatures.

Figure 27.3
Research with cold fusion device conducted at Los Alamos, NM in 1989. Photo by D. Hurtak.

The Pons-Fleischmann Process

It was originally thought that, as the voltage is applied across the electrodes through electrolysis, the heavy water (D_2O) is split into oxygen and deuterium (Pons and Fleischmann, 1989). The deuterium atoms are absorbed into the palladium at octahedral sites on the crystal lattice while oxygen accumulates at the platinum anode. The deuterium density is greater than that of liquid hydrogen.

The fusion reaction is catalyzed by the deposition of D^+ and metal ions from the electrolyte at (and into) the negative electrode. The deuterium atom ionizes with its electrons entering the band structure of the palladium. After various times of charging (or "aging"), the palladium rod is supersaturated with

Figure 27.4
Model of a Cold Fusion Cell. Image courtesy of the Academy For Future Science.

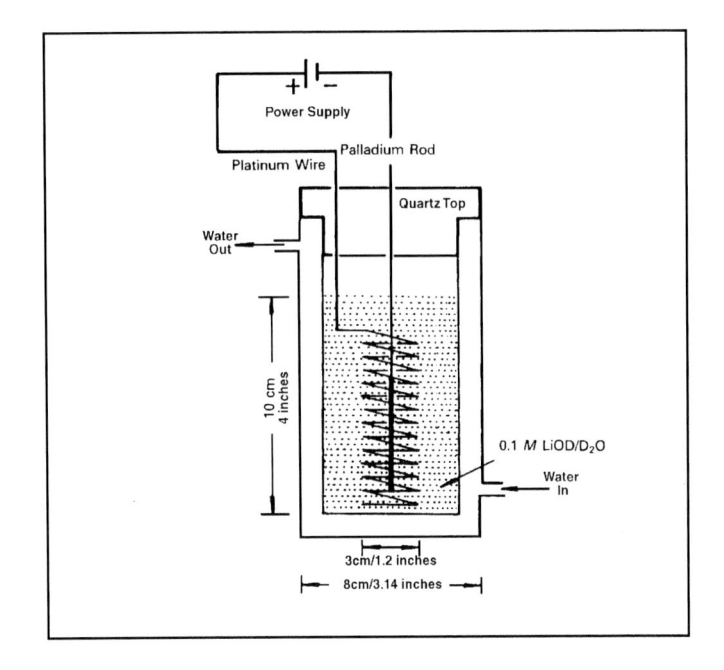

deuterons, and it has a crystal lattice structure like NaCl (King, 1989). All lattice sites are occupied, and the excess free deuterons form a "protonic fluid" which can aid electrical conduction. Thus, although metals such as palladium and titanium are used to support the fusion reaction, they are not consumed in the process of solid-state fusion. Instead the fuel consumed is the deuterium in the heavy water.

The Surface Model and Three-body Collisions

John Bockris also describes the "surface model" which does not consider that the fusion occurs within the electrode, but that the surface of the electrode might be the site of the reaction. He suggests that fusion reactions occur at specific points, or protuberance on the surface of the electrode (Bockris, 1989b). Here fusion occurs on the lattice, not within the lattice, whereby the lattice is a reservoir of deuterium providing enough raw material for the dynamic process that takes place even after the electrolysis is stopped (Glueck, 1993).

Jacques DuFour believes that when a transient electrical field is created by sparking through the gas between two disymmetrical electrodes, the surface layer of hydrogen isotopes builds a three-body collision of two hydrogen isotopes and one electron (DuFour, 1993). The accumulation of these species in a surface layer of the electrode metal can be explained by the known properties of sparks and of hydrogen isotopes in metal, implicating the weak electronuclear force that yields products completely different from those of hot fusion, whereby a deuteron is a two-nucleon system containing weak interactions. According to DuFour there is a whole class of nuclear fusion reactions at room temperatures, involving "three-body collisions" of two hydrogen isotopes and a neutrino, which through an indirect transition (virtual neutron states), have reactions favored by the high electron and proton concentrations existing in the metal and the high transient electrical field created by the sparks.

A controversy has arisen over the need for refined palladium that is relatively free of microscopic cracks in order for the "cold fusion" process to succeed. Several researchers claim that if the electrode has too many cracks it will fail to produce the excess heat. Contrary to this belief, Rainer Kühne in Germany postulates that it is the cracks within the electrode that are the trigger for cold fusion (Kühne, 1994). The crack hypothesis claims that the absorption of hydrogen gives rise to deformations and expansion of the metal lattice and that the formation of anions (metal ions) which allow for crack formations near the surface gives rise to deuterium absorption. Another controversy has also arisen—namely that the palladium metal to be used in successful "cold fusion" experiments needs to be "Type-A" palladium—i.e. rolled in an ammonia atmosphere (perhaps to increase the hydrogen (H_2) loading), and not rolled in an argon or inert atmosphere.

The Two-Step Mechanism Involving Electron Capture by a Deuteron or Lithium Atom

This model represents a coherent and semicoherent neutron transfer with increasing phonon coupling. It appears that on the surface of the Pd the D^+ can diffuse and combine with ingoing electrons where $2D^+ + 2e^-$ yields D_2 or the D ions can also stay on the surface and be independent of the electrons. Another theory proposed by J.C. Jackson and Budelov is that the neutron could be captured by the Pd metal nuclei and used to produce a different isotope of palladium and a gamma photon which could cause a photodistintegration of the deuteron and could liberate a neutron. The by-products would then be heat and electrons (Hagelstein, 1990).

Transmission Resonance

R.T. Bush has suggested that when a palladium lattice is fully occupied by deuterons, conditions are favorable to support laser-like actions where the deuteron-loaded lattice supports a type of resonating phenomena in which the probability of a traveling or "hopping" wave-like deuteron fusing with a target deuteron is increased significantly. Bush's theoretical model accounts for the heavy water heat effect and light excess heat effect from cold fusion. It provides a unique and highly novel mechanism to sufficiently enhance tunneling through the Coulomb barrier, as well as incorporating the role of lithium in electrolytic experiments.

The Collapse Ground State

If one could increase ω_{min} of the zero point field associated with the establishment of λ_{max} this could cause the electron to spiral inward to increase its angular velocity where $\omega'_o = \omega_{min}$, where ω is the frequency of absorbed radiation and ω'_o is the electron angular velocity. In some experiments light water or ordinary water has been used successfully to reproduce results similar to the Pons-Fleischmann model. According to Randell Hills, we may be viewing a catalysis process whereby the H electron is induced to undergo a transition to a lower electronic energy level than the "ground state" as defined by the usual quantum-mechanical model of the atom. Thus, stored energy in the atom is catalytically released.

The Tunneling Model

Tunneling has been considered a quantum mechanical phenomenon, where a particle whose energy is less than the potential energy of a barrier can overcome the barrier of electrical repulsion. Calculations by Rabinowitz and scientists at EPRI have shown that it is possible for the effective mass of the deuterium nuclei in a solid to be sufficiently less than the mass of deuterons in free space (Rabinowitz, 1990). This can increase the tunneling coefficient by many orders of magnitude.

By replacing the electron in a hydrogen molecular ion with a more massive charged particle, the fusion rate is greatly increased. Mario Rabinowitz of EPRI likens tunneling to a classical high jumper where an extended body can clear a barrier even when its energy is less than the potential energy of the barrier, if it can communicate with and be aided by the interaction on the other side of the barrier.

Nuclear interactions can be coherent when the difference in the phases of the wave functions of the compound nucleus states formed by overlap between the itinerant deuteron (neutron) and the lattice deuterons (nuclei) is an integral multiple of 2π (Vaidya,1993).

According to Charles Horowitz, the electrons in metallic hydrogen can be modeled as a Fermi gas of electrons and a crystal of nuclei. Palladium is a transition metal that in its alpha phase has a face-centered-cubic (fcc) lattice structure and a lattice constant of 3.89 Å and a nearest-neighbor distance of 2.75 Å fcc lattices in the orthohedral sites with the highest packing fraction of 1.0 - 1.5 Å. Under normal conditions, in D_2 gas or liquid states, the separation of the deuterium nuclei is 0.74 Å. However, for muon-catalyzed fusion to occur this must be at least 0.035 Å.

According to Adam Burrows, this would first

require that the deuterons (positive) and the deuteride (hybrid) exist not as atoms or molecules, but as screened positive charges with screening clouds having the required length (Burrows, 1989). However, this would still not be sufficient since cold fusion reaction rates also require the increasing of the tunneling integral by unity to increase the fusion rate. Moreover, a vacuum zero-point energy stimulated by a resonance effect that matches the palladium cathodes atomic mass may be required to create the proper tunneling potential.

A further expansion of tunneling comes when the centrifugal barrier is combined with the Coulomb barrier. Here penetration can be increased due to the resonance level between the Coulomb barrier and the centrifugal barrier.

The E-Cell Theory

According to the theory put forth by Gennady Fedorovich *et al.* the E-cell is a radiation defect of a crystalline lattice of a hydride which forms as a result of the capture of a thermal neutron by the nucleus of an atom. Here the reaction products leave the cell in 10^{-17}s which is shorter than the electron system (10^{-15}s). According to Fedorovich's calculation, to confine the surplus electrons in the E-cell, the pressure in the LiH crystal must be >10 to 20 Mbar, where the motion of the hydrogen nuclei form a collective movement and at some phases of the movement, the potential energy is transformed into kinetic energy, the nuclei approaching a distance of <0.1 Å (Fedorovich, 1993).

Jahn-Teller Symmetry Breaking and Hydrogen Energy in Gamma-PdD

Keith Johnson from MIT has proposed a chemical process which corresponds to an "internal phase change of the deuterium within the gamma-PdD lattice." He believes that the energy released is caused by the internal cyclic gamma-phase change of atomic deuterium to dideuterium. The heat produced is "latent" in that it is produced by repeated formation of the "interstitial sublattice" of the D-D bonds between the tetrahedral interstices in the gamma-PdD (Johnson, 1994). However, the Jahn-Teller effect is unstable and the cycle time for recombination is difficult to calculate. This process according to Johnson could generate heat at a rate of 17 to 1700 Watts/cm^3 Pd.

New Particle: The Iton Particle and Nattoh Model

J.F. Yang has suggested the possibility that a new neutral elementary particle may be forming, where the deuteron captures an electron and is transformed into a dineutron N; the deuteron-dineutron reaction would then account for the cold fusion. The Nattoh model proposes a reaction that involves plural hydrogen atoms and electrons. Matsumoto (1993) has observed ring spots caused by gravity decay of single and di-neutrons upon copper plates after the cold fusion reaction. The double iton could explain warming or "Heat after Death" phenomena that occurs up to three hours afterwards.

Some research has suggested that hydrogen ignition is occurring at the air-water interface. From preliminary results obtained by Matsumoto using the Nattoh model, they predict that cold fusion can occur using ordinary water. The model is based on the hypothesis that hydrogen clusters are trapped in tiny cavities such as cracks and compress themselves to an induced hydrogen-catalyzed fusion reaction. Here cold fusion occurs when the hydrogen pressure exceeds a critical value under electrical current flow. Matsumoto claims that a metal such as nickel which has low hydrogen permeability can be used whereby hydrogen clusters on the surface (Matsumoto, 1993).

FUTURE BENEFITS

According to Keith Johnson, if some of these theories are correct and 1 cm^3 of Pd is capable of yielding upwards of 1.7 kW of energy, this could eventually create 22 kW or 30 HP in automobiles with

Figure 27.5
The oceans provide enough heavy water to energetically sustain the world for hundreds of years.

the possibility of "water engines" electrochemically generating both heat and hydrogen for a fuel cell.

The world's oceans contain a large amount of readily extractable heavy water, sufficient to meet the global energy needs for hundreds and perhaps thousands of years. Heavy water production facilities will be needed. One gallon out of every 7,000 gallons of ordinary water is heavy water (deuterium oxide or D_2O). The energy equivalent of a gallon of heavy water is about equal to 300,000 gallons of fuel oil. The cost of production of one gallon of heavy water is estimated at less than $1,000 or less than one cent per gallon of oil (energy equivalent).

In terms of domestic heaters where an electric or natural gas water heater can cost on an average $250-$400 U.S. dollars per year, after installation costs and capital expenditures which would hopefully be achieved at current heater prices, the average cost of heating a 5.50 kW fusion-based water heater could be as low as $50.00 per year (Haag, 1990). In addition, the low neutron radiation is highly desirable because there is only a limited amount of harmful radioactivity that could be easily shielded even for home use.

Heating tap water from 40° F to a temperature of 158°F requires an energy input of 0.26 kWh per gallon of water. The average consumption for a family of four is 80 gallons per day, requiring 20.8 kWh of energy. The height of standard residential water heaters is 152 cm, a deuterium storing metal rod electrode having this height and a diameter of 1.3 cm with a heat generation rate of 50 W/cm^3 of electrode, a corresponding energy output of 0.050 kWh cm^3 could be achieved with a volume of 200 cm^3 of electrode material.

Over $8 billion per year is spent on fossil fuels for heating water in the United States. This represents 4% of our total energy needs. The nuclear fusion-based water heater could save up to 90% of this cost for consumers per year. The systems where industrials would be positively effected are: (1) Water heating; (2) steam generation for sterilization; (3) water distillation; (4) air conditioning; (5) cooking; (6) heating for greenhouses; (7) heaters for chemical processing plants; (8) heaters for various transportation vehicles (trains, planes, buses, trucks); (9) heaters for snow, ice removal; (10) heaters for swimming pools and hot tubs.

Web Sites And Home Pages

Several organizations are actively pursuing licensed commercial applications for their proven "cold fusion" technologies. Further information about these applications can be found at the Institute for New Energy web site at www.padrak.com/ine/.

Conclusions

The challenge before us is to move forward with the expansion of worldwide teamwork, the study of Li and Ni, reverse profiles for low nuclear concentrations, and to make a closer study of several elements such as Al, Bi, Ca, Dy, Gd and Sm that are considered the reaction products of requisite existence for Cold Fusion activity.

Many of these theories although different are similar suggesting that there may be a unifying mechanism behind cold fusion phenomenon, such as zero-point energy fluctuations. Clearly the challenge beckons our full attention.

---

1. Bockris, John (1989) "A Review of the Investigation of the Fleischmann-Pons Phenomena," *Texas A& M University*, p. 20.
2. Bockris, J., Packham, N., Wold, K.L., Wass, J.C. & Kainthia, R.C. (1989b.) "Production of Tritium from D2O Electrolysis at a Rd Cathode," *J. Electroanalyt. Chem.*, **Vol. 270**.
3. Bockris, J. & Lin, G.H. (1996) "Proceedings of the Low Energy Nuclear Reactions Conference," *Journal of New Energy*, **Vol. 1**, No. 1, Fusion Information Center, P.O. Box 58639, Salt Lake City, UT 84158-0638. www.padrak.com/ine/.
4. Burrows, Adam (1989) "Enhancement of Cold Fusion in Metal 'Hydrides' by screening of proton and deuteron charges," *Physical Review B*, **Vol. 40**, No. 5.
5. Bush, Robert T. (1994) "A Unifying Model for Cold Fusion," *Transactions of Fusion Technology*, December 1994, **Vol. 26**, pp. 431-440.
6. DeNino, A. *et al* (1989) "Evidence of Emission of Neutrons from a Titanium-D System," *Europhysics Lett.*, **Vol. 9**, p. 221.
7. DuFour, Jacques (1993) "Cold Fusion by Sparking in Hydrogen Isotopes," *Fusion Technology*, September 1993, **Vol. 24**, pp. 205-222.
8. Fedorovich, Gennady V. (1993) "A Possible Way to Nuclear Fusion in Solids," *Fusion Technology*, November 1993, **Vol. 24**, pp. 288-292.
9. Glueck, Peter (1993) The Surfdyn Concept: An attempt to Solve the Puzzles of Cold Fusion," *Fusion Technology*, August 1993, **Vol. 24**, pp. 122-126.
10. Gozzi, D. *et al* (1990) "Evidences for Associated Heat Generation and Nuclear Products Release in Palladium Heavy-Water Electrolysis," *Il Nuovo Cimento*, January 1990, **Vol. 103 A**, No.1, pp.143-151.
11. Gozzi, D. *et al* (1990) "Neutron and Tritium Evidence in the Electrolytic Reaction of Deuterium on Palladium Electrodes,"*Fusion Technology*, **Vol. 21**, p. 60.
12. Haag, Arthur (1990) *Personal discussions for Electrofusion, Inc*, Houston, in Honolulu, Hi, June 1990.
13. Hagelstein, Peter L. (1990) "Coherent Fusion Reaction echanism," *Proc. 1st Annual Conference on Cold Fusion*, March 28-31, 1990, Salt Lake City, Utah, p. 99.
14. Iyengar, P.K. (1989) "Cold Fusion Results in BARC Experiments," *Fifth Intern. Conference Emer. Nuclear Energy System*, Karlsruhe, Germany.
15. Johnson, Keith (1994) "Jahn-Teller Symmetry Breaking and Hydrogen Energy in Gamma-PdD "Cold Fusion" as Storage of the 'Latent Heat' of Water," *Transactions of Fusion Technology*, December 1994, **Vol. 26**, pp. 427-430.

16. Jones, S.E., Palmer, E.P. et al (1989) "Observation of cold nuclear fusion in condensed matter," *Nature*, April 27, 1989, **Vol. 338**, pp. 737-740.
17. King, Moray (1989) *Tapping the Zero-Point Energy*. Paraclete Publishing Provo, Utah, p.145.
18. Kühne, Reiner (1994) "The Possible Hot Nature of Cold Fusion," *Fusion Technology*, March 1994, **Vol. 25**.
19. Matsumoto, Takaaki (1993) "Observations of Meshlike Traces of Nuclear Emulsions During Cold Fusion," *Fusion Technology*, January 1993, **Vol. 23**.
20. McKubre, Michael C.H. et al (1994) "An overview of Excess Heat Production in the Deuterated Palladium System," August *1994 Intersociety Energy Conversion Engineering Conference*, pp.1478-1483.
21. Palibrods, E.& Glueck, P. (1991) "Cold Nuclear Fusion in Tin Foils of Pd," *Radioanal.Nucl. Chem. Letter*, **Vol. 154**.
22. Pons, S. & Fleischmann, M. (1989) "Electrochemically Induced Nuclear Fusion of Deuterium," *Journal of Electroanal Chemistry*, **Vol. 261**, 301.
23. Pons, S. & Fleischmann, M. (1990) "Our Calorimetric Measurements of the Pd/S Systems," *First Conference on Cold Fusion*, March 27, 1990, Salt Lake City, Utah.
24. Rabinowitz, Mario (1990) *Physics Letters*. **Vol. 4**, No. 4, pp. 233-246.
25. Rabinowitz, Mario (1990) "Cold Fusion: Myth Verses Reality," *IEEE Power Engineering Review*, January 1990, pp. 16-17.
26. Rothwell, Jed (1996) "One Kilowatt Cold Fusion Reactor Demonstrated," *Infinite Energy: Cold Fusion and New Energy Technology*, January 1996.
27. Sanchez, C. et al (1989) "Nuclear Products Detection During Electrolysis of Heavy Water with Ti and Pt Electrodes," *Solid State Commun.*, **Vol. 71**, p. 1039.
28. Silver, David et al (1993) "Surface Topology of a Palladium Cathode After Electrolysis in Heavy Water," *Fusion Technology*, **Vol. 24**.
29. Storms, E. (1991) "Review of Experimental Observations About the Cold Fusion Effect," *Fusion Technology*, **Vol. 20**.
30. Vaidya, S.N. (1993) "Comments on the Model for Coherent Deuteron-Deuteron Fusion in Crystalline Pd-D Lattice," *Fusion Technology*, August 1993, **Vol. 24**.

28

Sacred Geometry: Insights

Patrick G. Bailey, Ph.D.

There are many books and many articles on "Sacred Geometry." Some of the most fascinating facts described are the fundamentals that relate the geometrical constants *e*, *phi*, and *pi*, and their relationships to regular 2-D figures and 3-D Platonic solids—what they stand for and how these constants interact.

In two-dimensional geometry (2-D): the number *pi* [π] is defined as the ratio of the circumference of a circle to its diameter:

π = circle's circumference/diameter
 = 3.141592653590...

The number *phi* [ϕ] appears in many geometrical constructs, such as pentagrams, and is simply defined as:

$\phi = (1 + \text{SQRT}(5))/2 = 1.618033988750...$

And the number *e* appears in calculus and in growth equations, where the rate of growth (or decay) is proportional to the amount present, and is defined as:

$e = exp(1) = 2.718281828459...$

and is the base of the natural logarithms; where ln(*e*) is the natural logarithm (ln) of *e*, (in base *e*) and is equal by definition to:

ln(*e*) = 1

It is very interesting to see how these constants relate to each other in mathematical sequences, music, and in 2-D and 3-D geometry. For example, by definition: ϕ = 1 + 1/ϕ, which leads to the infinite series of (1+1/ (1+1/ (1+1/ 1+...,))) which should have solid references in the definitions of musical scales.

SEQUENCES

One of the simplest sequences known is one in which the next term is twice the previous term (1,2,4,8,16,32,....) known as a binary sequence. Another famous sequence is one in which the next term equals the sum of the previous two terms (1,1,2,3,5,8,13,21,34,...) known as a Fibonacci sequence. In any Fibonacci sequence, regardless of which two integers are chosen to start it, the ratio of any two adjacent terms always and eventually converges to ϕ [*phi*] (1.618...).

Phi even emerges from the mathematics of life. Suppose that a living organism is composed of cells that can divide at defined set intervals, based upon an internal clock. If the cells each divide into two cells during one interval, we have twice the number of cells in the next interval, forming a binary sequence, based on powers of 2, where the number of cells in the next interval (i+1) would be N(i+1) = 2 * N(i). If we assume that the life force of the parent cell is not enough to allow both daughter cells to divide in the next time interval, so one cell can divide while the other must wait one more time interval before dividing, then we obtain a Fibonacci sequence, based on powers of ϕ: N(i+1) = ϕ * N(i).

And also, if we assume that the number of cells that can be produced is always proportional to the total number of cells that are present, we obtain an exponential growth, based on the exponent $\exp(x)=e^x$: $N(i+1) = \exp(a*ti)\, N(i)$, where *a* is the growth constant and *ti* is a time measurement (e.g., this equation is used to calculate radioactive decay.)

Music

The 12 musical notes of music today form a unique sequence. By assuming that the energy of the next musical note is proportional to the frequency of the previous note (neutral, sharp, or flat note), we obtain the sequence for the frequency of note N(i) over one musical octave (e.g., for the 13 notes from C to C'):

$$N(i) = N(0) * \exp[\ln(2)*(i/12)] \text{ for } i = 0 \text{ to } 12$$

So we see that the ratios of the notes are thus uniquely defined, and we can define N(0) = A' (above Middle C) = 440 cps (cycles per second), which is the current standard as defined today. We also note the definitions of the octaves, where N(12) is twice that of N(0), or A" at 880 cps. A plot of this exponential growth and various definitions for each note using ratios of specific integers to approximate these mathematically exact musical ratios were presented in the past.

It is also interesting to plot these 13 notes on a clock face, beginning with N(0) at 12 o'clock and numbering clockwise. We see that all the notes correspond to the 12 clock numbers, and are all separated by 30°. The major chord C-E-G-C' could be represented by a triangle formed by connecting the numbers 12-4-7-12. However, the proper representation might rather be to draw that triangle inside the musical spiral formed by the above equation on a clock face (i.e. in polar coordinates). Perhaps there is a relationship between the shapes of the triangles that identify each chord, and the tonal effect of that chord.

> ... [I]t is in accord with observation and experiment that the musical interval which gives the greatest satisfaction to the greatest number [of people] is the 'major sixth,'

Sacred Geometry: Insights

Figure 28.1
Musical Spiral and Chord C-E-G-C. Drawing by Patrick G. Bailey.

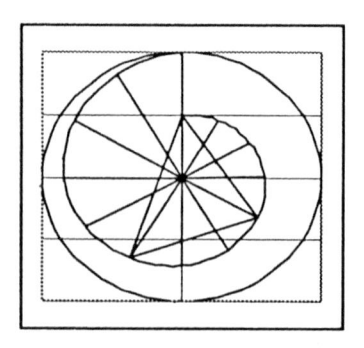

frequency 8:5 approximately [C':E]. This corresponds to the pleasure experienced in seeing the golden rectangle, the adjacent sides of which are in the ratio ϕ:1, which is approximately 8:5.

It is also the same as the major 6th or the keynote in *Rhapsody in Blue*.

2-D GOLDEN SPIRALS

One *Golden Spiral* that has often been defined as a "Sacred Geometry" is formed by connecting several quarter-circles of different sizes to create a spiral effect, with the size of the radius of the next circle being 1/ϕ more than that of the previous circle (known as *swirling Golden rectangles*). A true mathematical golden spiral would be an equi-angular spiral, which would have an equation similar to the musical note equation above, and would result in multiples of *phi* per revolution, rather than multiples of 2 as in the musical spiral. So the equation of a equi-angular Golden Spiral would then be:

$$r(\theta) = r(0) * \exp[\ln(\phi) * \theta/360]$$
for θ = 0 to 360 deg.

where theta is the polar angle that goes between 0 and 360° (one revolution), and the radius of the spiral, *r*, would then smoothly vary from r(0) to ϕ*r(0) per each

Sacred Geometry: Insights

Figure 28.2
Golden Spiral (equiangular). Drawing by Patrick G. Bailey.

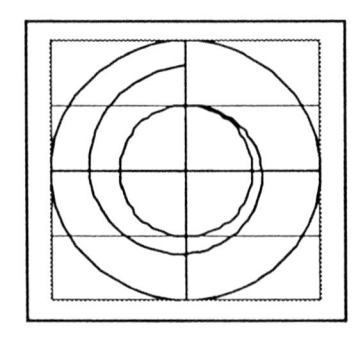

revolution.

Approximations of this pure mathematical spiral are seen everywhere in nature, in snail shells, sea shells, leaves, flowers, etc.[1]

As a result of related 2-D calculations, close approximations that relate *e*, *phi*, and *pi* have been found to be:

ϕ [approx.] = exp(ln(2)**2) [to -0.08 % error]
π [approx.] = 4/sqrt(ϕ) [to 0.10 % error]
e/π [approx.] = sin(60 deg.) [to -0.09 % error]

It is truly amazing how these seemingly independent sacred constants could be so closely and simply related!

3-D DOUBLE TETRAHEDRON

The number *phi* appears most strikingly in the pentagram (5-pointed star) and in the first Platonic Solid, the Tetrahedron, a 3-D pyramid composed of a triangular base and three sides to an apex having all sides of equal length. Such a solid will exactly fit into a sphere. When another inverted tetrahedron is placed inside the same sphere, and rotated 60°, the symmetrical solid thus formed is called a "Double Tetrahedron."

It is interesting that when viewing this solid from the top-most apex, a 6-sided "Star of David" (two superimposed equilateral triangles) is seen.

Sacred Geometry: Insights

Figure 28.3
Double Tetrahedron in a Sphere (top view above apex). Drawing by Patrick G. Bailey.

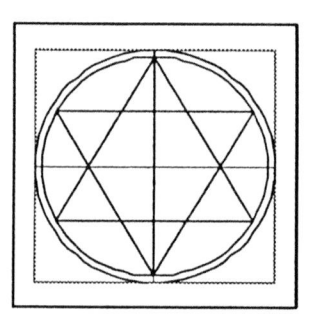

It can easily be shown that the radius of the circle that circumscribes this star is not the radius of the sphere, and is in fact equal to 2*SQRT(2)/3 (about 0.94) of the radius of the sphere. This is due to the fact that the bottom points of the upward apex tetrahedron do not lie in a 2-D plane of symmetry of the sphere (they are lower). Also, when viewed from the side, when looking at a protruding apex, one does not see a "Star of David." Due to these 3-D effects, if the radius of the sphere is defined as one, then the height of the 6 pointed star (side-view) will be 2, the height of each triangle will be 4/3, the lengths of the horizontal arms will be 4/sqrt(6), and the horizontal arms will be placed exactly 1/6 of the radius closer to the center of the sphere than in an exact 2-D "Star of David."

Also, as these arms extend 1/3rd of the radius below and above the center of the sphere, the latitude where these protruding apex points intersect the sphere is at arcsin (1/3), or 19.4712206°..., and is known as the

Figure 28.4
Double Tetrahedron in a Sphere (side view toward an apex). Drawing by Patrick G. Bailey.

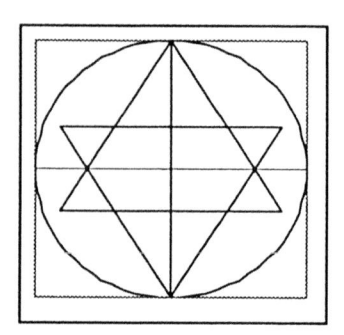

Sacred Geometry: Insights

famous "tetrahedral geometry" angle. Some researchers say that this latitude on planets is where certain special energy formations or conjunctions can appear, such as the famous "Red Spot" on Jupiter.

Also, we note that the tetrahedron, the first Platonic solid, exactly fits into a cube, the second Platonic solid, with its 4 apex points exactly fitting into 4 corners of the cube. So the 19.47 "tetrahedral physics" geometric angle is also applicable to "cube physics"—which goes to show that there is always another side to any point of view.

Now: What 2-D symmetrical shape could you use inside of a 2-D circle to closely approximate this 3-D tetrahedron 19.47° latitude angle? Look at any WW II US aircraft: Yes, it's a pentagram — at 18° latitude. Surprised?

THE GREAT PYRAMID: SQUARING THE CIRCLE

Herodotus, the great historian, is said to have learned from temple priests (in 440 BC) that the square of the height of the Great Pyramid of Egypt is equal to the area of each face.[2] As the square of ϕ is equal to $\phi + 1$ (from above), we can see that the proportions of the Great Pyramid's height, half-base, and apothem (from the apex to the mid-base) were respectively: sqrt(ϕ) : 1 : ϕ.

We should also note that these proportions were said to be valid during the time when the pyramid was covered with its smooth and polished limestone casing blocks, and the apex may or may not have been on top

Figure 28.5
Phi Ratio Pyramid
(side view). Drawing by
Patrick G. Bailey.

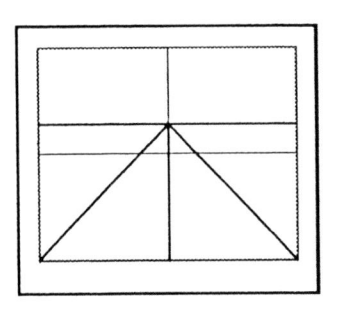

Sacred Geometry: Insights

of a solid capstone. So, we see that the square of the height (φ) is indeed equal to the area of one face (0.5*φ*2).

It is said mathematically that the squaring of the circle is an unsolvable problem. However, in these ratio units, the circumference of the base of the pyramid is 4*(1+1), or 8, and its height is sqrt(φ). If we draw a circle with a radius of that height [sqrt(φ)], we find that the circumference of that circle, 2*π*sqrt(φ), is very, very close to 8 (to 0.10 %)!

Figure 28.6
Phi Ratio Pyramid (top view) and Circle of Radius SQRT(Phi). Drawing by Patrick G. Bailey.

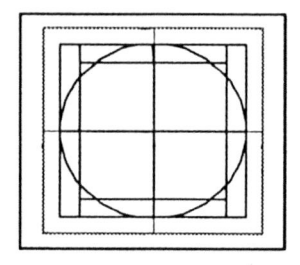

Also, since the area of a rectangle drawn from the pyramid's total base to its apex is 2*sqrt(φ), and this area is almost exactly equal to half of the area of a circle of radius sqrt(φ) [π*φ/2], and this latter area is exactly equal to the spherical surface of a quadrant of 90° (1/8 of a sphere's surface) THEN, with the Great Pyramid of Egypt (probably built between 7,000 to 2,500 BC), the ancient priests not only squared the circle, but effectively cubed the sphere.[2]

Some things never change, and many of these are sacred.

---

1. Huntley, H. E. (1970) *The Divine Proportion: A study in Mathematical Beauty*. Dover Pubs.
2. Tompkins, Peter (1971) *Secrets of the Great Pyramid*. Harper & Row.

29

Liberating Universal Constants: The Physics of Immortality

J.J. Hurtak, Ph.D., Ph.D.

Science and spiritual consciousness must in the end complement each other. An understanding of this congruence should be able to successfully surmount the most crucial problems facing the human community and the Earth. The false belief that a separation between science and spirituality, an illusion that split the human psyche and created a vacuum, occurred about 450 years ago in the West. There followed an ever-increasing stream of disciplines that are microcosmic but not holistic in perspective, and many of these disciplines are still in place today.

The deeper science looks at finding more integral answers, the closer it is coming to the existence of a unified force directed by a Divine field of energy. This Divine field cannot simply be present in this dimension, but must also permeate all dimensions, while at the same time defining "what is the nature of matter." Simply put, matter is energy, localized in the form of particles that have properties we currently define as mass, charge, and spatial extent in this dimensional reality.

We know that atoms in space demonstrate movement. The vibrating or "standing waves" of electrons around the nucleus represents continuous energy. In its quantum state, the angular momentum of the electron remains constant. But why is there this "constant", and is there some way to predict the constant even before it is measured? The fundamental laws of "known" physics depend on about 25 parameters, such as Planck's constant h, the gravitational constant G, and the mass and charge of the electron. It is natural to ask whether these parameters are really constants, or whether they vary in space or time.

The *gravitational constant (G)* has been intricately measured as $G = 6.670 +/- 0.005 \times 10^{-8}$ dyne-centimeter squared per gram squared (or approximately 10 m/sec^2). The graviton, the elementary unit that is said to cause this force of gravitation, is still unseen and unknown. Finding it would be equivalent to the discovery of the electron or photon (light particle). In truth, although there is a specific number for the gravitational constant, in theory the speed of gravity in Newton's Universal Law is unconditionally infinite[1]. Newtonian gravity can propagate with unconditionally infinite speed. This has confounded physicists, especially those who are examining "black holes"—for if nothing can escape the event horizon because nothing can propagate faster than light, how does gravity get out of a black hole?

The speed of light plays a major part in this small group of fundamental constants, where energy and mass are related by Einstein's equation, $E = mc^2$, which identifies an energy, E, as equivalent to a rest mass, m, multiplied by c^2, where c is the velocity of light. The speed of light c is perhaps the most famous constant. According to the US National Bureau of Standards:

$c = 299{,}792.4574 + 0.0011$ km/s,

but for the British National Physical Laboratory:

$c = 299{,}792.4590 + 0.0008$ km/s.

Regardless of what fraction you use, the speed of

Figure 29.1
*Albert Einstein
(1879-1955).*

light is said to be the same in all inertial frames of reference in all directions, and it is independent of the velocity of the source as well as the observer.

Einstein (1905) derived his equations from the research of J.C. Maxwell and Lorentz. Maxwell and Lorentz although both considering the existence of an "ether" ignored it in most calculations, hence the concentration on electromagnetic fields exclusively by Maxwell. Einstein, on the other hand, recognized the influence of not "free space," such as gravitational fields. For Einstein, free space (a vacuum) was a requirement for consistency, where all atoms and fields, including gravitational fields, would have to be removed because the velocity of light could change due to interactions between light and a medium.

What made Einstein famous was an "apparent" confirmation of this phenomenon which he had predicted by his general theory of relativity. Einstein calculated that a light beam, passing near to the Sun, would be bent 1.75 arc seconds. Half of this bending was caused by a change of the velocity of light (c), which he calculated as the *general theory of relativity* which deducts an equation for the velocity of "light" in a gravitational field. The second half was determined by the "curvature" of space, which related to the quantity of the present gravitational mass.

No matter how long or hard you push on a mass, you can never impart enough energy to it so that it reaches the speed of light, c. The only possible way such a thing can travel at the speed c and still have finite energy is if it had zero mass or if it became light. So we see that gravity and mass (m) play a central role in the formation of matter in the universe. If gravitational fields permeate all living systems, 'mass' becomes the metric distortion which gives rise to the observed effects we view as inertia.

Moreover, electromagnetic wave energy can propagate at the velocity of light, c, in free space (non-localized). Here electromagnetic waves as photons (light energy) can be represented by Planck's equation:

$$E = \frac{hc}{\lambda}$$

where h is Planck's constant, λ is the wavelength of the energy, and E is the energy associated with a photon in observer space.

Having an elementary particle, that exists in some form of matter or mass, creates non-free space. Planck was able to show the importance of gravity when he demonstrated that it was possible to construct a length, a time and a mass, by means of Newton's gravitation constant G, the velocity of light and the new Planck constant. In non-free space, the metric index, n, necessarily differs from unity. This causes the local velocity of light, v, as perceived by the observer, to differ from the free space value, c, as:

$$v = \frac{c}{n}$$

These equations are simply demonstrating that photons, or light which can be both particle and wave, can be affected by matter. This means that although there does exist a "constant" known as c, it has variables that must continually be accounted for, depending on the medium through which it is penetrating.

There is another constant worth noting, and that is the "fine structure constant" denoted by the Greek letter α (*alpha*) which shows the inherent strength of the electromagnetic (*em*) force, defined as the charge of the electron squared, divided by the product of Planck's constant (h) and the speed of light (c). The size of α determines how well atoms hold together.

How the constant α might vary again pin-points the real question: Do constants exist at all? Interest in the possible variations of α was spurred by Paul Dirac's large number hypothesis. Here again, one of the principal factors involves the gravitational force. Dirac's "Large Number" Hypothesis[2] is the ratio of the electric and the gravitational force between two electrons, which is about 10^{39}. Dirac pointed out that this number required the gravitational constant G to be

Figure 29.2
Johannes Kepler
(1571-1630).

a function of time and could relate to the age of the Universe in atomic units. Dirac suggested as early as 1937 (although it has not been proven) that this coincidence could be understood if fundamental constants—in particular, G—varied as the Universe aged, and that it is large because the universe is old.

Other models, including theories on quasars from John Webb at the University of New South Wales, and the Brans-Dicke theory of gravity, as well as some versions of superstring theory, also predict physical "constants" that vary.

How can variations exist?

If light can be slowed down by mass, it is most likely being held temporarily in a state that is constricted. If an elementary particle emits the photon (radiation) then it returns to its free-space mode. The speed of light has not changed. However, if we consider that the free-space mode is also a constricted medium ("empty space" is not actually empty) then we understand that the speed of light is not a constant except in this relativity. What is important here is the notion that matter and energy are truly interchangeable through the medium of space and time.

By breaking with this relativity, we can change the speed of light to not just be slower, but to speed up. Although faster-than-light force propagation speeds do violate the Lorentz invariant, they could be in accord with Einstein's theories. However, recognition of a faster-than-light-speed propagation of gravity may be the key to taking the thinking behind conventional physics to the next stage of its evolution.

Elementary particles themselves are confined by this "constricted medium" which is based on Supergravity (G) and Supermagnetism (M). That is why particles have specific values and why Mendeleev and Moseley were each able to predict the existence of certain unknown elements by calculating the atomic numbers as integers that followed a straight sequence. Bohr himself saw in such an interpretation of the atomic number "an important step towards the solution of a problem which for a long time has been one of the boldest dreams of natural science, namely, to build up an understanding of the regularities of nature upon the consideration of pure numbers." [3]

Pauli and Sommerfeld also appreciated an approach to physics that conceived of the universe not as a mechanism but as a pattern in numbers, or mathematical construct. We have now determined that the ratio between the strength of the electric and gravitational forces in an atom is 10^{39} (i.e., gravity and the electromagnetic force differ by 39 orders of magnitude). Professor Victor Stenger, Astronomy Professor at the University of Hawaii, has made correlations regarding that number and the ratio of a typical stellar lifetime to the time for light to traverse the radius of a proton which is also 10^{39}—a demonstration of the Anthropic Principle.[4]

Kepler also clearly understood the power of gravity and applied it to mathematics when he stated his Third Law of Planetary Motion (in 1619): "The square of the period of time it takes a planet to complete an orbit of the Sun is proportional to the cube of its mean distance from the Sun."

This demonstrates a relationship where P represents the sidereal period of the orbit in years and a is the semi-major axis of the orbit in AU (astronomical units); k is a constant which is unique for every body under consideration. Of course this constant is valid because it is a stable body and therefore provides us with a constancy of ratio:

$$a^3 / P^2 = k$$

where $k=1$; $a^3 = P^2$. For example, a planet like Jupiter that is 5 AU from the Sun would have an orbit of about 11.2 years, whereas planets closer to the Sun orbit more rapidly than those farther away.

Kepler's Third Law is a powerful tool for exploring the Universe and is still being used almost 500 years after Kepler lived, because it gives us a way to measure the absolute masses of planets and stars, including binary stars. Once we determine the mass of a star, we can estimate its intrinsic luminosity, its density, its size, etc.

Now, this all relates back to gravity. In fact, Newton adjusted one of Kepler's calculations. But if we add another dimension to gravity and realize that it may not be a localized force, then we will be able to use certain technological ways and means for gravity propulsion over very long distances, literally altering space and time, because we would have understood the essence of their constructs.

Distance would thus essentially become null and void. We will travel in control of the gravity waves which are powerful enough to escape from blackholes, and we ourselves will be able to travel through wormholes, by tunneling. It also means that we may be on the threshold of exchanging information not only on the structure of the universe, but also on zero-point energy applications, allowing us to tap into a "free energy" source.

So we don't have to take the logic of a radio astronomer and look 20 or 30 light years downstream to find answers. We can look at the possibilities of joining the galactic neighborhood even by our interstellar devices in this generation! Which brings us back to our spiritual responsibilities, our evolution into *homo noeticus*. It is the *sine qua non* of our advancement with a new charter of nations amongst the stars. The closer we come to understanding nature, the closer scientists are also coming to God.

In his last major work, the *Harmonice mundi*, Kepler in a sense equated God and geometry, speaking of geometry as having existed before the creation of the world, as being coeternal with the Divine Mind. Since all of God's creation had to be in some way an emanation of God's own "being," Kepler concluded that "geometry is God Himself." Geometry, as he put it, "supplied God with a model for the creation of the world and was implanted into human nature along with God's image and not through man's visual perception and experience."[5]

Figure 20.3
Title page of *Harmonices Mundi* (1619) by Johannes Kepler. The page names all five books including, the last of which discusses astronomical harmonies.

Humankind has to come to terms with *anomalous* history. In many areas of life a new consciousness of a unified science has already arisen. An inner knowing of realities operating in our immediate solar system converted to new science may feed-back and change the way planet earth looks at itself.

The influence and power of science, medicine, and technology are now so enormous that scientists, physicians, and engineers bear an unprecedented responsibility for the future. Not only their knowledge and technical skills but also their consciousness is so critical to what we make of ourselves and our world in the next decades.

We commit ourselves to the realization that science and spirituality must unite. In essence, Earth cannot be changed for the better unless the consciousness of individuals is changed. Let us pledge to work for such transformation, in individual and collective consciousness, and be prepared to use the keys to the science of the future.

---

1. Misner, C.W., Thorne, K.S. & Wheeler, J.A. (1973) *Gravitation.* W.H. San Francisco: Freeman & Co., CA, p.177.
2. *Proceedings of the Royal Society,* (1938) London, 921, 165, 199-208.
3. Bohr, Niels (1934) *Atomic Theory and the Description of Nature.* Cambridge: Cambridge University Press, 103-4.
4. Nakamura, Takashi, Hideya Uehara, & Takeshi Chiba (1997) "The Minimum Mass of the First Stars and the Anthropic Principle," *Progress of Theoretical Physics,* 97, 169-171.
5. Kepler, J. (1620) *Harmonice mundi.* Book 4, chap. 1, in Werke, VI, p. 223.

30

Hydrogen: The Fuel For Future Transportation

J.J. Hurtak, Ph.D., Ph.D.

From the environmental point of view, hydrogen is an ideal energy source. Many experts consider hydrogen as the most attractive, single fuel for the future. There is every reason to believe that the transportation sector will become the major consumer of hydrogen in the next century and will require it in quantities which were undreamed of not too long ago.

HYDROGEN FUEL RESOURCES

Six conventional processes exist for acquiring hydrogen: (1) steam reforming of natural gas (methane), (2) partial oxidation of residual oil, (3) gasification of coal using the Texaco process, (4) gasification of coal using the Koppers-Totzek process, (5) steam-iron process and (6) water electrolysis which is preferable utilizing one of our largest renewable resources on the planet.[1]

Kennedy Space Center has become one of the largest users of liquid hydrogen (LH_2) and has plans to construct its own liquid hydrogen production plant, most likely involving the process of polygeneration, a process developed by Texaco Corporation for the gasification of coal to produce methane and other coproducts.

The Space Shuttle extensively utilizes LH_2 as a fuel and as a source for generating electricity for the Shuttle while in orbit.[2]

In comparing the six processes described above, steam reforming of methane is currently the most economical process and can yield the following resulting components:[3]

Component	Volume %
H_2	74
CO	18
CO_2	6
CH_4	2

from the reaction:

$$CH_x + 2H_2O + heat/energy \longrightarrow (2 + 1/2X)H_2 + CO_x$$

when using methane: heat = approx. 1500° F and 250 psig.

Any use of a nonrenewable resource should be avoided making water electrolysis the only industrial hydrogen production process which does not necessarily rely on fossil energy. In water electrolysis, the main source of hydrogen is derived from breaking the chemical bond of H_2O. By adding acids, water becomes an electrolyte with a large number of free ions. The positive ions consist of ionized hydrogen atoms (protons) surrounded by a cluster of water molecules. One gallon of water has a hydrogen energy content of about 52,000 BTU which is just less than one-half the 119,000 BTU contained in one gallon of gasoline.[4] The electrical energy required can be derived from fossil energy, nuclear, or solar energy.

Specifically, water electrolysis involves the splitting of water into hydrogen and oxygen by passing a direct electrical current through water that has been made electrically conducting by the addition of hydrogen or hydroxyl ions (e.g., aqueous potassium hydroxide) as the electrolyte. By passing a large current through potassium hydroxide (KOH), for example, hydrogen is generated by the negative electrode connected to a direct-current supply and oxygen is generated at the positive electrode in the form of gas bubbles.

In this process the cathode reaction is:

$$2H_2O + 2e^- \longrightarrow H_2 + 2OH^-$$

the anode reaction is:

$$2OH^- \longrightarrow \tfrac{1}{2} O_2 + H_2O + 2e^-$$

The total reaction can be summarized as:

$$H_2O \longrightarrow \tfrac{1}{2} O_2 + H_2$$

Crude hydrogen produced by electrolysis is approximately 99% pure and may not require further purification. The drawbacks of water electrolysis are that it requires higher quality energy in the form of electric power, yielding limited efficiency, and requiring large expensive electrode surfaces. With electricity at a base cost of $.049/kWh, the hydrogen production cost is still about $6.57/$10^3$ SCF ($20.36/$10^6$ Btu).[5] Oxygen production can be separated for possible use and provides an additional credit to the economics of the process.

Solar energy is being studied as an adjunct to both electrochemical and thermochemical processes to improve hydrogen production efficiencies. During combustion of water, 33kWh/kg^2 of energy is released as heat or, in the case of fuel cells, directly as electric current. Attempts to produce hydrogen from solar energy by photolysis of water are coming closer to achieving a practical level of cost/utilization. Cleaving water molecules by direct application of heat requires a temperature of approximately 2500° C. By exploiting the photoelectric effect of semiconductors (e.g., silicon), electricity can be obtained without a detour via heat processes and mechanical energy. This direct route to

Hydrogen: The Fuel For Future Transportation

Figure 30.1
Solar energy is being studied to improve hydrogen production efficiencies. Image courtesy of NASA.

conversion of solar energy to electricity is realized in solar cells. This main focus in the development of new solar cell technologies (thin-film cells, amorphous semiconductors) reduces production costs for solar generators. Germany's DFVLR has developed along with Saudi Arabia, a project known as HYSOLAR which has already tested both 10 kW and 100 kW plants for hydrogen production. HYSOLAR combines the electrical properties of a solar generator with an electrolyzer, where 95% of the generator power can be coupled into the electrolysis.[6] Here the photo-electrochemical conversion of solar to chemical energy is a one step process. A semiconductor acting as a photoelectrode in an electrolysis type cell arrangement is exposed to sunlight, thereby producing an internal photocurrent. This current immediately drives the electrochemical reaction at the contact surface between electrode and electrolyte. In principle, the photo-electrochemical process represents a simpler technological approach to water splitting since an external intermediate generation of electricity is thereby avoided. Problems faced by the HYSOLAR researchers include corrosion, predominantly of the O_2 electrode.[7]

Most solar systems are only 10-12% efficient, dish energy conversion systems such as the Stirling dish gensets manufactured by United Stirling of Sweden has shown as high as 28% efficiently and similar systems were developed during the late 1970s at Edwards Air Force Base and later by Southern California Edison and EPRI. Each dish can be produced for less than $10,000 with a 20kW-output unit or just under $200 dollars per installed kW lowering the cost of the photovoltaic-electrolytic process.[8]

Ortenheim and Lundquist developed a different approach towards the water electrolysis process where water is thermally dissociated in oxygen and hydrogen in a high current arc plasma. Part of the energy for producing the high temperature plasma was taken from a conventional electric energy source, part from solar radiation focused on and absorbed by the arc plasma.[9] The feasibility of the method was demonstrated, but the existing financial resources did not permit a quantitative evaluation of the method.

Ortenheim and Lundquist suggested that a finely dispersed cloud of water mist should be charged with the highest possible positive charge on each droplet. The mist is then exposed to very repeated pulses or to a sinusoidally varying electric field of very high intensity. The applied field is added to the field caused by the droplet charge on one side of the droplet. On the other side, the fields have opposite direction and the resulting field is low. If the field strength on the first side reaches the ion emission limit one can expect hydrogen ions to be emitted from each droplet. The electromagnetic field could be caused by a powerful laser.[10]

The water molecule has an energy of formation

from atoms of 219 kcal/mole. The energy for dissociation of hydrogen is 118 kcal/mole. In a strongly ionized plasma the free plasma electrons interact with an atom immersed in the plasma in such a way that the binding energy of the electrons is decreased. The effect results in a shift of the frequency of the spectral lines from atoms in the plasma.

A similar effect is expected on the binding energy of atoms in a molecule immersed in water. The polarizability of the water molecules decreases the electric field around a charge (ion) in the water and the binding energy is decreased. Therefore, the removal of hydrogen from a water molecule in water is expected to require less energy than for a molecule in water vapor.

HYDROGEN IN GROUND TRANSPORTATION SYSTEMS

When cost effective systems for hydrogen production are achieved, hydrogen will be a prime candidate for fueling internal combustion engines because of its renewable nature and low pollutant emission characteristics. In 1978 a cooperative agreement was made between the University of Denver and Ergenics of New Jersey to produce an advanced prototype hydrogen vehicle using a Dodge D-50 pickup truck with a three-value combustion chamber in a Mitsubishi 2.6 liter MCA-Jet engine. After some revisions and additional development by Denver-based Hydrogen Consultants, Inc. (HCI) the vehicle was fitted with a 537 kg hydride system which was able to achieve 29 km/kg (18 miles) city and 57 km/kg (37 miles) highway using hydrogen fuel. The D-50 over a period of five days made a total of 18 trips in Denver city traffic having an average of 18 mph. Usual operating speeds were between 30-45 mph. Another short test run in 1988 was between Fort Collins and Castle Rock where the average speed was maintained at 52 mph.[11]

The D-50 research evolved into the Mitsubishi Rosa-25 passenger bus with a 2.4-liter Mitsubishi 4G53 engine developed by HCI (Denver) and sponsored by a joint project funded by Ergenics and Mitsubishi Motor

Corporation.[12] The University of Denver also co-sponsored development with Eimco Mining Company of Utah to create a mining vehicle utilizing a hydrogen-powered engine.

The Institute for Problems in Machinery at the Ukr SSR Academy of Science (Soviet Union) simultaneously tested an internal mixture formation using a swirl chamber hydrogen-fueled (LH_2) engine in comparison to an external mixture formation. They concluded that a swirl chamber diesel engine has a better prospect of being converted to hydrogen than other diesel engines because of the gradual increase of pressure in the cylinder, the good conditions of mixture formation at the compression stroke, reduction in the ignition delay period and the reduction of NO_x are a few of the reasons sited. They also reported no problems of a cold start.[13] The Soviet research lead to the development of a passenger van RAF-2203, a passenger car VAZ-2101, and a forklift that ran completely on stored LH_2.

Critical problems have been the storage and transport of hydrogen in the vehicle. The weight ratio of hydrogen and gasoline is only .37 calorific value, but hydrogen volume in normal state is 3,000 times as large as gasoline in liquid state. Therefore, although easy to use the liquid hydrogen storage is not acceptable for small passenger cars due to the following statistics:[14]

Component	Volume	Weight (kg)	Tank(kg)	Total(kg)
Gasoline	30	22	5	27
Methanol	62	49	8	57
LH_2	117	8.2	65	73

High pressure bottle storage (HP) or Metal Hydrides (MH) are more suitable. Until recently MH had an insufficient discharge pressure for injection, but since 1989 this has been overcome through the work of Daimler-Benz (Stuttgart). Now vast qualities of hydrogen can be safely stored in relatively small spaces. Since about 1970, scientists have been using certain metal alloys for storing the gas as metal-hydrogen compounds. Daimler-Benz began its research

Hydrogen: The Fuel For Future Transportation

Figure 30.2
Hydrogen van as debuted in Russia. Photo by D. Hurtak.

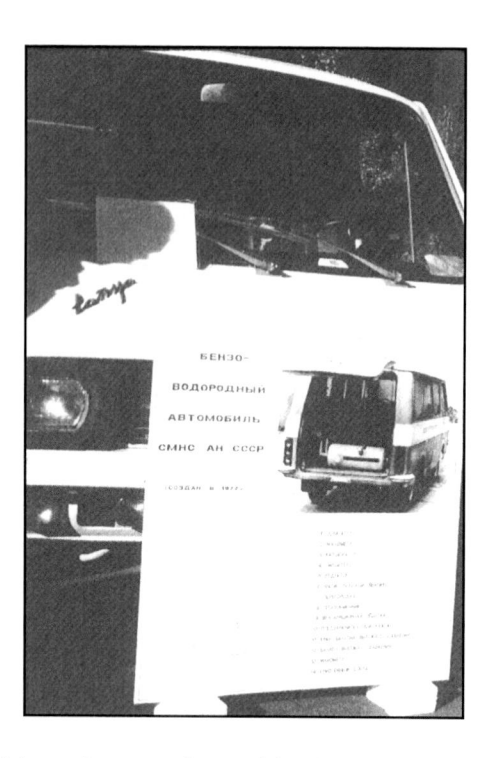

in 1974 into the use of metal hydrides where gaseous hydrogen is absorbed by metal powder in tubes forming the hydrides. One of the first alloys was a combination of lanthanum and nickel, $LaNi_5$. It is cheaper and safer than cryogenic storage. The chemically bound hydrogen is released by gently heating the hydrides. Problems exist with the high weight of the hydride in lightweight automobiles, however in buses or trucks the extra weight is less noticeable.[15]

Due to extensive research efforts during the past five years, the development of hydride storage tanks suitable for vehicle application has lead to the development of the alloy TiZrVFeCrMn (Code 5800) which was a milestone in this field.[16] The hydrogen storage unit is designed as a shell and tube exchanger. The tubes containing the hydrogen bonded to the metal are surrounded by water which absorbs the heat transfer. The metal hydride has a maximum hydrogen capacity of 1.8% by weight and provides sufficient hydrogen pressure for vehicle operations. A tubular heat exchanger has proved to be the best solution for a vehicle storage tank where the hydride material is inside the tubes and the tubes are surrounded by a fluid flow.

Other studies by the Max Plank Institute for Coal Research in Germany developed a preparation of magnesium hydride doped with various transition metals such as Ni resulting in a compound with excellent storage, hydrogenation/dehydrogenation and cycling characteristics.[17]

Research advances in fuel injection and a high temperature bicomponent system have made hydrogen one of the safest fuels for ground (and air) applications. New methods developed for a hydrogen injection engine will bring air into the cylinder and compress it, improving the response or concentrated time of firing to less than 200 micro seconds. Throughout the development of hydrogen-fueled engines various external and internal mixture formation methods have been used. Although both engines have their advantages most researchers have decided that the internal combustion engine with late fuel injection has provided the best options.

A typical problem arises when hydrogen is ignited by a spark which although demonstrates an extremely

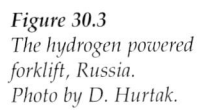

Figure 30.3
The hydrogen powered forklift, Russia.
Photo by D. Hurtak.

low energy in a wide inflammable range, its self-ignition temperature is so high that it is difficult to apply the compression ignition. Methods such as injection hydrogen into a cylinder while valves are closed to prevent backfire allows the heat content for the mixture to be increased by 20% compared to gasoline. In spite of problems such as irregular combustion, noise, increased NO_x emissions and requirement of advanced injection and storage systems, this technique is applicable to both four and two stroke engines and also to diesel engines.

AIRCRAFT TRANSPORTATION SYSTEMS

In April 15, 1988, the Soviet Union demonstrated the Tupolev TU-155 passenger aircraft that was able to fly on hydrogen, stored on board in a liquid form. The aircraft was a TU-154 that has its starboard Kuznetsov NK-8 turbofan engine modified to burn LH_2. The Tupolev, a medium sized jet transport, was completely powered by the hydrogen engine during a 21 minute flight. The plane contained a 15 cu. meters (4,000 gallons) liquid hydrogen tank in the aft.[18]

In studies involving passenger aircraft, hydrogen has been stored on board in liquid form because liquid is the minimum density state when the storage container is included. At standard pressure, liquid hydrogen has a boiling point of -253° C and must therefore be stored in containers with highly effective insulation. Vaporization amounts to a high of 1-2% per day, especially under pressure.[19]

In the TU-155, a sealed bulkhead in front of the tank was used in conjunction with higher pressure in the rest of the cabin to keep the hydrogen fumes from entering the forward cabin. The tank was pressurized to 1.5-2 atmospheres although it was difficult to maintain a constant fuel pressure.

A heat exchanger next to the boost pump used ambient air to heat the hydrogen to a gas at -100° C (-148° F), before being fed to the engine. The engine is throttled by valves controlling the liquid and gaseous hydrogen before and after the heat exchanger.

Due to the size of the tank only a limited number of seats were available on the aircraft and the tank held only two hours of fuel.

In addition to modifying existing passenger aircraft, there is also the need for high speed passenger and cargo planes as follow-ons to the Concorde. These aircraft would be larger because most studies show the requirements for 250-300 passengers for an economical 12,000 km transport. Once under production, hydrogen fueled planes should cost no more than $500 million (1990) each and would have a minimum commercial life of 500 flights requiring 292,000 lbs per flight of slush hydrogen (containing ice particles which are 15-20 times more dense than the normal boiling-point of liquid hydrogen with an 18% higher ability to absorb heat[20]) at a cost of $.50/lb.[21] With modern trade relations, immediate access across the Pacific, to South America and to southern Africa will require high speeds and long ranges.

Sonic boom and ozone depletion in the stratosphere have joined economics as crucial design factors. Aircraft above Mach 2 are known to release damaging NO_x into the atmosphere. To reduce NO_x a rich burn, quench, lean burn combustion system can be used where fuel is vaporized and mixed with air ahead of the flame so that all fresh mixtures enter at the air-to-fuel ratio, or a rich mixture that will not form NO_x is created and then air is rapidly added to make it lean. Leftover fuel consumes carbon monoxide and soot produced by the rich burn. Another process is to shorten the combustion as in the ATREX expanded cycle ATR turbojet engine where NO_x can also be reduced by reducing the high temperature residence time to a value where the non-equilibrium NO_x concentration, of very slow forming NO_x, and the fast hydrogen reaction are at equilibrium values.[22]

Research at Langley Research Center, has shown that small aircraft can reduce sonic booms to acceptable levels. NASA Langley's goal for the High Speed Civil Transport program is set to reduce NO_x emitted per pound of fuel burned to 5-10 g/kg. compared to 50-60 g/kg. for the Concorde. There appears to be two regions that permit low overpressure [less than 1. psf], or shock free overpressure signature. One region is for smaller sized aircraft flying up to Mach 2. The other region is for very large aircraft (300 Mg or larger) flying at high altitude above Mach 4.[23]

Gulfstream Aerospace Corporation also has conceived of an aircraft that would carry 10-15 passengers over a 5,000 naut.-mi range at speeds up to Mach 2 designed to meet the needs of the Pacific Rim in the early 21st century. Sukhoi Corporation has joined the supersonic market with aircraft designs that would operate economically both at Mach .8 and Mach 2 with a range of 7,000km.[24]

SPACEPLANES

A hydrogen engine will allow aircraft to takeoff and climb into space, as well as maneuver in suborbital and orbital flight delivering three times as much energy per pound as present aviation fuels, while providing a reduction in the weight of airplanes by a factor of 25 per cent. Future aircraft using hydrogen are estimated to operate at Mach 25 above 100,000 feet (i.e., 146,000 miles per hour). Such aircraft could carry a crew of pilots not only to any point on earth in less than two hours, but hypersonic airbreathing vehicles are capable of carrying 15,000 lbs into Low Earth Orbit (LEO) having a flight rate of 100 flights per year. These vehicles could be designed to take off and land at civilian or military airports and to cut the costs of a shuttle-style launch by over 50%.

America's X-30 NASP (National Aerospace Plane) plans to use hydrogen-fueled scramjets as part of a mid-range engine which will allow it to accelerate with additional rocket engine configurations up to Mach 25 flying at 20 miles above the earth. It is being tested at Wright Patterson Air Force Base and is the size of a 727. Below Mach 4.5, the X-30 propulsion module will probably operate under subsonic combustion conditions. The mid-range of Mach 4.5-6 regime will be a transition area, where simultaneously subsonic and supersonic combustion techniques will have to be used."[25] To date, the propulsion of the X-30 has only been confirmed in numerical wind tunnels that exist only in computer-aided CFD (computational fluid dynamics).

Other hydrogen fueled aircraft are: Sänger[26], Hytex, HOPE, Hermes[27], HOTOL[28], Buran[29].

CONCLUSION

Hydrogen has consistently proven to create a powerful rapid explosion for high performance power engines and with new advances in hydrogen research development, offer greater safety, performance, combustion, at less cost and with greater expandability than any other presently-utilized fuel source.

Judging from the readily available sources of hydrogen it is no exaggeration to say its availability, future cost possibilities, and best of all, environmental suitability makes it the best choice for new energy horizons. The hydrogen utilization may be of importance to almost every individual on Earth because it will involve the preservation of the global energy balance, the quality of the air, water and soil we all depend on—as well as the expansion of trade, which effects the standard of living of hundreds of millions of people. A hydrogen economy will be one of the keys of the 21st century.

---

1. Steinberg, Meyer and Cheng, Hsing, (1988) "Modern and Prospective Technologies for Hydrogen Production from Fossil Fuels," Brookhaven National Laboratory.
2. Mellow, Arthur (1990) "Propellants and Combustion" *Aerospace America*. December 1990.
3. Steinberg, Meyer, op. cit.
4. Braun, Harry W. "Solar Stirling Gensets for Large-Scale Hydrogen Production."
5. Steinberg, Meyer, op. cit.
6. HYSOLAR (1989) published by the DLR, KACST.
7. Ibid.
8. Braun, Harry W. "Solar Stirling Gensets for Large-Scale Hydrogen Production."
9. "Production of Hydrogen from Water,"(1986) *Conference Review 16*,

September 1986.
10. Ibid.
11. Zweig, R.M. and F.E. Lynch, (1988) "Hydrogen Vehicle Progress in Riverside, California" *Hydrogen Energy Progress VII*, Proceedings of the Seventh World Hydrogen Energy Conference, Moscow.
12. Ibid.
13. Kudryash, A.P. *et al* (1988) "Peculiarities of Hydrogen-Fueled Diesel Engine Performance" *Hydrogen Energy Progress VII*, Proceedings of the Seventh World Hydrogen Energy Conference, Moscow.
14. Furhama, Shoichi (1988) "Hydrogen Engine Systems for Land Vehicles," *Musashi Institute of Technology*, Japan.
15. Graff, Gordon (1983) "Hydrogen Energy Creeps Forward" *High Technology* May 1983.
16. Fuecht, F. *et al*. (1988) "Perspectives of Mobile Hydrogen Application," Daimler-Benz AG, Stuttgart.
17. T-Raissi, Ali *et al* (1990) "Hydrogen Storage Research at Florida Solar Energy Center," *Hydrogen Laboratory*.
18. "Soviets Test Hydrogen-Powered Transport, Plan Demonstrated" (1988) *Aviation Week and Space Technology* May 30, 1988.
19. Hurtak, J.J. (1988) "Hydrogen: The Fuel for the Future," *Hydrogen Energy Progress VII*, Proceedings of the Seventh World Hydrogen Energy Conference, Moscow.
20. Slush hydrogen: manufactured by the so-called freeze/thaw method that is now being tested in California. A vacuum is drawn on the liquid hydrogen in a 500 gal. dewar that will be used in the contract work until triple point pressure is reached (about 1.0 psia). As pumping continues, ice forms at this point on the surface of the liquid. The dewar is then repressurized slightly above the triple point pressure (about 10 torr), and the sheet of hydrogen ice that has formed detaches itself from the tank wall and sinks to the bottom of the dewar. Slush hydrogen is 15-20 times more dense than normal boiling-point liquid hydrogen and its ability to absorb heat is about 18% higher which will greatly reduce the size of the craft. The advantages of longer storage, reduced insulation, reduced tank venting, smaller tank, and lower operating pressure all are signifiant.
21. Stine, G. Harry and Hans, Paul C. (1990) "Economic Considerations of Hypersonic Vehicles and Spaceplanes," *The Enterprise Institute Inc*. Phoenix, Arizona.
22. Mellow, Arthur op cit.
23. Czysz, Paul (1990) "Foreign Spaceplanes," *AIAA*.
24. Report from Le Bourget, (1989) "Sukhoi, Gulfstream to Study Supersonic Business Jet," *Aviation Week and Space Technology*. June 26, 1989.
25. Kandebo, Stanley W. (1989) "Pratt Demonstrates Low-Speed Propulsion, Concept for NASP," *Aviation Week & Space Technology*, June 26, 1989.
26. *Sänger Deutsche Aerospace*, Daimler-Benz Group.
27. Lenorovitz, Jeffrey M. (1990) "Company Formed to Manage Next Phase of Europe's Hermes Spaceplane Program," *Aviation Week and Space Technology*, November 12, 1990.
28. Czysz, Paul op. cit.
29. Ibid.

PART FIVE

CONSCI

OUSNESS

31

Paradoxes, Paradigms, & the Para-Rational

Jeffrey Seth DeRuvo, M.A.

History reveals there once was a paradigm in which the universe was perceived to operate as a great mechanical clock. This clock was constructed and wound by the Cosmic Clockmaker who was, most assuredly, not in the clock. Standing outside our ticking universe was the eternally unknowable God. Humans, although inside the clock, were completely separate from the mechanics of the clock. The dialectical twins of mind/matter, man/machine, science/religion were born and raised in this time. All things were perceived to be distinct and separate from each other. The beauty and harmony of the universe were found in the precision and orderliness of the separate parts functioning together. Disturbances and incongruity were treated as mere surface messiness, akin to an unmade bed marring the cleanliness of the house. The task of science then, was to strip the bed and reveal the underlying law and orderliness governing the workings of all the parts. By utilizing rational, linear and logical methodologies which obviously mirrored nature's perfect functioning, all things could be explained and all laws could be derived.

Hints were given that perhaps the universe was

not so structured, nor so knowable as the Newtonian paradigm set forth. Heisenberg's Uncertainty Principle challenged the notion that all properties of a system could be discerned through scientific investigation, thereby introducing the concept of "probability" to the language of science. About the same time, Gödel's Incompleteness Theorem showed that mathematical language was only coherent within the system it seeks to describe. Yet, as much as these discoveries refuted the image of the cosmic clock, it persists in the collective consciousness much like brown withered leaves refusing to fall off winter trees.

Part of the problem lies in the ease and simplicity of linearity. Changes within linear systems and equations are predictable; so a small change here produces a small effect there. Logic and order dominate them, and there is a certain beauty in their precise simplicity. Moreover, they actually work: we send rockets to Mars using linear equations. Conversely, nonlinear systems and equations, are extremely complex and unpredictable, with no apparent order. They connote flux, chance, and random change. They appear illogical with no clear pattern or direction, hence most scientists and mathematicians swept them under the carpet.

A snow-capped mountain, the very picture of serenity, silence and stillness, suddenly tumbles when a hiker sneezes. That is a messy, nonlinear problem. How does a sneeze "cause" an avalanche? The mountain peak is a dynamical system, which means it is sensitive to feedback. There are innumerable influences upon the system, continually feeding back into one another. Wind, soundwaves, atmospheric pressure, clouds and snow, are all players here. Sudden shifts in any of them are extremely difficult to calculate and predict. However, if nonlinear equations are iterated or generated over and over millions of times, feeding the result of the calculation back into the equation, a previously hidden pattern emerges. This pattern, or fractal, reveals the dynamics of nonlinearity and mirrors the dynamic systems of nature.

Paradoxes, Paradigms, & the Para-Rational

Figure 31.1
Snow-capped mountains. Photo courtesy of the Academy For Future Science.

Paradoxically, order emerges from within chaos. But this order is of an inherently unpredictable sort.

Obviously, this was not possible to see before the advent of computers. For a long time, scientists could formulate nonlinear equations that modeled some of nature's complex processes, but they were unable to solve them. So, they took the easy way out and simply linearized all the nonlinear phenomena they could. This was the dirty secret of the rational mind: by linearizing the awkward terms in a nonlinear equation with a series of approximations to give a generalized picture of the process being studied, scientists neatly dismissed the behavior of "messy" natural phenomena. The turbulence, chaos, and uncertain factors that abound in nature were left for the day when science could amass enough information to categorize and connect them in one great picture. The house of science looked clean, yet its closets and drawers were overstuffed and about to burst.

With the help of the computer, the task of organizing and systematizing nature seemed within reach. But, it actually presented a great paradox—the machine born to serve the highest aspirations of the rational mind, served instead to ruffle the bed. The computer, much like the electron microscope and telescope before it, opened our vision to previously hidden worlds and gave birth to new sciences to explore them. The worlds revealed were chaotic, unpredictable, paradoxical yet hauntingly beautiful. These were the complex dynamical systems of nature herself; and the new science was chaology—-the study of chaos.

No longer could science aim to reduce nature to its component parts, exposing its inner logic and underlying order, for nature was now seen as a nonlinear dynamical system. That is, it consists of patterns of continual change which were fundamental to nature and not an aberration. The systems of nature were seen as irreducible wholes. Those troublesome, nonlinear equations which apparently fluctuated at random were revealed as images of awesome beauty. The tempestuous dynamics of waves and weather show, when plotted, an interrelatedness of an almost infinite number of influences. A holism was discovered

Figure 31.2
Sand Beach—National Lakeshore of Gary, IN.
Photo by L. Photiadis (1997).

in which everything influences, or potentially influences everything else, because all the parts that were perceived to be separate and distinct were in reality aspects of one dynamical system. So paradoxically, the messiness, which for so long plagued science became a science itself—not only of chaos but a science of wholeness.

The science of chaos and the study of fractals reveal a universe strikingly familiar to the poet, the romantic and the mystic. It is a mysterious universe of unpredictable patterns, chaotic order, and other paradoxes. In the words of one scientist, "Chaos is ubiquitous; it is stable; it is structured."[1] Surprise, chance, sudden luminosity and the sense of unity, characteristic of para-rational experience expressed within the arts, are mother's milk to the chaologist. With the slow death of the linear paradigm, we find the rational universe of science bleeding into the para-rational universes of art, music and mysticism.

Fractals, according to John Briggs, "describe the roughness of the world, its energy, its dynamical

Figure 31.3
"Finger of Creation"
by D. Hurtak (2000).

Paradoxes, Paradigms, & the Para-Rational

changes and transformations. Fractals are images of the way things fold and unfold, feeding back into each other and themselves."[2] Fractals visually trace the influences of seemingly insignificant events and the transformations that result. *The Four Quartets* by T.S. Eliot is an example of fractal geometry in literary form.[3] The impressions that it makes on ones mind have no apparently logical relationship, yet the rhythm of the images created by the word complexes has a transformative effect. Since it is nonlinear both in form and content, its effect is to free us from limited thought patterns. Eliot writes:

> Words, after speech, reach
> Into the silence. Only by the form, the pattern,
> Can words or music reach
> The stillness, as a chinese jar still
> Moves perpetually in its stillness.

Figure 31.4
"Shekinah" (Detail)
12 x 16, Acrylic by
L. Photiadis © 1999.

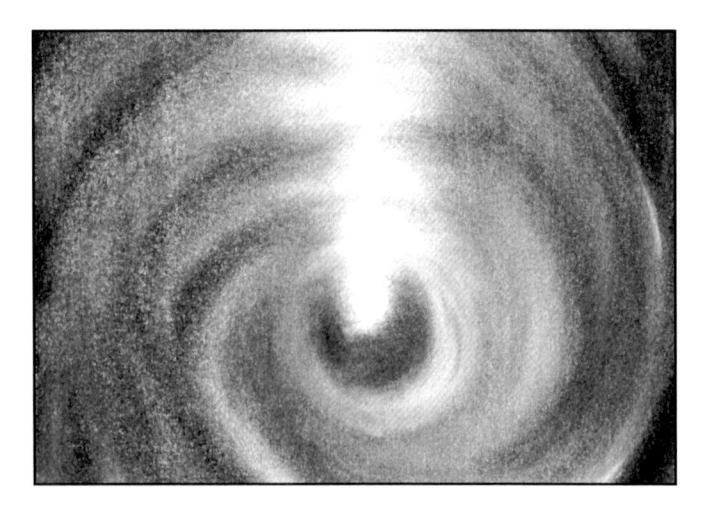

Eliot recognized that the pattern (fractal) created by word complexes was the key to overcoming the limitations of linear language, that is language which unfolds in time. This, too, is an important notion.

The opening concept of time, in *Four Quartets*, is presented syllogistically:

> Time present and time past
> Are both perhaps present in time future,
> And time future contained in time past.
> If all time is eternally present
> [then] All time is unredeemable.

But here our mind is catapulted beyond three-dimensional logic into an underlying spiritual realm where past, present and future merge. Logic, being a science of cause and effect, must remain linear; it must remain rational. But can reality be known in its totality through logic and reason? Not if "all time is eternally present," for if it is, then we are forced into other means of knowing. Logic, being sequential, only works in time. We are trapped and bound by knowledge derived sequentially and empirically. The concept of linearized life, for example, is inaccurate since it is not a total representation of reality. Our self worth, our inherent value, is greater than a lifelong sum of fragmented experiences.

The imposed pattern is the prevailing paradigm which structures our reality and limits our potential to experience truth. Sequential knowledge derived

Figure 31.5
Three spiral galaxies.

through choice and selectivity is, by its very nature, limited. Fortunately, there is sudden luminosity, the awareness of infinities within the finite. There is a somethingness which is beyond the realm of rational consciousness. The existence of this spiritual consciousness is the wholeness (the infinity) which is greater than the sum of the parts. It pours into and fills our minds as it flows from a mysterious effulgent place. There is no rationale for the sudden luminosity. Just as there is no rationale to the influences and images that flow from the poem. Yet they have an effect within the mind of the reader. The mind, like a computer which directs the pixels and displays the images, arranges feelings into beautiful array of meaning. Here science admonishes the subjective experience of poetry. Feelings are indulgent respites from the harried world, but science claims objectivity as the true bedrock of knowledge. The memory of duality and separateness, of humanity's independence from nature persists, while the memory of who we truly are is lost.

The revelatory vision, the prophetic insight and divine inspiration, while rare, come as a spring filling the dry pool of humanity. Thus we see the interconnectedness between humanity and the cosmos, and the value of subjectivity.

> Dry the pool, dry concrete, brown edged,
> And the pool was filled with
> water out of sunlight,
> And the lotus rose, quietly, quietly,
> The surface glittered out of heart of light,
> And they were behind us,
> reflected in the pool.
> And a cloud passed and the pool was empty.

The lotus, the Buddhist symbol of enlightenment, emerges from the dry, malillumined world and brings with it its own light. The clouds drift and the pool is now empty. Meanings and images come and go like forgotten dreams. The truths of life blossom fully and clearly, then disappear amidst the cacophony of living.

The prophetic vision is non-rational, and therefore it is labeled as just another awkward term in the non-linear equation. Reality then becomes a series of approximations and generalizations. This is repeated in religion as well as science. In religion, only those terms in the equation that fit the local religious paradigm are used. The visions, insights and subjective experiences which upset the cart are discarded. What remains is a miniscule part of the totality of life.

Applying, chaos theory to history shows that the linear concept of cause and effect so prevalent in the western historical paradigm, is incomplete. Locating event "A" which triggered event "B" in any historical context is myopic as well as misleading. The rational western approach studies specific causes of war and peace, progress and stagnation; while the eastern teachings, in particular, the Bhagavad Gita and Tao Te Ching, seem to look at history in terms of cycles and flows of knowledge and ignorance, good and evil, positive and negative, with no specific event or person singled out as a turning point. Chaos theory, likewise, looks to patterns of change within entire systems and acknowledges the role of chance in the flow of nature.

The para-rational concepts of the Bhagavad Gita's Dharma and the Tao are in line with chaos theories which recognize that the patterns of change and variations in the flow of dynamical systems result from innumerable and often unknown influences. Thus, history is viewed as changes in flow pattern rather than a linear sequence of seemingly significant events. The linear concept of evolution is challenged, as is echoed by Eliot:

> A people without history
> Is not redeemed from time,
> for history is a pattern
> Of timeless moments.

Again the pattern, or fractal, emerges from the dynamics of a non-linear system.

The concept that everything in the universe could

Paradoxes, Paradigms, & the Para-Rational

Figure 31.6
"*Celestial Voyage*"
4 x 6, Acrylic & Collage
by L. Photiadis © 2000.

be understood, labeled and compartmentalized, nourished the intellect yet starved the heart. The ego encouraged intellect which labels and quantifies in an effort to know all things, created a sense of separation between the individual and the Cosmos. This separation cramps the heart and emotions which seeks connectedness. Thus, the great rift between science and mysticism. The intellect rejects subjective experience in favor of structure and certainty. Hard, cold facts drive the machine of science, thus the para-rational, the nonlinear, the Great mystery, and God are relegated to the back of the bus.

The cosmology of chaos, a future science, reveals a strikingly new and different universe. It is a universe of connectedness, of interdependence long known by the mystics and poets. We explore a new model of reality which gives permission to enjoy what we cannot accurately predict and control. Here descriptions are limited and quantifiers are not precise. It is a universe where sudden leaps are the norm and order is illusory. Here the ego is humble and silent.

But is this truly chaos, or is it creativity? What scientists have discovered, in the iteration of non-linear equations, may be the mechanics of creation. The process by which dynamical systems feed back to the strange attractor, and then flow forth with a new, yet familiar creation is much like inspiration in art. Creativity is inherent in the dynamics of life. Is this not the depth of the message of the Avatars? Krishna unfolds the mechanics of non-linear dynamics when he states, "Curving back upon my own nature, I create again and again."[4] And the words of the Creator come through the prophet Isaiah, "For here I am creating new heavens and a new earth; and former things will not be called to mind, neither will they come up into the heart. But exult you people, and be joyful forever in what I am creating" (Isa 65:17).

For the new paradigm to incorporate rational and para-rational perspectives, a different cosmology is needed. The para-rational perspectives give expression to the sudden illumination which pours into the mundane world. Yet, the rational perspective presents a three-dimensional material cosmology. Thus, a cosmology of paradox, like spirit itself, which is mysteriously both completely transcendent to the world and completely immanent in the world, must be formulated. A paradigm shift away from the need to quantify, and into the need to express the great mystery in an individual creative way, is now taking place. We experience the fractal complexity of the dynamic earth, and the ordered chaos of the cosmos, with its multiple mansion worlds, reflecting the multiple dimensions of the infinite Self.

As our vision becomes stronger and clearer, so shall we come to acknowledge the para-rational at the core of complete knowledge. Linear logic and reason has its place in the scheme of things, but we must go beyond that illusion to gain real insight as to why we are here, and where we are going. As Eliot remarks:

> And all shall be well and
> All manner of thing shall be well

> When the tongues of flame are in-folded
> Into the crowned knot of fire
> And the fire and the rose are one.

---

1. Gleick, James. (1987) *Chaos: Making a New Science.* New York: Penguin Books, p. 23.
2. Briggs, John. (1992) *Fractals: The Patterns of Chaos.* New York: Touchstone, p. 76.
3. Eliot, T.S. (1943/1971) *Four Quartets.* New York: Harcourt, Brace, Jovanovich, Pub.
4. Sargent, Winthrop (ed.).(1984) *The Bhagavad-Gita.* New York: State University of New York Press, p. 384.

32

The Holographic Paradigm: Mind & the Awareness of Multiple Realities

Marcus Weber, M.D.
(Candidate)

In 1946, interested in the workings of memory, neurosurgeon Karl Pribram studied Karl Lashley's experiments on rats. After having been trained to perform a variety of tasks the rats were subjected to the surgical removal of different minute portions of the brain in an attempt to discover which part was responsible for the "memories" [not functions] of the learned tasks. The surprising result of the experiment was that there was no single location whose removal would eradicate the memory. Was memory not localized in specific brain sites, but distributed all over the brain? In the mid-1960s Pribram wrote an article on the construction of a hologram that provided a possible explanation to these findings.

Construction of a hologram is based on the phenomenon of interference which occurs when waves ripple through each other. Coherent laser light is especially good in creating interference patterns; a single laser light is split into two separate beams. The first beam is bounced off the object to be photographed and creates—with the second beam that is allowed to collide with the reflected light of the first one—an interference pattern that is recorded on a piece of film. The image on the film has no similarity to the object,

Figure 32.1
A hologram is an interference pattern created by two beams of light colliding that is then recorded on a piece of film.
"Water Blossom" 3 x 5, Photographic image by L. Photiadis (2002).

but as soon as another laser beam is directed through the film at the correct angle, a seemingly three-dimensional image of the original object appears. Another remarkable aspect of the hologram is that the entire image can be reconstructed from any small portion of the film, although with increasingly smaller portions the images will get hazier. If this phenomenon has something to do with memory, every part of the brain could contain all of the information necessary to recall a complete memory.

With the holographic concept came the possibility of explaining a series of mind-phenomena, e.g., recall and forgetfulness, and the photographic memory. Holograms possess a fantastic capacity for information storage: a one-inch-square of film can store the amount of information contained in 50 Bibles. When a piece of holographic film with multiple images is tilted back and forth in a laser beam the various images appear and disappear. To recall, then, would mean to activate the memory pattern at the right angle; to forget, failing to find the right angle. Individuals with photographic memory could, with reference to the holographic model, have access to large regions of their memory hologram; individuals with less vivid memories to a smaller region.

A crucial characteristic of a hologram is that things seem to be located where they actually are not. When we look at something, the image of it is on the surface of the retina, and yet we perceive it as being in the world-out-there. In fact it is a neuro-physiological process in the brain that creates this illusion. Now, if the picture of reality in our brains is not a picture at all but a hologram, then which is the true reality—the seemingly objective world of the observer, or the blur of interference patterns recorded by the brain?

For physicist David Bohm, the whole universe is structured like a hologram. With the discovery that an electron possesses no dimension and shows characteristics of both waves and particles, came the realization that colliding wavelike electrons could create interference patterns. Bohm found that electrons in plasmas did not behave like individuals but as part of a larger whole. Vast numbers of electrons produced surprisingly well-organized effects and could behave like an amoeboid creature which enclosed impurities in

Figure 32.2
According to physicist David Bohm, the whole universe is structured like a hologram.

a wall. The seemingly haphazard movements of individual electrons in metals produced a highly organized overall effect of oceans of particles which he called "plasmons." In 1952 Bohm proposed the "quantum potential," a hypothetical field that like gravity pervades all of space, but unlike gravitational or magnetic fields does not diminish. While classical science had always viewed the state of a system as the result of the interaction of its parts, the "quantum potential" explained that the behavior of the parts was organized by the whole.

Bohm's theory indicates that on a sub-quantum level all points in space are equal to all other points in space. With this property of nonlocality Bohm could explain the behavior of twin particles without contradicting special relativity's statement that nothing could be faster than the speed of light. Imagine a fish in an aquarium. Two television cameras are directed towards the aquarium's front and side and record what is going on. When the fish is moving, the cameras show synchronic events of two seemingly different fish, as if they were instantaneously communicating with one another. But in fact no "communication" is taking place, for both images refer to a common ground, a single higher-dimensional actuality—a three-dimensional fish in contrast to the two-dimensional projections of the cameras. This model could also be in accordance with the decay of two particles. On the basis of the "quantum potential" that underlies all of space (and time), all particles are non-locally interconnected, and all things are part of an unbroken web that is as real as matter.

Apart from nonlocality on the subquantum level, Bohm was also interested in the question of order. He found matter in very different degrees of order which implied that there was possibly no end to hierarchies of order in the universe, and that the things we perceive as disordered were, from a higher viewpoint, eventually highly ordered. In 1980 Bohm published his book *Wholeness and the Implicated Order* in which he describes the assertion of a universe working on

Figure 32.3
The revealed (explicate) reality is an illusion formed on the basis of the hidden (implicate) reality. Photo by L. Photiadis (1999).

holographic principles. The unfolded (revealed) or explicate reality of our everyday lives is, like a holographic image, actually an illusion formed on the basis of a deeper order of existence, a more primary enfolded (hidden) or implicate level of reality which brings forth all objects and appearances of our physical world in much the same way that a piece of holographic film brings forth a hologram. Bohm understood all manifestations in the universe as the result of countless enfoldings and unfoldings. The universe is like a giant hologram, ever active and dynamic, a holomovement of a multidimensional order, in contrast to a static piece of holographic film.

Wholeness means, in terms of the implicate order, to understand the universe not as being composed of parts, but to recognize the underlying unity, just as the different geysers in a fountain all arise from the same underlying source of water. An electron that is manifest to our senses, then, is not an elementary particle, but merely an abstraction of the holomovement that unfolds at a particular location. The very track of an electron is an orderly series of stages of unfoldment and enfoldment maintained by the implicate nature. Not only space and time but everything in the universe is part of a continuum. This explains how particles can shapeshift from one kind of particle to another or from a wave to a particle. We are the same as everything around us, and the apparently separate things are like ripples or vortices in a river. Every portion of the universe, every cell of our body, enfolds the whole just as every portion of a hologram contains the image of the whole.

Consciousness is present in various degrees of enfoldment and unfoldment in all matter. Animate and inanimate matter are inseparably interwoven. Life and intelligence are enfolded in all of matter, in energy, time and space, in the fabric of the entire universe and everything else; we abstract this out of the holomovement and mistakenly view it as separate. If observer and observed ultimately are the same thing, the observer, in a sense, is the observed. Thought, feeling, desire, attention, perception, understanding, that is, the whole mental and psychic life and consciousness according to the holographic concept, is a process of matter which, like all matter, is located in the implicate order and manifests into any explicate order, but as a more subtle aspect of the holomovement.

The origin of the holographic universe is a non-manifest source which rests in something that is far beyond it. One can imagine a universe that fades out to something beyond matter and consciousness and what could be called spirit. Considering the shortest wavelength of wave-particles of the gravitational field in empty space, one would compute the amount of energy in a cubic centimeter of space to be far beyond the total energy of all the matter in the known universe. In this vast sea of cosmic energy, a wave pulse could have brought forth our universe and, furthermore, there could be many other such universes. Matter is that with which we have contact through our senses, our instruments and our mind. A field is still matter. Spirit, compared with that, in all cultures is understood as something that has created matter and life (e.g., a plant starting as a seed can be regarded as a set of information).

The mind thinks it has reached what is and conceives itself as deriving from there. It thinks that the manifest and non-manifest make the whole, and that the whole goes just one step beyond the mind. But, if the spirit is beyond reach of mind, how could we go as far as this—beyond the manifest and non-manifest—when our mind might say that this is not possible? To comprehend a solution, Bohm would introduce the idea of an active intelligence beyond all energies of the non-manifest which ignores the mind's filtering effect and even changes the matter of the brain itself, transforming the mind as well. The more subtle level has the power to transform the less subtle, but the more coarse does not know what to do with the more subtle.

The obsolete explicate perspective of traditional science, conceiving the world as consisting of ever smaller fragments, reflects itself in the fragmentation of humankind into nations, religions, groups, families with isolated individuals who disintegrate into further fragments. Bohm sees in this conception the origin of chaos, violence and destruction. But just as the manifest world is one with the non-manifest order, on a deeper level the consciousness of humankind is one. For this reason the collective problems of humankind enter the individual who, however, in connecting to the cosmic totality, may sort out the collective pollution.

And what is the source of compassion and love? Bohm explains that the whole construction of the implicate order is a bridge. However, one has to cross the bridge and leave it behind, leaving behind thought, the whirling in the manifest and the conditioning of the non-manifest, in order to reach the underlying void that makes consciousness a vehicle or instrument of totality—of intelligence, compassion, truth. The way out of chaos is through meditation which actually transforms the mind; nothing that is produced in our consciousness can replace this transformation.

Transformation is scarcely recognized by

Mind & the Awareness of Multiple Realities

Figure 32.4
David Bohm explains the whole construction of the implicate order as a bridge that one must cross and ultimately leave behind. Image by the Academy For Future Science.

subscribers to scientific skepticism. But why for thousands of years, one has to ask, have monasteries and communities existed that allowed countless individuals to experience other states of consciousness? Why have people from every culture throughout history reported inner visions and other realities that are inaccessible to anyone who does not experience them directly? In view of the holographic concept of an implicate order of many inter-penetrating systems, entities and universes of whose dimensions we can only have an idea, the time may be coming when we will realize the inadequacy of attempting to continue scientific inquiry purely on the basis of visible and measurable reality.

---

1. Bohm, David (1983) *Wholeness and the Implicated Order*. Ark Paperbacks, London.
2. Gardener, Howard (1985) *The Mind's New Science*. Basic Books, Inc. New York.
3. Talbot, Michael (1991) *The Holographic Universe*. Harper Collins, New York 1991.
4. Wilber, Ken (1982) *The Holographic Paradigm and Other Paradoxes*. Shambhala Publications, Inc. Boston.

# 33

New Perspectives for Consciousness Evolution: At the Intersection of Science & Mysticism

Michelle D. Godfrey
M.A. Candidate

Structure and fluidity, matter and energy, perspective, awareness, transition, reflection… this is the stuff of consciousness, the functions and process of growth. And it is the key interest of Western scientific fields of psychology, physics and biology. But, even as the mind-body question turns up solid scientific answers to what was previously relegated to the mystical and magical, one particularly elusive question remains—what is consciousness? Why, and how, do we experience our world and ourselves?

It's a fool's question. Even the wisest among us can yet only approximate a theory (if "theory" is even an appropriate means of understanding consciousness). Masters in the East direct us to spiritual practice in discipline and patience so we might simply experience consciousness as subjective initiates. But the Western mind fidgets under secrets, and consciousness is the most elusive of them all.

Thus we embark on a hero's journey. Armed with reductionist tools of science, we approach the beastly problem of consciousness with uncomfortable ignorance and vulnerability. We draw the psychology sword and are reduced to explaining mind and behavior in terms of the action of the brain and nervous system. Picking up biology, we now understand the nervous system in terms of atomic physics and the interaction of basic neurotransmitter elements such as carbon and nitrogen which carry intelligent signals. Wielding the sword of physics, which is now most fully understood in terms of quantum mechanics, we realize that mind is a primitive component in atomic activity. And so, back to psychology, we have traveled an epistemological circle.

Why is consciousness so elusive to the Western mind? What have we missed, and just what are we trying to explain? Can consciousness ever be fundamentally understood in the light of day, outside of the privacy of subjective experience?

Given the tense relations between Western science and religion, it may seem highly improbable for our scientists to discover, let alone acknowledge, a "spirit" or "creator" as having a primary role in a theory of consciousness. Yet a reductive explanation of consciousness is so counter-intuitive. But perhaps that is a premature assessment. We may be able to propose a more inclusive theory.

To capture the fullness of consciousness, in quasi transcendental terms as understood by sages, a theory would have to account for consciousness's unity as well as its multiplicity. It would explain why consciousness is both unique to persons and shared

Figure 33.1
Will the Western mind ever fully grasp consciousness?
"Zen" 30 x 40, Tempera by L. Photiadis © 1998.

among them (i.e., why each of us experiences the color red, even though our individual experiences of red may differ). Sure enough, science is already moving toward such "multiple" theories—light is understood best in some cases as a particle, in others as a wave; electrons can be understood as both entities and fields. So maybe a theory of consciousness can include, simultaneously, details relevant to the "me" experiencing, the "you" or "other" experiencing, and also that of "we" experiencing collectively or as a species.

The problem for science, which is by default the predominant wisdom tradition of the Western world, is in admitting complexity. Our habit for paradigms resists it. But new ideas about complexity and chaotic systems in nature may soon crack the paradigmatic egg, and allow new ideas to be brought to the table of consciousness studies.

BREEDING COMPLEXITY

Many scholars now believe that complexity is the hallmark of evolution. In eukaryotic cells, for example,

Figure 33.2
Model of a Eukaryotic cell. Image by the Academy For Future Science.

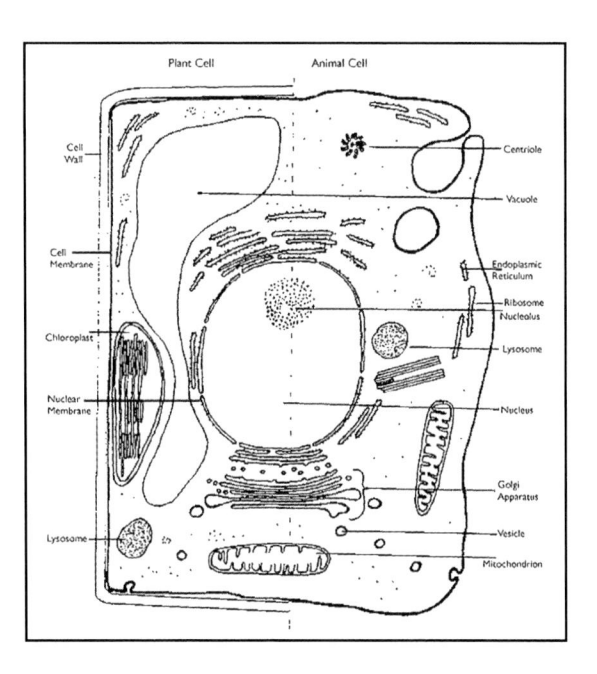

each level of complexity (growth) is a new and distinct system, with its own autonomy, patterns of interaction, and environment. And each level is an energy gain over the previous one. So increased complexity means increased cooperation between subsystems, which leads to the formation of emergent higher-order, autopoietic (self-creating) systems. This kind of evolution may be applicable to the evolution of consciousness. (See Allan Combs's *The Radiance of Being* for more discussion of autopoietic systems.)

The human brain is not as new as the human. It is an ancient structure with evolutionary layers, primarily three subsystems—the brain stem (reptilian brain), the central forebrain (paleomammalian brain) and the neocortex (neomammalian brain). The systems are active simultaneously, and can be thought of as three ancient attractor basins. Still, the three "brains" remain mostly independent of each other, with observable unique signatures and electrical patterns. This creates a tendency for the modern brain to be pulled in several directions at once. Thus "multiplicity" (complexity in the subsystems) and "unity" (the holistic brain) operate simultaneously in human thought processes.

Paleo-neurologist Harry J. Jerison proposed that the brain is a weaver of reality. Within that reality all the events of a lifetime take place. Reality, in a sense, can be thought of as a belief system, or a collection of processes—a complex system for ordering three-dimensional space, linear time, and coherent objects out of chaos-infused sense-data. This implies that the brain is not simply an organ which produces thought, but, at least for humans, its processing involves coordination of multiple thought patterns, and it remains flexible even in the presence of habits of mind (basins of attraction which draw thoughts into predictable patterns).

That begs the question: just how flexible are we willing to be with our "reality?" Eastern adepts report that pure consciousness, when it is experienced (for it takes great patience and diligence), feels far more "real" than the material reality we are accustomed to.

Even if we come to understand consciousness in terms of simultaneous complexity and unity, how ready will we be to accept the paradox? What sort of energy push will we need to jump the wall of our current habits of mind about consciousness?

EVOLUTIONARY DIRECTIONS

The Eastern-Platonic view of reality is a top-down version of evolution: There is an ultimate template of consciousness (and life in general) which precipitates down into material creation. So the work of consciousness growth implies activation of that form or divine substance, in whatever supply it may be available to us, and moving up into finer, broader levels of conscious experience.

Henri Bergson, evolutionary theorist and recipient of the 1927 Nobel Prize for Literature, put it this way: evolution is propelled by a subtle, non-material force which "insinuates" into organic matter, and consciousness operates as an evolutionary pressure. Each advance of the nervous system gives the organism larger choice, and allows consciousness to pass more freely. Thus, he says, the purpose of evolution is to free up consciousness from the structure of organic matter, and it is achieved by the development of large, flexible nervous systems (which are better equipped to handle complexity).

Teilhard de Chardin further realized what chaos

Figure 33.3a
Henri Bergson, French Philosopher (1859-1941).

Figure 33.3b
Pierre Teilhard de Chardin, visionary French Jesuit, paleontologist, biologist & philosopher (1881-1955).

theorists have just recently demonstrated: small amounts of energy can make a big impact on a complex form, which effect is to draw the organism into greater complexity, i.e., forwards. He believed the evolution of physical complexity is accompanied by the evolution of quality in conscious experience. In today's terms, then, large computers might someday give rise to conscious experience; it's just a matter of how complex we can make them. (But de Chardin did not favor reductionist explanations of consciousness which are assumed by the Artificial Intelligence community today).

However, most modern biologists would deny any "directionality" to evolution. Organisms don't "try" to evolve, they say—nature does the work by filtering out the productive variations from among the many random variants created by mutations and genetic mixing. This is a bottom-up view of evolution: its final product is a result of what has gone before. Douglas Hofstadter in *The Mind's I* (1981) calls it "upstream causality," synonymous with reductionism. "Hard scientists" who adhere to it are concerned with predicting what will happen based only on current causes—nothing "downstream" need be taken into account to understand reality. Perhaps the thought is that nature has selected out any previous causes and they are no longer relevant.

The top-down view, according to Hofstadter, is "downstream causality," which is synonymous with a teleological perspective—that organisms have a "goal" in evolution, and causality is projected backward in time. It is similar to "holism," except that in holism, causality arises from within the organism and flows from the outside whole inward toward its parts.

The "hard science" view—reductionist, bottom-up—is mechanistic and simplistic. The "soft science" view—teleological, holism-goalism, top-down—is complex and (says Hofstadter) soul-friendly. If there is hope for a Western wisdom tradition which can adequately address consciousness growth, the more complex "soft science" approach will be the productive path. Is it a surprise that, in academic circles, those who choose "soft science" approaches are often called "fools" by their "harder" colleagues?

We are now collectively at the transition point between bottom-up and top-down evolutionary cycles. The reductionist methodology for knowledge-as-wisdom has differentiated our minds from its Origin. The next stages will see human consciousness becoming more fluid and complex, more integrated to soul and the subtle bodies of being, and thus more closely identified with our creative source.

Consciousness Growth

Given a direction and a destination, what vehicle(s) may carry us to the next evolutionary stage of consciousness growth? In the top-down evolutionary direction, consciousness evolution occurs through successive realization of subtler planes of being... all that we are is already present within us; our task is to build it into our conscious reality. In the bottom-up direction, growth occurs moment-by-moment. The creator may be fully present in the process, but we have become separated from the creative source, and so the divine presence is limited to us, and we become aware of limited existence.

In the top-down view, lessons in consciousness are bricks to lay upon a foundation whose pinnacle draws ever nearer to the creative source. In the bottom-up view, our lessons dissolve the veils between us and the Divine. One approach builds structures, the other tears them down.

And indeed we can identify two types of wisdom traditions: ontic paths (most yogas), which emphasize realization of higher levels of being, and noetic paths (Buddhist schools), which strive for clearer, unobstructed insight. Ontic paths employ anabolic processes—building new structures; noetic paths employ catabolic processes—dismantling inhibitive structures.

Both can be understood in terms of chaotic processes. Ontic-anabolic growth is analogous to the rapid non-linear expansion of an organic system which

Figure 33.4a
The ontic path of Yoga emphasizes the realization of higher levels of being.

Figure 33.4b
The noetic path of sitting meditation strives for clear, unobstructed insight.

Images by the Academy For Future Science.

begins with just a few variables, and is given a "nudge" by the addition of just one more factor. This growth is constructive, progressive, steady. Noetic-catabolic growth may occur as a catastrophic bifurcation—a unique point in the life of a complex system in which a sort of "critical mass" causes the system to break into two directions, indicating a decision to be made (like that between the proverbial "high road" and "low road"). It is spontaneous, powerful and emergent.

Both processes are appropriate to a particular space and time in the life of the system. And each has associated pathologies. In ontic paths, subtle energies may awaken before the student is adequately prepared. Noetic varieties involve misunderstanding ecstatic experience, when the student mistakes raptures of subtle realms with ultimate realization itself. In this case, the student has the illusion that limiting structures have completely dissolved, perhaps out of wishful thinking, when they are actually still in place.

Ultimately Eastern wisdom traditions lead us to three dualities, or dimensions, of consciousness: ontic-noetic, anabolic-catabolic, constructive-emergent. How might these dimensions sharpen our three swords of psychology, biology, and physics? Do they have influence at all? Can physical "reality" of consciousness and its spiritual dimensions be reconciled?

David Chalmers in the Department of Philosophy at the University of Arizona wonders if consciousness exists independently of the physical world. Such an idea may lead us to the counter-intuitive notion that consciousness has no effect upon the physical world. If consciousness does exert causal affect upon the physical (likely so), yet remains independent of it (also probable), then we are left with a deep duality between the intrinsic and extrinsic features of physical reality. But underlying the dualism is a deeper monism: we get an integrated world of intrinsic properties connected by causal relations. And that amounts to an odd sort of 'materialism'—physical reality is all there is, but there is far more to physical reality than physical theory tells us about!

Dimensions of consciousness, then, may very well have causal impact on psychology, biology and physics (of course it seems that they do). But if that is true, in scientific terms we are faced with redefining our materialistic concept of reality. Which means that a new Western approach to consciousness may involve far more than just a path for internal, spiritual development—more than yoga or meditation or other personal growth tactics. In fact, the world in which consciousness grows—the world as we know it—will never be, and cannot remain, the same.

---

1. Chalmers, Davi (1996) *The Conscious Mind: In Search of a Fundamental Theory*. Oxford University Press.
2. Combs, Allan (1997) *The Radiance of Being: Complexity, Chaos and the Evolution of Consciousness*. Paragon House.
3. Dennett, Daniel C.(1992) *Consciousness Explained*. Little Brown & Co.
4. Gleick, James (1988) *Chaos: Making a New Science*. Penguin USA.
5. Hofstadter, Douglas R. (1985) *The Mind's I*. Bantam Books.
6. Jaynes, Julian (1990) *The Origin of Consciousness in the Breakdown of the Bicameral Mind*. Houghton Mifflin.

34

The World of Archetypes

Mario Schiess
Chairman of the Transvaal
Centre for Jungian Studies
Johannesburg, South Africa

That man is not only what he thinks he or she is, by now, is generally accepted. The concept of a "subconscious" originated long before Freud, Plato already expounded the idea. Schopenhauer wrote extensively about it, Carus published a book on it. Sigmund Freud, in his perhaps most accessible book *The Psychopathology of Everyday Life* really put it on the map. But the man who provided us with an anatomy of it was Carl Gustav Jung. In the process he re-christened it the "Unconscious" because the prefix "sub" has something inferior to it (as in, for instance, "sub-human").

Jung reasoned that the Unconscious besides being the "rubbish box of consciousness" as in Freud, contains the very highest impulses of humanity. Freud and Jung who were very close for a period of about seven years split over that question in 1913. In Jung's terminology the conscious part of ourselves, that part of us we know we are, became the ego, while the whole of our personality, the conscious plus the unconscious part, he termed the Self (more often than not spelled with a capital S). He found that a great portion of this Unconscious reached beyond the personal and he came up with the theory the "collective unconscious" for which he was severely attacked by most other psychologies. More and more, however, we find that the behavior of human beings cannot be convincingly explained without this concept of the collective unconscious.

In the Jungian opus we thus have two layers of unconsciousness, the personal unconscious and the collective unconscious. The word "complex" which was coined by Jung has found universal acceptance. Complexes are the contents of the personal unconscious. A complex is a cluster of ideas that form around a certain notion in the personal unconscious. For instance, if a person has experienced a really bad mother these experiences may all be repressed into the unconscious because facing them and remembering them all the time is just too painful. Everything that touches the field of "mother" may then be affected by the unconscious memories of that personal bad mother. This experience distorts everything that only remotely connects with the idea of "mother." One has, so to speak, no control over one's reaction to anything with the idea of mother, the "mother complex" colors one's reaction automatically. What touches "mother" is beyond one's conscious will, hence we speak of an autonomous "mother" complex. Strictly speaking one should call it a negative or morbid "mother" complex, because one can, of course, also have a positive one. All this in no way conflicts with the view of Freud.

As soon as the idea of a collective unconscious is introduced, things begin to get a little more complicated. The contents of the collective unconscious Jung called the "archetypes." Today a lot of people use the word with little idea what they are talking about. It is not all that different a notion to the "complex" except that it does not originate from personal experience. Archetypes are inherited, the collective unconscious is heritage, it is one's legacy of being human. Jung used to speak of "the two million year old man" implying that the wisdom of humankind is buried in each individual in that very collective unconscious. Jung, in a beautiful quote, puts it as follows:

Figure 34.1
Russian icon of Christ, a paramount archetypal figure.

Man's unconscious [...] contains all the patterns of life and behavior inherited from his ancestors, so that every human child is possessed of a ready-made system of adapted psychic functioning prior to all consciousness. In the conscious life of the adult as well, this unconscious, instinctive functioning is continually present and active. In this activity all the functions of the conscious psyche are prefigured. The unconscious perceives, has purposes and intuitions, feels and thinks as does the conscious mind. We find sufficient evidence for this in the field of psychopathology and the investigation of dream-processes. Only in one respect is there

Figure 34.2
Temple at Medinet Habu, Egypt. Photo by D. Hurtak.

an essential difference between the conscious and the unconscious functioning of the psyche. Though consciousness is intensive and concentrated, it is transitory and is trained upon the immediate present and the immediate field of attention; moreover, it has access only to material that represents one individual's experience stretching over a few decades. A wider range of "memory" is an artificial acquisition consisting mostly of printed paper. But matters stand very differently with the unconscious. It is not concentrated and intensive, but shades off into obscurity; it is highly extensive and can juxtapose the most heterogeneous elements in the most paradoxical way. More than this, it contains, besides an indeterminable number of subliminal perceptions, the accumulated deposits from the lives of our ancestors, who by their very existence have contributed to the differentiation of the species. If it were possible to personify the unconscious, we might think of it as a collective human being combining the characteristics of both sexes, transcending youth and age, birth and death, and, from having at its command a human experience of one or two million years, practically immortal. If such a being existed, it would be exalted above all temporal change; the present would mean neither more nor less to it than any year in the hundredth millennium before Christ; it would be a dreamer of age-old dreams and, owing to its limitless experience, an incomparable prognosticator. It would have lived countless times over again the life of the individual, the family, the tribe, and the nation, and it would possess a living sense of the rhythm of growth, flowering and decay. [*reference Chapter IX of Modern Man in Search of a Soul, by Carl Jung, (1933)*]

These archetypes, which are the contents of this collective unconscious, determine human behavior. To use the same example as for the "complex": in each individual resides also the "archetypal mother," an inherited idea of what a mother is and does. A mother does not have to be taught how to deal with a baby, that knowledge is instinctive, archetypal. More to the point

Figure 34.3
The Language of Symbol is a Language of Metaphor.
"Falling Water" 4 x 6, Acrylic & Collage by L. Photiadis © 2000.

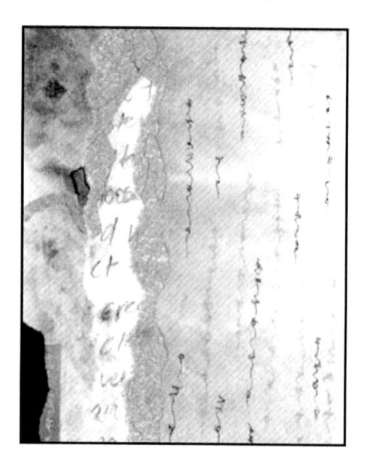

in each of us is also an inborn knowledge of what to expect of a mother. We expect nurturing and part of our growing up, or individuation as Jung called it, is to free ourselves from that archetypal expectation and not need nurturing all our life. Likewise the mother has to free herself from the archetype by letting her children go. The negative mother here manifests itself by the clinging, smothering mother who will hold on to her children all her life.

Much has been written on the question of what archetypes really are but the above hopefully provides an idea. The archetype is a very important concept particularly since it is the bottom line in strong emotion. Whenever an archetype is touched, stirring feelings result. The archetype is particularly involved in the phenomenon of "numinosity," a word coined by Rudolf Otto in his celebrated work *The Idea of the Holy* and defined as follows:

> The "numinous" is the deepest and most fundamental element in all strong and sincerely felt religious emotion...we shall find we are dealing with something for which there is only one appropriate expression, mysterium tremendum. The feeling of it may at times come sweeping like a gentle tide, pervading the mind with a tranquil mood of deepest worship. It may pass over into a more set and lasting attitude of the soul, continuing, as it were thrillingly vibrant and resonant, until at last it dies away and the soul assumes its "profane," non-religious mood of everyday experience. It may burst in sudden eruption up from the depths of the soul spasms and convulsions, or lead to the strangest excitements, to intoxicated frenzy, to transport, and to ecstasy. It has its wild and demonic forms and can sink to an almost grisly horror and shuddering. It has its crude, barbaric antecedents and early manifestations, and again it may be developed into something

beautiful and pure and glorious. It may become the hushed, trembling, and speechless humility of the creature in the presence of— whom or what? In the presence of that which is a Mystery inexpressible.

Archetypes and complexes express themselves most clearly in dreams. Freud held that: "Dreams are the royal road to the unconscious." Words are the means of expression of consciousness, the unconscious is almost exclusively silent, it expresses itself in images and dreams, our daily (or nightly) dip into the world of images. Although many people believe that they never dream it has been proved experimentally that everyone dreams four to five times a night during so called Rapid Eye Movement (REM) sleep. The problem is that most people do not remember their dreams and it takes a certain amount of training oneself to do so.

In order to understand what images say it is necessary to know the language of symbols. A symbol, in the Jungian opus, has a specific meaning, it is not a sign which is a construct of consciousness. To qualify as a symbol it must have its roots in the unconscious. Toni Wolff, Jung's chief assistant, explains it particularly well:

> Take a symbol in our own experience. We will immediately notice that the picture speaks to us. It does so because, inexplicably, we are touched by something that is only vaguely felt but recognized as meaningful quite apart from its depicted content. It is as if behind the visible an essence attracts the deepest levels of our being. The physical appearance is only the container for that which lies behind it, let's call it the metaphysical. The image is the picture of something else, something irrational that cannot manifest itself in any other way than by this image at this point in time. This manifestation or "becoming flesh" elevates the carrier of this image and makes him/it into

something holy, something symbolic.

This language of symbols has been called God's forgotten language, it is a language of metaphor. Gregory Bateson, the Nobel laureate in biology in an interview with Fritjof Capra said: "Metaphor. That's how this whole fabric of mental interconnections holds together. Metaphor is right at the bottom of being alive." Images, hence dreams, pictures etc. must not be interpreted literally. A cat in a dream is not only a cat, but a cat-as-symbol. As a symbol, aspects must be considered that have little to do with the animal cat. The cat has always been the familiar, as far back as the ancient Egyptians, who revered the cat-goddess Bast. Someone once said that people who want to give love have cats, those who want to receive love have dogs. Cats can be mini-predators. All these and more must be taken into account when looking at a cat as a dream image, as a symbol.

Another extremely important phenomenon much written about by Jung is that of projection. It is an automatic reaction and is described in New Testament language as "the speck in another's eye and the beam in one's own." Contents of one's unconscious, usually negative qualities (because one does not wish to have negative sides hence remains unaware, unconscious of

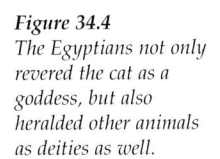

Figure 34.4
The Egyptians not only revered the cat as a goddess, but also heralded other animals as deities as well.

The World of Archetypes

them) are seen in projected form in other people. A miser, for instance, will not admit to being one but condemns any sign of miserliness in another. If that person then appears in his dream, the dream is trying to draw his attention to the fact that a miserly streak exists in him of which he is unaware.

As human beings it is now up to us to not only determine life's complexes but the archetypes that we share. As individuals who seek deeper answers, we must not only seek understanding, but also learn to release ourselves from the negative aspects within and without through the universal concepts of understanding, wisdom and forgiveness.

The genius of Jung was to underscore the spiritual or luminal part of the mind, wherein humanity could awaken from its long "unconscious" sleep into the light of Self discovery, life as part of God. The mind awakened to its archetypal symbols could breakthrough the memory and limbic unconsciousness of physical birth and understand the cosmic wholeness of Life.

---

1. Freud, Sigmund (1953-74) "The Psychopathology of Everyday Life," **Vol. 6** of *The Standard Edition of the Complete Works of Sigmund Freud,* James Strachey (Ed.) *et al* The Hogart Press & the Institute of Psychoanalysis, London.
2. Jensen, Ferne, C. G. Jung, Emma Jung, & Toni Wolff (1982) *A Collection of Remembrances.* San Francisco: Analytical Psychology Club of San Francisco (Eds.).
3. Otto, Rudolf (1958) *The Idea of the Holy.* Oxford University Press: Oxford.

35

Threads in the Holographic Tapestry of Consciousness

Ben Taylor, Ph.D.
Educator and Psychotherapist

Consciousness as a concept is as old as the human ability to use symbols (language), to think (manipulate the symbols), and to express ideas (communicate). However, there is academic agreement that scientific method and research has had limited success in explaining and measuring this complex phenomena. The strong influence of behavioral psychology in the early Twentieth Century resulted in the use of reductionistic approaches limited primarily to specific physical states or activities of consciousness. The big problem, according to David J. Chalmers[1], is that there are no acceptable theories to provide the foundation for the research and quantification of the unique and personal experience of consciousness in the individual person. In this scientific vacuum we return to the philosophical and religious ideas of consciousness.

There are many levels of consciousness, which might be visualized as a series of concentric ripples moving outward on a lake of cosmic consciousness. Though different from other forms of life in that it uses symbolic thinking, imagination, reflection, and intuition, expanding human consciousness is just one of the circles forming between the microcosm and the macrocosm. All creation is connected to a shared

Figure 35.1
His Holiness,
The Dalai Lama.

source, and the closer we get to the source, the lesser is the illusion of separateness, and the closer the proximity to ultimate truth.

Any discussion or description of human consciousness would include terms such as awareness, enlightenment and mysticism. Awareness is one of our essential gifts, giving us the capacity to value, to appreciate, to know and to discern. Enlightenment, in Taoism and Buddhism, describes the process and attainment of spiritual harmony with the universe. The present Dalai Lama described the path of enlightenment as involving the determination to be freed from cyclic existence and to achieve the correct view of emptiness.[2] Mysticism, according to J.J. Hurtak, is not an academic process alone, but *"the phenomenon of transcendence through altered levels of experience and reception."*[3]

In order to address the realization that there are many different threads in the holographic tapestry of consciousness, it is necessary to highlight some of the important qualities inherent in the fabric:

INTENTION OR WILL

We have already mentioned the idea of intention or determination as outlined by the Dalai Lama. Human will, or intention, when aligned with Divine Will, is the catalyst for the mind and results in heightening consciousness in a way that enhances connectedness and creativity. When we decide or choose our path to higher consciousness, our intention is like a flashlight illuminating our way.

FAITH

The act or state of believing unshakably in the existence of the Supreme Being without proof, is surrendering to God. Pure faith is the surest and straightest road to God. According to Fr. Thomas Keating: *"the essence of mysticism is the path of pure faith. You do not have to feel it but you have to practice it."*[4]

ABIDING IN THE WILL OF GOD, OR SURRENDERING

By surrendering oneself to God, which is an act of faith, you are consenting and receiving so that the process of transformation can be experienced in your innermost being where God dwells. One is entering a relationship with the Divine.

WISDOM

Webster's International Dictionary defines wisdom as *"the effectual mediating principle or personification of God's will in the creation of the world."* Wisdom is needed as we search for the transformation of ourselves, of humankind, and of this planet. David A. Cooper suggested that true wisdom does not come from without but within. It is exemplified by the way we live through our direct experiences.[5]

LOVE AND COMPASSION

The Bible is full of references to these words and these concepts. For example, Mark 12:30 and 31: *"thou*

Threads in the Holographic Tapestry of Consciousness

Figure 35.2
"Love is the center of human life."
—H.H. Dalai Lama.
Image by L. Photiadis (2002).

shalt love the Lord thy God with all thy heart and all thy soul and with all thy mind and with all thy strength....and Thou shalt love thy neighbor as thyself." Also, in John 13:34, Jesus told us to "*love one another as I have loved you.*"

The Dalai Lama spoke of the importance of wisdom and compassion, and of the Buddha's emphasis on establishing a working balance between a good brain and a good heart. He also stated that love is the center of human life. A famous quote attributed to Martin Luther King Jr. is especially applicable to the world today: "*Darkness cannot drive out darkness; only light can do that. Hate cannot drive out hate, only love can do that.*"

Additional threads may include, but not be limited to: truth, knowledge, forgiveness, patience, humility, honesty, understanding, grace, righteousness, and peace. The Kabbalah, the ancient Jewish mystical tradition of hidden knowledge, describes the Tree of Life as the manifestation of the Divine Will containing ten emanations called Sefirot, which express divine attributes. Though named as attributes of God, they can be defined in terms of human experience, because we too are created in the Image of God. These ten Sefirot are: Crown, Kingdom, Foundation, Wisdom, Victory, Understanding, Mercy, Beauty, Splendor, and Strength.

But what are we to do with these wonderful threads and ideas of consciousness? What tools and techniques do we need to practice and perfect, so that we may experience personal consciousness expansion and become agents for comprehensive transformation?

There are many pathways leading in the direction of the union of consciousness with the divine, and the sources are too numerous to mention. However, the following resources delineate several of these

Figure 35.3
Pacific Coast Trail
Marin, CA.
Photo by J. Martín
(2001).

pathways: In the Eastern teachings, both the *Keys To Enlightenment* by Geshe Tsultim Gyeltsen,[6] and *Kindness, Clarity and Insight*, by the Dalai Lama, include specific practices and meditations for the Path of Enlightenment. In the Judaic teachings, *God Is A Verb*, by David A. Cooper includes The Path of Tzaddik (Jewish Enlightenment). Finally, for the Christian approach, a recommendation is *Open Mind, Open Heart*, by Thomas Keating, who presents a complete context and detailed explanation of contemplative prayer and centering prayer.

It is important to highlight some of Keating's ideas, experiences and thoughts for the reader. He states that each person should pick a spiritual practice that adapts to one's particular temperament and natural disposition. Then, one should surrender and let Spirit lead.

Contemplative prayer is not a type of relaxation but rather a method of moving our developing relationship with God to the level of pure faith. Keating states clearly that contemplative prayer is not a charismatic gift, although the devotee may be contemplative and have the gift at the same time. It also is not a parapsychological or psychic phenomenon. Contemplative prayer is based upon the belief and faith that the presence of the Spirit is in us, prays in us, and that we consent. In this context, prayer is the putting aside of thoughts and detachment from them. It is also the offering of ourselves to God. Contemplative prayer is part of a dynamic process that initiates the participant into a deep, living relationship with the Divine. Keating gives the reader specific guidance when the release of unconscious energies occurs, or when the false self, shadow self or counterfeit self interfere with the process. He guides you in the reduction of "performance anxiety," which tends to put one in a future context, instead of the "Be here now" of the moment.

Keating gives an overview of the history of contemplative prayer, particularly its separation into the three parts of discursive meditation, affective

Figure 35.4
Contemplative prayer is the practice of silent interaction directly with God. Drawing by the Academy For Future Science (2002).

prayer (both of which rely heavily upon the rational mind and right hemisphere of the brain), and contemplation. Between the 15th and 16th Centuries, contemplative prayer lost its place in the church, and thus this silent interaction directly with God was eliminated. About one hundred years ago, the process of reintegration of contemplative prayer began in the church. Thomas Keating has played an important role in this revival process.

Centering prayer is the specific term he has chosen for this renewal based on the traditions of contemplative prayer, and Keating gives step-by-step guidance into the method of centering prayer. This includes the ways to reduce ordinary obstacles to contemplation, so that during the time of prayer one's attention is centered on God's presence within. One is taught to turn off the ordinary flow of thoughts and emotional patterns and open up to a new world of reality. Numerous questions by practitioners of the centering prayer method are asked and answered, and these provide valuable insights into the typical issues that arise through this approach. Clearly, this method of prayer opens our awareness to the Spiritual level of our being and facilitates our personal transformation in ways unique to each individual.

Some of the more valuable insights include how to monitor one's progress on the path to higher consciousness and connection. For example, a Christed person can be growing internally but not be aware of the growth. Plateaus and boredom may occur which might discourage the participant, and ideas and explanations are given on this issue.

The participant is encouraged to depend less on outer signs of growth and to be more accepting of the Spirit and Kingdom within. The process of Spiritual growth usually means facing the challenges of personal and emotional baggage, including the "counterfeiting self." Finally, progress in the spiritual journey is manifested by the unconditional acceptance of other people, especially those with whom we live.

As the challenges on our planet today grow in such dramatic and visible ways, each individual has the opportunity to be the key that opens the vault to the inner riches of our higher holographic consciousness. As we evolve and connect with our divine counterpart, may we take up our specific mission and role in the Divine plan so that *"Thy will be done on earth as it is in heaven."*

---

1. Chalmers, David J. (1996) *The Conscious Mind: In Search of a Fundamental Theory*. Oxford University Press.
2. Dalai Lama, His Holiness, Tenzin Gyatso (1988) *Kindness, Clarity & Insight*. Ithaca, New York: Snow Lion Publications.
3. Hurtak, J.J. (1997) "Future Science: Inductive Inference or Inductive Linkage?" *Future History*, **Vol. 2:6**, The Academy for Future Science.
4. Keating, Thomas (1992) *Open Mind, Open Heart*. New York: Continuum Publishing Co.
5. Cooper, David A. (1997) *God Is A Verb*. New York: Riverhead Books.
6. Geshe Tsultim Gyeltsen. (1989) *Keys to Great Enlightenment*. Los Angeles: Thubten Dhargye Ling.

36

Seeking Higher Consciousness

Gerald H. Vind, M.A.
Former New Technologies
Staff, Northup Corporation

As scientific investigations have probed the nature of subatomic particles, it has become clear that the presence and awareness of the investigator limits the discoveries. In other words, our thoughts and the very nature of consciousness are part of the answer to our questions. At the farthest reaches of scientific investigation, we discover that we are really looking back at ourselves. At the smallest units of the microcosm we find the multiple infinities of the macrocosm.

Joseph Chilton Pearce describes a triune structure of our human brain, a trinity of three parts that function together as a singular mind. This triune structure and the interaction of the three subunits is important to understanding our relationship to higher consciousness:

> We have three distinctly different neural structures within what we once thought was a singular brain.... These three structures in our skulls represent the major neural systems developed throughout evolutionary history, through which we inherit all accomplishments that precede and led to...a quantum-leap of additional potential we have not yet developed.[1]

The three distinctly different parts of our brain are:

1. The R-system (for reptilian) or brain stem which encompasses our sensory-motor system and all basic physical processes.

2. The limbic system, or "old-mammalian brain," which wraps around the reptilian brain to transform the crude instincts of the R-system, giving an adaptable and powerful intelligence. This system is also the area of feeling or emotions.

3. The neocortex—five times bigger than the two lower parts combined—providing intellect, creative thought, analytical and computational thought. When developed it provides compassion, empathy and love. It is also our gateway also to transcendental experience.

The limbic system integrates the three parts of the brain into a single whole system directing attention to the higher or lower brain functions. Thus, it can block our higher brain functions when it acts in a survival mode.

The illusive nature of consciousness, once a matter of philosophical speculation, has established an important presence in the field of quantum physics. In a paper published several years ago, Stuart Hameroff, collaborating with quantum physicist Roger Penrose, advanced a theory that the extensive network of intracellular microtubules can explain the remarkable ability of our brain to perform the incredibly complex, yet seemingly simple, task of recognizing a human face. Even with some 100 billion neurons and an average of some thousand synaptic junctions per neuron, there is not enough computing capacity to perform the complex pattern recognition processes we take for granted. Hameroff outlines the cellular mechanism for coupling to some form of higher level functioning[2] in which microtubules appear to form a computer within

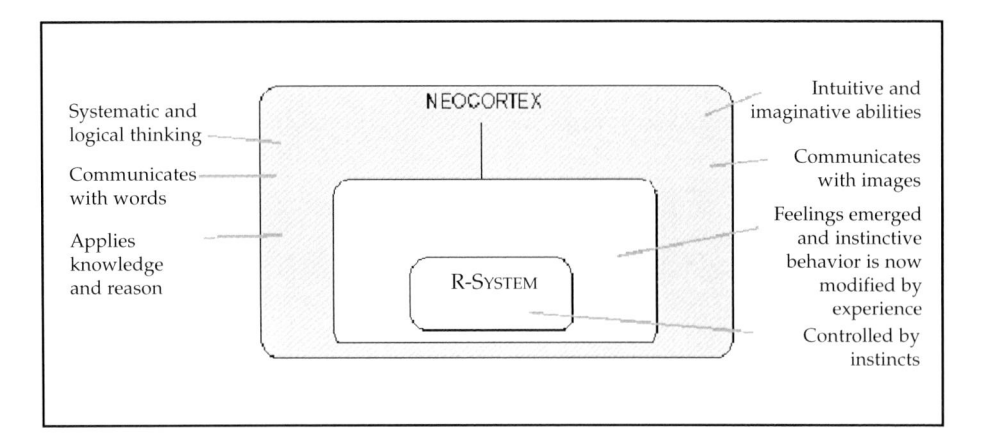

Figure 36.1
The three parts of the human brain and their functions. Schematic courtesy of Gerald H. Vind.

Diagram labels:
- NEOCORTEX
- R-SYSTEM
- Systematic and logical thinking
- Communicates with words
- Applies knowledge and reason
- Intuitive and imaginative abilities
- Communicates with images
- Feelings emerged and instinctive behavior is now modified by experience
- Controlled by instincts

a computer, so to speak, providing a biomolecular quantum-level coupling within every cell, coupling it to higher levels of existence, as well as potential resonance coupling to other cells.

Microtubules are inelastic tube-like polymers that assemble from tiny molecular filaments that form into tiny tubes of uniform diameter (30 nm) from filament strands constructed from two complementary protein subunits (alpha and beta tubulin). It is interesting that microtubules are bioactive in the range of acoustic frequencies. Do microtubules have some bioacoustic resonance response to information contained within sounds?

In the broad spectrum of sounds that are processed by our ears, there is a specific group of sounds that are called phonetic, and the term phoneme is used to define the smallest unit of sound out of which words are formed. All the letters of our alphabet and all syllables are phonemes comprising most, but not all, of the fifty phonemes accounted by researchers as the building blocks of all languages, old and new. None of the thousands of languages in the world use all fifty phonemes.

About 25 years ago scientific investigations discovered an innate language connection in humans. Researchers found that from the seventh month of pregnancy and continuing into the neonatal period

Seeking Higher Consciousness

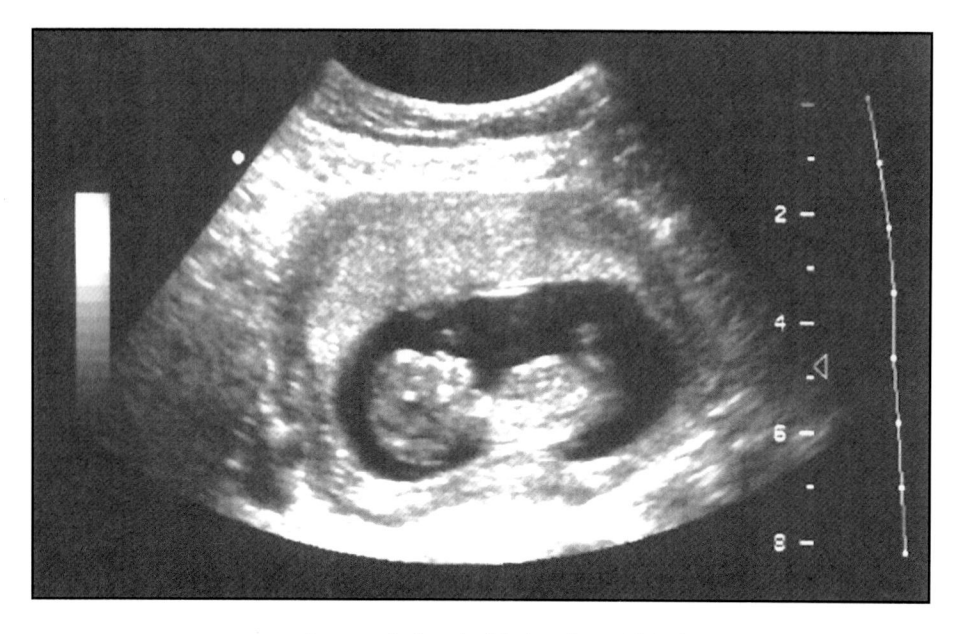

Figure 36.2
Scientific investigations have discovered that in vitro infants respond with precise muscular movements to each of the 50 phonemes. This process begins about 7 months into the pregnancy and continues through the neonatal period after birth.

after an infant's birth, that all infants responded with precise muscular movements to each of the fifty phonemes. Specific muscle groups appear to be "hard wired" to respond to specific phonemes, with the same muscle responding to the same phoneme each time it sounds. The response is immediate; there is no time lag. This is present before language learning takes place, and provides the foundations for subsequent language experiences.[3]

By birth, then, the sensory-motor structures that form the foundation of language are fully formed to respond to all fifty phonemes, even though we subsequently learn languages that use less than the total pool of phonemes. The structure of the human larynx is complex and far superior to the vocal structure of other creatures permitting us to form all of the fifty phoneme sounds. (Neanderthal man had a larger brain than we have, but lacked our vocal structures). However, the human languages, and the cultures that transmit language, are limited in that they do not use all fifty of the existing phonemes.

Additionally, in examining the structure of the inner ear, Alfred Tomatis found that all of our human perceptual senses are integrated or coordinated through the acoustic nerve.[4] This means that spoken language is intimately involved in, or influences, all of our perceptual processes.

The spoken word is certainly central to human access to higher intelligence and ultimately to God. But access to higher intelligence requires more than words—it requires the meaning of those words. The meaning of a word has two parts: connotative and denotative. There is an emotional content to all language. In addition to the denotative or cognitive meaning of a word, there is also a connotative meaning linked to emotional associations. And so it is important to look at how our brains process our thoughts and feelings.

Joseph LeDoux, professor of psychology and neuroscience at New York University, has found that the cognitive information from our life experiences is stored in the brain's neocortex. However, the human emotional memory that includes feelings and associated physiological responses, is stored in an area of the limbic system known as the amygdala. This is the part of our memory that makes it emotional, the true feeling content of our lives. LeDoux says that our memories about emotions are just facts, but it is our emotional memories that give the emotional quality to

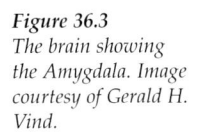

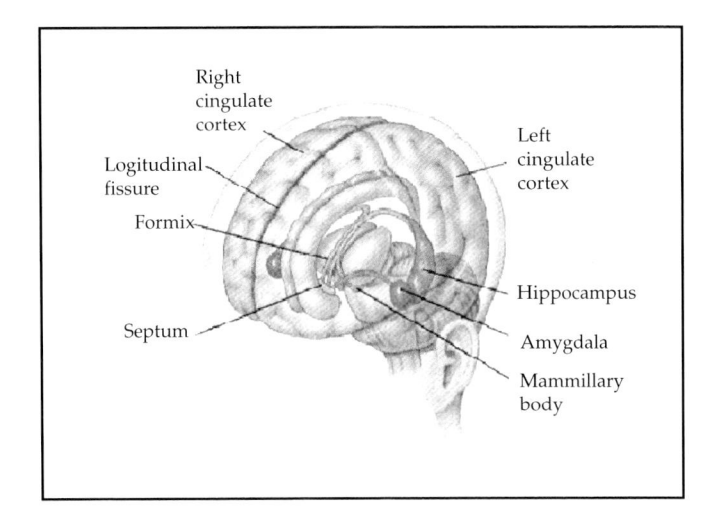

Figure 36.3
The brain showing the Amygdala. Image courtesy of Gerald H. Vind.

Figure 36.4
Meditation is now recognized as an effective way of quieting the emotional activities of the brain. Image by the Academy For Future Science.

any of our memories. Somehow our brain fuses the two parts together into a seamless whole so that it seems that they are coming from the same place.[5]

It is now known that the limbic system's amygdala can register the emotion of fear without any cortical involvement. This is explained by recent discoveries that some neural pathways carry sound signals from the ear directly to the amygdala. Direct sensory data from the thalamus allows us to respond quickly without first analyzing the data. Then, as more information reaches the amygdala from the cortex, we can analyze the situation to determine if there truly is a threat.

Messages from the amygdala then trigger the adrenal gland to produce adrenaline (epinephrine). The adrenaline release causes increased heart rate and other physiological preparations to fight or flee. This discovery explains how we can be deeply anxious and fearful without knowing why; the amygdala is conditioned to fear reactions when there is no apparent reason. Because of the complexities and uncertainties of our world, there is a tendency for us to establish chronic reactive patterns of fear and anxiety. These patterns influence how we approach life and perceive the world.

The amygdala operates almost as a switch that turns off input from the higher brain functions of the neocortex (80% of our brain) when it activates in a fear pattern. Only when we quiet our limbic system through relaxing activities, meditation or prayer, can we receive input from our higher brain functions.

The amygdala responds primarily to emotional input, and it is difficult, if not impossible, to reason the amygdala into open receptivity to higher brain functions. Meditation entered into cultural prominence 2,600 years ago when Siddhartha became the Buddha by finding enlightenment, and meditation is now recognized as an effective way of quieting the emotional activities of the brain.

Six centuries later, Jesus preached love and forgiveness, and these are two effective ways of quieting fear and anger—even of reprogramming our

Figure 36.5
When we open the doorway to higher consciousness, we can more fully experience our relationship with God. Doorway at Macchu Pichu. Photo courtesy of L. Photiadis (1997).

amygdala. Beyond any controversy of the historical Jesus and the divine Jesus, it is clear that Jesus did provide us with a new paradigm through which we can open ourselves to transcend mental-emotional constraints to access higher brain functions.

We could say that God stands at the door closed by the amygdala and knocks. Why do we not answer the knock? When we open that doorway we approach a higher level of existence—the experience of our relationship with God. The Christ can become our amygdala "doorway opener." I cannot avoid speculating about a parallel in our brain to the triune unity of the Father, Son and Holy Spirit where the Son operates within our limbic system, opening us to fully experience a higher consciousness.

---

1. Pearce, Joseph Chilton (1992) *Evolution's End*. Harper, San Francisco, pp. 42-51.
2. Hameroff, Stuart (1995) "Microtubules, Coherence, Consciousness," *Letter* dated May 15, 1995, to Psyche-D, at http://psyche.cs.monash.edu.au Also: Hameroff, S.R. & Penrose, R. "Orche-strated reduction of quantum coherence in brain microtubules: A model for consciousness," *Toward a Science of Consciousness*, Contributions from the 1994 Tucson Conference, Hameroff, Kaszniak, & Scott (Eds.), MIT Press, Cambridge, 1996.
3. Conrad, William, & Sander, Louis (1974) "Neonate Movement is Synchronized with Adult Speech; Interactional Participation & Language Acquisition," *Science*, Jan. 11, 1974, pp. 99-101.
4. Tomatis, Alfred (1991) "Chant, the Healing Power of Voice and Ear," *Music, Physician for Times to Come*, (1991) Campbell, D. (Ed.), Quest, Wheaton.
5. LeDoux, Joseph E. (1992) "Emotion & the Amygdala," *The Amygdala: Neurobiological Aspects of Emotion, Memory & Mental Dysfunction*. Aggleton, J.P. (Ed.), Wiley-Liss, New York, pp. 339-351.

37

The Greater Unity of Sacred Geometries

J.J. Hurtak, Ph.D., Ph.D.

The ancient artisans projected the universal patterns of active intelligence found in nature, the meditative sounds of inner consciousness and the geometries of the mind, into all that was man-made, creating a sacred architecture. Through a sacred canon of proportion and geometry, number and form, the principles of the fundamental unity of reality were crafted into our art and language, artifacts and temples, even our social structures (as in North India and Iran). There was no absolute distinction between the sacred and the profane that would later occur in Western art and architecture. All was a reflection of universal order and harmony, a microcosm, designed to remind and reconnect us to the Spirit that is the cause of and in all things.

The encoding of ancient wisdom attunement is most evident in the remains of ancient cities and temples, from the pyramids of Egypt, Mexico and China, stone circles and stupas, to Gothic cathedrals and Indian dance circles in the American southwest. In the words of the Rg Veda, "In the realm of the creator god, Indra, there exists a net, woven with pearls at the intersections, so positioned by enhanced display that each reflects all the others." In mandalas and

The Greater Unity of Sacred Geometries

Figure 37.1
Ancient near eastern temple, showing spiraling stupas. Bangkok, Thailand. Photo by D. Hurtak.

interconnecting circles with sacred words, this was consistently applied all over the globe as an expression of the divine interacting with human consciousness.

The form of the Temple was based upon the archetypal image of life and the macrocosmic universe in relationship to the Divine Man, the Anthropos, the "ideal human image." In the East, this was the Buddha, or Krishna; in the West, the archetypal heavenly man, "the Adam Kadmon" of the biblical scriptures exemplified in the risen Christ. Man, since he was created in the image of God, was thought to have parts and functions of his body in the form of sacred patterns exemplifying the whole universe. The purpose of a physical, social and symbolic environment was to connect humankind to higher, more integrated states of being: to relate us to our common humanity, connect us to this universe, and unite us to the source of our being and vitality. In being self-actualized, the consciousness is expanded, the emotions balanced and the body healed and made whole, allowing for the "end" of life to be the complete acquisition of supernature.

Today in the speeding contours of a technical society making rapid decision at every turn, we are operating as a species out of balance with the deeper intuitive skills within ourselves and our world. We have not only lost touch with our planet, our heritage

Figure 37.2
Utriusque Cosmi, Vol. II,
Oppenheim, 1619, by
Robert Fludd.

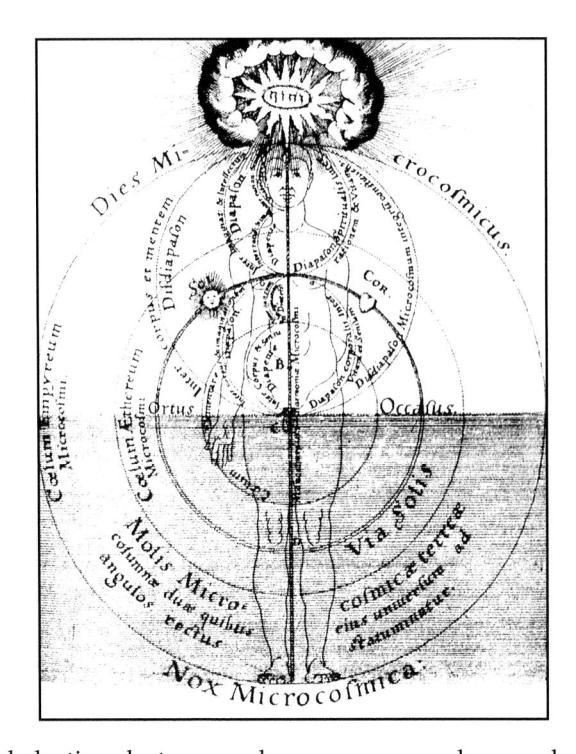

and destiny, but we make war on ourselves and our environment, forgetting that what we do to it, we ultimately do to ourselves. In effect, we have superceded God. Standing in the shadow of the dinosaur we mock the cosmos, treading a path of destruction, if not in the image of nuclear holocaust then in environmental pollution, with almost total disregard for the whole of life and the living tradition of service with which we share this planet. This was not always the case. In addition to the equivalent of the five Platonic solids many of the ancient societies made use of the mysterious circle.

The ancient circular structures for measurement marking the arrival of the summer solstice and various star alignments go back more than 7,000 to 8,000 years. They accurately reflect the movements of the heavens and the global nature of the earth through complex measuring systems. We are just beginning to find the pieces. From the stone circle at Rujum al-Hiri east of the

The Greater Unity of Sacred Geometries

Sea of Galilee to a proto-Stonehenge stone circle at Nabta, Egypt near the frontier with Sudan, humanity has erected structures as long as 8,000 years ago. Nabta, for example, is a highly specialized megalithic stone work where each standing stone of more than forty stones in circular patterns functioned as a very early astrophysical computer system by the ringmakers who recorded history in stone (See also Granögger, *Stone Circles, Sky Circles, Sound Cirlces: New Evidence on Global Round Numbers*, this edition, Chapter 5). Included in these unique designs of star and solar calculators are the Great Circle of Zimbabwe, the great circle at the Cahokia Mounds in Illinois and those found in the area of Okinawa, Japan.

On the other side of the planet, while recently working with anthropologists in the deserts of Australia (1998), my colleagues came across a series of perfect interlocking circles within circles. It would be difficult to grasp the purpose of the size and complexity of the circles from the ground level each averaging more than two hundred meters across. Aerial pictures taken of the geometries reminds one of the plains of Nasca. This matrix of circles can be

Figure 37.3
Nazca drawing of a spider spanning over 140 feet (43 meters).
Image by the Academy For Future Science.

The Greater Unity of Sacred Geometries

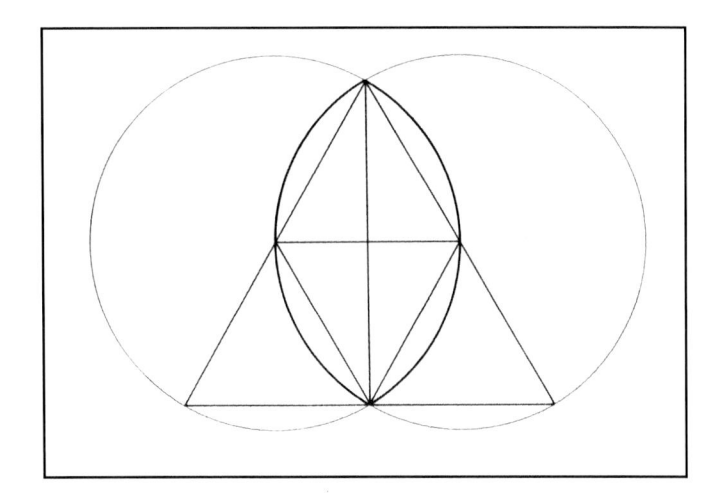

Figure 37.4
Simple form of the vesica pisces, created by the overlapping space between two circles. Image by the Academy For Future Science.

bounded by three nested equilateral triangles, giving rise to nine points. The circles can be combined to create larger overlapping and superimposed geometric circles as the vesicas pisces, demonstrating ongoing life where a singular circle is not the end, but the beginning. This Australian circle series appear to be also a variation of the Pythagorean Tetractys, seeking to detail the mathematical organization of the macro- and micro-details of the universe. The geometric figures represented multiple closure of temporal patterns that can combine 24 external circles with numerous other circles and horizontal and vertical hypersphere extensions showing the unending flow of time. We interpret this overall geometric figure to represent the geometry of one quantum unit of pure space.

According to renown shamanistic painter Malcolm Jagamarra from the remote area of Warlpirt in the desert outback of the Northern Territory of Australia, the circle is continually used as the overriding social symbol of life. Religious people continually sit in circles through their life, noting where uncles and grandmothers sit within the plane of the circle. The same can be said of indigenous peoples throughout the Third World who use the "culture circle" or medicine wheel to define qualitatively greater or lesser degrees of cultural, ethnic, spiritual, and life-style diversity

The Greater Unity of Sacred Geometries

Figure 37.5
Australian Dreamtime picture depicting the Circles of Life. Drawing by Malcolm Jagamarra.

than was accepted in formal housing structures used by Europeans. Throughout the Northern Territory of Australia, large family areas can be found in interlocking stone circles. In pictures of Bali's wana wana, the stone marker surrounded by two flowing snakes, symbolizes the sign of life and the power of life. In water dreaming and in Ngopa lightning dreaming, the use of circles is necessary to form a prominent form of energy continuity between the physical world, the social world, and the higher spiritual worlds.

Our planet with its respective solar system and galaxy exists in a type of circle arrangement, but so does the structure of the cranium that holds the brain (in the mid-coronal plane). We swim in outer space as astronauts and inner space as psycho-nauts. The view that man is a microcosm is finding renewal in the scientific speculations that the universe is like a hologram, meaning that the pattern of the whole is holographically encoded in every part. From the atom to the galaxy, the same laws of physics apply everywhere, with the underlying unity being as a holographic interference pattern of the fundamental field of vibration. Every state of being, every level of organization, from atom to flower to star, occupies a characteristic plane of frequency pattern. These are essentially vibrational forms having unique corresponding frequency signatures creating, fields of geometry. Thoughts, emotions and dreams are energy and are therefore essentially vibrational in nature. As such they have form and pattern. The planes of consciousness are like frequency bands. Attunement to a dimension or state of being is a matter of sympathetic resonance to the corresponding frequency pattern that takes one into the broad spectrum of living options.

Contemporary scientists, like neurophysicist Karl Pribram and mathematicians like Peter Plichta and Hartmut Müller have proposed a unified working model showing that the universe unfolds in repetitions of numbers emanating from cycles or circles. And, like a hologram, each part exhibits the whole. To apply this to our consciousness field, our own mind can be considered a field around the brain in which memory exists undifferentiated everywhere within the larger field and, ultimately, the cosmos.

Many creative forms derive from a perception which is essentially the neural interaction with an interference pattern of expanding electrical wave fronts arriving from the sense organs. Looking at the cellular and subcellular levels we see similar dynamics where microstructures function with a fourth state of matter throughout the geometric organization of the human body. The self-regulation systems are geometric patterns working as loops ensuring a signal image that effects multiple body systems. If both mind and the universe are holographic, then we may be living within a great thought, or as the mystics say, in the Divine Reality.

The Greater Unity of Sacred Geometries

*Figure 37.6
Can humanity accept the awesome responsibility for the maintenance of "spaceship earth"?
Image courtesy of NASA.*

To what end does the sacred circle serve if created by Divine Thought? There are several considerations regarding the circle of sacred interconnectedness that is found in all life and which can lead not only to the understanding of the symbolism of the Divine, but to the awakening of direct participation. The first is the idea of planetary stewardship, of accepting an awesome responsibility for the maintenance of Buckminister Fuller's "spaceship earth." Such views suggest a global systems approach to energy and resource management, leading us to more holistic human ecology practices based on living environmental habitats and life protection in a new transnational context.

The second notion is that of global consciousness, of recognizing not only that the earth is a single holistic circle, but that humanity is one whole being. In a world becoming a global village, shrinking from the effects of modern transcommunications and high speed networks, we are beginning to think and act globally as one global mind. We must begin to understand that at the level we connect to the planet's being, there is no 'we' or 'they,' only us. When one is starving, we all are starving. What happens to any part of us ultimately affects us all. Differences in race, culture or belief are destined to give humanity the diversity of life experiences necessary for the evolution of the whole where each skeletal part is united into one being on mother Earth. Implied here is a fractal economics of starting a politics of common goals and caring rather than of security and protectionism, a society free of hunger, poverty and ignorance. The international work can be focused in partnerships, e.g., in U.N. programs, State of the World Forums, educational innovations of world citizenship, eventually becoming the leaven of inspiration within organizations working with environmental associations, the World Health Organization, non-governmental organizations, and genuine ecumenical work.

The third aspect is ultimately the most important. It is synthesis of the first two themes in the context of a Divine Plan that recognizes that we are all spiritual beings, sharing a common Creator and higher destiny. We are beginning to see ourselves endowed with purpose, as well as with love and intelligence. With the intense search for other intelligent forms of life, we are awakening to the idea that we share this universe with a vast variety of other evolving beings. Now we need to develop the perception and sensitivity to live with other forms of intelligent life existing on many levels of reality not currently accessible but which nonetheless feel the effects of our hearts and minds by virtue of sharing the energies and qualities of a living God. It requires an expansion of consciousness that understands not only humanity but the whole planet and the whole universe as a living being existing in an ocean of forms.

I believe the hidden denominator of all things rests upon consciousness as the field for pattern discernment and ongoing creativity. Humanity will have to learn to move from its so-called "materially oriented axis" to the adoption of an attitude which falls more nearly under the heading of the "methodology of pattern in field theory concepts," the in-depth meaning of which has yet to be understood. If this pattern can be held for the creation of actual life in new space, it will convey sacred geometry as a clue to the myriad geometries through which the human can operate with the well-executed thought-forms of the divine in human clothing. In grasping the interpenetration of divine form and human debris at the Angel's feet of our lives on earth—the cycle of renewal and rebirth is possible.

---

1. Müller, Hartmut (2000) "Global Scaling: Die globale Zeitwelle," *Raum&Zeit* **Vol. 107,** September/Oktober 2000, pp. 48-59.
2. Penrose, Roger (1994) *Shadows of the Mind: A search for the missing science of consciousness*. Oxford: Oxford University Press.
3. Plichta, Peter (1995) *Gottes geheime Formel: Die Entschlüsselung des Welträtsels und der Primzahlencode*. München: Albert Langen/ Georg Müller Verlag.
4. Pribram, Karl. H. (1993) "Rethinking Neural networks: Quantum Fields and Biological Data," In *Proceedings of the first Appalachian Conference on Behavioral Neurodynamics*. Hillsdale, New Jersey: Lawrence Erlbaum Associates, Publishers.

38

Age Eleven Speculations

Gerald H. Vind, M.A.
Former New Technologies
Staff, Northup Corporation

Is our present human evolution reaching the end of a cycle? Are there internal forces that will soon bring about drastic changes? We are reaching a point in our individual and collective development where far too many of our old ways do not work, and it is becoming increasingly necessary for us to create and adapt to new ways.

In his book *Collapse of Complex Societies*, Joseph Tainter presents the view that the fall of societies, such as Roman, Mayan, etc., all share the common element of diminishing returns, where the marginal return for each additional unit of effort declines to the point of societal collapse. Tainter expresses concern that our present society has achieved a level of complexity such that the economic overhead for maintaining the bureaucracy of our contemporary society is becoming so great that our survival is threatened.[1]

Our complex industrialized world is in a time of great innovation, change, and increasing instability. As our remarkable information-technology revolution accelerates change at all levels, those who are most set in their old ways will have the greatest difficulty adapting to rapidly changing conditions.

This collective inability to make major changes,

Figure 38.1
Myelination of neurons in the brain is a process that takes place in children at age eleven. Image by the Academy For Future Science.

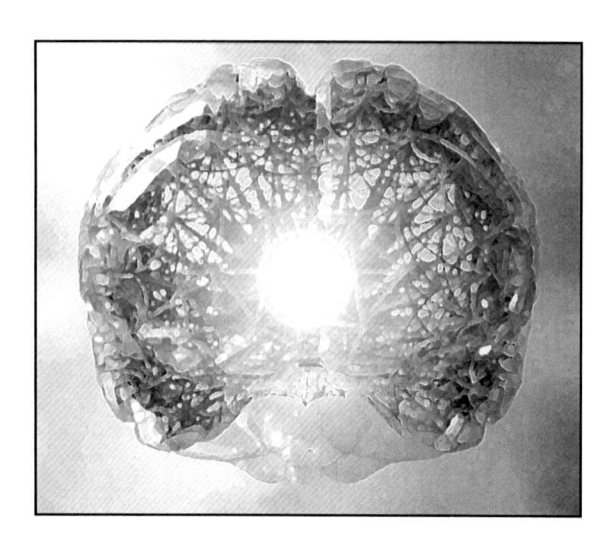

and to undergo adaptive restructuring, can leave us unprepared and unable to cope with new and perhaps dangerous circumstances. But could the development of dangerous circumstances for humankind be part of a vastly larger developmental process? Is there some collective process we are all going through that will bring about the sudden onset of major changes?

Consider the possibility that each of us have within our brains the pattern for our human evolution. Thus, humans may be collectively recapitulating the developmental process of the individual human brain. Joseph Chilton Pearce, in his book titled *Evolution's End*, explains the developmental growth process of the human brain.[2]

Brain growth spurts take place *in utero*, at birth, and at the beginnings of each stage of child development. By around age six this fundamental world-self-language system is complete, and nature turns to the development of the neocortex, ushering us into the world of intellect, logic, and reasoning. At age eleven, however, instead of a brain growth spurt, nature releases a chemical in the young brain that dissolves all undeveloped neuronal fields. Eighty percent of the neural mass of the brain disappears, and we end up with the same brain weight we had at eighteen months.[3]

The neuronal fields that survive nature's

Age Eleven Speculations

housecleaning at age eleven are those that have developed and have become covered by a protective sheath of myelin. Myelination of neurons in the brain is a function of their utilization. Thus, unutilized and undeveloped neuronal fields are cleaned out in order to make room for new intelligences that are to develop after age eleven.

As we accelerate through our present societal growth spurt, pause now and consider this question: Has our collective human development reached age eleven? Are we about to undergo a collective housecleaning, in order to make room for new intelligences that will develop subsequently?

Are there those who are proposing, advocating, or encouraging major reductions in the human population? Let us examine one somewhat obscure example, the *Georgia Guidestones*. Some 20 years ago in the remote setting of Elberton County, Georgia (about one hour east of Atlanta), a mysterious monument was created and unveiled to the public. Called the *Georgia*

Figure 38.2
The mysterious Georgia Guidestones located in Elberton County, GA bear their cryptic message for humanity in eight contemporary languages.

415

Guidestones, the large granite structure comprises six pieces of Pyramid Blue Granite averaging 26-tons each. The monument is inscribed with a Message for Mankind in eight active contemporary languages (English, Russian, Mandarin Chinese, Arabic, Hebrew, Hindi, Swahili, and Spanish) as well as four ancient languages (Egyptian hieroglyphics, Babylonian cuneiform, Classical Greek, and Sanskrit). The four ancient languages repeat the admonition: "Let these be guidestones to an age of reason."

The main message, repeated in eight languages, begins with:

> Maintain humanity under 500,000,000 [one twelfth of the Earth's present population] in perpetual balance with nature; guide reproduction wisely—improve fitness and diversity; unite humanity with a new living language; rule passion—faith—tradition.

The message continues with admonitions for such things as fair laws, reason, social duties, etc., and concludes with: "Be not a cancer on the earth—leave room for nature..."

The people of the Elberton Granite Finishing Company, who fabricated and constructed the monument, were paid for their work by mysterious sponsors. They and other local people had contact with only one person, a well-dressed man known only as R.C. Christian. Mr. Christian told them the sponsors of the Georgia Guidestones project would forever remain anonymous.[4]

The message presented by the *Georgia Guidestones* appears to be from those who fit the role of "Earth stewards"—those who offer guidance, albeit obscure guidance, and who are making a public declaration presumably to guide or influence humanity. The important question about guiding humanity seems to be: Is anyone listening?

There are two levels of listening: the external world of human discourse and interaction, and the inner world of inner-awareness or spiritual relationships. Unfortunately, most of humanity is so concerned with survival in the external world, that the inner world has been ignored.

The late Julian Jaynes, in his book titled *The Origin of Consciousness in the Breakdown of the Bicameral Mind*, details a thesis that human consciousness changed significantly between 1,000 and 2,000 BCE. The primary thesis of his book, greatly simplified here, is that our present human consciousness is essentially left-brained, meaning that language is processed primarily in three regions of the left hemisphere of the brain: 1) The supplementary motor cortex (on the top of the left frontal lobe) is mostly involved in articulation of language, 2) Broca's area (at the back of the left frontal lobe) handles articulation, vocabulary, inflection, and grammar, and 3) Wernicke's area (mainly in the posterior left temporal lobe) embraces vocabulary, syntax, meaning, and understanding.[5]

Jaynes puzzled about all of the speech-brain functions operating in the left lobe, when the right hemisphere is also capable of all speech functions, and notes that a few ambidextrous people have speech developed in both hemispheres. He speculated that in ancient times (circa the time of the Biblical patriarch Abraham) human consciousness was more whole-brained. Jaynes suggested that the corresponding area in the right hemisphere (called the hallucinatory area) might have organized admonitory experiences where people "heard the voice of god," and transferred these experiences to Wernicke's area.

Paul Devereux also speaks of this ancient change in human consciousness as having a profound influence on western civilization. In his studies, observing a lowering of human behavior and achievement in the latter part of the Bronze Age and continuing into the Iron Age, Devereux said it was like watching a light go out:

> Certainly, there were wise men, and their colleagues that doubtlessly kept some of the

Age Eleven Speculations

Figure 38.3a
Early Bronze Age shaft-hole axe from Marston.

Figure 38.3b
Early Iron Age earthenware head excavated near Lydenburg, South Africa.

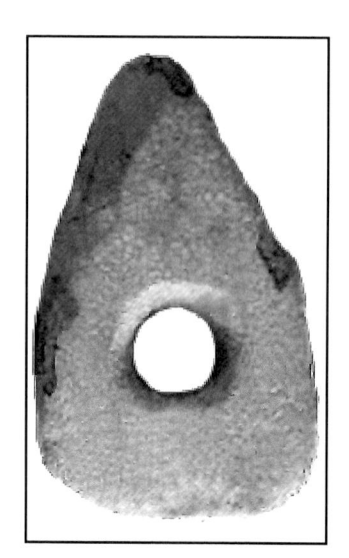

[higher] Knowledge alive, but the whole society was no longer informed by wisdom and visionary knowledge. Society no longer had a direct channel to supernormal knowledge; priests had to be used as intermediaries, [higher] priests who had themselves lost the understanding of how to activate the outer mechanisms to present their inner visions.[6]

The ego-centered self-awareness we know today did not exist in ancient humans. As human consciousness shifted from the ancient whole brain to a left-dominant brain function, individual self-awareness became dominant. Jaynes believed that ancient human consciousness was much less autonomous and lacked the self-awareness that we assume today to have always been present. Devereux, however, sees ancient human consciousness as simply more in harmony with nature (Gaia). Devereux calls for an alteration of our perceptions of the world around us, an "ecopsychology" that will reestablish our harmony with the natural world.

It is worth noting that the complex issues of brain

laterality are far from scientific agreement and remain the subject of ongoing scientific study. Reviewing the current research, John McCrone observes that, while there has been much confusion on brain laterality, the bulk of evidence indicates that the left-brain hemisphere is organized with a bias to local concerns, while the right hemisphere is biased toward global concerns. (In a small percent of the population this laterality is reversed, and with the ambidextrous it is balanced.)[7]

Brain laterality research is very complex and still in an early phase of development, yet research to date indicates that human consciousness is much more complicated than the simplistic left-right caricature embraced by today's popular culture. The most important consideration is how the parts of the brain complement each other, and how they function together as a whole.[8]

There can be no doubt that the consciousness of most of the civilized world has evolved from ancient times into our current insulated self-awareness. Perhaps we may now be ready to re-embrace wholeness in our connection with higher intelligence, a process of becoming increasingly reconnected to the collective consciousness field that already includes us all.

Although much of human consciousness today is dominated by the left-brain functions, we still retain the open portal for extra-sensory communication through the right-brain region corresponding to Wernicke's area, the so-called hallucinatory region. This area is presently dormant in most of us. When we become able to access higher and non-linear forms of communications and start reclaiming our whole brain in order to become a whole person, some important considerations need to be addressed about the nature of that higher consciousness, and our personal relationship with it. Carl Gustav Jung observed:

> In the realm of consciousness we are our own masters [current self-centered consciousness]... But if we step through the door of the shadow

we discover with terror that we are the objects of unseen factors.[9]

Our shadow, as Jung called it, is our disowned self, the disowned material buried deep within us that we hide from our self and from others. Buried, but not powerless; our perceptions can be altered by our shadow material. One who sees Satan under the bed, so to speak, is seeing the projection of his own fear-filled shadow material, and many people remain vulnerable to manipulation, influence, and even control by people who operate knowledgeably on the disowned parts of a target individual.

Most of us are unaware of the vestiges of an earlier whole-brain, low-ego-awareness organization and so, as we open to our wholeness, we must be prepared to undergo a truth process, confronting what is inside us as well as outside. We must be willing to illuminate

Figure 38.4
According to Jung, our "shadow" is our disowned self, buried deep within the unconscious.
Image by the Academy For Future Science.

and embrace our own shadow material. When we come from an inner state of unconditional love that accepts all that we are, and have been, we can successfully make that embrace. Without a process of personal centering in unconditional love (total self-acceptance without evaluation or judgement), the terror of our unseen factors cannot be confronted successfully.

From this personal center of unconditional love we can further empower ourselves with the awareness that our human consciousness has evolved through software changes (learned behavior), rather than through some evolutionary biological or physical change. It is therefore within our human potential to edit or rewrite our own personal biocomputer software.

It is within our power to open, illuminate, and reprogram ourselves to be able to achieve the best of our full human potential, and in this process we also become more aware of the potential for abuse or misuse of newfound or rediscovered abilities. Our growing wholesomeness as individuals creates a unified field effect that expands the collective human consciousness field.

Since the tragic events of September 11, 2001, our world has entered an era of newly perceived threats to our existence as a species. However real, these threats must be held in a larger context in order for us to remain open to higher consciousness. Emotional, pre-conscious reactions of anger and fear, arising from our unexplored shadow self, will incapacitate the higher brain functions and keep us locked in our negative emotions.

External threats should not keep us from entering a new level of transcendent human awareness. More and more of us are experiencing a new meaning of life, a new reality emerging from our personal spiritual unfolding. While this is a personal process, it is but one element among millions in a growing wave of consciousness expansion. This wave is expanding individuals beyond the confines of convention and orthodoxy into a transcendent spiritual connection.

Our personal spiritual development leads us to a living ascension in which we open our whole being to walk with continuous divine guidance.

Recalling the opening thoughts of this article, our spiritual development may be viewed as age-eleven myelination. And thus evolved, we will be more fully prepared for whatever unfolds in our future reality. Indeed, we may rediscover our ability to influence our future reality more directly by the collective alignment of our positive creative human intention.

---

1. Tainter, Joseph (1990) *Collapse of Complex Societies*. Cambridge U. Press Paperback.
2. Pearce, Joseph Chilton (1993) *Evolution's End*. Harper San Francisco, p. 99.
3. Pearce, Ibid.
4. Information on the Georgia Guidestones & Elberton Granite Finishing Company is available through Elberton County Chamber of Commerce, 148 College Avenue, Elberton, GA, 30635. Phone: 706-283-5651.
5. Jaynes, Julian (1990) *The Origin of Consciousness in the Breakdown of the Bicameral Mind*. Houghton Mifflin, reissue as paperback.Julian Jaynes (1923-1997) taught at Princeton and achieved a dedicated following for this controversial book (his only book).
6. Devereux, Paul (1996) *Earth Lights Revelation* (out of print). Also: *Re-Visioning the Earth: A Guide to Opening the Healing Channels Between Mind and Nature*.
7. McCrone, John (1999) "Left Brain, Right Brain," *New Scientist*, July 3, 1999. Also: Farber, B.(1999) *Going Inside: Tour Around a Single Moment of Consciousness*.
8. McCrone, Ibid.
9. Jung, Carl Gustav (1969) *Essays on a Science of Mythology*. Princeton University Press, Reprint edition.

Awareness & Self-Determination versus the Technification of Knowledge on the Net

J.J. Hurtak, Ph.D., Ph.D.

Today, in the midst of the Internet revolution, every human initiative can use technical means to express itself. There are several important elements in our consideration of the widening focus of humankind's relationship with technology. First, and most important, for large numbers of people, the technological elites of the pre-Internet era screened out whatever did not lend itself to technical expression, limiting the soul's content to the basic needs existence. Such expressions as accountability and self-awareness remained a purely private matter, with little importance to the technical society.

In the 1950s and on into the 1970s, with no apparent planning, the American passion for technology and gadgetry became functionally associated with the creative arts. While it is hardly surprising that a small and highly-talented group in the world of performing and visual arts should instinctively utilize the most sophisticated artifacts of science and technology available, scarcely anyone familiar with the arts would have expected high-minded scientists and engineers to enter into a free and enthusiastic collaboration with a new generation of commercial artists. During the same period, development of technology in totalitarian countries had enormous significance for creative arts based on mass-movements.

The eras have changed, but the struggle between the free soul and the mind bonded to the technification of knowledge is still being played out. The avant-garde artist through cinematography, computer-generated graphics, lasers, etc., has been subject to the imprint of technification. The global web blurs the balance of art, consciousness, culture and technology with images of death and violence which dominate the screen.

A second observation is that the hubris of technology has compelled a rigid conformism. With the blossoming of technology, human initiative was reduced to the lowest common denominator and is, in effect, without higher cosmic awareness, limited to the technological power brokers. A quiet struggle still continues behind the scenes that could be called that of the mind-soul or "free spirit" versus the technification of knowledge in the global commons. The penetration into one's personal life by manipulators using services still in their embryonic stage on the Internet has caught the free society off guard and exposed a personal vulnerability that affects the entire Internet.

A third observation of the growing reliance on

Figure 39.1
The struggle between the free soul and the mind bonded to the technification of knowledge still continues.

Figure 39.2
High technology has largely replaced humanity's quest for spiritual values.

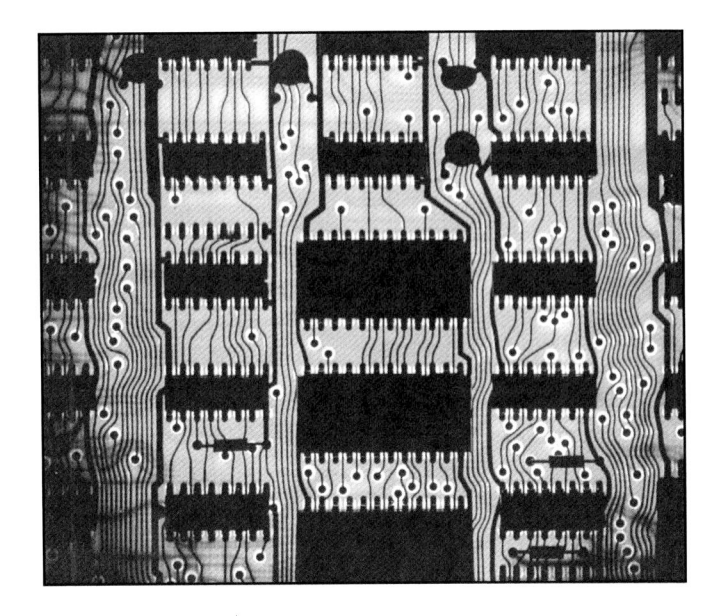

technology for all levels of problem-solving is how high technology, exemplified in the computer chip, has largely replaced humanity's quest for spiritual values with automata that evoke what many feel to be a shallow examination of the fate of the ecstatic impulses and phenomena of the human spirit. It is not difficult to observe that the "ecstatic phenomena" of computer screens proliferate in proportion to the technification of society. Computer networking plays an important role in modern society, but not the role usually assigned it; it now functions not as cause, but as effects of technical beingness.

Historically, in combining Communism or Fascism with technology, it is clear that the mythmakers controlling the masses presupposed a psychological basis, namely that people adhere to systems because these systems respond to something "true" in them. But this truth is certainly not very specific, since different sorts of people adhere to them. At the same time, no truly "popular government" can produce closed systems of belief; the requirements for closed-mindedness refute spontaneous mental breakthroughs. Nor should it be said that the Russian soul and the

Chinese soul were naturally "predisposed" to totalitarian systems, any more than the American to capitalist thinking.

It is nevertheless a debate whether the emergence of the modern deterministic supertechnological society will remain in the hands of a democratic open-minded liberal infrastructure with minimal managerial elites. Will the masses obey a new state of physical laws and mechanisms for conveyance of trust, and autonomous technology in exchange for the process of taking over the traditional values of every society? Without a global ethic of individual rights there will continue a silence on the most pressing humanistic issues. For example, we can explore the many options we have to resolve the ecological challenges humanity faces by reducing what Professor Paul Ehrlich[1] at Stanford University has researched compiling the equation:

$$\text{human future} = \text{population} \times \frac{\text{per-capita consumption}}{\frac{\text{technology}}{\text{efficiency}}}$$

We can either decrease the numerator or increase the denominator on the right-hand side of this equation through future science.

There are many exceptions in the rush to use technology amorally. Modern technology in pluralistic hands (via the computer workstation and Internet) was a successful tool of change in the second stage of opening Russian society to a Western-based market economy. Children by the millions can now have their consciousness raised and be given higher value-centered experiences of life if the right teachers and mentors can guide them in an "electronic school house." The "chat room" can be especially effective in preventing the "killing of dialogue"—the suppression of free speech by a cadre of ideologists—allowing for discussions that are in open disagreement. Vast satellite systems can almost freely download libraries to the children of the world, in a terrestrial paraphrase of the

Figure 39.3
Children across the planet now have the opportunity to raise their consciousness and be given higher value-centered experiences through the "electronic school house." Photo courtesy of the Academy For Future Science.

availability of higher, spiritual knowledge to the non-rigid mind.

Pointedly stated, there is a real information struggle taking place behind the scenes: Knowledge elites without "souls," who use immoral content, strive to break the back of target populations through manipulations of exoteric and esoteric developments. Opposing them are non-hidden mature human beings, aware of their potentials and limitations, who incubate and educate inner values and share in the vision of plenitudes beyond the confines of misery for a positive future.

These observations on technological manipulation of information confirm Professor Douglas Hofstadter's[2] research that the more restrictive the social mechanisms in a society, the more exaggerated are the associated ecstatic phenomena. The restrictions imposed by techniques on a society reduce the number of ways in which religious, psychic and new scientific energy can be released. In many of the closed societies that populate parts of Africa and South America, there are a plurality of ways in which mental energy can be channeled, but a self-serving technical society without soul is hazardous. Human spiritual and mental energies can, on the other hand, synergize and widen focus from immediate personal gains to the benefit that can accrue to the world community, promising happiness for each and every one of us through infinite combinations of knowledge. The result is ecstatic phenomena of unparalleled intensity and duration. If a sufficient number of people share the conviction that knowledge expansion is unconditionally soul-based in sharing, then the world will transform itself from restrictive, object-center knowledge systems.

In today's technical society, visual magic and mystical techniques that traditionally were in opposition are all mutually satisfied by the vitality of the new arena of spell-binding computer graphics: generally on the side of capturing young people's mind with dehumanizing death scenarios that rival ancient Rome's preoccupation with death. This means that each individual has a harder time to make his or her contribution to the functioning of the entire society according to talents and possibilities of rising above heavy metal games. The old mind-set tries to maintain its mystique while possessing and dominating the inner nature of humanity.

Is it necessary to evoke spiritual powers when machines can produce much better results? Technologies can encourage and develop within us the phenomena of "awesomeness"—the ability to perceive the mind as a bio-computer using its own "light-ware" to bring new expressions of all domains of knowledge. In response human consciousness has to develop towards a global mind, if we are to go beyond what Albert Einstein said of the previous age, that it is characterized by a perfection of means and a confusion of ends.

New knowledge that does not inspire one "to think cosmically and act globally" promotes, unfortunately, what could be called an indispensable alienation from the multidimensional self. The thinking soul is uprooted and the identification of the individual is encumbered with a singular ideology. Whether man identifies with an abstract "father figure" of a corporation behind the web, or with a mechanistic "terra-byte farm" of thousands of computers giving human genome instructions and assembly, he sacrifices his birthright.

Figure 39.4
Is the technological "Golden Age" really a progressive advancement or are we being misled along the information "super-highway?" Image by the Academy For Future Science.

If we take a hard, unromantic look at the coming age which is advertised to us by technocrats as a "Golden Age," we are struck with the incredible naivete of the generation of engineers and scientists on the one-track mind of the super-highway. They say they will be able to shape and reshape human will, desires, and thoughts so that we may scientifically arrive at certain efficient, pre-established collective decisions. They claim they will be in a position to develop certain collective desires, to constitute certain homogeneous social units out of aggregates of individuals, and even persuade people to renounce having any children. At the same time, they speak of assuring the triumph of freedom and of the necessity of avoiding dictatorships at any price.

On the positive side, the good news is that the approaching transformation of consciousness can touch everything from personal tutoring at home to distant learning for millions of people. Humanity unquestionably needs global citizens with an authentic sense of responsibility and autonomy based on real images on the web, posted by non-profit experts and foundations, of how the domains of biology, the human being, life on earth, the solar system, and life forms of intelligence in the universe are converging in our lifetime through teaching, processing, listening and watching. We need a fuller expression of a knowledge based on an awareness of human love and compassion, and on the insight that the well-being of the individual depends on the well-being of the global community.

When we step back, we should be seeing the computer as a tool for supplementing humanity's creative ability. The most exciting thing is not the design of new technology in computers, or even new computers, but the creation of synthetic images from vast knowledge sources, and the creation of art. The computer simply becomes a method of doing things much more rapidly. You try a million things and one of them is all right, except that with a computer you can do a million things in a second instead of a million things in a million years. We live at a time when new and ingenious teaching programs on the Internet must be sought through those involved with spiritual-scientific dialogue, who can bring hundreds of domains together for experiences of the living universe and with respect for the designs of the Most High.

Let us return to the roots of consciousness and the vitality of the soul that shaped Western civilization. Let the mind be freed from the heavy metal scenarios by beginning to forge alternative pathways of scientific and spiritual dialogue and find a genuine cross-cultural experience that recognizes a Divine purpose. Our civilization can be free from the limitations we have placed upon our world filled with true inspiration, hope and a future connected with a cosmos of living intelligence. In effect, we come closer to God by coming closer to humankind with eternal values. This is the challenge of Metatronic science in overcoming the technological mind!

---

1. Ehrlich, Paul R. (1968) *Population Bomb*. New York: Ballantine Books.
2. Hofstadter, Douglas R. (1979) *Gödel, Escher, Bach: An Eternal Golden Braid*. New York: Basic Books.

40

The Organized Consciousness Universe

Gerald H. Vind, M.A.
Former New Technologies
Staff, Northup Corporation

Our conscious awareness develops from the fundamental process of our perception of light and sound. The light we observe comes mainly from the radiation of photons from things, and each photon results from an electron releasing a tiny portion of energy called a quantum. There are no fractional quantum units (no fractional photons), yet light has a dual existence as both particle and wave. Physicist Fred Allen Wolf has popularized this paradox with his observation that the human eye, when adapted to darkness, can detect a single photon.[1]

Since as either a quantum wave or as a photon particle there is only "oneness" as a unit of energy, when that photon is detected by the eye's retina, the wave properties that were simultaneously radiated from the source must cease to exist. Somehow, the rest of the radiating quantum wavefront "knows" instantaneously when one point is detected. Furthermore, this "knowing" occurs also simultaneously or faster than the speed of light (which is the speed of the radiating wavefront). The crucial factor in the transformation from a propagating wavefront to a photon seems to be the act of conscious detection of this microcosmic event.

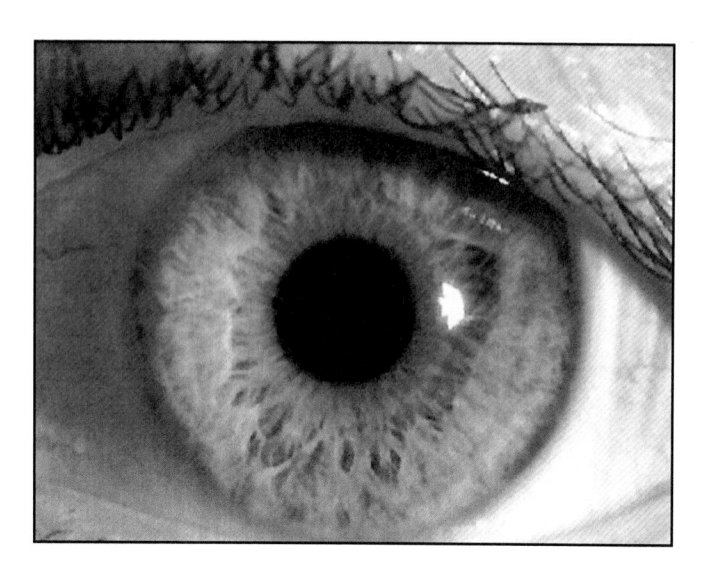

Figure 40.1
The human eye, when properly adapted to darkness can detect a single photon.

Quantum physics has led us to an awareness of a hyperdimensional or multi-dimensional reality, and yet contemporary science is limited by present definitions of our greatly expanded reality. There is a prevalent epistemology that "we can only know the physical reality within our space-time continuum" and that all else is unmeasurable, unknowable, and has no true reality. However, to talk of "reality," we must examine it as a psychological map of our own making, in which we create our own individual reality. What purports to be real are our belief structures that operate within a larger set of agreements by which we humans experience our lives together.

Reality is an individual experience of physical things and events, and there is a social fabric of agreement that provides the larger context for our individual experience of reality. Individual belief systems are harmonized in our cultural experience, and most of us do not challenge or deviate from this social fabric of agreement. We learn at an early age that there are penalties for going against the established order or rules; multidimensional journeys to other realities can get one in trouble. However, enough people in agreement can form their own system, order, or religion.

Quantum physics has developed enough agreement that another paradigm shift is taking place. Most have earlier moved beyond the view of classical (Newtonian) physics, that of an "observed reality," to a contemporary physics view wherein the act of observing (measuring) changes reality. Now, however, we are entering a new era of physics where we are part of the reality we perceive, and we too change, along with what is observed. This new view might be referred to as transformational physics.

There is another paradigm shift that has taken place recently, that has to do with the organization and ordering of forces. The belief that self-organization was the exclusive property of living systems has changed, because self-organizing forces are observable in "non-living" things such as ocean currents and weather patterns. The concept of self-organizing systems was popularized some fifteen years ago by Erich Jantsch, in his book, *The Self-Organizing Universe*:

> Self organization is the dynamic principle underlying the emergence of a rich world of

Figure 40.2
Self-organization is a principle that manifests itself in many natural structures.
Arches National Park, Moab, UT. Photo by L. Photiadis (1998).

forms manifest in biological, ecological, social, and cultural structures. But self organization does not start with what we call life. It characterizes one of the basic two classes of structures which may be distinguished in physical reality, namely the dissipative structures that are fundamentally different from equilibrium structures. Thus, self organization dynamics become the link between the animate and inanimate. Life no longer appears as a thin superstructure over a lifeless physical reality, but as an inherent principal of the dynamics of the universe.[2]

Even earlier, in 1963, this distinction between self-ordering and dissipative structures (between animate and inanimate) brought Illia Prigogine a Nobel Prize in chemistry through distinguishing that the force of disorder (entropy) causes structures to dissipate and disintegrate. This disordering force has a coexistent companion force that is observed in all living things, that is, the property or capability of increasing order and complexity. So, we exist in a dynamic tension between order and chaos, between centropy and entropy. Perhaps this is touching on something as fundamental as consciousness and energy.

Let us consider, for a moment, an example of the physical evolution of structure: Protein molecules are manufactured inside the cell, and they have self-organizing abilities to come together in ordered structures. The tertiary fold in proteins gives them a crystal-like structure, and they form themselves into lattices or arrays with the molecules aligned as dipoles (called electrets). Collagen protein arrays, for example, organize themselves into characteristic twisted patterns to form cartilage, fascia, ligaments, tendons, etc. Keratin molecules organize themselves into the characteristic patterns of epidermis, hair, and nails.
Once protein structures are formed into arrays of tissue, they acquire physical properties of whole structures, a significant property of which is their

Figure 40.3
Self-organizing protein molecules have the ability to come together in ordered structures. Image by the Academy For Future Science.

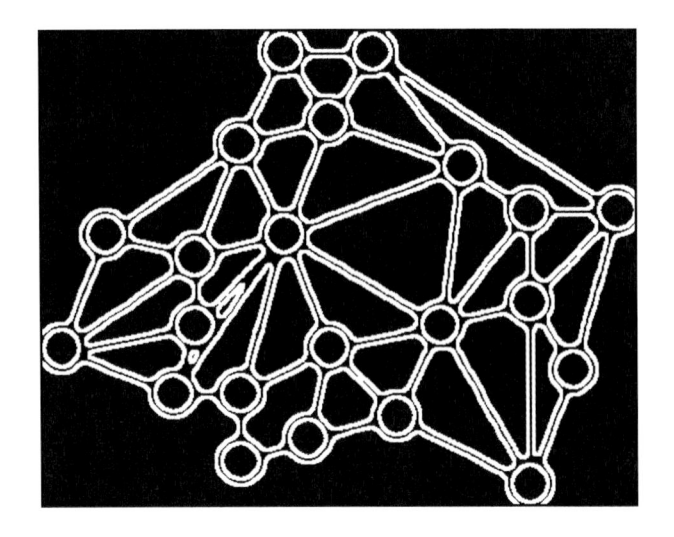

piezoelectric effect—their ability to convert mechanical motion into electrical impulse, and conversely to convert electrical stimulation into mechanical movement. Many tissues of the body have piezoelectric properties, including bone and skin.

The physical movement of most tissues produces an electrical impulse that generates magnetic and electrical fields radiating from the source of the impulse. Electrical signals are received and converted to mechanical movement, and the biological quantum effect of the mechanical movement corresponding to one photon is something called the phonon, or acoustic wave. The constant interaction between photons and phonons can be seen as a molecular-level of communications that provides the organization and feedback necessary to sustain biological activity. This produces electrical fields, magnetic fields, and quantum fields that are transmitted and received throughout the cellular structures through protein macromolecules.

Professor Franco Bistolfi (Genoa, Italy) describes this energy transduction as the fundamental point of exchange between electromagnetic and mechanical oscillations or waves:

Living matter is made up of highly ordered cooperative molecular systems which have solid state characteristics such as biological membranes, the crystal like tertiary structure of globular proteins, and the orderly assemblies of monomorphic globular proteins forming filamentous electrets... Protein macromolecules are to be considered not only as three dimensional structures, but also as sources of electromagnetic radiation... Oscillating processes in living matter must be considered both from the biochemical and biophysical point of view... The activity of both intracellular and extracellular biostructures must also be seen as a process of optical and infra-optical electromagnetic radiation emission, giving rise to complex bioresonance interactions by which various biomolecules recognize each other.[3]

Thus, the most fundamental level of life energy in living tissues is found in the constant interactions of molecular systems oscillating between quanta of electromagnetic energy (photons) and mechanical/acoustical waves (phonons). This interaction produces a constant exchange and flux at the molecular level.

Different molecular structures each have a characteristic oscillatory (vibrational) rate and, much like a bunch of crickets, molecules are constantly "chirping" their identity and location. The fundamental nature of life energy is information, and this information is modulated in electrical fields, magnetic fields, and quantum fields that interact in resonant patterns and harmonics that flow throughout (and beyond) the body. Information is a vital part of the process of self organization.

We all started as a single cell (zygote) which grew into an enclosed self-regulating system of some 100 trillion cells. As the one cell divides again and again, an organization that comes from more than the codon patterns of the DNA appears. Messenger-RNA does

The Organized Consciousness Universe

Figure 40.4
The human physical body exists within a "morphogenic field." Image by the Academy For Future Science.

not carry enough information to the ribosomes (where proteins are manufactured) to complete the tertiary fold which determines the biological properties of a protein. Something larger than the individual cell, and perhaps larger than the physical body, provides living systems with a form-guiding influence.

The physical part of us comes and goes. We replace one molecule with another many times in the lifelong metabolic process of turning food into bodily tissues and excreted waste. The actual physical integrity of our bodies is an illusion, since the actual molecules of our skin, blood, etc., differ from month to month. What is uniquely us is our informational system, the template of life-energies that maintains our physical form. Rupert Sheldrake calls this "morphic resonance" and "morphogenic fields."[4] In other words, our physical body exists within a larger form-generating body.

Dr. J.J. Hurtak sheds some light on this matter, in documents on file with The Academy For Future Science, in which he considers that we may exist as five energy bodies, and that these bodies operate together, from the physical to higher dimensional realms. In a view that differs from the simple tradition of physical, emotional, mental, spiritual, and causal bodies, Dr.

The Organized Consciousness Universe

Figure 40.5
There are five energy body vehicles that interconnect with the corporeal vehicle of humanity.
"Five Bodies" 5 x 5, Acrylic & Collage by L. Photiadis © 2002.

Hurtak explains these five energy bodies as vehicles: the five potential energy vehicles that interconnect with the corporeal vehicle of Man.[5] Of these five vehicles, the two basic ones that are within and around our physical body are sound and light: the Epi-Kinetic Body and the Electromagnetic Body.

In studying these "five bodies," there exists a relationship between physical and quantum level biological processes, between microscopic and macroscopic, that make up our collective energy field. The Epi-Kinetic Body operates upon the level of kinetic vibration (primarily low frequency acoustic energy). The Electromagnetic Body is a dynamic harmonic expression of the electromagnetic spectrum of our bodies as we absorb and radiate photons. These two bodies emerge as collective forms of the fundamental molecular-level processes of all of our molecules "chirping" their identity and location.

These two energy bodies, like sound and light interact biologically with each other through piezoelectric conversions of one form to another. They also operate within a larger reality, a hyperdimensional or subtle-energy body. This subtle energy body relates to what Dr. Hurtak calls the Eka Body, "a Higher Consciousness Body...which is a collection of many plus and minus relativities..., a consciousness that sustains a direct relationship to the physical vehicle." This third of the five vehicles, thus, is a body of consciousness that transcends our space-time reality.

We know alignment and harmonic resonance occurs throughout nature from the smallest photon to the water molecule. And since our body is over 90% water, we also have that same resonance. Recently, in his investigations into the effects of hyperdimensional fields, Glen Rein found that relatively high levels of information can be stored in water.[6] His experiments used self-canceling coils to create scalar or hyperdimensional fields, and he was able to produce certain physical effects in water.

The resonance can be explained by new quantum field theories, where coherent domains exist between dipoles. Dipoles are molecules with an electro-positive and (-) negative polarity. Dipoles are not only found in proteins; every water molecule is a dipole. The long-range interaction between biological dipoles is characterized by their capacity for accessing "zero-point energy". They are far from equilibrium, they are non-linear, and they have a flux going through them. This symbiosis between nature and supernature is the realm of the Eka Body, infinitely larger than our light-bound physical world. A new theory in physics called Super Radiance attempts to explain the propagation of electromagnetic fields in hyperdimensional terms, or as Hurtak would call it "Superluminal Light." Moreover, the last two bodies Hurtak locates as the inner and outer Superluminal Light consciousness bodies that function principally in higher realities, and are not dependent on physical reality.

Humanity is entering some "stimulating" times, going through something that is building or increasing our consciousness and spiritual energy. Some have difficulty integrating change into their lives, and they increase the dysfunctional patterns that cause them pain and suffering. This dysfunction has its roots in our disowned responsibility to our life experiences. C.G. Jung referred to this disowned material as one's "shadow," and explained how our inability to confront and take responsibility for our own shadow has a way of projecting that disowned negativity into the world around us. This shadow realm is the realm of the counterfeit spirit, where the profane masquerades as the sacred.

At the same time, the cultural hypnosis that grips us all is beginning to lift for more and more individuals. Truth and responsibility are the pillars supporting the doorway to a positive new millennium. The levels of human awareness and spiritual sensitivity are increasing, and this allows us to see through the old lies and deception. Now is the time in which we must work on revealing the truth within and around us. It is time to recognize that we are all destined to return to the Light, and that we are all in the process of becoming beings of Light, being transformed in the Light, where we are destined to serve a higher sacred purpose.

---

1. Wolf, Fred Alan (1981) *Taking the Quantum Leap*. New York: Harper & Row.
2. Jantsch, Erich (1980) *The Self-Organizing Universe*. New York: Pergamon.
3. Bistolfi, Franco "Energy Transduction in the Bioconductive Connectional System (BCS): A Meeting Point for Electromagnetic and Mechanical Oscillations," *Journal of the Bio-Electric Magnetics Institute*, **Vol. 2**, No. 2.
4. Sheldrake, Rupert (1988) *The Presence of the Past*. New York: Time Book Co.
5. Hurtak, J.J. (1996) *The Five Bodies*. Los Gatos: The Academy For Future Science.
6. Rein, Glen "Anomalous Information Storage in Water," *Proceedings of the New Energy Conference*, Texas A&M University, October, 1996.